Communications
in Computer and Information Science   942

Commenced Publication in 2007
Founding and Former Series Editors:
Phoebe Chen, Alfredo Cuzzocrea, Xiaoyong Du, Orhun Kara, Ting Liu,
Dominik Ślęzak, and Xiaokang Yang

Editorial Board

More information about this series at http://www.springer.com/series/7899

Hector Florez · Cesar Diaz
Jaime Chavarriaga (Eds.)

Applied Informatics

First International Conference, ICAI 2018
Bogotá, Colombia, November 1–3, 2018
Proceedings

Editors
Hector Florez ⓘ
Universidad Distrital Francisco José de
Caldas
Bogotá, Colombia

Jaime Chavarriaga ⓘ
Universidad de Los Andes
Bogotá, Colombia

Cesar Diaz ⓘ
Universidad de Bogotá Jorge Tadeo Lozano
Bogotá, Colombia

ISSN 1865-0929   ISSN 1865-0937 (electronic)
Communications in Computer and Information Science
ISBN 978-3-030-01534-3   ISBN 978-3-030-01535-0 (eBook)
https://doi.org/10.1007/978-3-030-01535-0

Library of Congress Control Number: 2018956560

This Springer imprint is published by the registered company Springer Nature Switzerland AG
The registered company address is: Gewerbestrasse 11, 6330 Cham, Switzerland

Preface

The First International Conference on Applied Informatics (ICAI 2018) aimed to bring together researchers and practitioners working in different domains in the field of informatics in order to exchange expertise and discuss the perspectives of development and collaboration.

ICAI 2018 was held at the Universidad de Bogotá Jorge Tadeo Lozano in Bogotá, Colombia, during November 1–3, 2018. It was organized by the Information Technologies Innovation (ITI) research group that belongs to the Universidad Distrital Francisco José de Caldas and the Data Engineering and Intelligent Systems (ID & SI) research group that belongs to the Universidad de Bogotá Jorge Tadeo Lozano. In addition, ICAI 2018 was proudly sponsored by: University of Central Florida, Springer, ACIS, Cyxtera, itPerforma, and Manar Technologies.

We received 81 submissions on informatics topics such as data analysis, decision systems, health-care information systems, IT architectures, learning management systems, mobile information processing systems, robotic autonomy, and software design engineering. Authors of the 81 submissions came from the following 14 countries: Argentina, Brazil, China, Colombia, Ecuador, Germany, India, Lithuania, Mexico, Namibia, Nigeria, South Africa, Spain, and USA. Moreover, 11 of the 81 submissions are international collaborations.

All submissions were reviewed through a double-blind peer-review process. Each paper was reviewed by at least three experts. To achieve this, ICAI 2018 was supported by 82 Program Committee (PC) members, who hold PhD degrees. PC members come from the following 20 countries: Argentina, Austria, Brazil, Canada, China, Colombia, Ecuador, France, Germany, Latvia, Luxembourg, Mexico, The Netherlands, Romania, Spain, Sweden, Switzerland, UK, USA, and Uruguay. Based on the double-blind review process, 27 full papers were accepted to be included in this volume of *Communications in Computer and Information Sciences* (CCIS) proceedings published by Springer.

Finally, we would like to thank Jorge Nakahara, Alfred Hofmann, Leonie Kunz, and Raghuram Balasubramanian from Springer for their helpful advice, guidance, and support in publishing the proceedings

November 2018

Hector Florez
Cesar Diaz
Jaime Chavarriaga

Organization

General Chairs

Hector Florez   Universidad Distrital Francisco José de Caldas, Colombia
Cesar Diaz   Universidad de Bogotá Jorge Tadeo Lozano, Colombia
Jaime Chavarriaga   Universidad de los Andes, Colombia

Organizing Committee

Ixent Galpin   Universidad de Bogotá Jorge Tadeo Lozano, Colombia
Olmer Garcia   Universidad de Bogotá Jorge Tadeo Lozano, Colombia
Rafael Hernandez   Universidad de Bogotá Jorge Tadeo Lozano, Colombia
Carenne Ludena   Universidad de Bogotá Jorge Tadeo Lozano, Colombia
Edgar Ruiz   Universidad de Bogotá Jorge Tadeo Lozano, Colombia
Edgar Vargas   Universidad de Bogotá Jorge Tadeo Lozano, Colombia

Workshops Committee

Jaime Chavarriaga   Universidad de los Andes, Colombia
Olmer Garcia   Universidad de Bogotá Jorge Tadeo Lozano, Colombia

Publication Chair

Hector Florez   Universidad Distrital Francisco José de Caldas, Colombia

Program Committee

Fernanda Almeida   Universidade Federal do ABC, Brazil
Diego Angulo   Universidad de los Andes, Colombia
Andres Aristizabal   Universidad de Bogotá Jorge Tadeo Lozano, Colombia
Oscar Avila   Universidad de los Andes, Colombia
Jorge Bacca   Universidad Distrital Francisco José de Caldas, Colombia
David Becerra   McGill University, Canada
Xavier Besseron   Université du Luxembourg, Luxembourg
Dominic Bork   Universität Wien, Austria
Francisco Brasileiro   Universidade Federal de Campina Grande, Brazil
Robert Buchmann   Universitatea Babes-Bolyai, Romania
Raymundo Buenrostro   Universidad de Colima, Mexico
Monica Castañeda   Universidad de Bogotá Jorge Tadeo Lozano, Colombia
Jaime Chavarriaga   Universidad de los Andes, Colombia
Erol Chioasca   University of Manchester, UK
Cesar Diaz   Universidad de Bogotá Jorge Tadeo Lozano, Colombia

Diana Diaz	Wayne State University, USA
Helga Duarte	Universidad Nacional de Colombia, Colombia
Silvia Fajardo	Universidad de Colima, Mexico
Mauri Ferrandin	Universidade Federal de Santa Catarina, Brazil
Hans-Georg Fill	Universität Bamberg, Germany
Hector Florez	Universidad Distrital Francisco José de Caldas, Colombia
Efraín Fonseca	Universidad de las Fuerzas Armadas ESPE, Ecuador
Ixent Galpin	Universidad de Bogotá Jorge Tadeo Lozano, Colombia
Paulo Gaona	Universidad Distrital Francisco José de Caldas, Colombia
Kelly Garces	Universidad de los Andes, Colombia
Maira Garcia	Universidad EAN, Colombia
Olmer Garcia	Universidad de Bogotá Jorge Tadeo Lozano, Colombia
Leonardo Garrido	Tecnológico de Monterrey, Mexico
Matias Gerard	Universidad Nacional del Litoral, Argentina
Cecilia Giuffra	Universidade Federal de Santa Catarina, Brazil
Raphael Gomes	Instituto Federal de Goiás, Brazil
Jānis Grabis	Rīgas Tehniskā Universitāte, Latvia
Guillermo Guarnizo	Universidad Santo Tomas, Colombia
Antonio Guerrero	Universidad de Colima, Mexico
Jens Gulden	Universität Duisburg-Essen, Germany
Cesar Hernandez	Universidad Manuela Beltran, Colombia
Ta'id Holmes	Deutsche Telekom Technik GmbH, Germany
Gilles Hubert	Institut de Recherche en Informatique de Toulouse, France
Manfred Jeusfeld	Högskolan i Skövde, Sweden
Monika Kaczmarek	Universität Duisburg-Essen, Germany
Dimitris Karagiannis	Universität Wien, Austria
Rodrigo Kato	Universidade Federal de Minas Gerais, Brazil
Daniel Katz	University of Illinois Urbana-Champaign, USA
Samee Khan	North Dakota State University, USA
Paula Lago	Universidad de los Andes, Colombia
Robert Laurini	Knowledge Systems Institute, USA
Maria Leitner	Universität Wien, Austria
Marcelo Leon	Universidad Estatal Península de Santa Elena, Ecuador
Tong Li	Beijing University of Technology, China
Sandra Londoño	Universidad del Valle, Colombia
Orlando Lopez	Universidad El Bosque, Colombia
Carenne Ludena	Universidad de Bogotá Jorge Tadeo Lozano, Colombia
Thomas Luft	Lehrstuhl für Konstruktionstechnik, Germany
Jose Marquez	Universidad del Norte, Colombia
Juan Mendivelso	Universidad Nacional de Colombia, Colombia
Osval Montesinos	Universidad de Colima, Mexico
German Montoya	Universidad de los Andes, Colombia
Jose Moreno	Institut de Recherche en Informatique de Toulouse, France
Iván Mura	Universidad de los Andes, Colombia
Sergio Nesmachnow	Universidad de la Republica, Uruguay
German Obando	Universidad del Rosario, Colombia

Contents

IT Architectures

Learning Management Systems

Mobile Information Processing Systems

Robotic Autonomy

Software Design Engineering

Data Analysis

Digital Observatory of Social Appropriation of Knowledge of a Territory

Leidy Alexandra Lozano$^{(\boxtimes)}$
and Guillermo Antonio Gaona-Ramirez$^{(\boxtimes)}$

IS-PCE, Floridablanca, Santander, Colombia
la.lozano51@uniandes.edu.co, ggaonar@gmail.com

Abstract. The social appropriation of knowledge (SAK) of a territory is gotten when a society achieves development and applies science, technology and innovation to generate social and economic development.

A Digital Observatory SAK, is a means of using the concepts of visual data analytics (VA) and business intelligence (BI) and based on a proposed conceptual model, seeks to make available to the population and intuitive form, scientific and technological knowledge of a territory.

In this way, it seeks to stimulate the creation and consolidation of spaces for the understanding, reflection and debate of solutions to social, political, cultural and economic problems. Additionally, it is sought that the population can make their own, knowledge such as useful and necessary elements for their benefit and advantage.

This article presents the description of the proposed conceptual model to observe, analyze and monitor the SAK of a territory and how this model is embodied in an interactive web page accessible to the community.

Keywords: Social appropriation of knowledge · Decision making
Data analytics · Indicators

1 Introduction

The social appropriation of knowledge (SAK) is a process implying that scientific and technological knowledge is available to the population in a common scenario and language for the Society. Therefore the human being can make his own, useful and necessary elements of knowledge that will benefit and profit [1].

In an organization making a decision receives help of different tools as Visual analytics (VA) and Business Inteligence (BI). The generation of knowledge is the result of the combination of reliable and repeatable data obtained from different bases correctly organized and managed. It gives BI the opportunity to detect tendencies and arrangements, signals in several stages of analysis. [2, 3]

Alternatively, VA present the options for easy understanding in different stages that present the information in many ways. VA gives tools to work with information to obtain alternatives of analysis when selection, alliances, arranges and purifying are applied to the data collected and organized, creating an environment of fast visual analysis. [4, 5]

© Springer Nature Switzerland AG 2018
H. Florez et al. (Eds.): ICAI 2018, CCIS 942, pp. 3–15, 2018.
https://doi.org/10.1007/978-3-030-01535-0_1

The Digital Observatory SAK, is a medium that using the concepts of visual VA and BI; and based on a proposed conceptual model, seeks to stimulate the creation and consolidation of spaces for understanding, reflection and debate of solutions to social, political, cultural and economic problems, where the population is involved with the social groups that generate knowledge and, in the generation and use of technological and scientific knowledge.

For the creation of the Digital Observatory SAK, initially a conceptual model was created that allowed to observe the social appropriation of the knowledge of a territory. For this, existing models were considered such as the integral command and strategic maps of Kaplan and Norton, the Skandia Navigator model of Edvinsson and Malone and the model developed by José Maria Viedma called CICBS model (Cities'Intel-lectual Capital Benchmarking System). Additionally, the concepts of social and eco-nomic development of the territory and the problems or needs perceived from the community were included.

Subsequently, based on the concepts of VA and BI, we proceeded to design a web application that would allow both, the population with scientific and technological knowledge, and the Society in general could access the information of their territory to understand and analyze the different thematic issues in the proposed conceptual model.

In this way, the Digital Observatory SAK can be considered as both an SAK tool and a means to observe, analyze and monitor the SAK of a territory.

The article present in Sect. 2 a description of an Observatory conceptual model, and in Sect. 3 it is shown how each concept that makes up the conceptual model is shown on the website developed. Finally, Sect. 4 contains the conclusions and future work.

2   Conceptual Model

The SAK is a topic that has been discussed in Colombia since 1993 [6]. Since then, it has generated concern for the scientific communities, governments and the media, leading them to take it as a social commitment of the community [1]. However, generating indicators to assess the SAK level of a territory has not been so easy [6, 7].

Considering that the objective to measure is the development of the capacities that people have to resort to knowledge as well as scientific and technological practices and incorporate them into everyday life to solve their problems, taking advantage of them for their benefit [8], to generate the conceptual model, different existing models that focus on measuring intellectual capital were evaluated.

From the adaptation of these models, other important concepts were taken into account: the economic and social development of the territory, the problems or needs perceived from the community and the projects developed in the region.

The revised models that served as the basis for the creation of the conceptual model of the observatory are presented below and the description of the proposed model is presented later.

2.1 Background

Organizations, like territories, have tangible and intangible resources to meet market requirements. Intangible assets, symbolized by intellectual capital, are the main generator of value and have become the fundamental basis for the generation of wealth for any business community [9].

In the review of literature, there is a diversity of authors and definitions of intellectual capital. However, there are some elements in which it is agreed: "(a) refers to intangible resources or assets, (b) includes resources and capabilities, (c) implies combination and dynamism, and (d) has a strategic nature as a source of competitive advantage" [10].

In the same way, "there are several models of intellectual capital that seek to identify it, know how it is created, measure it through a set of variables and indicators and manage it from a dynamic perspective" [9].

The conceptual model of the observatory was constructed taking as reference the most important aspects of some of these models, among them, the Skandia Navigator model of Edvinsson and Malone [12], the integral command and strategic maps of Kaplan and Norton [11] and the CICBS model (Cities'Intellectual Capital Benchmarking System) developed by José Maria Viedma [13].

Both the Kaplan and Norton strategic command model and comprehensive maps, such as the Skandia Navigator model, are focused on making measurements of intellectual capital in an organization. Each one defines the components that make up the intellectual capital and from there they propose how to measure these components. However, there is evidence of scarcity in topics on the management of intellectual capital that specifically target the regions or cities.

Unlike the previous models, the CICBS model (Cities'Intellectual Capital Benchmarking System) developed by José Maria Viedma, is based on the Skandia Navigator model but focuses on measuring the intellectual capital of a specific territory or city specific. This model is composed of two stages: the general model and the specific model of management of the Intellectual Capital of Cities. First, it seeks to measure and manage the intangible assets of the city or territory and the second, seeks to measure the intellectual capital of each of the relevant productive sectors of the territory [13].

In its two stages, it must pass through the identification of the vision, essential activities, essential competences and indicators that are classified in the 5 categories of intellectual capital of the Skandia Navigator model (financial capital, process capital, market capital, capital of renovation and development and human capital). This model is closer to the requirements of the ASC Observatory, however, the measurement of the productivity of the territory and not the social appropriation of knowledge predominates.

2.2 Conceptual Model OSAK

Starting from the hypothesis that the ability of a population of a territory to incorporate into their daily lives, the knowledge and scientific and technological practices and taking advantage of them for their benefit and improving the development indicators of their territory, it was defined as the first dimension to be visualized in the ASC observatory: Social and economic development. For this, the variables Innovation, Competitiveness,

Productivity, Social Welfare and Sustainability were chosen (Fig. 1). Each of these variables is observed from the different indices already defined for its measurement.

In the case of Innovation, the IDIC information (Index of innovation for Colombia) is analyzed with the objective of comparatively measuring the generation and appropriation of knowledge and innovation of the territory [14]; for Competitiveness, there is the Departmental Competitiveness Index (Private Competitiveness Council) that has the objective of measuring, in a robust manner, different aspects that affect the level of competitiveness of the departments in Colombia [15]. In the case of Productivity, GDP per Capita is observed; for Social Welfare, the Human Development Index (HDI) and for Sustainability the Sustainable Development Goals (SDO).

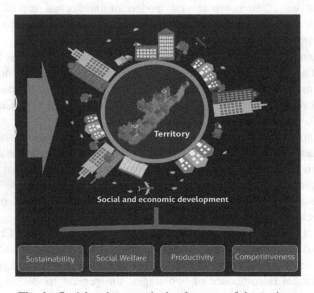

Fig. 1. Social and economic development of the territory

In order to better understand the territory, the observatory extends its statistics at the systems level (health, education, Science, Technology and Innovation (STaI) and productive systems). The systems are understood as an organized structure of human, environmental and economic resources that respond to the needs or problems of the territory. Each of these systems is composed of levels or services for which the problems or needs are observed, the attention capacity to respond to these needs and the intellectual capital they possess (Fig. 2).

The attention capacity is observed through two variables: coverage, which seeks to achieve the totality of the population that requires the services of the system and quality which is understood as the degree of satisfaction of said population.

Intellectual capital is the specific knowledge possessed by the resources of the system and that is required to execute its processes and generate value. The more intellectual capital in the system, the greater the capacity of the system to meet the needs of the territory. This capital is observed through three variables: Structural capital, relational capital and human capital.

Human capital represents competencies (knowledge, skills and talents); attitude (motivation, behavior and behavior) and intellectual agility (innovation: capacity to build new knowledge, imitation: ability to perceive innovation in the external environment to be applied in the internal environment, adaptation and presentation) of the population [16].

Structural capital is constituted by organizational capital (processes, decision-making systems, management systems and leadership) and technological capital and infrastructure (software, databases, laboratories, etc.).

Relational capital refers to internal relationships (among system actors), external relations (relationships between systems) and the community.

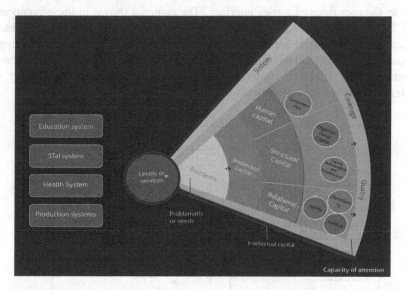

Fig. 2. Systems: Problematic, intellectual capital and attention span

Finally, it is very important to analyze those scenarios (congresses, seminars, etc.) and actions (projects) that are being developed in the territory and apply science, technology and innovation to increase the intellectual capital of the systems. Issues, improving their attention capacity and therefore responding in a better way to resolve the needs and problems of the territory to generate social and economic development.

3 Digital Observatory for Monitoring the Social Appropriation of Knowledge of a Territory

Based on the conceptual model described above, and following the strategy to develop a digital Observatory of Public Health Integrating Business Intelligence and Visual Data Analytics [17], the digital observatory was designed to monitor the SAK of a territory.

Additionally, the observatory was intended to be used as an SAK mechanism by the population of the territory and could be used by the scientific community and decision makers to observe the SAK of the territory. Therefore, it was very important to introduce the concepts of VA. To achieve this, it was intended to provide easy-to-use and interactive visual interfaces that will help in the exploration of information. Likewise, options were included to manipulate the data (filter, group, sort, eliminate, refine, among others), interact easily and quickly with them, and allow the visualization of multiple dimensions.

The application was designed using the architecture pattern MVC (Model View Controller). In this architecture, all the components of the system are divided into three large groups. The model, which is located on the server, is responsible for managing all the business logic, including the CRUD functions with the system database. The views, which are rendered in the client's browser, are responsible for displaying the information to the user through a user interface. The contents shown in these components are of 3 types: static content, dynamic geo-visualization, and InfoVis (Information visualization). Finally there are the controllers who are in charge of communicating the previous two: the view and the model. These views generate requests that pass through the controller who delivers them to the corresponding components in the model, who ultimately respond to the requests (Fig. 3).

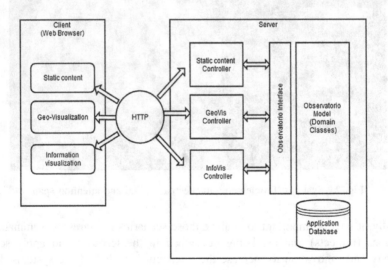

Fig. 3. Architecture

The application was based on Java technology for the design of its components using the Grails development framework and the Groovy language as a base. The database used was Postgres with its postgis spatial module and communication with the system was done through JDBC drivers. For the presentation layer, the application is divided into two: static presentation and dynamic presentation. For the static part, HTML5 is used, and for the dynamic part Leaflet and D3 are used as libraries for presentation of geo-spatial information and InfoVis respectively. For the management of geographic information, the postgis and geoserver extension is managed as a map server (Fig. 4).

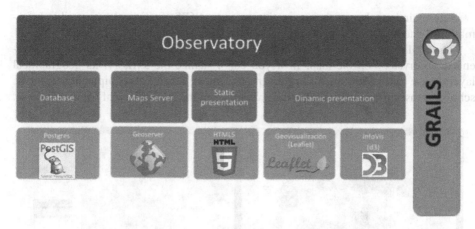

Fig. 4. Development technology

A selection and collection of information from different sources was carried out, which was processed to offer updated and good quality data (complete and consistent) that allowed for the discovery of patterns and trends, the generation of knowledge, monitoring of indicators and in general different types of analysis.

For the feeding of the database, a selection and collection of information from different sources was carried out Among the sources of information are the DIAN, the education secretary, the ICFES, Colciencias, the private competitiveness council, the government of Huila, among others. For each of these sources a specific ETL process was carried out to unify concepts and formats and be able to offer good quality information.

The navigation menu in the form of a tree is on the left side of the web page as shown in Fig. 5. Upon entering the observatory, the first thing that is shown is the explanation of the conceptual model.

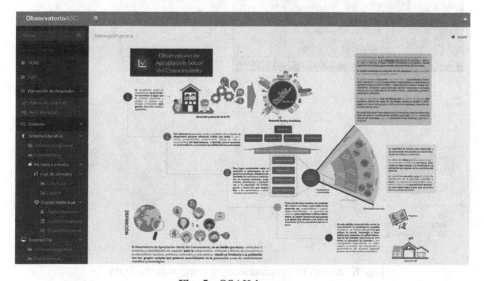

Fig. 5. OSAK homepage

The main branches of the navigation tree are: SGIS (Statistical Geographic Information System), Development dimension, Systems and general information.

The SGIS section (see Fig. 6) allows you to view the information of the georeferenced observatory on the map. In it you can visualize the territory, its geographical layers (base cartography such as rivers, roads, among others), its equipment (hospitals, schools, museums, among others), the problems and the information of some indicators.

Fig. 6. SGIS (Geographic and statistical information system)

In addition, it allows different operations to be carried out on geographic information, such as searching for attributes (name, location, type, etc.), filtering information according to a drawn area, consulting for proximity, drawing indicators on the map, among others (see Fig. 7).

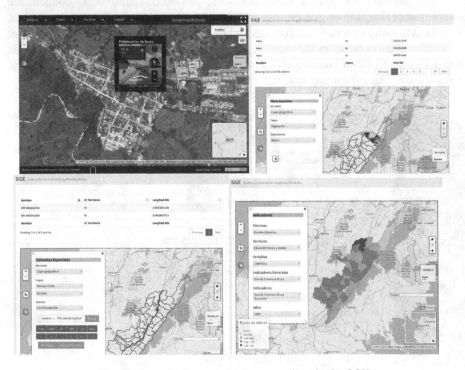

Fig. 7. Results of geoprocessing operations in the SGIS

The second section corresponds to the development dimension. In it, you can find all the information on social and economic development indicators. This visualization allows the user to observe the state of the variables that define the development dimension of the territory: Innovation, Competitiveness, productivity, social welfare and sustainability and observe the municipal profile developed by the DNP of each municipality (see Fig. 8).

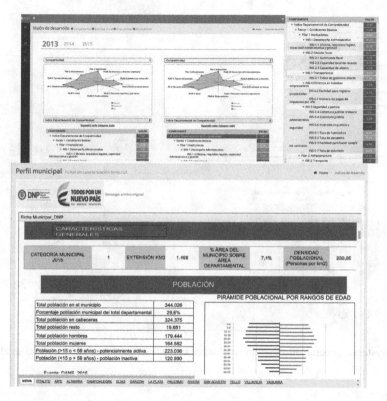

Fig. 8. Development dimension. Competitiveness, productivity, social welfare and sustainability.

The third section corresponds to the systems. For each system (Education, Science, Technology and Innovation (STaI), Health, etc.) we have the following subsections: general information, which conceptualizes the system; problems and needs, that geo-referencing the different problems identified in the territory; attention capacity, which shows the indicators of coverage and quality; and intellectual capital, which allows analyzing the indicators of relational capital, structural capital and human capital (Fig. 9).

Each of these sections offers a variety of interlaced graphics, which allow you to easily filter information to be able to do different types of analysis.

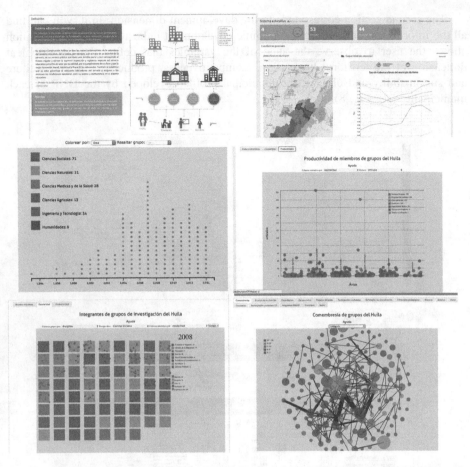

Fig. 9. Systems: general information, problems and needs, attention capacity and intellectual capital

Furthermore, in this section, the SKA scenarios and the STaI projects that are being developed in the territory can be observed (see Fig. 10).

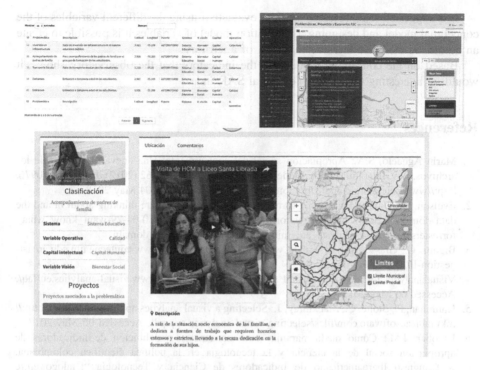

Fig. 10. Scenarios and SKA projects of the territory

4 Conclusion and Future Work

As the SAK is a topic that has generated concern for the scientific communities, governments and the media, and the definition of a set of indicators that can measure the SAK in a territory, which is not an easy process, the proposed conceptual model, the proposed model becomes a contribution of great importance.

With the proposed model, the components that should be considered for the observation of the Social Appropriation of Knowledge of a territory were selected: economic and social development of the territory (innovation, competitiveness, productivity, social welfare and sustainability), territorial systems (capacity of attention: quality and coverage, intellectual capital: human, structural and relational capital, problems or needs perceived from the community) and the SAK scenarios and projects developed in the region.

Having included the concepts of Visual Data Analytics (VA) and Business Intelligence (BI) to create the digital observatory that followed the conceptual model, it made the observatory available to the population and intuitively, scientific and technological knowledge of the territory.

It is necessary to perform user tests to evaluate quality attributes and be able to guarantee that the chosen analyzes are the most suitable for the target audience.

It is suggested to do research work to evaluate if using the different variables of the conceptual model and designing a correlation model of variables it is possible to create an automatic model to measure the SAK of a territory.

Based on the conceptual model and the indicators that the observatory shows, it would be interesting to create a Territorial SAK index.

References

1. Marín Agudelo, S.A.: Apropiación social del conocimiento: Una nueva dimensión de los archivos. Rev. Interam. Bibliot. Medellín (Colombia) **35**(1), 55–62 (2012). ISSN 0120-0976. http://www.scielo.org.co/pdf/rib/v35n1/v35n1a5.pdf. Accessed 04 May 2018
2. Evelson, B.: Want to know what forrester's lead data analysts are thinking about bi and the data domain? (2010). http://blogs.forrester.com/boris_evelson/10-04-29-want_know_what_ forresters_lead_data_analysts_are_thinking_about_bi_and_data_domain
3. Bigatti, C., Grasso, M.: Bi – data warehouse (2005). http://www.edutecne.utn.edu.ar/sist-gestion-II/Apunte%20BI.pdf
4. Visualanalytics.Eu.: What is visual analytics? (2012). http://www.visual-analytics.eu/faq/. Accessed 06 May 2017
5. Hanrahan, P., Stolte, C., Mackinlay, J.: Selecting a visual analytics application (2009). http:// mkt.tableausoftware.com/files/selecting-visual-analytics-app.pdf. Accessed 06 May 2017
6. Escobar, J.M.: Cómo medir naranjas con manzanas: La definición de indicadores de apropiación social de la ciencia y la tecnología en la política científica colombiana. X Congreso Iberoamericano de Indicadores de Ciencia y Tecnología "Diálogo entre productores y usuarios de información" San José de Costa Rica, 20–22 November 2017. https://drive.google.com/file/d/1EWStj7Qad07SbInlNruIOuRXX5deBXDi/view. Accessed 17 May 2018
7. Escobar, J.M.: La apropiación social de la ciencia y la tecnología como eslogan: un análisis del caso colombiano, Revista Iberoamericana de Ciencia, Tecnología y Sociedad -CTS, vol. 13, no. 37 (2018). http://www.revistacts.net/files/Volumen_13_Numero_37/Preliminares/ 03EscobarEDITADO.pdf. Accessed 17 May 2018
8. Ramírez, L.L., Rueda, X., Garcia, J.C., Gómez, M., Olivé Morett, L.: La apropiación social del conocimiento y sus indicadores: Una reflexión desde el análisis de las prácticas epistémicas. IX Congreso Iberoamericano de Indicadores de Ciencia y Tecnología (2013). http://congreso2013.ricyt.org/files/mesas/2fPercepcion/LazosRuedaGarcia.pdf. Accessed 17 May 2018
9. Fontalvo, T.J., Quejada, R., Puello, J.G.: La gestión del conocimiento y los procesos de mejoramiento. Dimens. empres. **9**(1), 80–87 (2011). https://dialnet.unirioja.es/descarga/ articulo/3797779.pdf. Accessed 30 May 2018
10. Naranjo-Herrera, C.G., Rubio-Jaramillo, J., Salazar-Mesa, L.M., Robledo-Martínez, A.V., Duque-Trujillo, J.: Indicadores de capital intelectual. Memorias **11**(19), 39–51 (2013). https://revistas.ucc.edu.co/index.php/me/article/view/108. Accessed 30 May 2018
11. Norton, D.P., Kaplan, R.S.: El Cuadro de Mando Integral. Grupo Planeta (GBS) (2009). ISBN 8498750482, 9788498750485
12. Edvinsson, L., Malone, M.S.: Intellectual Capital: Realizing Your Company's True Value by Finding Its Hidden Brainpower/ L. Edvinsson, M.S. Malone; pról. de Rich Karlgaard (1997)
13. Viedma, J.M.: CICBS: Cities' Intellectual Capital Benchmarking System (2003). http:// www.intellectualcapitalmanagementsystems.com/publicaciones/CICBStrad.pdf.   Accessed 30 May 2018

14. OCyT: Índice Departamental de Innovación para Colombia (IDIC) 2017 (2017). https://colaboracion.dnp.gov.co/CDT/Prensa/Publicaciones/Informe%20IDIC%202017.pdf. Accessed 06 June 2018
15. Consejo Privado De Competitividad: Índice departalmental de competitividad. https://compite.com.co/idc/. Accessed 30 May 2018
16. Molina, R., Argotte, L.P., Jácome, N., Domíngez, M.: Modelo de gestión por competencias: Conceptos básicos (2006). https://www.ineel.mx/boletin012006/act.pdf. Accessed 30 May 2018
17. Lozano, L.A., del Pilar Villamil, M.: Strategy to develop a digital public health observatory integrating business intelligence and visual analytics. In: Rocha, Á., Guarda, T. (eds.) Proceedings of the International Conference on Information Technology & Systems (ICITS 2018). ICITS 2018. Advances in Intelligent Systems and Computing, vol. 721. Springer, Cham (2018). https://doi.org/10.1007/978-3-319-73450-7_42

Evaluation of the Bias of Student Performance Data with Assistance of Expert Teacher

Cinthia Vegega[✉], Pablo Pytel, Luciano Straccia,
and María Florencia Pollo-Cattaneo

Information System Methodologies Research Group,
National Technological University of Buenos Aires, Buenos Aires, Argentina
cinthiavg@yahoo.com.ar, ppytel@gmail.m,
flo.pollo@gmail.com

Abstract. Machine Learning algorithms have many advantages and a great potential for solving complex problems in different domains. However, it is not "magical". One of its main difficulties lies in recollecting representative data of the domain in order to train the system, otherwise, its efficacy will be seriously compromised. Therefore, a method has been proposed to evaluate the collected data with the assistance of the available domain experts and determine whether it can be used. In this work, the method is applied to evaluate two versions of data gathered on the students' performance in an undergraduate program course. As a result, it is determined whether they can be used in the training of an Intelligent System that will foretell such performance.

Keywords: Intelligent systems · Machine learning · Training data
Education and technology · Bias

1 Introduction

Machine Learning algorithms have many advantages and a great potential for solving complex problems in different domains [1, 2]. In fact, according to Ethem Alpaydin [3], they can be compared to living beings due to their ability to self-adapt by learning from the data gathered. However, "Machine Learning is not magical; it cannot create something out of nothing" [4]. This means that it also has limitations in which, unlike traditional programming, the difficulty does not lie in how to program the logic that the software system must follow, but in having available representative data of the domain in order to train the system [5]. Only in this way may valid models be generated to be used in the implementation of an Intelligent System that solves the problem required [6]. As a consequence, the first stages of a project entail identifying, gathering, integrating, cleaning and pre-processing the available data [7].

However, gathering the necessary data that must be given to the algorithm is not a trivial task [4]. An example of this is the issue of determining the amount of historical information required to produce the best results [8]. According to [9], the typical answer to the question "how much data is required?" is "as much as possible", since the more data available, the easier it is to identify the model's structure. But, when conducting a real project, it is essential to set a limit to the amount of data to be applied [4].

© Springer Nature Switzerland AG 2018
H. Florez et al. (Eds.): ICAI 2018, CCIS 942, pp. 16–31, 2018.
https://doi.org/10.1007/978-3-030-01535-0_2

Although there are publications [8–11] establishing minimum requirements for the amount of data to be applied, these are considered excessively simplified since certain aspects, such as the underlying variability of the data or the characteristics of the problem domain, are ignored [9]. As a result, in order to define the amount of data to be used, it is first necessary to identify the sources available and to understand their characteristics [7]. Only in this way will it be possible to collect data that sufficiently represent the problem to be solved [3]. Otherwise, the efficacy of the Intelligent System will be seriously compromised. This is due to the fact that when the data collected is not sufficiently representative, they are said to have a "bias". This term is used in Psychology to refer to the tendency or prejudice shown by a person when perceiving and interpreting reality, thus distorting it. In Statistics, bias is used to refer to the difference between the value generated by the model and the expected value. In the case of Machine Learning, it refers to something similar to both disciplines. If the data are biased, then there is a risk that the Intelligent System would not be based on reality and will produce wrong outcomes [4]. In other words, algorithms might be being trained to solve a different problem from the one that should actually be solved.

Therefore, it is vital to know the biases associated to the data and to the Intelligent System in advance, so that they can be understood by future users in order to avoid misunderstandings and discrimination situations [12, 13]. It is not rare for developers with the best intentions to inadvertly produce Intelligent Systems with biased results, because even they may not sufficiently understand the problem, its context and the data so as to prevent unintended results [1]. The worst issue of this scenario is that the bias may be so subtle that it may remain undetected during tests [14]. If the system is then put into operation and the users blindly trust its results, this may result in sexism, racism or other forms of discrimination in the long term [15].

In this context, an adaptation of the Grid Repertory has been proposed in [16] to evaluate the collected data with the assistance of the available domain experts and determine whether it can be used. In this work, the proposed method is applied to a higher education institution course data in order to evaluate whether they are sufficiently representative to implement a future Intelligent System. For this purpose, Sect. 2 describes the data gathered and its context, whose evaluation is dealt with in Sect. 3. Finally, Sect. 4 presents the conclusions and the future line of work.

2 Context and Collect Data Description

The Facultad Regional Buenos Aires of Universidad Tecnológica Nacional (UTN-FRBA) at Argentina is a higher education institution providing education in engineering and other technical university programs. Among them is the "Information Systems Engineering" (ISI) undergraduate program [17]. At the first level of its Study Plan [18] is the "Systems and Organizations" course, which is part of its integration module and which has cross-curricular relations with all the levels of the Study Plan [19]. In addition, this course is mandatory for those students who have passed the entrance course to the program (approximately 800 students enrolled). However, since the dropout rate is approximately 30% in the first year of the program (only), it is important to provide mechanisms and interventions aimed at reverting that situation.

Among the factors contributing to this problem, this study seeks to address one of the most serious issues: students' lack of study during the course. As a result of this, many students fail the first term exam of the course (which they sit for near the end of the first term). In some cases, this causes so much frustration that students drop out of the course and enroll again the following year (thus resulting in an important delay in graduation) or, in more drastic cases, they drop out of the program altogether (thus increasing the university dropout rate).

For the reasons stated above, the implementation of an Intelligent System has been decided in order to offer a solution to the specific problems posed by the course. This system will include a module for the analysis of the students' level of knowledge on theory and practice topics of the course using information gathered from other modules. In this way, the module will be able to predict the students' performance throughout the course and identify their strengths and weaknesses, which is very important information for both the students and the teachers of the course. It is considered paramount for the system to provide results that are consistent with the students' normal behavior in the course. Thus, apart from gathering the historical data which will be applied to build the system, it is necessary to identify the general characteristics of the domain where the prediction is made. In addition, it is essential to detect situations or events that should be considered for which there are no data or the data available is not representative. Otherwise, the system might generate incorrect predictions, leading teachers or students to make wrong decisions.

The data collected to carry out the analysis can be classified into two versions: an initial version and an extended one. However, before describing them, a brief description of the course under study is presented. It is an annual course and therefore the theory and the practice developed throughout it are evaluated by means of two term exams. Should students fail to pass any of the topics in the syllabus, they have the possibility to sit again for those topics (up to two opportunities), in the corresponding make-up exams. The theory includes concepts related to the professional scope and the role of the Information Systems engineer, as well as the resolution of problems using Systems Methodologies. In turn, the practice includes the development of Organizational Charts and Process Charts in the first semester of the course, and the development of Administrative Circuits in the second term. A more detailed description of the topics taught can be found in the technical report [20].

In order to pass the course, students must pass all the topics (either in the term exam or in one of the two make-ups). Otherwise, they must retake the course. In addition, there are students who drop out of the course and who do not appear in the final course records (TPA) or they are disenrolled due to absenteeism.

Therefore, the data collected correspond to the results of the evaluations of students who took the course on Mondays, Tuesdays, Thursdays and Fridays in 2016. It is stressed that, regardless of the day on which the course is taught, the structure of the exams is similar since they are taught by the same teacher, so all the exams include the same types of exercises. As mentioned above, these data can be classified into two versions. The initial version includes only 14 attributes corresponding to 75 records of the students' performance both in theory and practice in the exams (term exams and make-ups) of the course as well as the course day and the academic status of the student (that is, whether they passed, they failed or directly do not appear in the final records due to absenteeism). Performance is identified using the values assigned by the teachers: Passed with Honors (AP_dist), Satisfactory Pass (AP), Passed with some errors (AP_err), Borderline Pass (AP_lim), Borderline Fail (NO_AP_lim), Failed (NO_AP), Topic Not Answered (NC), Student Absent in the Evaluation (AUS), and Topic that the student does not need to answer (NA, which is used for make-up exams only). Due to format reasons, these data are not transcribed in this document but are instead presented in the 'Datos Originales' (Original Data) sheet of the spreadsheet available in [21].

On the other hand, the second version of data is referred to as "extended" since it details the results for each topic of each exam (for example, in the Practice section of the first term exam, the results for Organizational Charts and Process Charts are indicated). In addition, 51 records of students were added so these data have a total of 126 rows and 23 attributes, which are detailed in the 'Datos Originales' sheet of the spreadsheet available in [22].

3 Results of the Application of the Proposed Method

The results of the application of the method proposed in [16] to evaluate the initial version of the data (Sect. 3.1) as well as the extended version (Sect. 3.2) are presented below. More detail can be found in the technical report [20].

3.1 Evaluation of the Initial Version of the Data

With the aim to show the operation of the proposed method, a detailed description of all the steps applied to this dataset is provided below. Many of these results cannot be included in this document so they are shown in the spreadsheet available in [21].

- **Phase A: Design of the Grids**
- **Activity A.1- Data Preparation**

The data to be used include 14 attributes mentioned above which can be seen in the 'Datos Originales' (Original Data) sheet of [21]. Furthermore, in the 'Estadisticas Datos Originales" (Original Data Statistics) sheet, general statistics of such data are included. Since there are no null or void values, cleaning them is not required and since they are in a single file, integrating them is not required either. However, since the attributes are not numerical, it is necessary to convert them. To that aim, the conversion table shown in the 'Conversion a Continuos' (Conversion to Continuous) of [21] is applied thus obtaining the results shown in the 'Datos Continuos' (Continuous Data) sheet [21]. After the latter are obtained, the next activity follows.

- **Activity A.2- Data Segmentation**

In this activity, numerical attributes are segmented. To this aim, the data are imported in Tanagra [23] and the first 4 operators of the process indicated in the 'Proceso Tanagra' (Tanagra Process) sheet [21] are applied. A distribution of 3×2 neurons (i.e. a requested maximum of 6 clusters) resulted in a distribution of three clusters with less than 10 tuples ($c\_som\_1\_3$, $c\_som\_2\_1$ and $c\_som\_2\_3$), as it can be observed in the 'Res Kohonen' (Result of Kohonen) [21] sheet. Furthermore, a new attribute called *Cluster_SOM_1* indicating the ID of the cluster assigned to each tuple was added. This new structure, included in the 'Datos Segmentados' (Segmented Data) sheet [21], will be used in subsequent activities and it shown in Table 1.

Table 1. Number of tuples assigned per cluster

Cluster	Cluster ID	Number of tuples
N° 1	c_som_1_1	22
N° 2	c_som_1_2	16
N° 3	c_som_1_3	1
N° 4	c_som_2_1	7
N° 5	c_som_2_2	24
N° 6	c_som_2_3	5

- **Activity A.3- Design of the Elements Grid**

Using the segmented data obtained in the previous activity, the Elements Grid is generated. The Elements Grid is a 3×6 matrix since it has three columns that correspond to the values of the class (APRUEBA when the student pass the course, NO_APRUEBA when the student fails to pass the course, and NO_TPA when the student drops out of the course), and six rows corresponding to clusters (*c_som_1_1*, *c_som_1_2*, *c_som_1_3*, *c_som_2_1*, *c_som_2_2* and *c_som_2_3*). To complete the values of the matrix, the proposed steps are applied. To illustrate such steps, the definition of value V_{22} corresponding to class NO_APRUEBA and cluster *c_som_1_2* are presented below, as an example:

(a) The number of tuples is determined in the segmented data for class NO_APRUEBA and cluster *c_som_1_2*, which is equal to 12.
(b) The total number of tuples for class NO_APRUEBA, which is equal to 29, is also determined.
(c) The membership percentage is calculated using the following formula:

$$P_{22} = \frac{T_{22}}{\sum_{i=1}^{6} (T_{i2})} = \frac{12}{29} = 0,41$$

(d) Then the membership percentage is rounded to 4.
(e) Therefore, 4 is registered as value V_{22} in the matrix corresponding to the class and the cluster.

Likewise, the remaining values are completed, as it can be seen in the 'Parrilla de Elementos' sheet [21] obtaining, as a result, the grid shown in Table 2.

Table 2. Elements grid

	APRUEBA	NO_APRUEBA	NO_TPA
c_som_1_1	8	0	0
c_som_1_2	1	4	0
c_som_1_3	0	0	0
c_som_2_1	1	1	1
c_som_2_2	0	3	9
c_som_2_3	0	1	1

- **Activity A.4- Attribute Weighting**

In this activity, the segmented data from Activity A.2 are used again to apply the remaining 4 operators of the process indicated in the 'Proceso Tanagra' sheet [21]. Thus, using Tanagra, the numerical attributes are first converted into discrete (with two ranges of equal width for each one), and then, the conditional probabilities with operator Näive Bayes shown in the 'Res NaiveBayes' sheet [21] are calculated.

- **Activity A.5- Design of the Characteristics Grids**

The two Characteristics Grids (the Direct and the Opposite) are generated from the conditional probability tables obtained in the previous activity. They have a 6 × 13 structure since there are six cluster values indicated as columns and 13 attributes, as rows. As it can be seen in the 'Parrilla de Características' sheet [21], this is performed with all the combinations to obtain the grids shown in Tables 3 and 4.

Table 3. Direct grid of characteristics

	c_som_1_1	c_som_1_2	c_som_1_3	c_som_2_1	c_som_2_2	c_som_2_3
CURSO	5	8	10	1	0	10
C1_P_PRACTICA	1	5	0	3	9	10
C1_1R_PRACTICA	9	4	10	7	9	10
C1_2R_PRACTICA	10	8	10	10	10	8
C1_P_TEORIA	6	9	10	6	10	10
C1_1R_TEORIA	3	7	10	10	10	10
C1_2R_TEORIA	8	8	10	10	10	10
C2_P_PRACTICA	4	9	10	4	10	10
C2_1R_PRACTICA	8	8	10	10	10	10
C2_2R_PRACTICA	8	8	10	10	10	10
C2_P_TEORIA	3	8	10	7	10	10
C2_1R_TEORIA	7	8	0	10	10	10
C2_2R_TEORIA	8	10	0	10	10	10

Table 4. Opposite grid of characteristics

	c_som_1_1	c_som_1_2	c_som_1_3	c_som_2_1	c_som_2_2	c_som_2_3
CURSO	5	3	0	9	10	0
C1_P_PRACTICA	9	5	10	7	1	0
C1_1R_PRACTICA	1	6	0	3	1	0
C1_2R_PRACTICA	0	2	0	0	0	2
C1_P_TEORIA	4	1	0	4	0	0
C1_1R_TEORIA	7	3	0	0	0	0
C1_2R_TEORIA	2	3	0	0	0	0
C2_P_PRACTICA	6	1	0	6	0	0
C2_1R_PRACTICA	2	2	0	0	0	0
C2_2R_PRACTICA	2	2	0	0	0	0
C2_P_TEORIA	7	3	0	3	0	0
C2_1R_TEORIA	3	2	10	0	0	0
C2_2R_TEORIA	2	0	10	0	0	0

- **Phase B: Formalization and Analysis of the Grids**
- **Activity B.1- Classification of the Elements**

Once the grids are available, they are classified starting from the Elements Grid (generated in activity A.3). First, the distances between columns are calculated (that is, elements or classes) using the Manhattan distance formula [24] with the values in Table 2. Thus, the remaining distances are calculated, then the Matrix of Distances of Elements in Table 5 are obtained. As it can be observed, by considering the absolute differences between the classes, only the distances on the diagonal are indicated because the distances under it are equal. Using that matrix, clusters are formed by applying the minimum distance criterion. In this case, the minimum distance is 10 and thus joins NO_APRUEBA with NO_TPA; then, the distance matrix is updated as shown in Table 6. Since there are only three classes, with this new matrix, only group APRUEBA remains to be joined with group [NO_APRUEBA, NO_TPA] to finish. This means that, while the difference between NO_APRUEBA and NO_TPA is 10, the largest similarity of APRUEBA with these two classes is equal to 15 (the graphic representation of this is shown in activity B.3).

Table 5. Matrix of distances between the elements

	APRUEBA	NO_APRUEBA	NO_TPA
APRUEBA		15	19
NO_APRUEBA			10
NO_TPA			

Table 6. Matrix of distances of the elements after the first cluster

	APRUEBA	[NO_APRUEBA, NO_TPA]
APRUEBA		15
[NO_APRUEBA, NO_TPA]		

- **Activity B.2- Classification of the Characteristics**

  Similarly to the previous activity, the matrix of distances is generated for the attributes or characteristics of the grids obtained in activity A.5. Notwithstanding this, since there are two grids, a Direct one associated to the first pole of attributes and, an Opposite one associated to the second pole, in this case, for each combination, it is necessary to calculate two distances (d_1 and d_2) using also the Manhattan distance formula. Thus, the Matrix of Distances d_1 and d_2 of the Characteristics is obtained, which can be observed in the 'Distancias de Caracteristicas' (Distances of Characteristics) sheet of [21]. As it can be seen, the d_1 values are located above the diagonal and the d_2 values, below it. Since it is necessary to have one single distance to form the clusters, d_1 and d_2, should be unified taking the lower for each combination. That means that, for each combination of attributes, the minimum value is taken between the value below and above the diagonal. Then, the values below the diagonal are discarded, thus obtaining the unified Matrix of Distances (included in the same spreadsheet). Finally, with the unified matrix, the clusters corresponding to the minimum distance criterion are formed in the same way as with the elements.

- **Activity B.3- Interpretation of the Results**

  From the clusters obtained in activities B.1 and B.2, the Ordered Tree of Elements and the Ordered Tree of Characteristics are generated, which are available in the 'Interpretacion Elementos' (Interpretation of Elements) sheet and the 'Interpretacion Caracteristicas' (Interpretation of Characteristics) of [21]. The interpretation of such trees is included below:

- Analysis of the Ordered Tree of Elements: In this tree, 2 groups were generated. The students who failed the course (NO_APRUEBA element) show a behavior more similar to those who drop the course (this is the reason why they are not included in the final course record or TPA, NO_TPA element), than to the students who pass the course (APRUEBA element). Notwithstanding this, the similarity is slight since they meet at a distance of 10.
- Analysis of the Ordered Tree of Characteristics: In this case, 8 groups were generated, 4 major ones and 4 with individual characteristics. The first major group (GP1) includes identical characteristics which are the results of the Theory section of the first semester in the second make-up exam with the results from the Practice section of the second semester in both make-up exams. On the other hand, the second major group (GP2) includes the similar characteristics (with a distance of 3) corresponding to the results of the Theory section of the second semester in both make-up exams. The third group (GP3) corresponds to quite similar characteristics (distance of 4) to the Theory section of the first semester in the first make-up exam and, Theory of the mid-term test of the second semester. Finally, with the same degree of similarity as the previous case, the fourth group (GP4) has the Theory section of the mid-term test of the first semester together with the Practice section of the mid-term test of the second semester.

  For these major groups, the following clusters are generated. The results of the Practice section of the first semester taken in the second make-up exam are added to

GP1, with a distance of 4. Groups GP3 and GP4 meet with a distance of 5 and meet the GP1's previous cluster at distance 6. Then, the Practice of the first make-up exam corresponding to the first semester is added to this cluster at 9. The Course is added at 15, and finally, at 17, the last characteristic, which is the results of the Practice taken in the mid-term test of the first semester, is added

- **Activity B.4- Discussion of the Results**

To finish the procedure, a meeting is held with the teacher of the courses (who, in addition, is Chair of the course), whose data were collected, and he takes the role of domain expert to discuss the results obtained in the previous activities and interpreted in activity B.3.

First, the teacher is presented with the analysis of the ordered tree of elements and its explanation and interpretation. With regard to the relationship found between students who fail the course and those who are not included in the TPA (Final Course Records), the expert states that the behavior of students who drop the course and are not included in the TPA is more similar to those who do not pass. According to the teacher, if a student is disenrolled it means they have had too many absences (otherwise, the office of the registrar would not have excluded them from the attendance list). It is not common for a student who missed many lessons to pass all the topics included in the first mid-term test (since most of the students who pass the first mid-term test have participated and done all the tasks required in class). On the other hand, the few students who pass all the topics included in the first mid-term test will most probably do well in the second mid-term test. This is because the students who have passed almost all the topics in the first mid-term test try harder and pass more topics in the second mid-term test. However, a student who has to sit for many test topics in the second make-up exam of the first semester will find it difficult to pass the topics of the second mid-term test. This means that they will not sit for the following make-up exams and will drop the course.

Once the validity of the clusters for the students' behavior is agreed, there follows the analysis of the attribute clusters. So the expert is shown the ordered tree of characteristics and its interpretation. The expert expresses his disapproval due to the way the topics are represented since he expects a specific analysis of each topic and not a more general analysis of the theory and practice. However, the discussion on the groups detected is held anyway and the following results are obtained:

- To consider that the attributes forming the first major group (C2_1R_PRACTICA, C2_2R_PRACTICA and C1_2R _TEORIA) show certain similarity. Taking into account that Systems Methodology is included in the theory of the first semester and Administrative Circuits is included in the practice of the second semester, it should be noted that these topics are more difficult and they are usually passed in the making-up instances. Regarding Methodology, the teacher allows the students to hand in a draft describing the topic (those students who hand in the draft greatly increase their chances of passing the topic). However, almost nobody hands it in before the mid-term test, and instead they hand it in the make-up instance. In turn, the students say that Administrative Circuits is very difficult "because you have to study by heart" but, according to the expert, it is a wrong idea.

- Regarding the second major group (C2_1R_TEORIA and C2_2R_TEORIA), the expert assumes that this cluster is due to the similar performance of the students in the Theory in the make-up exams of the second semester. Many students believe that reading the Theory in the last week is enough but then, they realize it is too much to study and during the exam, and they get confused. Therefore, these students pass in the make-up instance. However, the expert points out that he does not agree on the cluster of the third major group (C1_1R_TEORIA and C2_P_TEORIA). According to the expert, the student who passes the Theory in the first mid-term test has great chances of passing the Theory of the second mid-term test, but, if they have not passed the Theory of the first mid-term test, it is difficult for them to pass the second. Then, according to the expert, the relation should be established between attributes C1_P_TEORIA and C2_P_TEORIA.
- The fourth major group (C1_P_TEORIA and C2_P_PRACTICA) would not make sense either, since the Practice of the second semester (Administrative Circuits) depends more on the Theory of the second semester and on the fact that the student has done well in Process Charts (included in the Practice of the first semester). Generally, it is difficult for the student who has not passed Process Charts to pass Administrative Circuits. For the expert, it is essential to understand Process Charts if the student wishes to sail through Administrative Circuits.
- For the two attributes that meet later (C1_1R_PRACTICA and C1_2R_PRAC-TICA), the expert shows indifference (neither does he accept nor he rejects the way the cluster was performed).
- On the other hand, although the day of the week when the students attend the course (CURSO) should have no influence on the results of the exams, it often happens that there are courses with a larger number of students who are re-attending than new students and in those courses students tend to fail or drop more often than courses made up of new students only. In addition, due to administrative issues, sometimes there is a whole course made up of students who had a direct admission, who have a much better performance than regular first-year students. For example, in 2016, students from the Friday courses showed a better performance than those from Monday courses. Therefore, an implicit and indirect relation between the course and the general performance of the students may be detected but a specific one related to a particular topic cannot.
- Finally, the expert assumes that the Practice of the first mid-term test (C1_P_PRACTICA) is the last attribute to be clustered because it includes both Organizational Charts and Process Charts, the two topics the students most pass in the mid-term test. If a student reaches the second make-up exam due to those two topics, then they are most likely to fail the course.

Due to all the problems detected for the attributes, it is concluded that this dataset is not representative of the students' behavior in the course. These data show several biases that could generate incorrect results in the Intelligent Systems trained using such data. Consequently, it was decided to generate a new version of the data (the so called 'extended' version) including more examples and incorporating more details regarding the attributes to be used. The evaluation of these data is developed in the following section.

3.2   Evaluation of the Extended Version of the Data

Due to the problems detected in the initial version of the data, it was decided to extend them both in the number of rows and in the detail of attributes, which are also evaluated as described below. Again, many of the results cannot be included in this document, and therefore, they are shown in the sheet available in [22].

- **Phase A: Design of the Grids**
- *Activity A.1-Data Preparation*

This version of the data includes the 23 attributes that can be fully accessed in the 'Datos Originales' sheet of [22]. Furthermore, in the 'Estadisticas Datos Originales' [22] tab, the general statistics of these data are included. Here again, there are no null or void values so it is not required to clean them and since they are in a single file, it is not necessary to integrate them either. However, since the attributes are not numerical, they must be converted. To do so, the conversion table indicated in the 'Conversion a Continuos' sheet is applied, thus generating the results shown in the 'Datos Continuos' sheet [22] to continue with the following activity.

- *Activity A.2- Data Segmentation*

The prepared data are imported in the Tanagra tool [24] to be segmented through the application of the process's first operators indicated in the 'Proceso Tanagra' sheet [22]. To generate a detailed or fine enough segmentation, a 3×3 output neuron distribution was used for the RNA Kohonen SOM (that is, with 9 maximum clusters). The resulting distribution of the tuples in the clusters are in the 'Res Kohonen' [22] sheet, and the ID of the cluster assigned for each tuple is indicated in the 'Datos Segmentados' sheet [22].

- *Activity A.3- Design of the Elements Grid*

Applying the steps defined by the procedure on the segmented data of the previous activity, the 3×9 grid is generated as shown in the 'Parrilla de Elementos' sheet [22].

- *Activity A.4- Attribute Weighting*

Again, with the segmented data of A.2, the remaining operators of the process indicated in the 'Proceso Tanagra' sheet [22] are applied. That is, first, the 22 attributes are transformed into discrete values and then, the Näive Bayes operator is used to generate the conditional probability tables presented in the 'Res NaiveBayes' sheet [22].

- *Activity A.5- Design of the Characteristics Grids*

To finish this phase, the two grids corresponding to the attributes are then generated through the steps defined by the procedure and the conditional probability tables generated before. As it can be observed in the 'Parrilla de Caracteristicas' [22], these matrices have a structure of 9×22 formed by the nine values of clusters indicated as columns and the twenty-two attributes as rows.

- **Phase B: Formalization and Analysis of the Grids**
- *Activity B.1- Classification of the Elements*

In this phase, the clustering of the elements is performed. To this aim, it is essential to calculate their distance using the 'Parrilla de Elementos' sheet [22]. As a result, the matrix available in the 'Distancias de Elementos' sheet [22] is obtained.

- *Activity B.2- Classification of the Characteristics*

A similar process is repeated with the attributes, using the direct and opposite grids ('Parrilla de Caracteristicas' sheet of [22]) generated in the previous phase. With these two grids, the matrix of distance which can be seen in the 'Distancias de Caracteristicas' sheet is generated. Then, the distances on the diagonal are unified generating the matrix of unified distances included in the same tab.

- *Activity B.3- Interpretation of the Results*

From the clusters obtained in activities B.1 and B.2, the Ordered Tree of Elements and the Ordered Tree of Characteristics, which are available in the 'Interpretacion Elementos' sheet and the 'Interpretacion Caracteristicas' sheet of [22], are built. The interpretation of such trees is included below:

- Analysis of the Ordered Tree of Elements: In this tree, 2 groups can be found like in the initial version of the data. The students who fail the course (NO_APRUEBA element) show a more similar behavior to those who drop the course (this is the reason why they are not included in the final course record or TPA, NO_TPA element) than those who pass the course (APRUEBA element). Notwithstanding this, the similarity is very slight since they meet at a distance of 13.
- Analysis of the Ordered Tree of Characteristics: For this group, two major groups and nine groups of individual characteristics were generated. For the first major group (GP1), the most similar characteristics correspond to the results of the topics Systemic and Linear Thinking (PLS), Administrative Circuits and Theory in the second make-up exam (second semester) because they meet at a distance of 3. Then, at a distance of 4, the results of Organizational Charts in the second make-up exam and Theory in both make-up exams are added (the latter exams belong to the first semester). In addition, with a distance of 4, the results of Process Charts and Systems Methodology join for the second make-up exam of the first semester. These two subgroups meet later at 5, including the results of Administrative Circuits in the first make-up exam (second semester).

In the second major group (GP2), the results of Administrative Circuits and Theory in the second semester mid-term test meet at a distance of 5. The PLS results of the mid-term test of the second semester meet the Systems Methodology results of the first make-up exam of the first semester at a distance of 8. These two subgroups then join at a distance of 11.

On the other hand, five characteristics are added to GP1 between distances 6 and 11 while only one is added to GP2 at 13. Both groups meet after a distance of 14. Finally, the results of Process Charts and Organizational Charts of the first semester's mid-term test are the ones which differ the most (they meet at 16 and 22, respectively). However, the most different characteristic corresponds to the Course, which is added at a distance of 26.

- *Activity B.4- Discussion of the Results*

To finish the procedure, a new meeting is held with the teacher of the course who takes the role of domain expert to discuss the results obtained in the previous activities. Since the ordered tree of elements of this data version is similar to that obtained through the initial version of the data, its validity remains. It is only mentioned that in this new version, the similarity between the students who fail and those that are disenrolled is somewhat lower (in the initial version, they are unified at distance 10 and in this version, at a distance of 13), to which the expert does not object.

Instead, the ordered tree of the characteristics is completely different so it must be fully analyzed again. It should be noted that this time the expert is satisfied with the attributes since they properly represent each of the topics as he uses them. From the analysis of the groups detected, the following responses were obtained:

- In the first major group, the first attributes to unify correspond to the results of the second make-up exam in the second semester (C2_2R_PLS, C2_2R_CIRCUITOS and C2_2R_TEORIA), that is, to the last exam sat for by the students to determine whether they will have to re-take the course or not. According to the expert, the students who fail in passing many topics in the first make-up exam are not likely to pass all the topics in the second make-up exam. Then, if a student is sitting for the second make-up exam for all the topics, they will likely have to re-attend the course (either because they did not pass or because they dropped out). On the contrary, if it is a student who studied hard, they will have probably passed the three topics in the term test or in the first make-up exam, so they will not need to sit for those topics in the second make-up exam. Therefore, the clustering of these three attributes can be deemed correct since their behavior is similar.
- The attributes corresponding to some of the results of the Theory and Organizational Charts make-ups in the first semester are added to the previous attributes with a slight difference (C1_1R_TEORIA, C1_2R_TEORIA and C1_2R_ORGANI-GRAMA). According to the expert, this occurs because students who passed the Theory of the first semester (between the term test and its first make-up) are not likely to reach the second make-up exam of the second semester (in general, the students' performance improves in the course of the year). However, if a student reaches the second make-up exam having failed Organizational Charts, this student will probably have to sit for the Theory of the first semester, and it is almost certain that they did not pass the second term exam (which has an influence on the attributes of the first cluster).
- Independently of the previous attributes, the results of the second make-up exam for Process Charts and Systems Methodology (C1_2R_CURSOGRAMA and C1_2R_METODOLOGIA) are unified. Methodology is usually the most difficult topic to pass in the first semester since, as it was mentioned in the previous evaluation, the students just hand in the draft in the make-up instance. Since many hand in the draft before sitting for the make-up instance, the pass rate grows

exponentially, remaining only a few students for the second make-up exam (which is the normal behavior in the case of Process Charts). This means that most of the students who reach the second make-up exam with Methodology are those who have not handed in the draft yet, that is, the students who are postponing the study of the topics and therefore, they also have trouble with Process Charts.

- All these attributes then meet with the first make-up of Administrative Circuits (C2_1R_CIRCUITOS) that, as it was mentioned, is the most difficult topic of the second semester for the students to pass. This causes the results of the first make-up exam to have a low level similarity with the previous attributes. The same happens with the five attributes that are added later (C1_P_METODOLOGIA, C1_1R_ORGANIGRAMA, C1_1R_CURSOGRAMA, C2_1R_TEORIA and C2_1R_PLS), to which the expert is indifferent (he neither accepts nor he rejects the way the clustering was performed).

- In the case of the second major group, the results of Administrative Circuits and Theory of the second term test are clustered (C2_P_CIRCUITOS and C2_P_TEORIA), which are later added to the cluster between Systems Methodology in the first make-up exam and PLS in the second term test (C1_1R_METODOLOGIA and C2_P_PLS). For the expert, these clusters make sense. On the one hand, a student who passes Administrative Circuits often passes the Theory of that term test, and vice versa, the student who does not know Administrative Circuits does not know the Theory either. On the other hand, PLS is a topic which the students often pass in the term test (it is the easiest topic of the second term test), so the performance is similar to that of Methodology in the first make-up exam (as it was mentioned, most of the students study the topic for the make-up test).

- The groups above mentioned meet at a distance of 14, which does not generate any special opinion from the expert.

- The remaining attributes correspond to the Practice of the first term exam (C1_P_CURSOGRAMA and C1_P_ORGANIGRAMA) which in the evaluation of the initial version was also the last attribute to be clustered (C1_P_PRACTICA). Therefore, the same behavior remains because those are the topics which have the highest pass rate. The difference in the distance at which these attributes meet lies in the fact that Organizational Charts is often easier than Process Charts so the pass rate is slightly higher (the student who passes Process Charts is very likely to have also passed Organizational Charts). That makes Process Charts differentiate even more from the remaining topics in terms of the students' performance.

- Finally, the most different characteristic corresponds to the day in the week when the students attend classes (CURSO). As it was mentioned in the previous evaluation, this is because of the implicit and indirect relation between this attribute and the general performance of the student, which is not associated to any particular topic.

Consequently, it is concluded that the new data version is representative of the students' behavior in the course. Therefore, this data version can be used for the implementation of the Intelligent System (through a Bayesian Network or an Artificial Neuronal Network).

4 Conclusions

In this work, an adaptation of the Grid Repertory technique was applied to evaluate the data gathered on the students' performance in an undergraduate program course, and to determine whether they can be used in the creation of an Intelligent System that will foretell such performance.

From the analysis performed, the initial version of the data (more general and limited) shows biases that generate differences in the relationships preconceived by the teacher. Thus, the data were extended (providing more detailed in the attributes and more examples), which are considered sufficiently representative and, therefore, useful to be applied in the implementation of an Intelligent System that allows the students' performance in the course to be predicted. Notwithstanding this, this does not mean that the extended data are not biased, but that the bias of the data is consistent with the normal behavior of the students of this course in particular. So, if these data were used to predict the students' behavior in other courses, they would obviously not be useful.

Future lines of work include the construction of the Intelligent System with an extended version of the data to confirm the results of the evaluation performed.

References

1. Obama White House. Preparing for the Future of Artificial Intelligence. Executive Office of the President, National Science and Technology Council (NSTC) & Office of Science and Technology Policy (OSTP). Obama White House Archives (2016)
2. Shah, J., Tambe, M., Teller, A.: Artificial intelligence and life in 2030. One Hundred Year Study on Artificial Intelligence: Report of the 2015–2016 Study Panel. Stanford University (2016)
3. Alpaydin, E.: Machine Learning: The New AI. MIT Press, Cambridge (2016)
4. Domingos, P.: A few useful things to know about machine learning. Commun. ACM **55**(10), 78–87 (2012)
5. Domingos, P.: The Master Algorithm: How the Quest for the Ultimate Learning Machine Will Remake Our World. Basic Books, New York (2015)
6. Cohen, P.R., Feigenbaum, E.A.: The Handbook of Artificial Intelligence, vol. 3. Butterworth-Heinemann, Los Altos (2014)
7. Trujillano, J., March, J., Sorribas, A.: Aproximación metodológica al uso de redes neuronales artificiales para la predicción de resultados en medicina. Med. Clin. (Barc.) **122**(s1), 59–67 (2004)
8. Walczak, S.: An empirical analysis of data requirements for financial forecasting with neural networks. J. Manage. Inf. Syst. **17**(4), 203–222 (2001)
9. Hyndman, R.J., Kostenko, A.V.: Minimum sample size requirements for seasonal forecasting models. Foresight **6**(Spring), 12–15 (2007)
10. Raudys, S.J., Jain, A.K.: Small sample size effects in statistical pattern recognition: recommendations for practitioners. IEEE Trans. Pattern Anal. Mach. Intell. **13**(3), 252–264 (1991)
11. Stockwell, D.R., Peterson, A.T.: Effects of sample size on accuracy of species distribution models. Ecol. Model. **148**(1), 1–13 (2002)
12. Collins, N.: Artificial intelligence will be as biased and prejudiced as its human creators. Pacific Standard, 1 Septiembre 2016

13. Crawford, K.: Artificial Intelligence's White Guy Problem. The New York Times (2016)
14. Datta, A., Sen, S., Zick, Y.: Algorithmic transparency via quantitative input influence: theory and experiments with learning systems. In: Proceedings of 37th IEEE Symposium on Security and Privacy (2016)
15. Dujmovic, J.: Opinion: what's holding back artificial intelligence? Americans don't trust it. MarketWatch, 30 Marzo 2017
16. Vegega, C., Pytel, P., Pollo-Cattaneo, M.F.: Repertory grid based method to assess the data to train machine learning algorithms. Actas de Ingeniería, vol. 3, pp. 377–397. Revista Oficial de la Conferencia Internacional de Ingeniería INGENIO (2017). ISSN: 2463-0128
17. Universidad Tecnológica Nacional – Facultad Regional Buenos Aires. Perfil Profesional del Ingeniero en Sistemas de Información. DISI (2008)
18. Universidad Tecnológica Nacional – Facultad Regional Buenos Aires. Programa la carrera Ingeniería en Sistemas de Información (Plan 2008). DISI (2008)
19. Universidad Tecnológica Nacional – Facultad Regional Buenos Aires. Programa de la asignatura 'Sistemas y Organizaciones'. DISI (2008)
20. Vegega, C., Pytel, P., Pollo-Cattaneo, M.F.: Evaluation of data through the repertory grid method. Technical report GEMIS-TD-2017-02-TR-2018-02 (2018). http://grupogemis.com.ar/web/evaluation-of-data-through-the-repertory-grid-method/
21. Vegega, C., Bazet, A., Pytel, P., Pollo-Cattaneo, M.F.: Resultados de la aplicación sobre los datos de alumnos de Sistemas y Organizaciones del año 2016. Reporte Técnico GEMIS-TD-2017-02-TR-2017-06A (2017). https://goo.gl/EbdbDC
22. Vegega, C., Bazet, A., Pytel, P., Pollo-Cattaneo, M.F.: Resultados de la aplicación sobre los datos extendidos de alumnos de Sistemas y Organizaciones del año 2016. Reporte Técnico GEMIS-TD-2017-02-TR-2017-06B (2017). https://goo.gl/N3Khrb
23. Rakotomalala, R.T.: data mining software for academic and research purposes. In: Actes de EGC 2005, RNTI-E-3, vol. 2, pp. 697–702 (2005)
24. Black, P.E.: Manhattan distance. In: Dictionary of Algorithms and Data Structures, National Institute of Standards and Technology (NIST), U.S. Department of Commerce (2006)

Social Media Competitive Intelligence: Measurement and Visualization from a Higher Education Organization

Olmer García[1(✉)], Oscar Granados[1], and Fran Romero[2]

[1] Universidad Jorge Tadeo Lozano, Bogotá, Colombia
olmer.garciab@utadeo.edu.co
[2] Universidad del Bosque, Bogotá, Colombia

Abstract. Competitive Intelligence (CI) is a valuable tool that allows organizations to have information relevant to their environment, allowing them to anticipate changes, identify opportunities and focus on innovation. Implement useful methods for the control and systematic monitoring of the impact generated in social networks, is very useful in the context of the CI. This article proposes a methodology designed to process the information obtained about the activity of various Twitter accounts linked to the same institution. The first analysis, based on structured data of the twitters, lets to identify graphically how to find relations between the accounts data over the time. After that, it is presented how Natural Language Processing (NLP) using machine learning techniques could be used to visualize, classify and group the information. The methodology was tested with public data from a university through cloud computing services, so an CI analysis is performed for the institution. As result, we found the identification of crucial discussion topics within the analyzed community is highlighted, as well as the proposal of a control panel for monitoring the various associated accounts.

Keywords: Social network · Competitive intelligence · Machine learning
Natural Language Processing

1 Introduction

The information contained in social networks is the largest and most dynamic data based on human behavior, which offers new opportunities to understand people, communities and society in general [1]. Additionally, there is a lack of methodological strategies to manage information from social networks [2]. To solve this problem, the analysis of the data collected from the publications generated by different Twitter accounts linked to the same organization, as well as the responses and reactions to them, constitute a valuable input for CI strategies.

The information visualization generated from the publications on social networks, particularly on Twitter, seeks to provide visual representations of the complexity inherent in the textual data. For example, in [3], they make a proposal to visualize the behavior of feelings in the timeline based on data processing techniques and machine learning.

H. Florez et al. (Eds.): ICAI 2018, CCIS 942, pp. 32–44, 2018.
https://doi.org/10.1007/978-3-030-01535-0_3

Literature has several approaches to analyze feelings and the construction of opinions. Many analyses of information from social networks use Data mining techniques [4], which use various unstructured data analysis techniques from Twitter to show their usefulness in identifying patterns. De Boom [5] uses clustering algorithms on sets of tweets with semantic information, generating a proposal to improve the detection of events. [6], present a methodology based on semantic grouping on the hashtags extracted from a set of tweets, allowing discovering relevant information in the field of Oncology. [7], propose a method of gathering the users of a social network based on a measure of centrality weighted on a graph. The analysis of feelings and opinions based on the Web articulates different situations that users present when they interact in the social network [8–11]. Additionally, several algorithm techniques have identified approaches for analysis of emotions [12–15] and the processes where anxiety, affections or passions can direct feelings towards a particular situation that influence behavior and addressing of social networks [16, 17].

This article proposes to analyze the tweets through Natural Language Processing (NLP), which "is an area of research and application that explores how computers can be used to understand and manipulate natural language text or speech to do useful things." The method of analysis selected use machine learning defined as an essential subjection of Artificial Intelligence (AI), which aimed to design algorithms that allow computers to evolve behaviors based on empirical data [18]. In this case, the empirical data is raw tweets, which are the input of the algorithms presented in this article.

The learning problem looks for a general rule that could explain the examples even if only a limited size of samples exists. These algorithms can be divided into supervised and unsupervised. The first one requires known the target or label expected for the data used to teach to the algorithm. These methods include for example made a sentimental analysis or try to predict which tweets will have more impact (likes and retweets) in the future. The second one, it used in this article, try to arrange the input data, with the possibility of extracting some "structure" from them. If the structure exists, it is possible to take advantage of this redundancy and find a concise description of the data representing specific similarity between any pairs of objects [19].

In the following text, the first section introduces the methodology to process the tweets produced by a higher education organization and generate the visualization of the data to identify the critical discussion topics within the community of the organization. The following section presents the results to analyze the CI of the organization. Finally, the last section shows the conclusions and future studies.

2 Methodology

The adoption of CI strategies as result the information analysis from social networks starts with the contents evaluation, where opinions and feelings expressed by users are grouped. This aim is the design of a continuous cycle of planning, collection, processing, analysis, dissemination and, feedback of the results [20].

The information used to carry out the analysis comes from Twitter®. For its part, the analytical tool is R®, which provides several libraries focused on the statistical analysis of texts and natural language processing. In addition, it provides libraries with functionalities to connect to social networks and download information from publications in bulk. Through an instance of R Server®, using the Microsoft Azure® HDInsight services, a script was executed that downloads information from users and stakeholders and inserts it into an instance of MySQL®, also implemented using the MS Azure® services.

In the case of Twitter®, the information generated by fifteen active accounts linked to the Jorge Tadeo Lozano University was analyzed, namely: @UtadeoMediateca, @UtadeoCaribe, @Utadeo_edu_co, @tadeolab, @TadeoCrossLab, @tadeo_investiga, @Oyeme_UJTL, @LaBrujula_UJTL, @FEconoAdmUtadeo, @EgresadosTadeo, @EditorialUTadeo, @CulturaUtadeo, @ConfucioBogota, @AuditorioFabioL, @CODIGO_URBANO.

Twitter provides an API that allows applications written by third parties to connect to an account and massively download user information and published tweets. First, it is necessary to create an App on Twitter and connect using the OAuth protocol to access the data. After, a library in the specific language, twitteR [21], in this case, allows the use of the API through the call to specific methods to obtain the information of published tweets as well as of the users and hashtags. twitteR also allows using the search features provided by the social network.

The public information available to each user corresponds to Name, Twitter id, personal URL, user description, location, number of friends and followers, language and number of publications. On the other hand, for each published tweet is possible to obtain the following information: Twitter id, text, creation date, user information that generated it, place of generation, number of re-tweeted, number of times marked as favorite, language, and id of the tweet to which it responds.

In a first methodological approach to search of relevant knowledge, about 250,000 tweets generated by friends and followers of target groups were downloaded and analyzed. This approach was not practical because most tweets were related to personal issues and outside the interest of the university; On the other hand, downloading all this information demands a considerable cost in time, given the restrictions imposed by the Twitter API (approximately five tweets per second).

A more practical way to carry out the analysis is to focus on the tweets that the diverse groups have published, and from there, to evaluate the response, they have had from their followers. Figure 1 shows the simple count of the tweets generated by each group during each month of the year 2017.

To focus more efficiently on the publications that have generated the most significant impact among the friends and followers of the different groups, we chose to assign a factor that measures the likes and retweets received as a proportion of tweets sent in a specific month as it is presented by (1). This value will be called the impact.

$$Impact_i = \frac{likes_i + retweets_i}{tweets_i}, \quad i = January, february, \ldots \quad (1)$$

Based on the impact calculated for each month, it can be identified the months in which there was more activity. In this way, the analysis focused on the publications generated by groups in those months. Figure 2 shows the calculated impact for each group in each of the months of 2017.

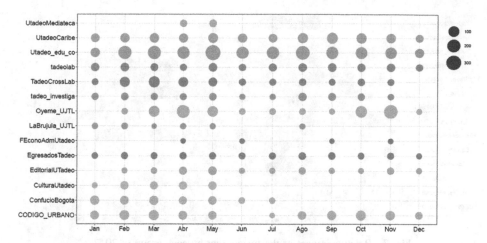

Fig. 1. Number of tweets generated by each group for the year 2017

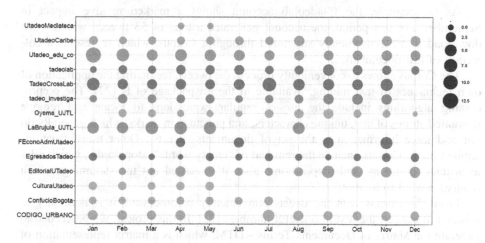

Fig. 2. Likes and retweets as a proportion of the total of tweets sent by each group.

The relative impact of different publications is measured, comparing likes and retweets received in each month as a proportion of the total of likes and retweets received in the analysis period, the year 2017 for this case (2).

$$RelativeImpact_i = \frac{likes_i + retweets_i}{\sum_i likes_i + retweets_i}, \quad i = January, \ldots \quad (2)$$

Using values calculated from (2), the heat map generated shows the relative impact of the tweets sent by each of the groups in each month -see Fig. 3-. The areas painted a more intense blue indicate the months in which the publications aroused the highest interest of friends and followers; this information is quite useful to concentrate the subsequent analysis on these periods.

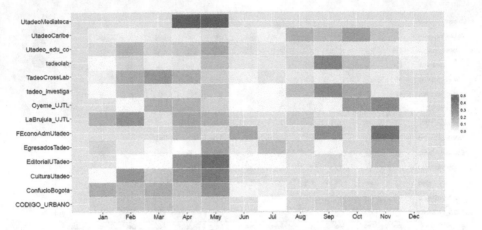

Fig. 3. Relative impact of the tweets sent by each group in 2017.

As an example, the @tadeolab account shows a marked relative impact in September. For this period, the account generated a total of 53 tweets, which, once downloaded, are conveniently structured through a Corpus, which represents a collection of text documents.

The Corpus allows to conveniently process the tweets, facilitating the application of own techniques of text mining, available in the tm package of R [22]. The preprocessing algorithms include the use of regular expressions to locate and remove unwanted strings of text, unique characters, and punctuation marks, which generally do not add more information to the set of documents -tweets-. Other transformations applied on the Corpus, include the removal of "empty words" -stopwords-, which refer to articles, pronouns, and prepositions; also, it is carried out the stemming, which reduces a word to its root.

From the Corpus with the tweets conveniently preprocessed, it is necessary to proceed to convert the text into useful numbers [23]. In this project, we proceeded to generate the Matrix of Documents-Terms - DTM, which is a matrix representation of the tweets, in which each column corresponds one word and each row to a tweet. The *Nij* entries of the DTM count the times that the *ith* word appears in the *jth* tweet. This representation lets to carry out a statistical analysis of the texts, as well as for the application of classification and grouping techniques. Since the resulting DTM has many zeros, R allows decreasing the dimension using a specified dispersion factor. It is important to point out that the manipulation of the Corpus, for this small case has around 40,000 documents, as well as the DTM, whose dimension is approximately 40000×3200, could be carried out by implementing an R Server cluster on MS Azure.

Considering that the visualization of information constitutes an essential and characteristic input when implementing CI strategies, multiple presentation formats have been established and applied for the established results, such as word clouds, hierarchical groupings - dendrograms - and directed graphs.

Using the R package [22], lets to generate the word clouds shown in Fig. 4, which allows visualizing the most used terms for the case mentioned above.

Fig. 4. Most common terms for the @TadeoLab account in September 2017.

From the use of regular expressions, all the hashtags used in publications made have been extracted. The analysis of hashtags provides relevant information, allowing to identify topics that are a trend. The bar chart in Fig. 5 shows the most used hashtags in conversations that occurred in the account @tadeolab during September 2017. As the word cloud, it is evident that the terms related to an event called hactravel, are the ones that appear more frequently.

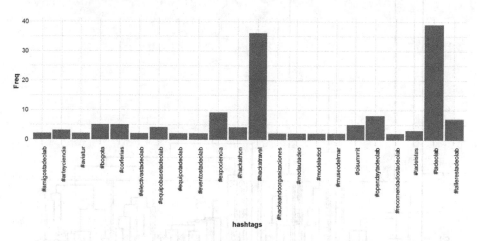

Fig. 5. Hashtags used in the @TadeoLab account in September 2017.

To identify the different topics, which groups and users are thinking during a specified period, in the first instance it is proposed to use unsupervised machine learning techniques. Specifically, the clustering technique, which is a process in which they form data sets that have similar characteristics, that create a cluster. Next, the two techniques used are presented.

In the first case, the hierarchical clustering algorithm seeks to group clusters to form a new cluster or divide an existing cluster, giving rise to two others; this process of agglomeration/division is carried out successively until a distance is minimized or similarity is maximized. Figure 6 corresponds to a dendrogram, in which the height gives the similarity between two tweets or groups of tweets - shown on the vertical scale - of the closest common node. Four subgroups are Blue highlighted, which the distance between its components is less than four units; To summarize each subgroup, a cloud of words has been generated, shown in Fig. 7.

On the other hand, the k-means algorithm has been applied to carry out a grouping by partitions. This algorithm requires knowing in advance the number of groups to assign, in this case, four groups. This number selected according to the Elbow method, in which the error function is plotted for different numbers of groups, identifying the point at which the aggregation of more groups does not represent a significant reduction in the variance. The visualization of the partitions uses reduction of the dimensionality through Principal Components Analysis - PCA, which let to generate a bidimensional diagram. In this way, despite the fact that there are more than 3000 dimensions with only two new dimensions, the highest possible variance of the data can be seen (22% in this case). Figure 8 shown the generated partitions. That algorithms and cluster visualization functions are available in the cluster package of R [7].

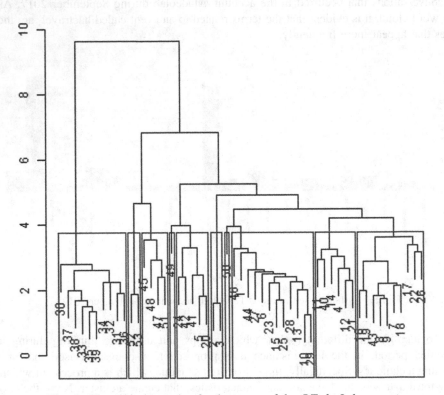

Fig. 6. Hierarchical grouping for the tweets of the @TadeoLab account

Fig. 7. Word clouds corresponding to each group in the hierarchical grouping

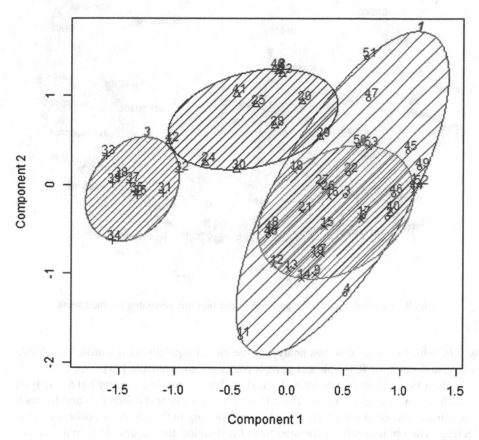

Fig. 8. Groups generated by the k-means algorithm. The two components explain 22% in the variation of the data.

The analysis described so far has been carried out again, but no longer using separate words, other than bigrams, which correspond to consecutive pairs of words. Analysis by bigrams allows a better semantic analysis of the texts [24]. For example, Fig. 9 shows a graph that allows to simultaneously visualize all relationships between

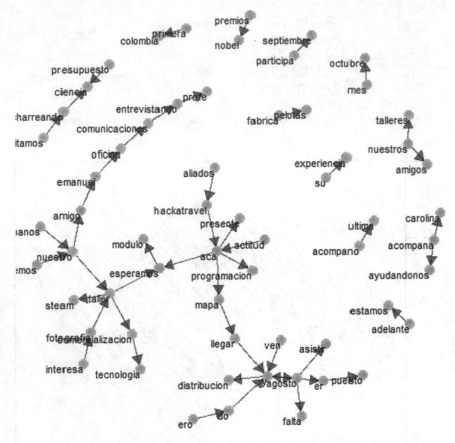

Fig. 9. Directed graph corresponding to the bigrams generated for the tweets

words, which is better than just analyzing the most frequently used words. To achieve this visualization in R igraph and ggraph packages are available [25].

Using the services of MS Azure for text analysis is possible to carry out an analysis of feelings about a set of tweets. The API receives a set of text documents and for each one returns a score in the interval [0, 1], corresponding to the degree of positivity of the feeling. The opinion score generated use classification techniques. The input characteristics of the classifier include n-grams, characteristics generated from syntax tags and word insertion.

When applying this analysis, Fig. 10 presents the results. The graph lets to conclude that There is a higher proportion of texts with a positive connotation.

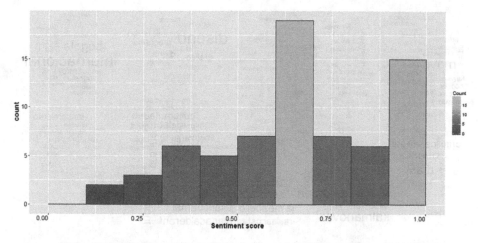

Fig. 10. Sentiment analysis for the tweets of the @TadeoLab account

3 Impact Over CI

The analysis described in the previous section was performed for each of the institutional accounts that were part of the study. From the results, some of the groups maintain a relatively constant activity in the social network, while others only publish sporadically, which influences the number of reactions -likes and retweets- that they obtain from their followers. On the other hand, towards the middle and the end of the year some accounts stop having activity, due to the absence of students during the holidays.

The use of the relative impact indicator turns out to be very useful to identify the topics that have aroused the most significant interest within the community. This indicator was performed for original tweets of each group, which is, those that are not retweets. Apart from the institutional accounts - @ Utadeo_edu_co and @ Utadeo-Caribe -, which are followed by almost all the students. Which generate a large volume of tweets, likes, and retweets, the accounts associated with research groups of the University stand out - @ Tadeo_Investiga, @TadeoLab, @ TadeoCrossLab-, whose publications generated many reactions, producing a positive impact within the virtual community.

In the case study, the topics that aroused the most significant interest revolved around "The Documentary Center" -a virtual photography exhibition on the center of Bogotá- China, the Fulbright chair, the Colombian region of Chocó and Cartagena. In the face of today's competition in the education sector, it is necessary to take more significant advantage of the information that emerges from social networks and from there strengthen these elements as part of a competitive strategy [26]. From the analysis carried out on the hashtags and the information thrown the grouping techniques used, a summary obtained show the topics that generated the most significant impact throughout the year or any period that one wishes to know (Fig. 11).

Fig. 11. Word clouds generated from grouping the tweets of @Utadeo_edu_co

In this sample, the unified use of a single account, as well as interaction from labels, strengthen the definition of a more successful communication strategy of the higher education organizations. It is possible to interact better in the social network based on positive comments of collective order and not only on an individual proposal based on adverse situations or comments that do not link the word network correctly as if the comments made from labels. For this reason, labels can be an active part to carry out a communication strategy in social networks successfully and thus make better use of information than tools to build a competitive intelligence based on the visualization of social network data.

The feeling analysis is also a useful tool to characterize the activity generated by groups and users. At the global level, the opinion polarity expressed is positively oriented, highlighting the notable impact generated by the accounts @ Oyeme_UJTL and the magazine @CODIGO_URBANO.

4   Conclusion

Analyze efficiently and systematically the activity generated in social networks enhance the knowledge about students, professors and interest groups linked to the higher education organization taken as a case study. This knowledge promotes the discovery of new opportunities, innovation, and better decision-making, significantly benefiting CI strategies.

The development of a methodology of analysis on the publications made by various Twitter accounts linked to the same institution, and the impact they generate becomes a valuable tool to address the communications strategy, emphasizing those topics and proposals that generate more significant interaction with the community and, in general, with the target audience.

Build and maintain a centralized control board to monitor the activity of the various social network accounts allows communication departments to have a continuous measurement on the impact they are generating, even helps determine those accounts let to generate some type of negative impact due to inactivity or inappropriate approaches that generate negative feelings.

While there are commercial tools in the market to monitor activities in social networks, the use of free software such as R and its multiple libraries available for connectivity with social networks and unstructured information processing is an excellent option to personalize the analysis. In this work, MS Azure® Cognitive Services has been used to analyze feelings, although it can be carried out using free-use tools.

References

1. Batrinca, B., Treleaven, P.C.: Social media analytics: a survey of techniques, tools and platforms. AI Soc. **30**, 89–116 (2015)
2. Brooker, P., Barnett, J., Cribbin, T.: Doing social media analytics. Big Data Soc. **3**, 2053951716658060 (2016)
3. Hoeber, O., Hoeber, L., El Meseery, M., Odoh, K., Gopi, R.: Visual Twitter Analytics (Vista) temporally changing sentiment and the discovery of emergent themes within sport event tweets. Online Inf. Rev. **40**, 25–41 (2016)
4. Khanaferov, D., Luc, C., Wang, T.: Social network data mining using natural language processing and density based clustering. In: 2014 IEEE International Conference on Semantic Computing (ICSC) (2014)
5. De Boom, C., Van Canneyt, S., Dhoedt, B.: Semantics-driven event clustering in twitter feeds. In: Making Sense of Microposts (2015)
6. Vicient, C., Moreno, A.: Unsupervised semantic clustering of Twitter hashtags. In: ECAI (2014)
7. Zudilova, T.V., Ivanov, S.E.: The clustering methods in graph models of social networks. Appl. Math. Sci. **11**, 1007–1017 (2017)
8. Christakis, N., Fowler, J.: Connected: The Surprising Power of Our Social Networks and How They Shape Our Lives. Little Brown and Company, New York (2009)
9. Chau, M., Xu, J.: Int. J. Hum. Comput. Stud. **65**, 57–70 (2007)
10. Liu, B.: Web Data Mining: Exploring Hyperlinks, Contents, and Usage Data. Springer, Liepzig (2011)
11. Pang, B., Lee, L.: Opinion mining and sentiment analysis. Found. Trends Inf. Retr. **2**, 1–135 (2008)
12. Allen, C., Machleit, K., Schultz Kleine, S., Notani, A.S.: A place for emotion in attitude models. J. Bus. Res. **58**(4), 494–499 (2005)
13. Chmiel, A., et al.: Collective emotions online and their influence on community life. PLoS ONE **6**, e22207 (2011)
14. DeSteno, D., Petty, R., Rucker, D., Wegener, D., Braverman, J.: Discrete emotions and persuasion: the role of emotion-induced expectancies. J. Person. Soc. Psychol. **86**, 43–56 (2004)
15. Prabowo, R., Thelwall, M.: Sentiment analysis: A combined approach. J. Informetrics **3**, 143–157 (2009)
16. Alkis, Y., Kadirhan, Z., Sat, M.: Development and validation of social anxiety scale for social media users. Comput. Hum. Behav. **72**, 296–303 (2017)

17. Wakefield, R., Wakefield, K.: Social media network behavior: A study of user passion and effect. J. Strat. Inf. Syst. **25**, 140–156 (2016)
18. Chen, C.L.P., Zhang, C.-Y.: Data-intensive applications, challenges, techniques and technologies: a survey on big data. Inf. Sci. **275**, 314–347 (2014)
19. Garcia, O., Diaz, C.: Machine learning applied to autonomous vehicles. In: Rabelo, L.B.S., Gutierrez, E. (eds.) Artificial Intelligence: Advances in Research and Applications, pp. 49–74. Nova Science Publications Inc. (2018)
20. Miller, S.H.: Competitive intelligence–an overview. Compet. Intell. Mag. **1**(11), 1–14 (2001)
21. Gentry, J.: Package 'twitteR' (2016)
22. Feinerer, I., Hornik, K.: Text Mining Package, R reference Manual, R-project.org (2014)
23. Richert, W.: Building Machine Learning Systems with Python. Packt Publishing Ltd., Birmingham (2013)
24. Schmidt, D., Heckendorf, C.: Guide to the ngram Package (2014)
25. Csárdi, G., Nepusz, T.: The igraph software package for complex network research. InterJournal, p. 1995 (2006)
26. Granados, O., Velez-Langs, O.: Competitive intelligence in the service sector: a data visualization approach. Commun. Comput. Inf. Sci. **852**, 1–9 (2018)

Towards Automated Advertising Strategy Definition Based on Analytics

Vladimir Sanchez Riaño, Cesar Diaz[✉], Carenne Ludeña,
Liliana Catherine Suarez Baez, and Jairo Sojo

Universidad de Bogotá Jorge Tadeo Lozano, Bogotá, Colombia
{vladimir.sanchez,cesaro.diazb,carennec.ludenac,liliana.suarez,
jairo.sojo}@utadeo.edu.co
http://www.utadeo.edu.co

Abstract. In today's world, advertising has become one of the most important aspects of modern life and has impacted society in many ways. We could say, that it has become embedded (even surreptitiously) into the human symbolic universe. On the other hand, social networks play an almost ubiquitous role both in message production and transmission, as well as providing unique insights not readily available through other channels. It is only natural then, to develop strategies capable of automating information retrieval and processing. Our main goal is the construction of an automated process for the constitution of an advertising strategy based on the use of social network data and user provided information. The underlying model considers text mining algorithms along with an innovative content-based decision process constructed in terms of theoretic-semiotic assumptions of pragmatism of Charles Sanders Peirce. We describe a practical application of the proposed methodology in order to obtain the required insights for the future construction of the advertising strategy of an academic institution in Colombia based on Facebook, Twitter and student-surveys as a first step in the development of an automated solution.

Keywords: Automated advertising · Social networks
Data analytics · Big Data

1 Introduction

Since the advent of modern advertising organizations, such as Leo Burnett, Rosser Reeves, Bill (William) Bernbach and David Ogilvy, advertising had not experienced a transformation as profound as it has in recent years. Advertising firms of the second decade of the 21st century must offer its clients not only persuasive communication solutions with a high degree of creativity, but also holistic solutions and technological developments.

This is quite a challenge for advertisers who need to find new more efficient methodologies, increasing data quality while improving retrieval time [8].

© Springer Nature Switzerland AG 2018
H. Florez et al. (Eds.): ICAI 2018, CCIS 942, pp. 45–59, 2018.
https://doi.org/10.1007/978-3-030-01535-0_4

The planning model proposed in this paper aims to be a significant contribution in the development of strategic and communicative intelligence because it integrates semiotic research, modern trends in market research and developments in data intelligence. This semiotic model of strategic planning proposes new processes, and, although it requires traditional and digital sources of information, it allows new ways to interpret and consume information from digital sources, aiming at an integrated marketing and communication solutions approach.

In this paper, we propose an innovative research methodology as an application of this new way to work in advertising planning models. For this, traditional research with social media analysis using big data tools are combined. In our approach, traditional research has a very low percentage of participation and we focus on search algorithms and text mining as well as word association methodologies for obtaining the insights required for the planning process in advertising. Our goal in the near future is to create a completely automatized process for planning advertising. For this, the first step is establishing an abstract Semiotic Planning Model which we describe in Sect. 2. We do not include particular examples as to not bias the general conception, but rather emphasize on the construction of a planning matrix which once fed with the required insights, meanings and information, provides the basis for the advertising strategy.

2   Advertising Semiotic Model

The advertising semiotic model has its theoretical foundation in the North American philosophical current called pragmatism. In general terms, pragmatism can be considered as a philosophical position that emerged in the late nineteenth and early twentieth century Cambridge United States, within a group of intellectuals who called themselves the "Metaphysical Club". In particular, we work from the perspective of C.S. Peirce, who called it pragmaticism [11] to differentiate it from its other club mates [7]. The central idea of this method is that the meaning of the concepts and therefore their significance processes is not established by the definition or familiarity with them, but through the practical effects of such concepts in the real world. These effects are transformed into beliefs understood as action rules and embodied in habits of sensation, action or reason. The model has six stages that are explained below.

2.1   Stage One: "Planning Objective"

In the process of implementation and execution of the planning model, the client or advertiser arrives with a clear objective, which expresses his need related to the product or brand [9]. Usually what a client wants is to increase their sales; however, it is important to validate this objective through the research processes and the context that the account team has had before (if there is one). This objective is analyzed by appealing to the context of the market and evaluating whether the objective is to solve the real needs of the product or brand. If it is not, the objective must be restated, to express a clear purpose that allows a location and strategic movements within the planning model.

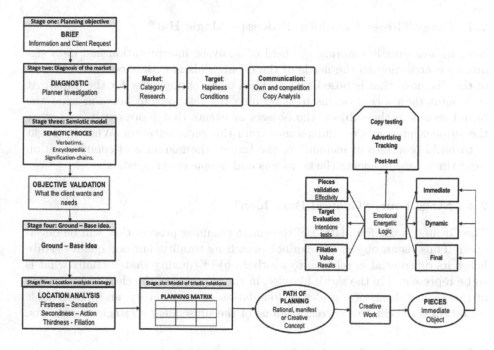

Fig. 1. Advertising planning semiotic model

2.2 Stage Two: "Market Diagnosis"

The meaning of the data collected in the research that the client has conducted or that has been made for the preparation of the planning, must be interpreted. Qualitative, quantitative studies, reviews, field visits, brand reviews, focus groups, ethnographies, digital eavesdropping, big data diagnostics, among others, were conducted. This done in order to separate or cross data and find new information beyond the apparent one. The three basic pillars are:

- Analysis of the *Target*: recipient intended to be reached by the product or service for which the advertising strategy is planned.
- Market category and Benchmarking: It is necessary to observe the direct competition and the one that "works as a substitute" supplying the necessity that the product or service fulfills. It is also important to determine where and in what channels the brand is in relation to the others, especially for market leaders.
- Communication strategies: In this final aspect, the strategy of the competition is observed, in terms of what type of characteristics, competitive advantages are communicated, in what tone and style the target is spoken. The tool in this process is the Copy Analysis.

2.3   Stage Three: "Semiotic Process - Magic Hat"

Here we are already entering the field of analysis, interpretation and data significance according to the needs of the client. This is understood as the result of the diagnosis that is posed as a problem or an opportunity for the brand. At this point the process begins to determine the relationship between what the brand means to the subject, the objects or events that represent it, and what the subject interprets or understands from this representation. What is sought is to build processes of meaning of the target, the market and communication from three base moments (facts, means and people encyclopedias).

2.4   Stage Four: "Ground Base Idea"

The Ground is the foundation of the entire planning process that will be developed. Thus, as an object one can not preach its totality, but one quality establishes its differential in relation to another object (quality that is finally what is to be represented in the sign); likewise, in the planning of the clear identification of the ground, basis of the idea or foundation of the strategy, an indispensable condition is to achieve a correct framing of the subsequent strategic movements.

2.5   Stage Five: "Location Analysis Strategy"

To determine where the brand is or if the product should be analyzed, the *Ground* and the destination determine the actions that the quadrants will take. The *Ground* will give entrance to the planning in the model, since it allows establishing the starting point around what needs to be communicated. This considers three levels

1. Firstness: need is to establish a sensible connection between the consumer and the product
2. Secondness: need is to reinforce the quality and emphasize the promotion and sale of the product
3. Thirdness: filiation processes and brand loyalty.

2.6   Stage Six: "Model of Triadic Relations"

The model is developed in a matrix of three columns and three rows that generates nine quadrants and ten strategic planning movements. In the rows, the Ground is located depending on whether the entry is by quality (Firstness), by action (Secondness), or affiliation/fidelization (Thirdness). In the columns is located *what do you want to communicate?* The second *How do you want to communicate?* Finally the third one. *What is the expected response?* With the entry of the Ground the matrix is as follows:

Once the Ground is defined, the following possible combinations are analyzed in Quality (or First), action (or second) and filiation (or third). The movements must always be in a horizontal movement at the same level of the row in the

PLANNING MODEL	What do you want to communicate?	How do you want to communicate?	What is the expected response?
Possible input of the Ground by Quality	→→→→		
Possible input of the Ground by Action	→→→→		
Possible input of the Ground by Filiation	→→→→		

Fig. 2. Planning initial matrix

direction towards higher levels and not towards the lower ones; this allows to establish ten possible movements. The movement that starts from the Ground of quality (movement one), has emphasis in the expectation and launching phases. The movements that start from the Ground of Action (movements two, three and four) have their emphasis in the launching and positioning phases, especially movement four, since the other two can be combined with the Ground of quality. The movements that start from the Affiliation/Loyalty Ground (movements five, six, seven, eight, nine and ten) have their emphasis in the branding phase [10], especially movement ten, since the other five can be combine with the Action Ground.

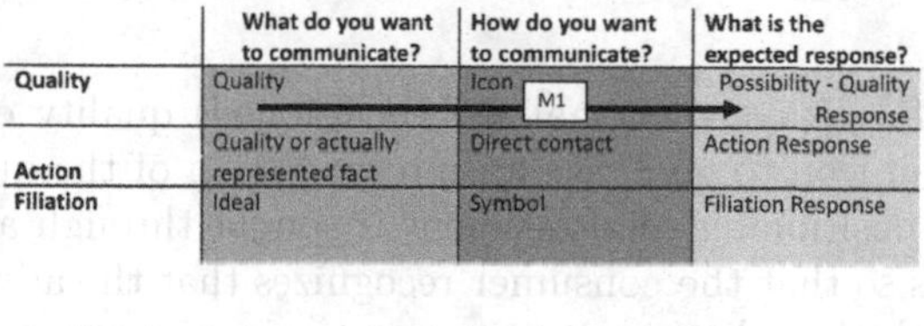

	What do you want to communicate?	How do you want to communicate?	What is the expected response?
Quality	Quality	Icon M1	Possibility - Quality Response
Action	Quality or actually represented fact	Direct contact	Action Response
Filiation	Ideal	Symbol	Filiation Response

Fig. 3. Movement 1: With the ground defined in Quality it's possible the following combination

Movement 1 (M1): Quality of a product represented through an icon to generate an interpretation of a quality that is possible to find in the product. The consumer is expected to recognize that the advertised product possesses the preached quality.

Movement 2 (M2): Real product represented through an icon to generate an interpretation of a quality embodied in the product. It is sought that, through iconic elements about the product and its main qualities, the consumer recognizes that the advertised product possesses the preached quality.

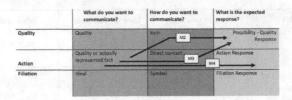

Fig. 4. Movements 2–4: With the Ground defined in action, exist the following possible combinations

Movement 3 (M3): Real product represented through an index to generate an interpretation of quality embodied in the product. It is sought that, through a direct contact with the product, the consumer recognizes that the advertised product possesses the preached quality.

Movement 4 (M4): The real product is represented through an index to generate an interpretation of real existence (the product really exists and actually fulfills that function). It is sought that, through a direct contact with the product, the consumer carries out the purchase of the product.

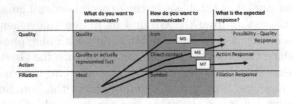

Fig. 5. Movements 5–7: Starting with the Ground, these are the possible combinations

Movement 5 (M5): A conventionalized (positioned) quality of a brand, represented through an icon to generate an interpretation of the quality embodied in the product. A positioning reinforcement is sought through a product representation processes so that the consumer recognizes that the advertised product possesses the preached quality.

Movement 6 (M6): A conventionalized (positioned) quality of a brand, represented through an index to generate an interpretation of quality or possibility in the product. A positioning reinforcement is sought through processes of direct contact with the brand so that the consumer recognizes that the advertised product possesses the preached quality.

Movement 7 (M7): A conventionalized (positioned) quality of a brand, represented through an index to generate an interpretation that the product really exists and generate the purchase decision and brand-loyalty. Purchase because of brand-loyalty is sought.

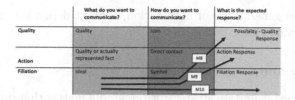

Fig. 6. Movements 8–10

Movement 8 (M8): A conventionalized (positioned) quality of a brand represented by symbols to generate an interpretation of the quality that is embodied in the brand. The expected response is of Quality; that is, the consumer is encouraged to reinforce the recognition that the loyal brand has the preached quality.

Movement 9 (M9): A conventionalized (positioned) quality of a brand, represented through symbols to generate an interpretation that the product really exists and generate the purchase decision and loyalty with the brand. The expected response is of action; that is, purchase for loyalty to the brand.

Movement 10 (M10): It is the aspired end-point for any product in terms of brand architecture, it is the moment of total branding. It is a conventionalized (positioned) quality of a brand, represented through symbols to generate an interpretation, an embodied habit of purchase or use. The expected response is the Top of mind, Top of heart and Top of hand advertising.

Through the selection of the movements in the matrix, we obtain the **Planning Path** that ends with the location analysis leading to a manifest (if it is firstness), a Conexial (if it is in secondness term) or a Rational (if it is thirdness). In any of the three cases, the creative concept that explains the planning path(s) is expressed. This concept is then given to the creative department with all the necessary information for planning.

The strategic planning developed through pragmatics becomes a process that helps visualizing and designing the plan on what the Ground will achieve in the product or the brand. This includes what to say, what elements to use in communication and what is the response you want to receive according to the input of the Ground in the planning matrix. It also marks the fulfillment of the brand objective, in order to take full advantage of the existing communication potential and, above all, take advantage of the semiotic process that makes the model different.

3 Analytics

In order to automate the process of obtaining insight from data ("magic hat" step) Social Network (SN) information was retrieved and analyzed as described as follows. In the general aim of automation, context dependent information is included user-defined information.

3.1 Category and Concept Matrix

As part of the word definition strategy, we created a matrix that describes all the variables that make up the service of the university. For this we created several large categories such as service, academics, administrative and so on. Then we created sub-categories to each category and variables to each sub-category. This matrix allowed us to understand better the positioning of the university in social media, we could know in which variables of service people are either more happy or more angry about. It was necessary to define for each variable a list of positive and negative words, positive and negative sentences that people could used to talk about the services. This list of words and phrases were mostly what was already in the dictionary but we increased the list with the results of a survey applied to the students of the university. The survey was anonymous and sought for a free student's expression about the services of the university. The strategy was organized in a series of steps which we describe below. The methodology follows five steps:

User Defined Page Selection for Analysis. The objective in this step is to find the pages of the university in Facebook, whether official or not, in which the content and the interactions were large enough to make a web scraping in the fifth step. In order to accomplish this objective we create the input for a user-defined page list and a first-draft dictionary with the most common words used in the selected pages to talk about the brand, classified as positive and negative words.

Observation and Monitoring of Selected Pages. The selected pages are monitored for a period of 15 days with the objective of increasing the list of common words and the context in which those words were used. Furthermore, this observation provided information about which pages were really susceptible to be analyzed. The result of this step was a shorter list of pages to analyze and a bigger set of words used by people to talk about the brand in analysis.

Dictionary Construction. A dictionary was created in which we included the common words used by people to talk about the brand or its services. As a starting point, this research defined positioning as a "means of finding the proper location" in the minds of a group of consumers or market segment, so that they think about a product or service in the "right" or desired way to maximize the potential benefit of the firm. Good brand positioning helps to guide marketing strategy by clarifying what a brand is all about, how it is unique and how it is similar to competitive brands, and why consumer should purchase and use it [5]. So, in the dictionary we included words and hashtags that University uses to communicate to students, workers and regular people the academic and non-academic activities/events, accomplishments, news, etc.

Information Retrieval. The dictionary provided the basis for automatic search of SN. We discuss information retrieval for two popular platforms, Twitter and Facebook, describing the basis of the automated procedure. The described procedures can be applied to other SN, according to the particular characteristics of each. Twitter: this SN is characterized by short texts, sometimes describing images or links, but in general, the main message is contained in text. In general also, this SN is not used as a specific way of relating to the brand, such as maybe writing on the FB page of the brand. Finding information specifically related to the brand and concepts pertaining the list of common words. Thus strategies involving Twitter must take this into consideration. In our case of study we considered rather a list directly involving the brand and then at the analytic stage applying filters related to list words or association strategies. Texts were retrieved using the twitter API linking to brand username and/or special hashtags provided by the brand. Facebook: this SN is characterized by short to medium texts, but in many cases refereed to images, videos or links which are unavailable for analytics, unless willing to consider processing attachments at the cost of a much more sophisticated analytics platform. Also, unlike Twitter, information from FB is oriented by the brand itself, thus introducing a concept bias. In our case, this led to the definition of two strategies of information retrieval. For the first, only comments (and comments of comments) related to brand posts were retrieved. The original message was kept only a reference. For the second, comments from brand-user communities were used, as well as comments from these. Whenever related to images, although the image was kept as a reference, only text related information was kept. Additionally, for the brand post, FB provided analytics concerning characteristics of each brand post (likes, reposts, number of comments, etc.) which were used in order to rank posts in different ways during analysis. Texts were retrieved using the FB API with a Python program.

Web Scrapping. The phrase "Information is power" attributed to the philosopher, writer, politician and lawyer Francis Bacon, allows you to deep this concept [1,2]. It is one of the main foundations to make the right decisions in management, based on the knowledge of the available data. "The massive data point to the beginning of a considerable transformation" [6].

Web Scraping gives the solution of the task of Copy & Paste, when it came to download information of websites and depending on this, build databases about some kind of knowledge, task that with the increase of information volume was almost an assignment impossible. The availability of data in a way public [3], of course, has generated various debates of what is appropriate and not the use of this information, that is why policies of privacy and protection of own data for each website and available in them, where stipulates, among other aspects, related matters with the use of information permits and/or prohibitions, so, when trying to use information on web pages [4], it is imperative to consult about their policies to apply the use of the information that is received from these pages. Web scraping is a technique that through a software can access the content of what is published on the Internet in the web browser. It can be automatic using an Internet bot or a Web Crawler.

3.2 Information Processing

Having finished the information retrieval process, standard text preprocessing was considered and analytics were performed over the pre-processed text. In particular, document term matrices were created for the preprocessed texts and further word analytics was based on these structures [12]. We briefly describe the procedure. All text processing and analysis was done in the open source statistical and analytical programming language R with packages tm, stringr, slam, wordcloud, topicmodels and Rgraphviz.

1. Text mining: Twitter and FB contents were pre-processed in order to eliminate non informative words based on a dictionary (Spanish), avoid synonyms, conjugated verbs, numbers, special characters, etc. [12]. Clean text was then used to create document term matrices using the tm package in R. Further processing for some applications such as topic analysis included selection of top %p percent of most frequent words.
2. Frequency analysis: this included analysis of most frequent words in whole corpus, or for subsets of corpus determined by subsets, such as most liked or more retweeted.
3. Word association: word association was considered for special words in the pre-configured list and for most frequent words in the corpus. Graph representation for word association of a selection of top interactions was also considered [12].
4. Message analysis: messages associated to most frequent words or words in the list were analyzed.
5. Topics: underlying topics were identified using Latent Dirichlet Allocation (LDA). Topics were associated to special words and messages aiming at recovering word-topic and special-word-topic associations as well as contextual meaning of each topic. For the latter, messages corresponding to top words identified with topics were examined. For this we considered Latent Dirichlet Allocation (LDA). Latent Dirichlet Allocation is a mathematical technique based on a hierarchical Bayesian model which creates underlying concepts, previously unknown, assigning conditional probabilities to words in documents. More precisely, the model assumes that the probability of finding a given word i in document j depends on a latent, unobserved topic k. The topic is related to documents and words by means of a certain latent variable $z_{i,j}$. This yields

$$P(w_i|d_j) = \sum_k (P(k|d_j)P(w_i|\beta_k)) = \sum_k P(z_{i,j} = k)P(w_i|\beta_k), \qquad (1)$$

and then, if $c_{i,j}$ is the observed proportion of word i in document j,

$$P(w_i, d_j) = P(d_j) \prod_k P(w_i, d_j)^{c_{i,j}}. \tag{2}$$

The model further assumes that $z_{i,j} \sim M_K(1, \theta_j)$ a K-dimensional multinomial distribution and $\theta_j \sim \text{Dirichelet}(\alpha)$ indicates the mixing proportion of the topics for each document. The model estimates parameters by maximum likelihood [12]. Implementation in R indicates top probability words for each topic. Number of topics is user-selected.

6. Network analysis: relation among messages (comments or tweets) were finally analyzed using network techniques. This allowed identifying central messages in terms of message degree or intrinsic ranking strategies such as likes or number of comments and retweets, degree distribution properties and clustering or modular behavior. Analysis were performed using the open source Graph analysis and visualization tool Gephi.

4 Application to a Real Case

The proposed methodology was applied to define brand identity for an academic institution in Colombia. For this information of two SN, Twitter and FB, was considered. Information retrieval was implemented as explained in Subsect. 3.1, taking into account for Twitter, the brand user name and around a dozen hashtags directly related to the brand and for FB the brand page and three other user-related pages, two of which were meme pages, thus mostly images and videos. In total, circa 1700 twits and 3700 FB original posts were used.

Preprocessing and analysis was done as described in Subsect. 3.2. As mentioned, text processing for FB is not related to actual brand page posts, but rather to comments related to these. In what follows we describe findings, which then fed the Planning model described in Sect. 2. Exact insights are not presented because of brand privacy issues. Although it was not in he scope of this work, the goal is achieving complete automation of the planning model.

4.1 Findings

Word Frequency. A first interesting result for brand identity purposes was the elevated frequency of proper names (see Fig. 7) in FB comments. This required additional filtering, but also brought to our attention to the fact that proper names are a conspicuous part of messages. Use of proper names was also observed for brand-user pages. Frequency results for Tweeter are also presented in Fig. 7 where this phenomenon is not present.

A second finding was the use of non-words ("jaja", "jajaja", meaning laughter, or analogous longer expressions) which required the introduction of additional filters. This is important for quality information retrieval and should be taken unto account when designing automated search protocols, taking into account characteristics of population under study.

Frequency count of selected common words are given for the analyzed pages. Table 1 gives a summary of top 10 counts for each page. It is quite interesting to observe that ordering of the several pages is quite homogeneous despite their different nature. However, as discussed below, frequencies must be dealt with caution as words do not necessarily have the original meaning implied.

Table 1. Frequency of words from common list.

Brand page		User page 1		User page 2	
Word	Frequency	Word	Frequency	Word	Frequency
universidad	25	semestre	18	universidad	229
calidad	8	horario	11	semestre	117
horario	6	cambio	4	horario	48
semestre	6	calidad	3	creditos	25
requisitos	4	plan	3	cambio	24
investigacin	3	cambio	24	taller	14
tadeolab	2	biblioteca	2	biblioteca	13
estudios	1	biblioteca	13	calidad	8
computadores	1	metodologa	1	investigacion	6
salones	1	magistral	1	plan	6

One of the interesting by products of frequency analysis was showing that the automation strategy must allow for a two way strategy: identifying words and frequencies in corpus related to chosen words, but also retrieving new words and concepts from corpus analysis.

4.2   Word Association

A word association graph for brand-user pages and comments is constructed as a weighted list of pairs. Information obtained by this means is very enlightening, offering the possibility of construction of new concepts, but most importantly understanding word meaning in context. It is out of the scope of this work to interpret the actual word association implications, but rather to show the kind of analysis which can be implemented.

4.3   Message Analysis

Most frequent words were analyzed in their context allowing for the discovery of no real interaction between some proposed concepts and meanings. For precision consider the words University or Library, which were initially acknowledged at face value. However, analysis of messages showed categories associated to physical references more than concepts, providing interesting insight as to creation of messages for brand identity purposes.

An important issue concerning message analysis and which we have not been able to address at present is that SN context information is many times associated to images. A manual inspection of course allows assigning correct meaning, but this leaves out the possibility of a totally automated process. Our designed method of analysis thus provides for most frequent terms from the list a visual inspection of associated images (or posts) by including in an intermediate text file the associated link address.

4.4   Topic Analysis

We show results for LDA with four categories in Table 2

Table 2. Frequency of words from common list.

Topic 1	Topic 2	Topic 3	Topic 4
biblioteca	profe	as	denuncias
educacin	personas	elecciones	record
uniformes	da	educacin	desvo
dos	dos	aprender	depo
procesos	rosario	da	personas
plataformas	wifi	moderno	presentado
gente	horarios	profesores	acuerdo
profesores	aos	aprendizaje	aprendo
gestin	debe	repotenciados	calidad
estudiantes	gimnasio	estudiantes	dos

4.5   Network Analysis

Network analysis provides insight related to, on the one hand, how strategies change from page to page, and on the other, how network composition changes according to ranking strategies. This information is used to help understand strategy design according to the nature of pages and kind of expected effect (comments, loves, positives, etc.).

Figure 8 illustrates this point. It shows the network associating original post to comments for the brand network and one of the brand-user networks. We see that the brand page is more hierarchical in nature. This same kind of behavior is true for networks constructed based on different ranking strategies.

Fig. 7. Wordclouds for comments of official FB brand page (l) and brand related tweets (r): FB comments shows high frequency of proper names

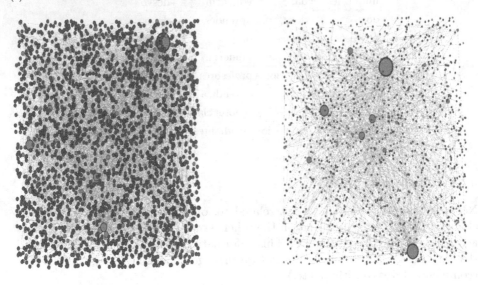

Fig. 8. Networks for brand-user (l) and official brand (r) ranked by number of comments

5 Conclusions and Future Work

This work is a first step towards building protocols to determine the scope of Big Data and automated information search from non traditional platforms such as SN in strategic planning. The steps for this planning model are thus intended as a way of automatically feeding the semiotic process with which people interact analyzing the way they are presented and expressed, generating valuable grounds for planning.

The projection of the planning model with the data obtained by research by analogous or digital analysis will contribute to the relationship between semiotics, advertising, strategy and technology. In this way research can be more responsive to the needs demanded by the contemporary world. The future of academia and scientific research in the fields of communication, marketing and advertising is marked by its ability to contribute significantly and concretely to the needs of advertising and marketing business processes, generating links with the industry and modernizing the mechanisms of academic training and seedling research and training of future professionals.

References

1. Hernandez Orallo, J.: Introducción a la Minera de Datos. Pearson Educación (2004)
2. Santos, R., Ruz, J.C., Gilbert, R., Karina: Mineria de Datos: Conceptos y Tendecias. Inteligencia Artificial: Revista Iberoamericana de Inteligencia Artificial, pp. 11–18 (2006)
3. Diaz, C.O.: Editorial MUTIS Journal, Computación de alto desempeño para Ciencias biológicas. v6,1. (2016). ISSN 2256-1498
4. Garcia y C. Diaz, O.: Artificial Intelligence: Advances in Research and Applications L. a. B. S. Rabelo y E. Gutierrez, Edits., pp. 49–74. Nova Science Pub Inc. (2018)
5. Keller, K.: Strategic Brand Management. Building, Measuring, and Managing Brand Equity. Pearson Prentice Hall, p. 98. (2008). Author, F.: Article title. Journal **2**(5), 99–110 (2016)
6. Mayer-Schonberger, V., Cukier, K.: Big Data. La revolución de los datos masivos. Turner Publicaciones S.L., Madrid (2013)
7. Peirce, C.S.: Essential Peirce. Bloomington and Indianapolis. Edited by the Peirce Edition Project, vols. 1 and 2. Indiana University Press (1998)
8. Tungate, M.: Adland: A Global History of Advertising. Gale Virtual Reference Library. Kogan Page Press, London (2007). ISBN 9780749452179
9. Scott, L., Celia, L.: Global Culture Industry: The Mediation of Things. Wiley, Hoboken (2007). ISBN 978-0-745-62482-2
10. Holt, D.B., Holt, D.B., Harvard Business Press, Muñoz, L., da Cunha, R., de Sousa Coutinho, M., de Cacegas, L., Herbert, M.E.H.: How Brands Become Icons: The Principles of Cultural Branding. Harvard Business School Press, Brighton (2004). ISBN 9781578517749
11. William, J.: Pragmatism: A New Name for Some Old Ways of Thinking. Dover Publications, Inc., New York (1995)
12. Srivastava, A., Sahami, M. (eds.): Text Mining: Classification, Clustering, and Applications. CRC Press, Boca Raton (2009)

Decision Systems

CHIN: Classification with META-PATH in Heterogeneous Information Networks

Jinli Zhang, Zongli Jiang, and Tong Li[✉]

College of Computer, Beijing University of Technology, Beijing, China
zhangjl86@emails.bjut.edu.cn, {jiangzl,litong}@bjut.edu.cn

Abstract. Most real-word data can be modeled as heterogeneous information networks (HINs), which are composed of multiple types of nodes and links. Classification for objects in HINs is a fundamental problem with broad applications. However, traditional methods cannot involve in heterogeneous information networks. These approaches could not involve the relatedness between objects and various path semantics. In this paper, we proposed a novel framework called CHIN for classification. It utilizes the relevance measurement on objects to iteratively label objects in HINs. As different meta-path performs different accuracy for classification, the proposed framework incorporates the weights of meta-paths. As our experiments show, CHIN generates more accurate classes than the other classification algorithm, but also provides meaningful weights for meta-paths for classification task.

Keywords: Classification · Meta-path
Heterogeneous information networks

1 Introduction

Information networks have a large number of objects and their relationships, which are universal in many domains [1]. For example, co-author networks and citation networks extracted from heterogeneous Information Networks [2], knowledge networks encoded in Wikipedia [3], and friendship networks extracted from Facebook. Most current studies [4–8] on information networks focus on homogeneous information networks, i.e., networks consisting of a single type of links and objects, such as co-user networks. However, many existing information networks are heterogeneous information networks with different types of entities and their relationships. For example, social networks contain multi-typed objects like users, blogs, and labels which have publish, forward and comment of relationships. Beyond social networks, bibliographic information network forms Heterogeneous Information Networks (HINs) consisting of different types of objects, such as authors (A), conferences (C), and papers (P).

Example 1 *Bibliographic Information Network.* A bibliographic information network almost contains multiple types of objects: papers, authors, and

© Springer Nature Switzerland AG 2018
H. Florez et al. (Eds.): ICAI 2018, CCIS 942, pp. 63–74, 2018.
https://doi.org/10.1007/978-3-030-01535-0_5

conferences and so on. Papers and authors are linked by the relation of "write" and "written by". There are "cite" and "cite by" relations between papers, "publish" and "published in" between papers and conferences.

The problems of classification is the most fundamental analytical techniques in a heterogeneous bibliographic network. In semi-supervised learning, classification can utilize the labeled objects and the relevance between objects to predict the unlabeled objects. Lots of applications have been found in classifying objects of HINs, such as community detection, link prediction and object recommendation. Considering the model of heterogenous information networks, such as the microblog networks that have multi-typed objects such as bloggers, messages, photos, advertisements and product pages. One could perform very effective community detection, link prediction, and object recommendation, if these objects can be classified according to bloggers' topic of interest. Classification has been widely researched and applied to lots of fields.

In this work, we propose CHIN that combines classification. The relatedness between same or different-typed objects can be measured by CHIN. By building the distribution of objects, objects can be grouped into the pre-specified classes. The main contributions of this work are:

- We give the weights of each meta-paths, which can effectively promote the task of classification and address their limitations on the scarce labels.
- CHIN built the distribution over nodes ranking to determine an object's optimal class membership.
- We conduct experiments to evaluate our algorithm on real datasets. The results show that our method is highly effective and achieve high classification precision.

The rest of paper is organized as follows. Section 2 reviews related work. Related concepts and formal problem definition are presented in Sect. 3. The proposed framework CHIN is introduced in Sect. 4. We analyze the experimental results in Sect. 5. At last, we conclude our study in Sect. 6.

2 Related Work

The technique of data mining on HINs has been done by a number of works. Compared with homogeneous information networks, HINs contain various types of objects and links, and have more complex topological structure and richer semantics [9]. Examples of homogeneous and heterogeneous information networks are respectively showed in Fig. 1(a) and (b). Figure 1(a) indicates audience homogeneous network having the same type of audience, and edges meaning relationship of comment and sharing the same movie. Figure 1(b) shows movie heterogeneous network containing four-typed objects like movies, audiences and comments with watching and comment relationships between them.

There many substantial attentions in Classifying networked data or objects in recent years. One is to operate on the structure of local and global networks,

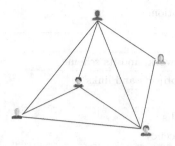

(a) Audience Homogeneous Network

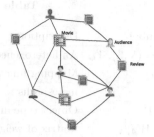

(b) Movie Heterogeneous Network

Fig. 1. Audience Homogeneous Network and Movie Heterogeneous Network

and the other is to use lots of prior labels in earlier studies such as [10–12]. However, most of these approaches were applied to homogeneous information networks, and there are not many models to directly be used to HINs.

Recently classification of HINs has become a new research direction. Collective classification [13] is the most frequently used method, which not only employs objects' feature representation, but also the structure of networks. Zhou et al. [14] proposed Learning with Local and Global Consistency (LLGC) to add sufficiently smooth coefficients the intrinsic structure, which was reflected by the labeled and unlabeled points in homogeneous information networks. Ji et al. [15] proposed GNetMine to deal with the classification task in HINs. In their work, the whole network was utilized for transductive classification. However, their approach does not distinguish label sets in different object types. The weighted-vote relational neighbor classifier (wvRN) [10,16] is another widespread method to determine the labels of objects by considering all the neighbors labels. Wan et al. [11] constructed classifiers by class-level meta-paths, which could derive relationship between objects. Ji et al. [11] put forward RankClass algorithm to integrate classification and ranking on objects in HINs. The higher ranked objects, the a more important role they play in the classification task. RankClass performs an iterative authority propagation to calculate the rank scores also with the link weights, then makes class prediction by calculating a posterior probability.

3 Problem Formalization

The background and preliminaries are introduced as follow. Table 1 lists some notations which are important and frequently used. Our definition of the information network in Definition 1 and definition proposed by Sun et al [9] are similar.

Definition 1 *Information Network. An information network is defined as a graph $G = (V,E)$ with an object type mapping function $\phi V \to A$ and a link*

Table 1. Symbolic description.

Symbol	Description
G = (V,E), T_G	An heterogeneous information network, and its schema
ϕ, ψ	Mapping function on the type of objects and links
P	meta-paths
A, R	Object type and type of meta-paths
M, $W_{A_i A_j}$	Matrix of weighted path and adjacency
$Rel(a_i b_j \mid P)$	Relationship following meta-path P among objects b_j and a_i
$P(x_i \mid k)$	Probability for object x_{ip} belonging to the class k
l_{ik}	Total number of objects labeled to k class belonging to type A_i
$\sharp x$	Number of x

type mapping function $\psi: E \rightarrow R$, where each object $v \in V$ belongs to one particular object type $\phi(v) \in A$, and each link $e \in E$ belongs to a particular relation $\psi(e) \in R$.

The network is a heterogeneous network, while the types of objects $|A| > 1$ or the types of relations $|R| > 1$; otherwise, it is a homogeneous network.

For a heterogenous information network, we give Definition 2 which represents the meta-level structure.

Definition 2 *Network schema [2,17]. The network schema, denoted as $T_G = (A,R)$, is a meta template for an information network $G = (V,E)$ with the object type mapping $\phi: V \rightarrow A$ and the link type mapping $\psi: E \rightarrow R$*

Different from homogeneous networks, different paths can connect two objects which are the same or different type. Different paths express different semantics which imply different similarities. Formally, these paths are called meta-paths, and the definition of it is the following.

Definition 3 *Meta path [1]. A meta path P is a path defined on a schema $S = (A,R)$, and is denoted in the form of A, which defines a composite relation*

$A_1 \xrightarrow{R_1} A_2 \xrightarrow{R_2} \dots \xrightarrow{R_l} A_{l+1}$, *which defines a composite relation $R = R_1 \circ R_2 \circ \dots \circ R_l$ between objects $A_1, A_2, \dots, A_{l+1}$, where $\circ$ denotes the composition operator on relations.*

Meta-path has connected objects and different meta-paths will have different semantic meanings in heterogeneous information network. In Fig. 1, meta-path APA (Author- Paper- Author) means authors who are collaborating on the same paper (i.e., co-author relation), while APCPA (Author- Paper -Conference-Paper- Author) shows that authors' papers are appeared in the same meeting (i.e., co-conference relation).

Definition 4 *Weighted path matrix. For a heterogeneous information network and its schema level representation, a weighted path matrix M for meta-path $P = (A_1 A_2 \cdots A_{l+1})$ is defined as $M = W_{A_1 A_2} \times W_{A_2 A_3} \times \ldots \times W_{A_l A_{l+1}}$, where $W_{A_i A_j}$ is the adjacency matrix between objects of type A_i and A_j. $M[x_i, y_j]$ represents the number of path instances between objects $x_i \in A_l$ and $y_j \in A_{l+1}$ following meta-path P, and $M[x_i, y_j] = M[y_j, x_i]$*

4   The CHIN Algorithm

In this section, we use a graph-based regularization framework to formulate the problem. To solve the optimization problem, we proposed efficient computational schemes.

4.1   The Framework of CHIN

The general framework of CHIN is described first, then the detail of the algorithm is explained.

- Step 0: Initialize the distribution of each class ranking by the prior labeled objects, i.e., $P(x|A_i, k)^0, \forall i = 1, \ldots, m, k = 1, \ldots, K$
- Step 1: Compute the relatedness between source object v_i and target object v_j following meta path $P : Rel_P(v_i, v_j)$
- Step 2: Based on the training data set $\mathcal{L}$ to compute the weight θ_p of p according to optimize an objective function $\mathcal{O}$; Integrate correlation matrices
- Step 3: Update the distribution of each class ranking, i.e., $P(x|A_i, k)^t, \forall i = 1, \ldots, m, k = 1, \ldots, K$
- Step 4: Repeat steps 1– 3, until convergence for all $v \in V$
- Step 5: Calculate each object's posterior probability.

4.2   Measuring the Relatedness Between Objects

The relationship among objects following the meta-path plays a important role for classification of objects. For that, we need to calculate similarity in source and target objects in the meta-path. Given a meta-path $P = (A_1 A_2 \cdots A_{l+1})$ such that source object A_1 and target object A_{l+1} are different objects type, then for adjacency matrix only between objects of type A_1 and target A_{l+1}, the relatedness between source object $a_{1i} \in A_1$ and target object $b_{(l+1)j} \in A_{l+1}$ is:

$$Rel(a_{1i}b_{(l+1)j} \mid P) = \frac{w(a_{1i}, b_{(l+1)j})(\frac{1}{d(a_{1i})} + \frac{1}{b_{(l+1)j}})}{\frac{1}{d(a_{1i})}\sum_j w(a_{1i}, b_{(l+1)j}) + \frac{1}{b_{(l+1)j}}\sum_i w(a_{1i}, b_{(l+1)j})} \quad (4.1)$$

where $w(a_{1i}, b_{(l+1)j})$ denotes number of paths connecting a_{1i} and $b_{(l+1)j}$, and is also the value of weighted matrix $M[a_{1i}, b_{(l+1)j}]$. $d(a_{1i})$ and $d(b_{(l+1)j})$ are respectively degrees of object a_{1i} and $b_{(l+1)j}$.

$$M^P[i,j] =\mid (p \mid (p \vdash P)) \wedge (p \text{ relates } x_i \text{ and } x_j) \mid \qquad (4.2)$$

$$P(x_{ip}|A_i,k)^0 = \begin{cases} 0 & \text{otherwise} \\ \frac{1}{l_{ik}} & \text{if data object } x_{ip} \text{ is labeled to be k-th class} \end{cases}$$

where the total objects' number of type A_i labeled to class k is denoted by l_{ik}.

4.3   Graph-Based Regularization Framework

In a HIN, let $\mathbf{M}_{ij}$ be an $n_i \times n_j$ relation matrix corresponding to graph G_{ij}. $M_{ij,pq}$ denotes as the p-th row and q-th column of $\mathbf{M}_{ij}$, representing the weight on link $< x_{ip}, x_{jq} >$. Undirected graphs satisfies the conditions such that $\mathbf{M}_{ij} = \mathbf{M}_{ji}^T$, that are we consider. The weights on the links are as follows:

$$M_{ij,pq} = \begin{cases} 0 & \text{otherwise} \\ 1 & \text{if data objects } x_{ip} \text{ and } x_{jq} \text{ are linked together} \end{cases}$$

In a heterogeneous information network, linked-objects usually have the same rank scores and labels. Therefore, we used the linked neighbors to iteratively update each rank score on object. We can specify the initial ranking distribution of objects labeled class k. The initial ranking $P(x_{ip}|A_i,k)^0$ is initialized as a uniform distribution, as following:

$$P(x_{ip}|A_i,k)^0 = \begin{cases} 0 & \text{otherwise} \\ \frac{1}{l_{ik}} & \text{if data object } x_{ip} \text{ is labeled to be } k-th \text{ class} \end{cases}$$

Following a similar theoretical analysis to [15,18], the class prediction on labeled objects should be similar to their pre-assigned labels, and two linked objects are likely to be assigned the similar labels based on the consistency assumption. Minimize the following objective function which could guarantee the prior knowledge and let $P(x_{ip}|A_i,k)$ be as consistent as possible with the link information:

$$\begin{aligned} obj(P(x_{ip}|A_i,k)) \doteq &\lambda_{ij} \sum_{p=1}^{n_i} \sum_{q=1}^{n_j} M_{ij,pq}(P(x_{ip}|A_i,k) - P(x_{jq}|A_j,k))^2 \\ &+ \alpha_i \sum_{p=1}^{n_i} (P(x_{ip}|A_i,k) - P(x_{ip}|A_i,k)^0)^2 \end{aligned} \qquad (4.3)$$

It is likely to [11], we could prove that minimizing objective function $obj(P(x_{ip}|A_i,k))$ can converge to a closed form solution:

$$P(x_{ip}|A_i,k)^t \doteq \frac{\lambda_{ij}M_{ij,pq}P(x_{jq}|A_i,k)^{t-1}) + \alpha_i P(x_{ip}|A_i,k)^0)}{\lambda_{ij} + \alpha_i} \qquad (4.4)$$

To keep a uniform ranking distribution, $P(x_{ip}|A_i,k)^t$ is normalized to satisfy $\sum_{p=1}^{n_i} P(x_{ip}|A_i,k)^t = 1, \forall i = 1, \ldots, m, k = 1, \ldots, K$ after each iteration.

4.4 Weight Learning of Meta-Path and Correlation Matrices

We used training data set to optimize an objective function $\mathcal{O}$, which can learn the weight θ_p of each meta-path p. We maximize the correlations of that share the same labels and minimize the correlations of objects that are given different labels:

$$\mathcal{O} = \max_{\theta} \sum_{x_i, x_j \in \mathcal{L}} \left(sign(x_i, x_j) \sum_{p} Rel_p(x_i, x_j) \right) - \lambda \|\theta\|_2^2 \qquad (4.5)$$

Here λ is the regularization parameter and $\| \cdot \|$ is the ℓ^2 norm. The objects' relatedness is computed by Rel_p under meta-path p_k. Equation (4.6) shows the definition of the function $sign()$ in Eq. (4.5).

$$Sign(x_i, x_j) = \begin{cases} -1 & otherwise \\ 1 & if\ x_i\ and\ x_j\ share\ the\ same\ label \end{cases} \qquad (4.6)$$

In order to obtain θ_p, we firstly compute partial derivative of $\mathcal{O}$, then set those derivatives to 0.

$$\theta_p = \frac{1}{2\lambda} \sum_{x_i, x_j \in \mathcal{L}} \left(Sign(x_i, x_j) \cdot Rel_p(x_i, x_j) \right) \qquad (4.7)$$

5 Experiments

To show the viability and the effectiveness of the proposed framework CIIIN for classification of objects in heterogeneous information networks, we utilized real-world heterogeneous network datasets: DBLP "four-area" dataset[1] which is a bibliography database. We compare the performance of CHIN with the algorithms of HetPathMine, LLGC and wvRN.

5.1 Description of Datasets

DBLP database is a computer science bibliography database, and it can be modeled as a HIN. The heterogenous network comprises of four types of objects, i.e. Author (A), Conference (C), Paper (P) and Keywords (K). The three different connections between different four objects represent as bidirectional links. For example, links among authors and papers show that some authors co-write the paper; therefore, the links are undirected links. The DBLP dataset in our experiments is a subset of full DBLP dataset, which involves major conference in four research areas: Datamining, Database, Artificial Intelligence and Information Retrieval. The dataset contains 14376 papers (P), 20 conferences (C), 14475 authors (A), and 8920 keywords (K). The 170794 different direct links: P-C, P-A, and P-K. The labeled datas are 4057 authors and all

---

[1] http://www.cs.illinois.edu/homes/mingji1/DBLPfourarea.zip.

20 conferences. As the higher length meta-paths, the more noisy to the classification task. The length of meta-paths is up to four. We consider the set of meta path $\mathcal{P} = (APA, APAPA, APCPA, APTPA)$, as shown in Table 1.

Table 2. Length of meta-paths.

Meta-path	Length
Author-Paper-Author (APA)	2
Author-Paper-Author-Paper-Author (APAPA)	4
Author-Paper-Conference-Paper-Author (APCPA)	4
Author-Paper-Term-Paper-Author (APTPA)	4

The objects' label information must be given to evaluate the accuracy in the classification task. In this paper, we implement classification on authors as the number of authors' labels are the most in the three nodes. The most of important thing is that we can obtain useful conclusions by the test based on a huge number of authors.

5.2 Classification Algorithms

To evaluate the performance of the proposed framework CHIN, we use three other classification algorithms: LLGC, RankClass, wvRN.

- Learning with Local and Global Consistency (LLGC). LLGC is a graph-based transductive algorithm for homogeneous information networks. It utilizes the local and the global structure of networks to classify the nodes.
- RankClass is a ranking-based iterative classification framework, which applies in heterogeneous networks.
- Weighted-vote Relational Neighbor Classifier (wvRN). wvRN is a simple relational predictive model that utilizes only the local network structure to classify the nodes.

LLGC and wvRN are usually used to classify the nodes as baselines method. However, these two models are only utilized on homogeneous networks. To compare with our proposed model CHIN, the heterogeneous networks were changed into homogeneous networks under different specified meta paths, which only consist of the type objects for classification.

5.3 Results and Analysis

Comparison of CHIN Using Four Meta-paths

In order to evaluate the performance of the proposed model, we utilize accuracy. Accuracy computes the algorithm of right numbers of unlabelled objects. Equation (5.1) is the definition of the accuracy:

$$Accuracy = \frac{\sharp Correctly\ classified\ objects}{\sharp unlabelled\ objects} \qquad (5.1)$$

We study the performance evaluation of CHIN on DBLP, which is established based on extension meta path set $\mathcal{P}$. We randomly select $x\%, (where\ x = 3, 5, 7\ and\ 10)$ of the labelled objects as the prior knowledge. In the DBLP experiments, we conduct classification on the rest of authors by the labelled authors as prior knowledge. To apply LLGC and wvRN on a heterogenous information network, we transform a HIN into a homogeneous network first. In this work, as discussed above, λ_{ij} indicates which the important links. In this work, all the types links are considered as the shame important, so we set $\alpha_i = 0.1, \lambda_{ij} = 0.2$ following [12]. It is good enough to verify the validity of our algorithm.

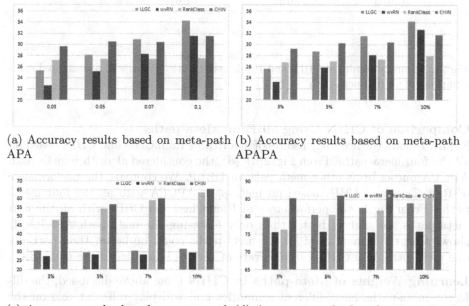

(a) Accuracy results based on meta-path APA

(b) Accuracy results based on meta-path APAPA

(c) Accuracy results based on meta-path APTPA

(d) Accuracy results based on meta-path APCPA

Fig. 2. Results of accuracy of classification for author based on different meta-paths

In Fig. 2(a)–(d) shows the accuracy of classification for authors based on the meta-paths: APA, APAPA, APTPA, APCPA. From the results, it is clear that the proposed measure CHIN performs better as compared to LLGC, wvRN and RankClass following all four meta-paths. When there are different training datas, CHIN shows stability and has almost the same performance. For the four algorithms, meta-path APCPA gives the best performance of accuracy in classification. Meta-paths APA and APAPA perform not good as others meta-paths, as they do not capture the semantics between different types of objects.

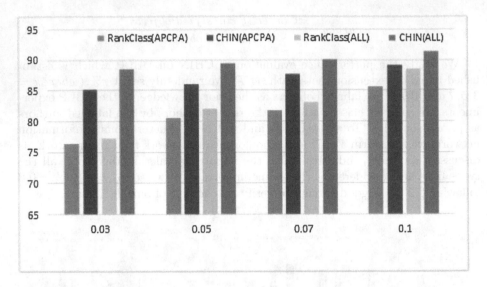

Fig. 3. Accuracy results of CHIN and Rankclass for APCPA as well as weighted combinations of all the meta-path.

Comparison of CHIN Using all Four Meta-paths

Figure 3 shows the accuracy results of algorithms RankClass and CHIN based on all the four meta-paths. From Fig. 2(a)–(d), the considered algorithm meta-path APCPA outperforms other meta-path in DBLP. We compare the performance of RankClass and CHIN based on meta-path APCPA with all the four meta-paths. From Fig. 3, the performance of RankClass and CHIN with all the four meta-paths are slightly better than only following the meta-path APCPA. It shows that the semantics of all the meta-paths could be better than partially one meta-path, and CHIN can integrate of various semantics in the networks.

Learning Weights of Meta-paths in CHIN From above discussed, the different meta-paths have different semantics and will play different role on the classification. To leverage various different semantics meta-paths, we need to learn the weights of meta-paths. The meta-path which lead to good classification should be assigned to bigger weights. CHIN could learn the weights between different meta-paths, and would assign higher weight to the meta-path which has the better performance.

Figure 4 shows the accuracy of CHIN corresponding to different meta-paths for DBLP dataset. Note that some meta-paths are not useful for the task, and both wvRN and LLGC are not used to HINs. We use RankClass to compare with CHIN. Table 2 shows the weights of meta-paths by CHIN. From Table 2, the meta-path APCPA was assigned the highest weight, as APCPA has performed best in the classification task; however, the weight of meta-path APA has assigned only around 0.001–0.015 since its poor performance for the classification (Table 3).

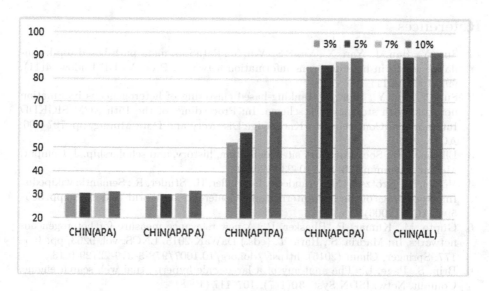

Fig. 4. Accuracy of CHIN corresponding to different meta-paths.

Table 3. Weights of meta-path.

Meta-path	Weights
Author-Paper-Author (APA)	0.001–0.15
Author-Paper-Author-Paper-Author (APAPA)	0.01–0.1
Author-Paper-Conference-Paper-Author (APCPA)	0.8–0.94
Author-Paper-Term-Paper-Author (APTPA)	0.001–0.2

6 Conclusions

In this paper, we studied the task of classification in heterogenous information networks. For classification on objects, a novel classification algorithm called CHIN is proposed to iteratively classify objects in HINs. CHIN could automatically learn the weight each meta-path, and select the meta-paths for effect classification. CHIN also incorporates the relatedness between objects, which expresses the different semantic meanings. Experiments on the real DBLP conducted in this paper illustrate the superiority of our method comparing to the previous methods. In order to verify our algorithm's effectiveness, we plan to apply it to more different heterogenous information networks in the future. Also, the proposed framework could extend to more general classification problem that an object has not only one label, for example, multi-label classification problem.

Acknowledgments. This work is supported by National Key R&D Program of China (No. 2017YFC08033007), the National Natural Science of Foundation of China (No. 91546111, 91646201) and Basic Research Funding of Beijing University of Technology (No. 040000546318516).

References

1. Sun, Y., Han, J., Yan, X., Yu, P.S., Wu, T.: PathSim: meta path-based top-k similarity search in heterogeneous information networks. Proc. VLDB Endow. **4**(11), 992–1003 (2011)
2. Sun, Y., Yu, Y., Han, J.: Ranking-based clustering of heterogeneous information networks with star network schema. In: Proceedings of the 15th ACM SIGKDD International Conference on Knowledge Discovery and Data Mining, pp. 797–806. ACM (2009)
3. Ellison, N.B.: Social network sites: definition, history, and scholarship. J. Comput. Mediat. Commun. **13**(1), 210–230 (2007)
4. Völkel, M., Krötzsch, M., Vrandecic, D., Haller, H., Studer, R.: Semantic wikipedia. In: Proceedings of the 15th International Conference on World Wide Web, pp. 585–594. ACM (2006)
5. Gupta, M., Kumar, P., Bhasker, B.: A new relevance measure for heterogeneous networks. In: Madria, S., Hara, T. (eds.) DaWaK 2015. LNCS, vol. 9263, pp. 165–177. Springer, Cham (2015). https://doi.org/10.1007/978-3-319-22729-0_13
6. Brin, S., Page, L.: The anatomy of a large-scale hypertextual web search engine. Comput. Netw. ISDN Syst. **30**(1–7), 107–117 (1998)
7. Li, J., Ge, B., Yang, K., Chen, Y., Tan, Y.: Meta-path based heterogeneous combat network link prediction. Phys. A Stat. Mech. Appl. **482**, 507–523 (2017)
8. Santiago, A., Benito, R.M.: Robustness of heterogeneous complex networks. Phys. A Stat. Mech. Appl. **388**(11), 2234–2242 (2009)
9. Gupta, M., Kumar, P., Bhasker, B.: DPRel: a meta-path based relevance measure for mining heterogeneous networks. Inf. Syst. Front., 1–17 (2017)
10. Macskassy, S.A., Provost, F.: Classification in networked data: a toolkit and a univariate case study. J. Mach. Learn. Res. **8**(May), 935–983 (2007)
11. Wan, C., Li, X., Kao, B., Yu, X., Gu, Q., Cheung, D., Han, J.: Classification with active learning and meta-paths in heterogeneous information networks. In: Proceedings of the 24th ACM International on Conference on Information and Knowledge Management, pp. 443–452. ACM (2015)
12. Ji, M., Han, J., Danilevsky, M.: Ranking-based classification of heterogeneous information networks. In: Proceedings of the 17th ACM SIGKDD International Conference on Knowledge Discovery and Data Mining, KDD 2011, pp. 1298–1306. ACM, New York (2011)
13. Pio, G., Serafino, F., Malerba, D., Ceci, M.: Multi-type clustering and classification from heterogeneous networks. Inf. Sci. **425**, 107–126 (2018)
14. Zhou, D., Bousquet, O., Lal, T.N., Weston, J., Schölkopf, B.: Learning with local and global consistency. In: Advances in Neural Information Processing Systems, pp. 321–328 (2004)
15. Ji, M., Sun, Y., Danilevsky, M., Han, J., Gao, J.: Graph regularized transductive classification on heterogeneous information networks. In: Balcázar, J.L., Bonchi, F., Gionis, A., Sebag, M. (eds.) ECML PKDD 2010. LNCS (LNAI), vol. 6321, pp. 570–586. Springer, Heidelberg (2010). https://doi.org/10.1007/978-3-642-15880-3_42
16. Macskassy, S.A., Provost, F.: A simple relational classifier. Technical report, New York Univ NY STERN School of Business (2003)
17. Sun, Y., Han, J.: Mining heterogeneous information networks: a structural analysis approach. ACM SIGKDD Explor. Newsl. **14**(2), 20–28 (2013)
18. Shi, C., Li, Y., Zhang, J., Sun, Y., Philip, S.Y.: A survey of heterogeneous information network analysis. IEEE Trans. Knowl. Data Eng. **29**(1), 17–37 (2017)

Decision Model for the Pharmaceutical Distribution of Insulin

Mariana Jacobo-Cabrera, Santiago-Omar Caballero-Morales[✉],
José-Luís Martínez-Flores, and Patricia Cano-Olivos

Universidad Popular Autonoma del Estado de Puebla,
17 Sur 711, Barrio de Santiago, 72410 Puebla, Pue., Mexico
mariana_jl04@hotmail.com, {santiagoomar.caballero,
joseluis.martinez01,patricia.cano}@upaep.mx

Abstract. In this work, we studied the problem of the efficient distribution of insulin, as it is a product of first necessity for the Mexican citizens with diabetes. In contrast to other pharmaceutical products, insulin must be transported with optimal conditions which restrict its distribution time. Similarly, warehousing and production costs must be considered in the supply, storage and distribution decisions given its obsolescence or damage risks. To address this problem, we propose a decision model that integrates distribution within the supply and storage aspects of the insulin supply chain. For this case, we considered variables such as warehousing costs, transportation costs and times, and decisions regarding route and inventory planning. For the development of the integrated decision model, we extended on the capacitated vehicle routing problem (CVRP) model and the Economic Order Quantity (EOQ) model of logistics and supply chain management. When the integrated model was tested on a distribution instance of 100 pharmaceutical retailers, we obtained a more suitable distribution of insulin considering time restrictions and operational warehousing and transportation costs. Thus, the proposed model can be considered for improvement of distribution decisions for other products or retailers in the pharmaceutical industry.

Keywords: Supply chain · Warehousing · Route planning · EOQ
CVRP · Pharmaceutical industry · Distribution

1 Introduction

Distribution is an important aspect of the supply chain. It is focused on the efficient management of the flow of materials (raw materials, components, sub-assemblies, finished products and supplies) throughout the supply chain. Thus, distribution or logistics is focused on improving planning, organization and control of the movement and storage processes that facilitate the flow of materials and products from the production point (source) to the consumption point (destination) to satisfy a specific requirement (demand) at the lowest cost, with the best quality at the most appropriate time. Therefore, the strategic supply implies considering the whole market, and the

© Springer Nature Switzerland AG 2018
H. Florez et al. (Eds.): ICAI 2018, CCIS 942, pp. 75–89, 2018.
https://doi.org/10.1007/978-3-030-01535-0_6

different current and potential suppliers. Its planning is relevant to reduce transportation costs, times and all the related costs that do not generate value to the product.

Within this context, the supply system for medicines is crucial for the availability of pharmaceutical products in drugstores and hospitals, being constituted as the support of the pharmaceutical services and pharmaceutical attention [1]. The pharmaceutical distribution must assure that the product placed in the market supports the characteristics certified by the laboratory.

For this, pharmaceutical products need to be distributed within short periods of time with specific conditions like: appropriate temperature and humidity levels to guarantee its optimal conservation, avoid direct contact to sunlight, appropriate tracking and visibility [2]. Due to this aspect, efficient distribution must be performed to reduce damage costs, warehousing problems, product losses and obsolescence, and delivery times.

Particularly, insulin is a vital product for people with chronical diseases such as pancreatic insufficiency or diabetes. Insulin is a hormone that is produced by the pancreas in response to high levels of nutrients in the blood stream. Its main function is to regulate the concentrations of glucose and lipids in the blood stream to facilitate their proper processing by the human body. In addition, it regulates the metabolism of carbohydrates and lipids [3]. If there is a deficiency of insulin, the body cannot process these elements efficiently, leading to liver and kidney failure, blindness and amputations.

Currently, demand of insulin is increasing due to the high levels of diabetes (type 1 and type 2) in different countries [4]. In North America, including Puerto Rico and Mexico, the current number of people with this disease is 37 million. In Central America, the rest of the Caribbean, Center and all of South America, the amount is 24 million. China stands out with 98.4 million and India with 65.1 million. Africa will increase from 2013 to 2035 to 41.4 million. In general, Central and South America will get an estimated increase of 60% within the following decades [5]. While actions are taken to decrease the growth rate of diabetes, currently the supply of insulin is essential for the wellbeing of patients with this chronic disease.

In Mexico, distribution of this product requires planning because insulin is a product which needs special handling conditions: storage temperature between $1.5°$–$8°$, do not freeze or expose to the sunlight, do not expose to temperatures greater than $30°$ and if insulin has been exposed to heat it must be destroyed [6]. Thus, efficient supply strategies must be considered to ensure the efficient distribution of this product, paying attention to storage and transportation costs.

Accordingly, the decision of supply and distribution must be a multi-objective strategy where distribution times must be reduced in accordance to reducing inventory costs. This leads us to formulate a decision model to address these objectives with the following contributions:

- Given the restriction in temperature, it is necessary to take precautions regarding the transportation time. Therefore, the decision model for route planning considers a time restriction for the delivery of the product in optimal conditions.
- The decision model integrates an inventory model with a vehicle routing model to optimize transportation and inventory management costs.

2 Development of the Decision Model

As previously discussed, efficient distribution of insulin requires the integration of different aspects of the supply chain. In this regard, the inventory supply strategy must minimize risks of obsolescence, stockout and excess of inventory. Once that this strategy is established, the task of minimizing transportation times and costs can consolidate the distribution strategy.

In order to accomplish these strategies, we considered logistic models for route planning and inventory control. Then, we proceeded to extend these models to consider the aspects of insulin distribution and warehousing. In this section, we present the technical background of these base models and then we describe the adaptation and extensions for the integrated decision model.

2.1 Technical Background

Capacitated Vehicle Routing Problem (CVRP). Routing is an important aspect of logistics as it determines the most suitable strategies for transportation of goods to ensure the efficient supply of all industries. In this regard, Transportation Planning (TP) consists of strategies aimed to make the most efficient decisions about transport requirements and achieve their long and short-term objectives. Therefore, TP focuses on the design, evaluation and scheduling of facilities and transport resources through the development of specific planning models [7, 8].
Nowadays, Travel Demand Models (TDMs) are logistic techniques that support the development of efficient transportation strategies. Within these models, the Vehicle Routing Problem (VRP) is the most important routing model [8, 9].

The VRP defines K vehicles located at a central depot. These vehicles have to deliver discrete quantities of goods to n customers. The principal objective of the VRP is to minimize costs by obtaining optimal routes which start and end at this central depot (or warehouse) and deliver the goods to all customers without visiting a customer more than once (either by the same vehicle or by different vehicles). If the capacity of the vehicle is considered within the route planning, the VRP is termed as Capacitated Vehicle Routing Problem (CVRP) [10]. Figure 1 presents the main elements of the VRP: routes (each route is served by a single vehicle), customers, and a central depot.

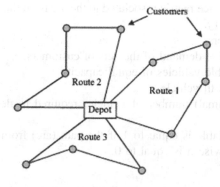

Fig. 1. Example of distribution network under the VRP.

Currently, many algorithms and models have been developed for different instances of the VRP such as: PDVRP (Pickup and Delivery VRP), PVRP (Periodic VRP), TWVRP (VRP with Time Windows), MDVRP (VRP with Multiple Depots), MDCARPFT (Multi-Depot Capacitated Arc Routing Problem with Full Truckloads), MDSDVRP (Multi-Depot Split Delivery VRP), 3L-CVRP (three-dimensional loading Capacitated VRP) [7, 8]. On the other hand, due to the NP-hard computational complexity of the VRP, the following solving algorithms have been developed: Genetic Algorithms (GA), Simulated Annealing (SA), Tabu-Search (TS), Ant Colony Optimization (ACO) and Savings (also known as Clarke & Wright) [11, 12].

The mathematical formulation of the CVRP model is described as follows [8]:

$$Minimize \sum_{i \in V} \sum_{j \in V} C_{ij} X_{ij} \qquad (1)$$

Subject to:

$$\sum_{i \in V} X_{ij} = 1 \quad \forall j \in V \backslash \{0\} \qquad (2)$$

$$\sum_{j \in V} X_{ij} = 1 \quad \forall i \in V \backslash \{0\} \qquad (3)$$

$$\sum_{i \in V} X_{i0} = K \qquad (4)$$

$$\sum_{j \in V} X_{0j} = K \qquad (5)$$

$$\sum_{i \notin S} \sum_{j \in S} X_{ij} \geq r(S) \forall S \subseteq V \backslash \{0\}, S \neq \emptyset \qquad (6)$$

$$X_{ij} \in \{0, 1\} \quad \forall i, j \in V \qquad (7)$$

Where:

- $G = (V, A)$: graph that represents the distribution network.
- $V = \{0, \ldots, n\}$: set of vertexes where 0 is the vertex or node that represents the central depot (in total, there are n customers).
- d_j: demand of each customer j (note that $d_0 = 0$).
- C_{ij}: cost, time or distance metric associated to the arc from the vertex (customer) i to the vertex (customer) j.
- $S \subseteq V$: set of customers.
- $d(S) = \Sigma d_i$: cumulative demand of the sets of customers.
- K: number of available vehicles of equal capacity.
- C_k: capacity of the k-th vehicle.
- $r(S)$: minimum (optimal) number of vehicles required to deliver all goods to all customers.
- $X_{ij} = 1$ decision variable is equal to 1 if the path (arc) from i to j belongs to the optimal route, otherwise it is equal to 0.

Equation (1) represents the objective function which consists on minimizing the cost metric associated to the routes. Equations (2) and (3) represent the restrictions that define that only one vehicle must visit a customer. Equations (4) and (5) define that the same vehicles that leave the central depot must return to it after the routes are served. Finally, Eq. (6) ensures compliance of the capacity restrictions of the vehicles and connectivity of all the complying routes.

Economic Order Quantity (EOQ). The standard EOQ model is one of the most important inventory control models. It aims to minimize inventory management costs associated to holding and ordering operations [13, 14].

In this context, the EOQ model determines the optimal lot size (number of units of product to be ordered or supplied) that minimizes total costs associated with the purchase, delivery and storage of the required product (i.e., raw material, sub-assemblies, final product, etc.) [13]. This model is characterized by the following assumptions [14]:

- demand is deterministic and constant over time (coefficient of variability less than 20%);
- lead time is fixed;
- there is no restriction on the lot size;
- there is no restriction on the storage capacity;
- the lot size is independent of the ordering cost.

The mathematical formulation of the EOQ model is presented as follows:

$$Q = \sqrt{\frac{2DCo}{Ch}} \tag{8}$$

Where

- D = accumulated demand throughout a planning horizon (i.e., annual demand).
- C_o = order cost per lot.
- C_h = holding cost per unit in inventory.
- C = unit cost (purchase cost or profit value per unit of product).
- Q = economic lot size that minimizes de total inventory cost TC throughout the planning horizon which is defined by:

$$TC = \frac{D}{Q}C_o + C_h\frac{Q}{2} + DC \tag{9}$$

2.2   Integration and Extension

As previously discussed, the distribution of insulin must consider special handling. Particularly, the following must be considered:

- The base unit of insulin is a vial of 100 UI/ml which lasts for about 28 days [6]. Thus, a user may need a new supply each 28 days. This can be considered as the life cycle T of the insulin vial. Also, the vial has a standard cost C of 10 USD (200 MXN).

- Due to the life cycle T, from the time of production to the time of delivery at the drug store, distribution time should be short. In this case, a maximum transportation time for delivery t_{trans} must be defined.
- The standard dose cannot be exposed to temperatures higher than 30 °C and the optimal temperature must be within the range of 2 °C to 26 °C. In order to keep this temperature, some additional supplies may be needed. This cost can be expressed as C_{temp}.

With these considerations, the following information is defined:

- There is a transportation time between locations i and j defined as t_{ij}.
- d_i is the total demand to be covered for each drug store i during T.
- The distribution center or production plant is located at $i = 0$ (hence, $d_0 = 0$).
- The transportation cost, which depends of the transportation time, can include C_{temp} and be integrated within the order cost C_o. In this case, a transportation cost per unit of time Y can be multiplied by t_{0j} to estimate the transportation cost associated to a route between the drug stores j and the distribution center at $i = 0$.
- A vehicle assigned to serve a set of drug stores (customers) is assumed to transport the lots of size Q_i defined by the inventory supply strategy. In this case, it is assumed that distribution must be planned for the delivery of the first lots at each location j.
- A binary decision variable X_{ijk} can be set to 1 if the vehicle k serves the route between locations i and j, and be set to 0 otherwise.

In this way, the integrated decision model for the distribution of insulin can be expressed by the following mathematical formulation:

$$Minimize \sum_{j \in V} \sum_{i \in V} \sum_{k \in K} t_{ij} X_{ijk} \tag{10}$$

Subject to:

$$\sum_{i \in V} X_{ijk} = 1 \quad \forall j \in V \backslash \{0\}, k \in K \tag{11}$$

$$\sum_{j \in V} X_{ijk} = 1 \quad \forall i \in V \backslash \{0\}, k \in K \tag{12}$$

$$\sum_{i \in V} \sum_{k \in K} X_{i0k} = K \tag{13}$$

$$\sum_{j \in V} \sum_{k \in K} X_{0jk} = K \tag{14}$$

$$\sum_{i \in V} \sum_{j \in V} Q_i X_{ijk} \leq C_k \quad \forall k \in K, i \neq j \tag{15}$$

$$\sum_{i \in V} \sum_{j \in V} t_{ij} X_{ijk} \leq t_{trans} \quad \forall k \in K, i \neq j \tag{16}$$

$$\sum_{i \notin S} \sum_{j \in S} \sum_{k \in K} X_{ijk} \geq r(S) \quad \forall S \subseteq V \setminus \{0\}, S \neq \emptyset \tag{17}$$

$$X_{ijk} \in \{0,1\} \quad \forall i,j \in V, k \in K \tag{18}$$

The mathematical model of the time-constrained CVRP minimizes the transportation time t_{ij} for delivery of insulin. For a more comprehensive order cost, the transportation cost can be included within Co as follows:

$$Co_j^* = standard\, C_o + Yt_{0j} + C_{temp} \forall j \in V \setminus \{0\} \tag{19}$$

Where Co_j^* is the order cost for customer j considering a standard C_o plus the transportation cost to customer j from the central depot at $i = 0$ and the temperature control cost C_{temp}. Then, the inventory supply EOQ model can be expressed as:

$$Q_j = \sqrt{\frac{2d_j Co_j^*}{Ch_j}} \tag{20}$$

$$TC_j = \frac{d_j}{Q_j} Co_j + Ch_j \frac{Q_j}{2} + d_j C \tag{21}$$

As presented in Eqs. (19)–(21), it is assumed that each drug store or customer has specific order and holding costs. Evaluation of the distribution and supply strategy for each customer can be assessed by the total cost as described by Eq. (9).

3 Test Instance

To validate the decision model we designed a test instance by estimating the number of people who may need insulin within a region in Mexico. This was performed as follows:

- The current population in Mexico is 119'000,000 people. From this population, approximately 1 out of 10 adults has diabetes, the most common affectation that requires insulin [15, 16]. This is equivalent to 10% of the whole population.
- In the south region of Mexico diabetes has a prevalence of 11.1% (which is similar to the national estimate). Within this region we focus on the state of Puebla which has a population of 6'000,000 people (this is approximately equivalent to 5.0% of the total population).
- Particularly, the city of Puebla is the largest municipality within the state, representing 26.0% of the population (= 6'000,000 × 0.26 = 1'560,000 people) [17, 18]. If considering the national estimate of people with diabetes, this leads to 1'560,000 × 0.10 = 156,000 potential insulin users within the city of Puebla.
- From this maximum estimate of insulin users we can focus on 156,000 × 0.50 = 78,000 users. It is considered that each of these users, for a period of 28 days, would require one vial of 100 UI/ml.

- If 100 pharmaceutical retailers within the municipality of Puebla are considered, a mean demand of $78{,}000/100 = 780$ vials can be estimated for each retailer. This represents the estimate for d_i for the mathematical formulation described in Eqs. (20)–(21).
- The location of the distribution center was estimated by means of the Weber model for facility location [19]. Table 1 presents the locations of the retailers and the distribution center (#1 location).

In order to model the capacity restriction described by Eq. (15), the vehicle's capacity must be standardized in terms of the real product which is an insulin vial. In this case, vehicles with a loading dimension of 1.80 m $\times$ 1.80 m $\times$ 3.30 m $= 10.70$ m^3 are considered. If the dimension of an insulin vial is approximately 0.10 m $\times$ 0.10 m $\times$ 0.15 m $= 0.0015$ m^3, then each vehicle has a maximum capacity of approximately $10.70/0.0015 = 7{,}134$ vials. For this instance we consider the 60% of this capacity ($= 0.60 \times 7134 = 4{,}280$ vials).

An estimate for t_{trans} was obtained by considering the life cycle of a cooling supply within the vehicle. While personal cooling gear has been reported to keep insulin within safe temperatures for approximately 45 h, it is commonly used for few units (i.e., 4 insulin pens or 6 vials). Also, the cost of these supplies is over $450 MXN. For this case, standard cooling supplies such as ice bags are considered at a cost of $10.0 MXN per lot ($C_{temp} = \$10.0$) with $t_{trans} = 4.0$ h.

As presented in Eq. (19), besides a standard C_o and C_{temp}, the values for t_{ij} and Y must be estimated. For this purpose, we used the *Google Maps* tool to determine the distances (km) and travelling times (hours) between all locations reported in Table 1. This led to two square distance/time matrices with $101 \times 101 = 10{,}201$ elements. By considering the current cost of $18.0 per liter, the vehicle's performance of 14 km per liter and the average speed of 70 km per hour, Y was estimated as (70 km/hr) $\times$ (1 L/14 km) $\times$ ($\$18.0/1$ L) $= \$90.0$/hr. Finally, a standard $C_o = \$150.0$ MXN was considered for all retailers while a variable C_h was considered for each retailer. C_h was considered within the range of 1.0% to 5.0% of C as this depends of the facility of the retailer.

Table 1. Geographical locations of the pharmaceutical retailers: Lon = Longitude, Lat = Latitude

#	Lon	Lat	#	Lon	Lat	#	Lon	Lat
1	−98.2183	19.0395	36	−98.2095	19.0577	71	−98.2128	19.0394
2	−98.1737	19.0725	37	−98.2525	18.9824	72	−98.2206	19.0562
3	−98.2186	18.9721	38	−98.2177	19.0591	73	−98.2242	18.9981
4	−98.2489	19.0472	39	−98.1928	19.0076	74	−98.2771	19.0512
5	−98.1984	19.0492	40	−98.2431	19.0711	75	−98.1953	19.0305
6	−98.2298	18.9883	41	−98.2377	19.0058	76	−98.2579	19.0741
7	−98.2320	19.0846	42	−98.2382	19.1455	77	−98.2112	19.0391
8	−98.2113	19.0678	43	−98.2496	18.9922	78	−98.1801	19.0427

(*continued*)

Table 1. (*continued*)

#	Lon	Lat	#	Lon	Lat	#	Lon	Lat
9	-98.2226	19.0988	44	-98.2220	19.0642	79	-98.2529	19.0362
10	-98.1419	19.0280	45	-98.2603	18.9897	80	-98.2556	19.0303
11	-98.2020	19.0146	46	-98.1974	19.0529	81	-98.2556	19.0631
12	-98.1957	19.0046	47	-98.1554	19.0520	82	-98.2609	19.0481
13	-98.2047	19.0263	48	-98.2530	18.9811	83	-98.2319	19.0427
14	-98.1330	19.0429	49	-98.2255	19.0427	84	-98.2395	19.0676
15	-98.2047	19.0310	50	-98.1807	18.9676	85	-98.2064	19.0506
16	-98.2610	19.0199	51	-98.2748	19.1036	86	-98.2232	19.0419
17	-98.2675	19.0497	52	-98.1310	19.0583	87	-98.2502	19.0558
18	-98.2022	19.0744	53	-98.1675	19.0439	88	-98.2183	19.0593
19	-98.2101	18.9928	54	-98.2820	19.0675	89	-98.2006	19.0251
20	-98.2939	19.0748	55	-98.2670	19.0041	90	-98.2054	19.0327
21	-98.1974	19.0529	56	-98.2627	18.9797	91	-98.1774	19.0677
22	-98.1865	19.0382	57	-97.9055	18.9628	92	-98.2125	19.0232
23	-98.2199	19.0557	58	-98.1760	19.0185	93	-98.2200	19.0064
24	-98.2590	19.0979	59	-98.2627	19.0332	94	-98.2302	19.0110
25	-98.2490	19.0472	60	-98.2254	19.0387	95	-98.2501	19.0456
26	-98.1609	19.0598	61	-98.2495	19.0546	96	-98.2170	19.0233
27	-98.2133	19.0868	62	-98.2368	19.0273	97	-98.2519	19.0174
28	-98.1751	19.0649	63	-98.2193	19.0287	98	-98.1938	19.0409
29	-98.2037	19.0184	64	-98.2270	19.0437	99	-98.1985	19.0463
30	-98.2589	18.9753	65	-98.2369	19.0071	100	-98.1982	19.0237
31	-98.1927	19.0717	66	-98.2230	19.0543	101	-98.2048	19.0722
32	-98.2461	19.0115	67	-98.2325	19.0591			
33	-98.4366	18.9040	68	-98.2084	19.0276			
34	-98.2202	19.0562	69	-98.2035	19.0314			
35	-98.1967	19.0238	70	-98.2113	19.0360			

4 Results

Figure 2(a) presents the locations of the retailers (yellow markers) and the distribution center (red marker) as obtained with *Google Maps*. For comparison purposes in Fig. 2(b) the visualization of the locations with MATLAB is presented.

By considering the time matrix for t_{ij} and the costs previously described, the lot size Q_j and the inventory costs for each retailer were estimated by means of Eqs. (20)–(21). The results are presented in Table 2 (in this case, Eq. (21) was computed without the term d_jC because it represents the purchase cost and it is the same for all retailers).

With this data we proceed to determine the most suitable routes for delivery of insulin as stated by the formulation described in Eqs. (10)–(18). Due to the size of the test instance a near-optimal solution to the proposed CVRP model was obtained by adapting the hybrid Tabu Search – Genetic Algorithm (TS-GA) metaheuristic reported

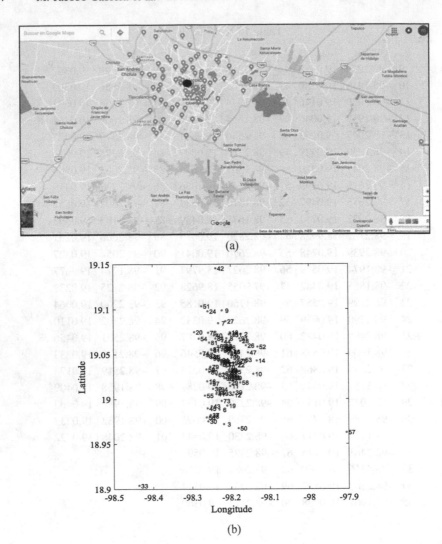

Fig. 2. Locations of pharmaceutical retailers and proposed distribution center: (a) Google Maps ®, (b) MATLAB ® (Color figure online)

in [20]. Implementation of the metaheuristic was performed with the software MATLAB.

The TS-GA metaheuristic was selected due to its capability to achieve a mean error rate of 5.27% for standard CVRP instances with more than 240 locations. This performance is very competitive within the context of metaheuristics for NP-hard problems. 10 runs of the metaheuristic were performed in order to obtain the most suitable solution for the insulin distribution problem. Table 3 presents the results for each of these runs including their execution time in seconds.

Table 2. Estimated lot sizes Q_j and total costs TC_j for each retailer j.

j	Q_j	TC_j	j	Q_j	TC_j	j	Q_j	TC_j
1	0	0.00	36	161	1601.96	71	355	708.95
2	365	729.72	37	164	1639.07	72	358	715.29
3	164	1635.40	38	359	716.97	73	162	1616.89
4	162	1616.28	39	362	723.93	74	367	733.83
5	358	715.57	40	362	723.65	75	160	1597.55
6	364	726.69	41	162	1612.56	76	364	727.80
7	364	726.69	42	168	1677.17	77	159	1583.06
8	361	720.04	43	365	728.90	78	162	1614.42
9	367	732.19	44	161	1606.32	79	364	727.80
10	165	1645.79	45	164	1639.07	80	163	1624.33
11	161	1608.19	46	161	1605.07	81	161	1608.19
12	162	1616.28	47	366	731.92	82	163	1626.17
13	361	721.99	48	164	1636.01	83	357	713.32
14	163	1627.40	49	160	1593.79	84	361	721.43
15	357	713.32	50	161	1609.43	85	358	714.17
16	364	726.97	51	376	750.59	86	355	709.94
17	364	726.69	52	374	747.91	87	162	1611.94
18	163	1621.87	53	163	1621.87	88	359	716.69
19	363	725.31	54	368	734.38	89	359	716.69
20	159	1587.47	55	365	729.17	90	357	713.32
21	161	1606.94	56	368	734.65	91	163	1626.79
22	360	718.65	57	185	1840.28	92	358	715.57
23	357	712.20	58	163	1623.71	93	162	1610.70
24	361	720.60	59	368	734.65	94	162	1610.08
25	364	726.97	60	355	708.81	95	363	724.21
26	164	1635.40	61	360	719.48	96	161	1600.71
27	366	731.92	62	161	1603.83	97	362	722.82
28	163	1629.86	63	160	1595.67	98	160	1598.18
29	360	718.92	64	159	1590.00	99	358	715.01
30	367	733.29	65	162	1616.89	100	359	717.25
31	364	726.97	66	160	1595.04	101	162	1615.66
32	360	718.92	67	360	718.65			
33	375	749.52	68	160	1598.18			
34	359	717.81	69	357	713.32			
35	359	717.81	70	159	1584.32			

As presented in Table 3 the TS-GA metaheuristic takes a minimum and maximum of 272 and 530 s respectively to provide a solution for the extended decision model. Within 10 runs or trials the metaheuristic provided a best solution with an objective function value (see Eq. (10)) of 3.96 h to serve a total of seven routes to deliver the requirements of Q_j for each pharmaceutical retailer. Figure 3 presents the details of this

Table 3. Results of 10 runs of the TS-GA metaheuristic: TTT = Total Transportation Time (hours), ET = Execution Time of the TS-GA metaheuristic (seconds)

Route	1	2	3	4	5	6	7	8	9	10
R_1	0.22	0.30	0.22	0.22	0.31	0.31	0.30	0.30	0.22	0.22
R_2	0.44	0.35	0.59	0.40	0.35	0.38	0.34	0.42	0.36	0.36
R_3	0.42	0.37	0.52	0.52	0.37	0.37	0.53	0.37	0.47	0.43
R_4	0.43	0.50	0.43	0.39	0.37	0.50	0.39	0.39	0.39	0.45
R_5	0.50	0.37	0.46	0.49	0.42	0.37	0.49	0.34	0.49	0.46
R_6	0.93	1.19	0.71	0.88	1.05	1.05	0.65	1.05	0.84	0.93
R_7	1.05	1.22	1.07	1.52	1.21	1.21	1.48	1.47	1.18	1.41
TTT	3.99	4.31	4.01	4.43	4.08	4.19	4.17	4.35	**3.96**	4.25
ET	316	319	287	323	311	530	302	272	299	385

solution. The minimum and maximum transit times are 0.22 and 1.18 h respectively, which are within the restriction for t_{trans}. Regarding vehicle utilization, in 6 out of 7 it is over 96%.

By considering the known performance of the TS-GA metaheuristic, and the consistency of this solution with the capacity and time restrictions of the distribution problem, it is assumed that the best solution obtained with the adapted TS-GA provides a very suitable alternative for the efficient delivery of insulin for the considered retailers. In the absence of a formal route planning, or if an empirical route planning is

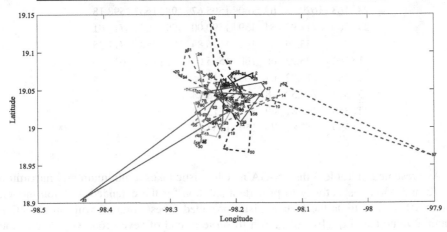

Fig. 3. Solution for the time-restricted CVRP

considered, it has been demonstrated that a near-optimal solution obtained with the CVRP is a more competitive strategy [8, 20].

Nevertheless, it is important to mention that information regarding the current distribution scheme is not available to quantitatively assess the improvement that can be obtained with this alternative solution. This is a complex scenario because the proposed model considers inventory and transportation costs and variables which are not commonly considered in practice but are important for the optimization of operational costs and reliability of distribution of vital goods such as insulin. This is discussed in the following section.

5   Conclusions and Future Work

Insulin is a vital product for people with chronic diseases such as pancreatic insufficiency or diabetes. Currently, demand of insulin is increasing due to the high levels of diabetes in different countries. Because the supply of this product is essential for the health of patients with this disease, its distribution times should be reduced according to the reduction of inventory costs. Also, insulin must be transported with optimal conditions which restrict its distribution time.

To address this situation, in this work we proposed an integrated decision model to support the determination of an efficient route planning to decrease distance, time and costs. The proposed decision model integrates time-restricted distribution with the supply and storage aspects of the product to meet the demand requirements of pharmaceutical retailers. Also, we provided a methodology to develop test instances for delivery of insulin or other medical supplies. This is an important resource for evaluation of scenarios and solving methods.

As discussed in Sect. 4, the model can provide route planning which maximizes the utilization of transportation and reduces distribution times, which is a key requirement for the delivery on insulin.

Although these results are encouraging, future work is needed to improve on the distribution of this vital product. As future work we consider the extension of the following points:

- A strategy for modelling the current distribution scheme is important to extend on the assessment of the proposed decision model. This can be also useful for the assessment of distribution scenarios under additional variables or restrictions.
- Currently all deliveries of insulin are considered to be performed in the same day. Future work can be focused on considering the distribution in different days, lots, or in specific days and shifts, adapting the route models of Periodic VRP (PVRP) or VRP with time windows (TWVRP).
- Instead of considering only one product (insulin) the model can be extended to consider more products which are equally vital for the health of people (multi-product model).
- Different additional supply and inventory costs can be included in the model. In example, the risk of not covering deliveries on time is not included in the standard EOQ model. Therefore, it can be extended to include costs of non-compliance.

- Regarding distribution, the model can be extended to consider zone or product restrictions on retailers.
- A mobile interface, which monitors the transfer times and temperature of the product, can be incorporated into a real-time management system to self-adjust the route planning as transportation conditions change.
- A dynamic model to estimate the transfer times based on the time in which the routing is done (forecast of times) can be integrated into the decision model.

References

1. Girón-Aguilar, N., D'Alessio, R.: Logística del Suministro de Medicamentos. Guía para el Desarrollo de Servicios Farmacéuticos Hospitalarios No. 5.2, pp. 1–34 (1997)
2. INVIMA. Buenas Prácticas de Almacenamiento y Distribución. Instituto Nacional de Vigilancia de Medicamentos y Alimentos (INVIMA): Dirección de Medicamentos y Productos Biológicos (2015)
3. Olivares-Reyes, J.A., Arellano Plancarte, A.: Bases moleculares de las acciones de la insulina. Red de Revistas Científicas de América Latina, el Caribe, España y Portugal 27(1), 9–18 (2008)
4. Tsilas, C.S., et al.: Relation of total sugars, fructose and sucrose with incident type 2 diabetes: a systematic review and meta-analysis of prospective cohort studies. CMAJ 189 (20), 711–720 (2017)
5. Mora-Morales, E.: Estado Actual de la diabetes mellitus en el mundo. Acta Médica Costarricense 56(2), 44–46 (2014)
6. Cobos-Campos, R., Salvador-Collado, P., Gómez Gener, A., Boj Borbones, M.: Estabilidad máxima de los medicamentos termolábiles fuera de nevera. Arán Ediciones, S. L. 30(1), 33–43 (2006)
7. Rojas-Cuevas, I.D., Caballero-Morales, S.O., Martínez-Flores, J.L., Mendoza-Vazquez, J.R.: Capacitated vehicle routing problema model for carriers. J. Transp. Supply Chain. Manag. 12, 1–9 (2018)
8. Durán-Méndez, M., Caballero-Morales, S.O., Martínez-Flores, J.L., Cano-Olivos, P.: Improvement of pick-up routes for an international shipping enterprise by using a heuristic method. Revista Latino-Americana de Inovação e Engenharia de Produção 4(6), 1–11 (2016)
9. Dantzig, G.B., Ramser, J.H.: The truck dispatching problem. Manag. Sci. 6(1), 80–91 (1959)
10. Carić, T., et al.: A modelling and optimization framework for real-world vehicle routing problems. In: Carić, T., Gold, H. (eds.) Vehicle Routing Problem, pp. 15–34. Intech (2008)
11. Kumar, S., Panneerselvam, R.: A survey on the vehicle routing problem and its variants. Intell. Inf. Manag. 4(3), 66–74 (2012)
12. Akhand, M.A.H., et al.: Solving capacitated vehicle routing problem using variant sweep and swarm intelligence. J. Appl. Sci. Eng. 20(4), 511–524 (2017)
13. Gordon, S., Gupte, J.: Overview of the classic economic order quantity approach to inventory management. In: The Business Age, pp. 1–16 (2016)
14. Agarwal, S.: Economic order quantity model: a review. VSRD Int. J. Mech. Civ. Automob. Prod. Eng. 4(12), 233–236 (2014)
15. UNIÓN. Estadística de diabetes en México 2017. El Universal: UNIÓN CANCÚN. http://www.unioncancun.mx/articulo/2017/11/13/salud/estadistica-de-diabetes-en-mexico-2017. Accessed 24 May 2018

16. Rojas- Martínez, R., Basto-Abreu, A., Aguilar-Salinas, C.A., Zárate Rojas, E., Villalpando, S., Barrientos-Gutiérrez, T.: Prevalencia de diabetes por diagnóstico médico previo en México. Salud Pública Mex. **60**, 224–232 (2018)
17. INEGI. Información por entidad: Puebla. Instituto Nacional de Estadística y Geografía (INEGI). http://cuentame.inegi.org.mx/monografias/informacion/Pue/Poblacion/default. aspx?tema=ME. Accessed 24 May 2018
18. Patiño-Tovar, E.: Territorio, Pobreza y Vida en el estado de Puebla. Liminar. Estudios Sociales y Humanísticos **1**(2), 43–58 (2003)
19. Stanimirović, P.S., Ćirić, M.S., Kazakovtsev, L.A., Osinuga, I.A.: Single-facility weber location problem based on the lift metric. FACTA UNIVERSITATIS (NIS) **27**(2), 175–190 (2012)
20. Garzón-Garnica, E.A., Caballero-Morales, S.O., Martínez-Flores, J.L.: Solution approach for a large scale personnel transport system for a large company in Latin America. J. Ind. Eng. Manag. **10**(4), 626–645 (2016)

Global Snapshot File Tracker

Carlos E. Gómez[1,2]([✉]) [ID], Jaime Chavarriaga[1] [ID], David C. Bonilla[1] [ID],
and Harold E. Castro[1] [ID]

[1] Universidad de Los Andes, Bogotá, Colombia
{ce.gomez10,ja.chavarriaga908,dc.bonilla10,hcastro}@uniandes.edu.co
[2] Universidad del Quindío, Armenia, Colombia

Abstract. Desktop clouds offer cloud computing services on desktops, simultaneously with users in interactive sessions. Users can affect the virtual machines execution for several reasons. For example, a user can turn-off or reboot the physical machine, or a user can execute demanding applications. A global snapshot of a distributed system is a fault tolerance strategy. In a previous work, we developed the Desktop Cloud Global Snapshot, which obtains the state of the whole system. In case of failure, it is possible to go back to the stored state and resume execution from that point. To recover the system from a global snapshot, we can use the same physical machines or others, if necessary. For this solution it is essential to have a file management system. As global snapshots are created, the number of files that must be handled grows making their management more complex. This article presents the Global Snapshot File Tracker, a software tool that is responsible for maintaining the record of the files that form the state of each virtual machine from its snapshots, and determining what files are required to replicate the state of the virtual machine if it is necessary to resume its execution on another host. The paper includes the background, the problem statement, the proposed solution, the developed solution, and the functionality and evaluation.

Keywords: Global snapshot · Checkpointing · Virtualbox snapshot Dependability · Reliability · Fault tolerance

1 Introduction

Desktop clouds such as CernVM [5] and UnaCloud [18] run virtual machines on desktop computers distributed along the private campuses. Using these platforms, researchers may execute scientific workflows where computations are performed on virtual machines (VMs) that run at the same time that programs started by the desktop users. Although these platforms take advantage of the idle resources in these desktops, they are susceptible to service failures derived from the presence of the users. Desktop users, for example, can turn-off or disconnect the computers. Therefore, these platform may result not reliable for scientists trying to perform large processing tasks.

© Springer Nature Switzerland AG 2018
H. Florez et al. (Eds.): ICAI 2018, CCIS 942, pp. 90–104, 2018.
https://doi.org/10.1007/978-3-030-01535-0_7

Recent researchers have been focused on supporting fault-tolerance strategies in these platforms. Alwabel et al. [3] proposed resource allocation algorithms that consider node failures, Blomer et al. [4] proposed a Global Filesystem for software and data delivery and Gómez et al. [8] have proposed global snapshots and virtual machine migrations as strategies for fault tolerance in desktop clouds. These solutions require a distributed tracking of the states of the virtual machines and of their snapshots. Regretfully, hypervisor software such as Oracle VirtualBox [16] do not support a distributed management of these information.

This paper introduces *Global Snapshot File Tracker (GSFT)*, our tool to manage the snapshot files of a set of VirtualBox machines. Basically, our solution is able to collect information from the virtual machine control files in each desktop, including both machine metadata (e.g., their name, their unique UUID identifier, and the machine configuration) as snapshot definitions. It analyzes and processes the *.vbox* definition file in order to gather in a single data structure the names of all the files that comprise the state of a VM, that is the *.vdi* virtual disk files and *.sav* files with the state of the memory at the snapshot time. The *GSFT* can be used, for instance, to create a *.csv* file with that information, to facilitate the execution of basic management operations on the snapshot files.

Rest of this paper is organized as follows: First, Sect. 2 includes a background for our work and Sect. 3 describes the problem statement and the research questions for this paper. Then, Sect. 4 explains our proposed solution, including the overview of the VirtualBox snapshots, the answers of the research questions and the motivation for the Global Snapshot File Tracker. After that. Section 5 describes the implementation and Sect. 6 reports the evaluation of our application. Finally, Sect. 7 concludes the paper and suggest the future work.

2 Background

Our solution aims to support desktop clouds that use VirtualBox to perform computations in the desktop computers by tracking the snapshots produced in these machines. This section introduced some concepts relevant to our work, namely, Desktop Clouds, Checkpointing and Global Snapshot Algorithms.

2.1 Desktop Clouds

Desktop Cloud (DC) is a form of cloud computing based on desktop computers [2,17]. It takes advantage of the idle computational resources on these desktops to manage the execution of fully functional VMs with their operating system and applications at the same time that the applications of users of these computers. DCs are designed to run the VMs without the users perceiving a decrease in computer performance or compromising their security [17].

Figure 1 shows a diagram of a DC. It is possible to observe that each desktop has a capacity occupied by the users and an idle capacity that can be used for the execution of VMs, which can be grouped into clusters forming the desktop cloud.

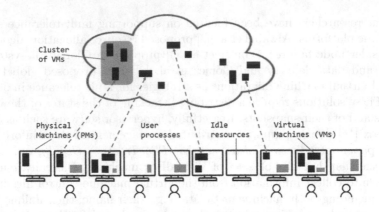

Fig. 1. Overview of a desktop cloud

Although, in a typical campus, the aggregate capacity of the idle resources in the desktops is significant [9], the use of not specialized and dedicated data centers turns desktop clouds more susceptible to failure in the service. Moreover, unlike cloud computing service providers, user presence using physical machines establishes different challenges to overcome: Users of desktops have priority in the use of resources, so their applications can affect the execution of the VMs running on the hosts. In addition, they can even shutdown or reboot the computers interrupting the execution of the VMs. As a consequence, desktop clouds are subject to service failures that do not exist in other platforms.

Recently, many authors have proposed strategies to implement fault-tolerance in desktop clouds: For instance, Alwabel et al. [3] proposed resource allocation algorithms that consider node failures, Blomer et al. [4] proposed a Global Filesystem for software and data delivery and Gómez et al. [8] have proposed global snapshots and virtual machine migrations as strategies for fault tolerance in desktop clouds. These solutions require mechanisms based on *checkpoints* or *snapshots*, to store the state of a VM, to restore its execution in the same or another desktop nodes.

2.2   Checkpointing

Checkpointing saves the state (a snapshot) of a system to resume it from that state when a fail occurs without having to start again from the very beginning. Naturally, if the system is resumed from a checkpoint, nothing performed on the system after the checkpoint was taken is included, so those modifications will be lost. Checkpointing can be full or incremental [1]. The first is the procedure through which every time it is invoked, it saves the complete state of the system. The second saves the system state from modifications after the last checkpoint instead of saving the entire checkpoint. So, it is necessary to keep the files of all previous checkpoints to be possible to resume the execution.

Virtualization-level checkpointing is a functionality (called snapshot) provided by all hypervisors, in which the entire state of a VM is stored in a storage

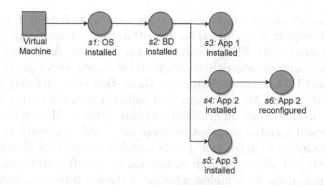

Fig. 2. Sample snapshot tree

medium to form a checkpoint with the possibility of using it later at any time to resume its execution from that state. A VM checkpoint stores the state of all disks attached to the VM, the memory state (if the VM is running when the snapshot is taken), and the metadata needed to configure the VM at the moment of resuming its execution [14].

Hypervisors such as Oracle VirtualBox, VMware Workstation and Microsoft HyperV stores each checkpoint in a *snapshot tree*. In these trees, there is a root snapshot with the initial state of the virtual. The other snapshots are stored with a relationship to their parent snapshot. Each snapshot may be the parent (the base) of one or more other snapshots. The Fig. 2 shows a sample snapshot tree. There root snapshot *s1* has the state when the OS was installed. The *s2* snapshot, based on the *s1*, has the state when a database was installed. Other *s3*, *s4* and *s5* snapshots are based on *s2* and represents the state when different applications was installed. Finally, *s6* keeps the state when one of the applications was reconfigured. When a virtual machine is running, its current state must be based on any of the snapshots in the tree.

Each hypervisor keeps track of snapshots and their dependencies in their own way. For example, Oracle VirtualBox stores the information corresponding to each snapshot in different sections of the *.vbox* file while the VMware Work-Station products do it in separate files. Although these hypervisors such can store snapshots of a single VM, they cannot save the state of a system distributed on multiple VMs.

2.3 Global Snapshot Algorithms

A *Global snapshot* is a copy of the state of a distributed system. In desktop clouds, it means a copy of the states of a set of VMs running on different desktops and of the communications among these machines. Creating one of these global snapshots is not a trivial task because it is not possible to assure that all the local snapshots are recorded at the same time [11] and the network communications not necessarily go through a central node [8]. Therefore, to obtain a global state, some coordination among the participants is required [12].

There are many algorithms and techniques used to implement it. For instance, Chandy and Lamport [6] proposed an algorithm to determining global states of distributed systems with FIFO communication channels. Afterward [12], based on Chandy and Lamport algorithm, presented his algorithm for distributed snapshots with non-FIFO channels that, later, Kangarlou et al. [10] simplified it and implemented it using VMs. However, that solution requires customized virtual switches that are not common in desktop clouds settings. More recently, Gómez et al. [8] proposed a global snapshot protocol for distributed systems running on VMs without virtual switches that can be applied to desktops clouds.

Both mentioned solutions, from Kangarlou et al. [10] and Gómez et al. [8], rely on VM snapshots. Any implementation of these solutions in desktop clouds requires to keep a track of the VM snapshots in different physical machines.

3 Problem Statement

In a distributed system, the global state (GS) comprises the set of the *local states* (LS) of each node or process in the system, along with the *channel states* (CS) of the communications among these nodes [6].

> **Global Snapshot.** In a distributed system with n processes, the global snapshot GS comprises the local state LS of each process and the channel state CS of each pair of processes: $GS = \langle \bigcup_{i=1}^{n} LS_i, \bigcup_{i,j=1}^{n} CS_{i,j} \rangle$

In a desktop cloud, the local states (LS) may be obtained by requesting to the hypervisor take an snapshot.

3.1 Local State (snapshot) in VirtualBox

As mentioned in the Sect. 2.2, the state of a VM at any given time is represented as a set of files. In VirtualBox, two files are used to create a VM with a single disk: a *.vbox* file with the configuration of the VM and a *.vdi* file with the virtual hard disk. An additional *.vdi* file is required for each additional disk Each time a snapshot of a VM is taken, the files are created: additional .vdi files are used to represent incremental changes on the disks and a .sav file is used to store the state of the machine. These files are stored with filenames that do not correspond to the name given to the snapshots.

As an example, Fig. 3, shows the files for a VM when six snapshots. It is not possible to determine which .vdi or .sav file correspond to each snapshot using only the snapshots. In addition the filenames cannot be used to determine the parent of each snapshot neither. Considering that we are interested on determining the minimal set of files that correspond to an specific snapshot, the file structure do not give use enough information.

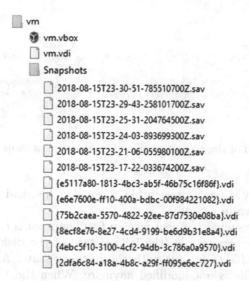

Fig. 3. Files of a virtual machine after six snapshots

3.2 Research Questions

To create tools that support global snapshots on desktop clouds using Virtual-Box, we posed the following research questions:

RQ1 How to determine and classify the files that make up a virtual machine when multiple snapshots have been obtained?

RQ2 Of all the files that make up a virtual machine when multiple snapshots have been obtained, which of them are needed to resume the execution of the virtual machine from a specific snapshot?

4 Proposed Solution

The analysis of the *.vbox* file is essential to answer the research questions. This file stores, not only the hardware specifications of the VM, but also the information corresponding to all its snapshots. This section describes the files that are created by VirtualBox when the snapshots are taken and shows the answer to our research questions: how to classify the files of a virtual machine and how to determine the files regarding an specific snapshot.

4.1 Overview of the VirtualBox Snapshots

Oracle VirtualBox offers functionality to obtain snapshots. Figure 4 shows an example of the VM file structure. When creating a VM with a single hard disk (called *vm* in this case), this is represented by two files, which are stored in the

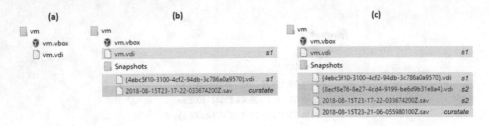

Fig. 4. Evolution of the virtual machine file structure as snapshots are taken

main folder: (1) a VM configuration file, a *vm.vbox* file, and (2) a virtual disk file, *vm.vdi*, as shown in Fig. 4(a).

Figure 4(b) shows what happens when a first snapshot is created. This snapshot consists of the *vm.vdi* file (the initial state of the disk) and a *2018-08-15T23-17-22-033674200Z.sav* file with the memory state. After the snapshot is taken, the disk file is not modified anymore. When the VM runs, an additional file is created to store any change to the hard disk. In our example, the {*4ebc5f10-3100-4cf2-94db-3c786a0a9570*}.*vdi* keeps the state of the disk. Each *.vdi* file stores the changes regarding the disk of their parent snapshot. Each of these files has information of its parent.

Figure 4(c) shows the files that represent the state of a VM after having obtained the second snapshot. Note that it is not easy to identify which are the two files (*.vdi* and *.sav*) correspond to each snapshot. In addition, in order to use or move one of the snapshots, it is necessary to determine not only the *.vdi* file of that snapshot but also all their parent disk files too. It is not possible to determine the files required to restore an snapshot by using only the filenames.

4.2   RQ1: How to Determine and Classify the Files that Make up a Virtual Machine When Multiple Snapshots Have Been Obtained?

As shown in Figs. 3 and 4, it is not possible to determine which files belong to each snapshot using the filenames. That information can be gathered from the *.vbox* file of the VM. This is an XML file conforming to a XSD schema definition provided by Oracle [15]. There are 112 different elements (tags) that may be used in that XML.

Listing 1 shows excerpts of the .vbox file for the VM described in Fig. 3. The *.vbox* file root is a `VirtualBox` tag. The first child element is a `Machine` tag that describes the virtual machine and shows the files with its current state. Among the descendent elements, there is a *HardDisks* tag that describes all the *.vdi* files. Each `HardDisk` can be a children of another `HardDisk`. That hierarchy of `HardDisk` elements shows, for each disk, which other disk is the parent.

Listing 1. Excerpts of the sample vdi.box file

```xml
<?xml version="1.0"?>
<VirtualBox xmlns="http://www.virtualbox.org/" version="1.14-windows">
  <Machine uuid="{0909f6e6-5527-4782-9f34-ce3e6988ebfd}" name="vm"
    OSType="Debian_64" currentSnapshot="{1020e46e-14bf-4a86-8ea4-d2d093224d3d}"
    snapshotFolder="Snapshots"
    lastStateChange="2018-08-15T23:32:02Z">
    <MediaRegistry>
      <HardDisks>
        <HardDisk uuid="{4a0e0fa2-1cde-4025-8549-dddedb5ce127}"
          location="vm.vdi" format="VDI" type="Normal">
          <HardDisk uuid="{4ebc5f10-3100-4cf2-94db-3c786a0a9570}"
            location="Snapshots/{4ebc5f10-3100-4cf2-94db-3c786a0a9570}.vdi"
            format="VDI">
            :
      </HardDisks>
    </MediaRegistry>
    :
    <Snapshot uuid="{2a0e6ffb-74bf-4402-9bbb-0fc32ca0f911}" name="snapshot1"
      timeStamp="2018-08-15T23:17:22Z"
      stateFile="Snapshots/2018-08-15T23-17-22-033674200Z.sav">
      <StorageControllers>
        <StorageController name="IDE" type="PIIX4" PortCount="2"
          useHostIOCache="true" Bootable="true">
          :
          <AttachedDevice type="HardDisk" hotpluggable="false" port="0"
            device="0">
            <Image uuid="{4a0e0fa2-1cde-4025-8549-dddedb5ce127}"/>
          </AttachedDevice>
        </StorageController>
      </StorageControllers>
    </Snapshot>
    :
    <Hardware>
    </Hardware>
    <StorageControllers>
      :
      <AttachedDevice type="HardDisk" hotpluggable="false" port="0"
        device="0">
        <Image uuid="{2dfa6c84-a18a-4b8c-a29f-ff095e6ec727}"/>
      </AttachedDevice>
      :
    </StorageControllers>
  </Machine>
</VirtualBox>
```

Below in the .vbox file, there are many **Snapshot** tags describing each snapshot. Among all their children elements there is a **StorageControllers** tag, where each StorageController can be attached to some media. The controllers uses the UUID (unique id) of the disks to determine which disk is attached. As the **HardDisk** elements, the **Snapshot** elements can be nested to describe the snapshot tree.

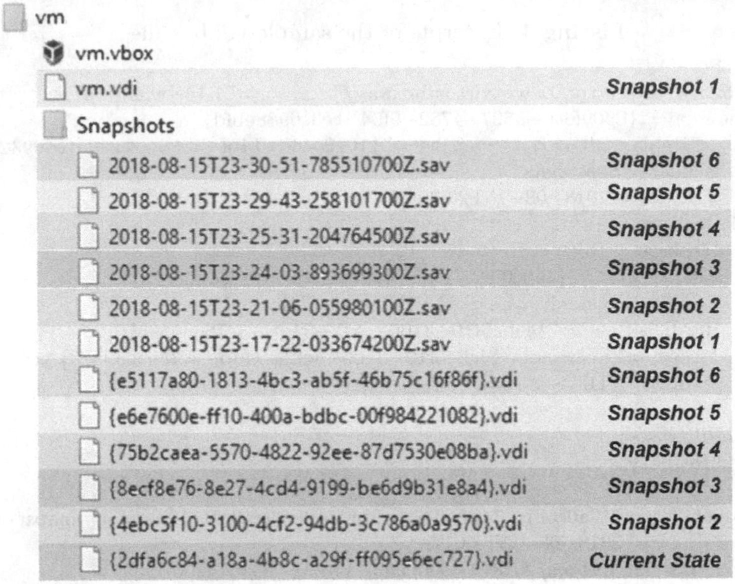

vm	
vm.vbox	
vm.vdi	*Snapshot 1*
Snapshots	
2018-08-15T23-30-51-785510700Z.sav	*Snapshot 6*
2018-08-15T23-29-43-258101700Z.sav	*Snapshot 5*
2018-08-15T23-25-31-204764500Z.sav	*Snapshot 4*
2018-08-15T23-24-03-893699300Z.sav	*Snapshot 3*
2018-08-15T23-21-06-055980100Z.sav	*Snapshot 2*
2018-08-15T23-17-22-033674200Z.sav	*Snapshot 1*
{e5117a80-1813-4bc3-ab5f-46b75c16f86f}.vdi	*Snapshot 6*
{e6e7600e-ff10-400a-bdbc-00f984221082}.vdi	*Snapshot 5*
{75b2caea-5570-4822-92ee-87d7530e08ba}.vdi	*Snapshot 4*
{8ecf8e76-8e27-4cd4-9199-be6d9b31e8a4}.vdi	*Snapshot 3*
{4ebc5f10-3100-4cf2-94db-3c786a0a9570}.vdi	*Snapshot 2*
{2dfa6c84-a18a-4b8c-a29f-ff095e6ec727}.vdi	*Current State*

Fig. 5. Meaning of files of a virtual machine after six snapshots

Figure 5 shows the meaning of the files for the sample VM. Although that information cannot be obtained from the filenames, it can be gathered from the *.vbox* file.

4.3   RQ2: Which Files that Make up a Virtual Machine Are Needed to Resume the Execution of the Virtual Machine from a Specific Snapshot?

Not all the files that are part of a VM are needed to resume its execution from the last snapshot:

.vbox file: The .vbox file maintains the configuration of the hardware for all the snapshots and the current state of the VM. This file is required to resume from any snapshot.

.vdi files: Since the *.vdi* files with the disks are differential with respect to its parent, it is necessary to determine all the ancestors in the hierarchy. This applies also for the last snapshot. Considering that the virtual machine may have a snapshot tree with multiple branches, it is possible that many *.vdi* files were not required to restore the last snapshot. Note that the *.vdi* corresponding to the current state of the disk is not required because it stores the changes that occur after the last snapshot.

.sav files: Regarding the state of the memory, the *.sav* file that correspond to the snapshot is the only required. All the other *.sav* files can be discarded or ignored.

Initial state of a VM. The initial state of a VM comprises the *.vbox* file and the *.vdi* files with the main disks: $S_0 = \langle .vbox, .vdi \rangle$

State of a specific snapshot. The state of a specific snapshot comprises the *.vbox* file, the corresponding *.vdi* files, their ancestors *.vdi* files and the corresponding *.sav* file: $S_i = \langle .vbox, .vdi_i, ancestors(.vdi_i), .sav_i \rangle$

5 Implementation

A prototype of the Global Snapshot File Tracker has been developed, which can be found in our repository [7]. It is a stand-alone application, and it is part of the storage system required for the global snapshot solution as a fault tolerance mechanism of a DC. GSFT is responsible for obtaining the necessary information to maintain the record of the names of the files that form the state of a distributed system that runs in a DC. This software can gather all the files required to resume the execution of any snapshots in a VM.

Our solution relies on the Simple API for XML (SAX) in the Java API for XML (JAX) [13] to process the virtual machine definition files. We traverse the structure in the *.vbox* files to obtain relevant and build an object structure with the information of the virtual machines, their snapshots and the corresponding files.

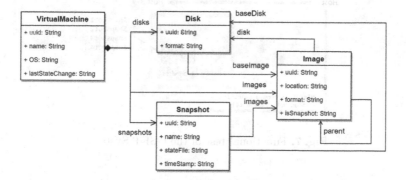

Fig. 6. Excerpt of the class diagram

Figure 6 shows an excerpt of the class diagram. The `VirtualMachine` represents each VM. It has a collection of `Disk` and `Snapshot`. The `Image` class represents each *.vdi* file. It has relationships that describes which `Disk` and `Snapshot` it belongs. In addition, it has a relationship to their parent `Image`.

We implemented a set of functional tests by processing multiple *.vbox* files. These tests cover multiple scenarios using VMs with different types of snapshot tress and diverse numbers of hard disks.

6 Functionality and Evaluation

This section shows a functionality test and reports the results of our preliminary evaluation. First of all we want to show the functionality of the developed software tool and then we will briefly talk about the time it takes to execute it.

6.1 Functionality

Experiment Design. Given a VM running on host A, we get six snapshots called *SnapshotN*, where *N* is the number corresponding to each snapshot. We want to migrate this VM to two different hosts. In host B, we want to recover the execution of the VM in the last obtained snapshot, while, in host C, we will resume the VM in a specific snapshot, the *Snapshot4*. Figure 7 illustrates the functional test of our system.

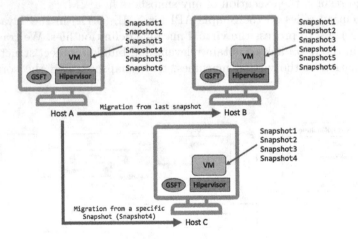

Fig. 7. Functional test of the GSFT System

To correctly resume the execution of the VMs from the mentioned snapshots, we need to know which are the files that should be migrated to the respective host. For this, we are going to use the GSFT system that we have developed.

```
java -jar gsft.jar vm\vm.vbox -f output01.csv
```

Fig. 8. GSFT command to obtain the file structure of a VM

Execution of the Experiment. The GSFT was executed on the *vm.vbox* file, which contains all the information of the VM. To obtain the file structure that make up the virtual machine, we use the command shown in the Fig. 8.

When executing the command, the file *output01.csv* is created with the file structure. In this file we can easily identify the meaning of each file within the composition of the VM, grouping each snapshot into a line. The Fig. 9 shows the result obtained.

Timestamp	Snapshot	Disk	Memory State
2018-08-15T23:17:22Z	Snapshot1	vm.vdi	Snapshots/2018-08-15T23-17-22-0336742002.sav
2018-08-15T23:21:06Z	Snapshot2	Snapshots/{4ebc5f10-3100-4cf2-94db-3c786a0a9570}.vdi	Snapshots/2018-08-15T23-21-06-0559801002.sav
2018-08-15T23:24:03Z	Snapshot3	Snapshots/{8ecf8e76-8e27-4cd4-9199-be6d9b31e8a4}.vdi	Snapshots/2018-08-15T23-24-03-8936993002.sav
2018-08-15T23:25:31Z	Snapshot4	Snapshots/{75b2caea-5570-4822-92ee-87d7530e08ba}.vdi	Snapshots/2018-08-15T23-25-31-2047645002.sav
2018-08-15T23:29:43Z	Snapshot5	Snapshots/{e6e7600e-ff10-400a-bdbc-00f984221082}.vdi	Snapshots/2018-08-15T23-29-43-2581017002.sav
2018-08-15T23:30:51Z	Snapshot6	Snapshots/{e5117a80-1813-4bc3-ab5f-46b75c16f86f}.vdi	Snapshots/2018-08-15T23-30-51-7855107002.sav
2018-08-15T23:32:02Z	{current}	Snapshots/{2dfa6c84-a18a-4b8c-a29f-ff095e6ec727}.vdi	null

Fig. 9. File structure of a VM

To resume the execution of the VM starting from the last snapshot, in host B, we need to know the list of files that must be migrated to be efficient in the use of the network. The software allows us to obtain it by means of the command of the Fig. 10.

```
java -jar gsft.jar vm\vm.vbox -f output02.csv -migrate
```

Fig. 10. GSFT command to obtain the list of files to migrate a VM in the last snapshot

Figure 11 shows the list of files needed to resume execution from the last snapshot. The result of the execution is stored in the file *output02.csv*.

Finally, for the migration to Host C and later resumption in the specific "Snapshot4" snapshot, we can use the command in the Fig. 12.

Again, the result is stored in a *.csv* file, which stores the list of files needed to be able to resume the execution of the VM in the specified snapshot (Fig. 13).

This test allows us to show the service provided by the developed software tool, answering the three research questions mentioned in the Sect. 3.

vm.vbox
Snapshots/{e5117a80-1813-4bc3-ab5f-46b75c16f86f}.vdi
Snapshots/{e6e7600e-ff10-400a-bdbc-00f984221082}.vdi
Snapshots/{75b2caea-5570-4822-92ee-87d7530e08ba}.vdi
Snapshots/{8ecf8e76-8e27-4cd4-9199-be6d9b31e8a4}.vdi
Snapshots/{4ebc5f10-3100-4cf2-94db-3c786a0a9570}.vdi
vm.vdi
Snapshots/2018-08-15T23-30-51-785510700Z.sav

Fig. 11. List of files to migrate a VM in the last snapshot

```
java -jar gsft.jar vm\vm.vbox -f ooutput03.csv -migrate -s Snapshot4
```

Fig. 12. GSFT command to obtain the list of files to migrate a VM in a specific snapshot

vm.vbox
Snapshots/{75b2caea-5570-4822-92ee-87d7530e08ba}.vdi
Snapshots/{8ecf8e76-8e27-4cd4-9199-be6d9b31e8a4}.vdi
Snapshots/{4ebc5f10-3100-4cf2-94db-3c786a0a9570}.vdi
vm.vdi
Snapshots/2018-08-15T23-25-31-204764500Z.sav

Fig. 13. List of files to migrate a VM in a specific snapshot

6.2   Preliminary Evaluation

The evaluation was carried out in order to determine the performance of the tool. The experiment was performed on a host that is usually used by a DC to run VMs. The experiment consisted of processing 10 .vbox files with one to ten snapshots, respectively. We measure the time it took for the system to generate the .csv file with the information of each snapshot, as shown in the Fig. 14

Figure 14 shows the analysis time of .vbox files, which had from one to ten snapshots. The average time for the analysis varies between 15 and 35 ms, with a linear behavior.

7   Conclusions and Future Work

In this tool paper we have presented the *Global Snapshot File Tracker*, a software tool developed to facilitate the management of the files that correspond to all the virtual machines running in all the computers in a desktop cloud. This software determines and classify the files that make up a virtual machine when multiple snapshots have been obtained. This facilitates the recovery of the execution of the virtual machines in the last snapshot or in a specific one. It can be used to

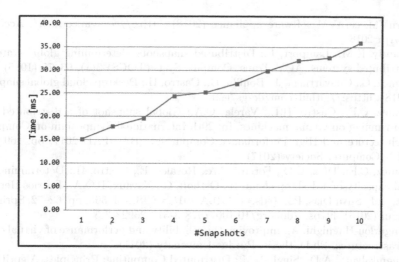

Fig. 14. Average time of analysis of .vbox files

migrate virtual machines by copying the minimal set of files required for a specific snapshot and implement other fault tolerance solutions for desktop clouds.

This paper reports a few functional tests for this application. Here we present the migration of the execution of a VM with six snapshots to other hosts resuming from the last snapshot and from a particular one. In addition, it reports some performance tests. Our public repository [7] has a larger set of functional tests.

As future work we intend to use the global snapshot file tracker within the system for managing files in our global snapshot solution. In addition, we are developing a solution to consolidate snapshots and reduce the number of files that must be copied and move to other machines, Finally, we are using our experience with VirtualBox to support other hypervisors used in desktop clouds, namely VMware Workstation and Microsoft HyperV.

References

1. Agarwal, H., Sharma, A.: A comprehensive survey of fault tolerance techniques in cloud computing. In: 2015 International Conference on Computing and Network Communications (CoCoNet), pp. 408–413. IEEE (2015)
2. Alwabel, A., Walters, R., Wills, G.: A view at desktop clouds. In: International Workshop on Emerging Software as a Service and Analytics (ESaaSA 2014), pp. 55–61 (2014)
3. Alwabel, A., Walters, R.J., Wills, G.B.: A resource allocation model for desktop clouds. In: Web-Based Services: Concepts, Methodologies, Tools, and Applications, pp. 356–376. IGI Global (2016)
4. Blomer, J., Buncic, P., Charalampidis, I., Harutyunyan, A., Larsen, D., Meusel, R.: Status and future perspectives of CERNVM-FS. J. Phys. Conf. Ser. **396**(5) (2012)

5. CernVM: cernVM software appliance (2018). https://cernvm.cern.ch/. Accessed 20 Apr 2018
6. Chandy, K.M., Lamport, L.: Distributed snapshots: determining global states of distributed systems. ACM Trans. Comput. Syst. (TOCS) **3**(1), 63–75 (1985)
7. Gomez, C., Chavarriaga, J., Bonilla, D., Castro, H.: Desktop cloud global snapshot (2018). https://github.com/dc-gs/gsft
8. Gómez, C.E., Castro, H.E., Varela, C.A.: Global snapshot of a distributed system running on virtual machines. In: 29th International Symposium on Computer Architecture and High Performance Computing, SBAC-PAD 2017, pp. 169–176. IEEE Computer Society (2017)
9. Gómez, C.E., Díaz, C.O., Forero, C.A., Rosales, E., Castro, H.: Determining the real capacity of a desktop cloud. In: Osthoff, C., Navaux, P.O.A., Barrios Hernandez, C.J., Silva Dias, P.L. (eds.) CARLA 2015. CCIS, vol. 565, pp. 62–72. Springer, Cham (2015). https://doi.org/10.1007/978-3-319-26928-3_5
10. Kangarlou-Haghighi, A.: Improving the reliability and performance of virtual cloud infrastructures. Ph.D. thesis, Purdue University (2011)
11. Kshemkalyani, A.D., Singhal, M.: Distributed Computing: Principles, Algorithms, and Systems. Cambridge University Press, Cambridge (2011)
12. Mattern, F.: Efficient algorithms for distributed snapshots and global virtual time approximation. J. Parallel Distrib. Comput. **18**(4), 423–434 (1993)
13. Oracle: JAXP-SAX API documentation. https://docs.oracle.com/javase/tutorial/jaxp/sax/parsing.html. Accessed 20 Apr 2018
14. Oracle: Oracle VM VirtualBox: User Manual Version 5.0.20. Oracle Corporation (2016)
15. Oracle: VirtualBox XSD schema definition (2017). https://www.virtualbox.org/browser/vbox/trunk/src/VBox/Main/xml/VirtualBox-settings.xsd. Accessed 20 Apr 2018
16. Oracle: Oracle virtualbox (2018). https://www.virtualbox.org/. Accessed 20 Apr 2018
17. Rosales, E., Castro, H., Villamizar, M.: Unacloud: opportunistic cloud computing infrastructure as a service. In: Cloud Computing, pp. 187–194 (2011)
18. UnaCloud: Unacloud: Opportunistic cloud computing platform (2018). https://sistemasproyectos.uniandes.edu.co/iniciativas/unacloud/. Accessed 20 Apr 2018

Health Care Information Systems

A System for the Acquisition of Data to Predict Pulmonary Tuberculosis

Juan D. Doria, Alvaro D. Orjuela-Cañón, and Jorge E. Camargo(✉)

Universidad Antonio Nariño, Bogotá, Colombia
{jdoria,alvorjuela,jorgecamargo}@uan.edu.co

Abstract. This paper presents a web system named TBDiagnostic for data acquisition, analysis and diagnosis of pulmonary tuberculosis. With the help of an artificial intelligence model, which generates a prediction of the diagnosis of tuberculosis, the system allows the user to generate a fast and accurate diagnosis of a person with symptoms of tuberculosis. The system allows to storage patient records and generate reports on these records. This system could help physicians who treat the disease especially in health centers and hospitals with limited infrastructure and data as it is the case of developing countries.

Keywords: Tuberculosis · Diagnosis · Acquisition
Artificial intelligence

1 Introduction

Today, technological advances make everyday life easier. The tools provided by information technologies can meet many needs in any field. For example, in medicine, software is used for reporting, data storage, analysis of results and diagnostics, among others. Pulmonary tuberculosis (TB) is one of the diseases with the highest number of patients worldwide. It is estimated that there are more than ten million new cases of TB per year. Diagnostic tests for tuberculosis is difficult because of the procedures that are performed to obtain a result are complex. The tuberculin test is one of the most common method worldwide, but obtaining reliable results takes up to one week [6]. With the help of information technologies, these procedures can be streamlined for the best care and treatment of patients.

This article presents a web-based tool (TBDiagnostic) for the acquisition and storing of TB data, which allows to predict the presence or absence of the disease. The system presented in this paper is part of a research project in the Universidad Antonio Nariíno in Bogotá, in which are participating co-investigators from Brasil. Additionally, in the project is involved physicians of Hospital Santa Clara located in Bogotá, who mainly participated in the definition of user to be implemented in the system and to validate it.

The paper is structured as follows, Sect. 2 presents the state of the art and related works in the field, Sect. 3 describes the software process performed to

H. Florez et al. (Eds.): ICAI 2018, CCIS 942, pp. 107–118, 2018.
https://doi.org/10.1007/978-3-030-01535-0_8

build the system, Sect. 4 presents each component of the system, and finally, Sect. 5 concludes the paper.

2   Related Work

In previous work, authors in [7] proposed to use TB surveillance tools, in line with the WHO's TB arrest strategy in 2006. WHO facilitates reports on TB control, establishing controls and parameters to treat tuberculosis, focusing on the advantages of using an electronic surveillance tool through the use of information technology. The article sets out three different tools (ETR.net, ENRS, eDOTS), which needed input from HIV-infected patients such as sex, age and type of TB; in other cases the type of HIV treatment.

Authors in [10] developed a software tool called "Electronic TB Register" based on the WHO/IUATLD data storage and reporting format. The tool allows to manage and monitor patients, generate reports on case detection, sputum conversion and cohort analysis generating tuberculosis trend graphs. Unlike TBDiagnostic, "Electronic TB Register" records data such as patient address, treatment start date, disease classification, patient category, regimen. Also the dates and results of the sputum microscopy. The software was implemented in five countries in southern Africa, and was successful in managing information with the support of each country's health information systems. In [3] authors explored the potential of web-based tools for TB treatment, monitoring, epidemiology and diagnosis. They evaluated the contribution of web technologies to TB diagnosis, incorporating diagnostic technologies in web environments. Also, using web environments for sending information such as images and X-rays, reducing response times and improving diagnostic accuracy. Keeping records of patients and their treatment was one of the advantages of the article.

Although there have been some works in the literature as it is shown in this section, our paper has the following contributions that have not beed addressed in previous works: (1) Acquisition tool: previous works do not offer a mechanism to acquire new records in a real medical scenario. Our tool offers the possibility to create new records to be studied; (2) TB prediction: our system integrates a prediction component that allows the user to predict if a patient has or not TB using a web interface, which was not identified in the existent works.

3   Software Engineering Process

In this section will be described the main aspects related to the software engineering process that was followed to develop TBDiagnostic.

3.1 Methodology

Some practices of the eXtreme programming (XP) methodology were used to develop the system. The following practices were selected:

- *User stories*: this practice consists in conducting meetings with business people to define what they want to be offered by the system. We conduct some meetings with medical personal of Hospital Santa Clara in which this user stories were generated.
- *Simple design*: this practice consists in designing software taking an approach of "simple is best", so when a new piece of code is written, programmers should ask themselves whether there is a simpler way to introduce such as functionality.
- *System metaphor*: this practice consists in representing each user story as simple as possible such that customers, programmers and managers can tell about how the system works. This was followed in the context of researchers and physicians involved in the project.
- *Whole team*: this practice consists in assuring that the "customer" is on hand all times and available for questions. In this project this role was played by the main researcher.
- *Continuous integration*: this practice consists in uploading every few hours to the source code repository the current version of the code of each programmer.

In the following subsections will be described each phase of the methodology that was conducted to develop the system.

3.2 Planning

In the planning phase we define user stories to specify what the system should do. At the same time, we review similar systems in the literature in order to obtain some ideas that allow to define such functionalities. As a result, a set of user stories were elucidated to be used as functionalities that the system should offer.

3.3 Design

In this phase, we built a set of mockups that best represent user stories, which allowed us to validate with the user whether those mockups are close to the expected functionality. Figure 1 shows one of the mockups.

In this phase we also built a set of UML diagrams such as components diagram, class diagram, sequence diagrams and use case diagrams. Figures 2, 3 and 4 presents the UML diagrams for use cases, class and components, respectively.

3.4 Development

TBDiagnostic was developed using Django, a web framework based on Python, and the PostgreSQL database engine.

Django Framework. Django is a web framework developed in Python that stands out for its speed, security and maintainability. It is a versatile framework that allows you to return content in any format (HTML, RSS feeds, JSON, among others) and connect to various database engines. It is scalable because it

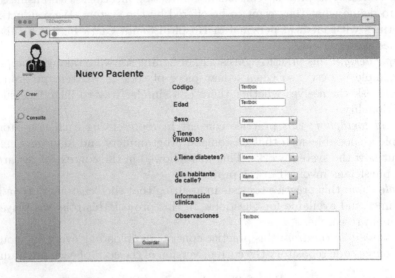

Fig. 1. Mockup for representing the user story related to create a new TB record. In this mockup information such as patient code, age, sex, diseases, and description is asked to the user.

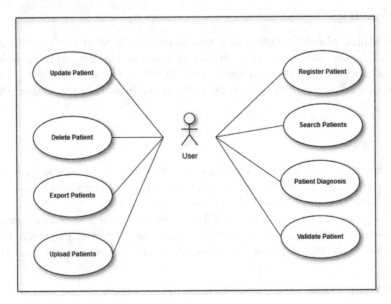

Fig. 2. UML use case diagram describing the main use cases of the system.

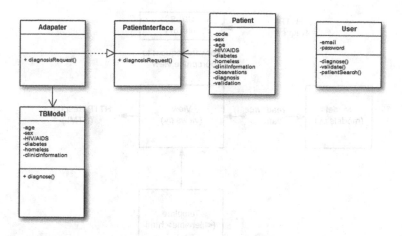

Fig. 3. UML class diagram that models the entities of the system.

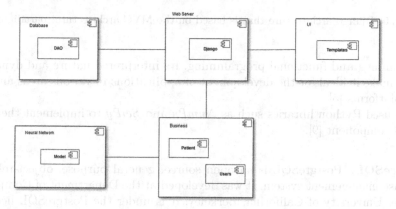

Fig. 4. UML component diagram representing components such as the data base, web server, user interface, prediction (ANN model), and business entities.

is based on a *shared nothing* architecture which means that each part is independent of the others, allowing it to be replaced or changed if necessary. Django is written using design patterns to encourage the creation of maintainable and reusable code [4].

It is based on the MVC (Model-View-Controller) architectural paradigm, following its premise of simplicity and code reuse, where the data corresponds to the model, the user interface corresponds to the view and the business logic to the controller [2]. The code separation in Django applications can be seen in Fig. 5.

Python. Python is a powerful, object-oriented programming language. It is a language whose syntax allows the code to be readable, and is also considered a multiparadigm language, because it supports object orientation, imperative

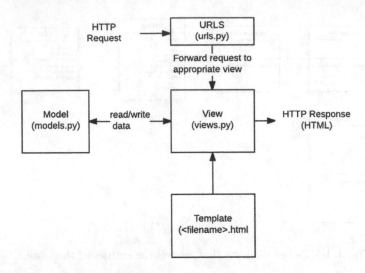

Fig. 5. Django architecture that is based on the MVC architectural paradigm.

programming and functional programming. Its interpreted nature and dynamic typing make it ideal for the development of applications in various areas and on most platforms [5].

We used Python libraries such as *NumPy* and *SciPy* to implement the prediction component [9].

PostgreSQL. PostgreSQL is an open source, general purpose, object-related database management system. It was developed at the Department of Computer Science, University of California, Berkeley. It is under the PostgreSQL license, which allows you to use, modify and distribute PostgreSQL in any way [8].

Django framework, offers the possibility of defining the data models directly in the project and by means of an ORM (Object-Relational mapping) performs the creation of the tables in the database. With Python code the models are created within the Django project and through a migration command offered by the framework, the tables are automatically created according to the models created in the project.

3.5 Testing

We build a set of functional tests to validate the system. A case test was built for each use case. Each test was executed by the researchers involved in the project, which allowed to fix some bugs that were detected.

3.6   Deployment

The system was deployed in a cloud machine of Digital Ocean, which offers virtual machines to deploy this type of systems. The virtual machine used to this project has Ubuntu Linux 14.04 with 8 Gb of memory.

4   System Description

TBDiagnostic can be separated into three different modules, in which the defined functionalities are developed. The modules are: patient registration module, patient search module and loading patient records module.

- **Creation module**: Module where the user can create patient records.
- **Consultation module**: A module where the user can consult the patient's records. In the records, the user can edit, perform a pre-diagnosis, validate the diagnosis and delete the record. In the query module you can also export the list of records to PDF or Excel.
- **Loading module**: Module where the user can load massive patient records using a CSV (Comma separated values) file.

4.1   Patient Registration Module

The patient registration module allows the user to create patient records. It is composed of an interface where the user can enter the data and by means of a button, store the data within the tool's database. The data on the form is:

- **Code**: text field, where the researcher can enter a unique value that identifies the patient.
- **Age**: numerical field, where the researcher can enter the age of the patient.
- **Sex**: Multiple choice field, where the principal investigator can define whether the patient is male or female, or no information is available.
- **¿HIV/AIDS?**: multiple choice field, where the principal investigator can enter whether or not the patient has HIV/AIDS, or no information.
- **¿Diabetes?**: multiple choice field, where the principal investigator can enter whether or not the patient has diabetes, or there is no information.
- **¿Is homeless?**: multiple choice field, where the principal investigator can define whether the patient is a street dweller or not, or whether there is no information.
- **Clinical information**: multiple choice field, where the principal investigator can define the diagnosis of tuberculosis based on clinical information, or no information is available.
- **Observations**: text field, where the researcher can enter observations about the patient.

The patient registration module is shown in Fig. 6, which ask the user for the patient information. Note that this information is recorded in the system and it is used then to predict if the related patient has TB.

Fig. 6. Patient registration module: the user enters information of the patient in a web form.

4.2 Patient Search Module

The patient search module allows the user to retrieve the list of patients stored in the system, as is shown in Fig. 7. In this module the user can entering the patient profile, search for patients in the search engine and export the list of records to Excel and PDF formats.

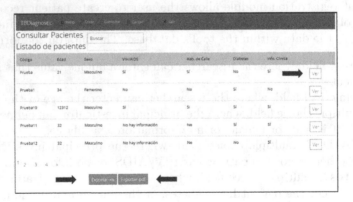

Fig. 7. Patient search module: the user can enter a set of keywords, which are used by the system to find matching records.

In the profile screen, the user can edit, pre-diagnose, validate or delete the patient record, as shown in Fig. 8. This according to the functionalities defined for the tool.

In the edit form, the user can update the data of a particular patient record and update the record in the database, as shown in Fig. 9.

The pre-diagnosis is a function for the user to use the artificial intelligence model to generate a prediction of the specific patient, as it is shown in Fig. 10. The result of the pre-diagnosis is given in two forms: a numerical value that

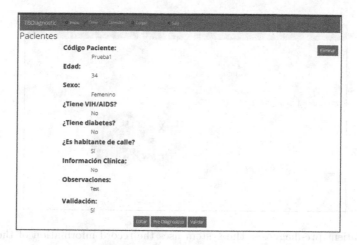

Fig. 8. Patient profile: patient details are shown to the user when he/she selects a patient record.

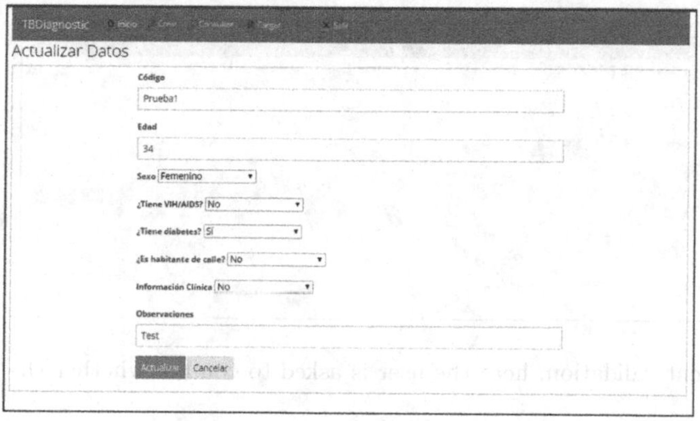

Fig. 9. Patient record edition: the user can modify information previously recorded.

means the patient's degree of tuberculosis, which is between 0 and 1, and the SOM map that means the patient's risk group, where the red risk group is high, the yellow risk group is medium and the green risk group is low.

The validation function is a functionality developed so that in the future medical staff can validate a patient's diagnosis. By keeping a record of a specific patient on the tool, a history can be kept; over time the patient may improve or worsen his or her condition through treatment and other procedures. Therefore, the diagnosis of pulmonary tuberculosis is validated, as shown in Fig. 11.

Finally, the user may delete a patient's record as needed. For instance, in the event in which an erroneous record was entered to the system. Figure 12 shows a screenshot of this functionality.

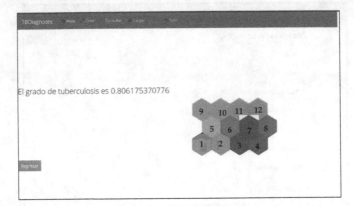

Fig. 10. Patient pre-diagnosis: the system uses the record information of the patient to predict the probability of having TB. The system shows a numerical value and the corresponding SOM map.

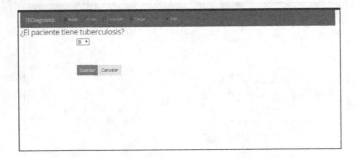

Fig. 11. Patient validation: here the user is asked to confirm whether the patient has TB.

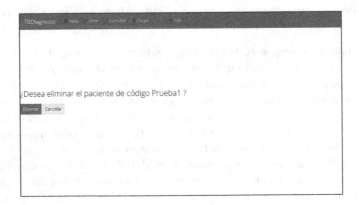

Fig. 12. Patient record elimination. The system ask the user a confirmation before record elimination.

4.3   Loading Patient Records Module

In the loading patient records module it is necessary to avoid accents and special characters. The user can upload massive patient records using a CSV (comma separated values) file. The CSV file must satisfy the following conditions:

- The file should be organized as follows: code, age, sex, HIV, diabetes, street dweller, clinical information and observations.
- Only CSV type files are allowed to be upload to the system.
- Avoid accents and special characters in the CSV file.

The loading patient records module is shown in the Fig. 13. It is worth noting that the user should selecting the CSV file from the file system of the computer in which is working.

4.4   TB Prediction Component

The machine learning model used by the prediction component is based on artificial neural networks (ANN). The architecture is depicted in Fig. 14 which is based on a multilayer perceptron with 3 layers of neurons: an input layer, a hidden layer and an output layer. The input layer is composed of 7 neurons, one

Fig. 13. Patient records loading: the user load massively patient records from a CSV file.

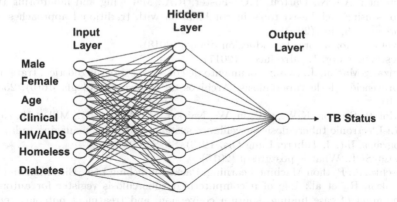

Fig. 14. Architecture of the artificial neural network used by the prediction component.

for each variable and the output layer is composed of a single neuron (which encodes the absence of disease with 0 and the presence of disease with 1). In the hidden layer, between two and ten neurons were used, one for each field of the patient's attributes. As an activation function, all neurons used a hyperbolic tangent function. The *resilient backpropagation* algorithm was used to train the ANN due to its low computational cost and speed.

It is worth noting that the details of the machine learning model such as training, testing, performance evaluation is presented in our previous work published in [1].

5   Conclusions and Future Work

This paper showed TBDiagnostic, patients can be monitored in a given environment and, through an artificial intelligence model, a diagnosis of pulmonary tuberculosis can be determined. The use of web applications makes it easier to manage and store patient data, and parameterized tools for diagnosis help medical staff to provide faster treatment.

In the future, the tool will be extended to allow the generation of graphs of the historical data stored in the database, among other functions that will be identified later. The graphical interface is also planned to be improved to make it more intuitive for the user. The aim is to improve the artificial intelligence model, allowing the diagnosis generated to be not only for pulmonary tuberculosis but also for other types of tuberculosis, such as the pleural, first of all. This with the aim of making the tool's diagnostic functionality more robust.

References

1. Orjuela-Cañón, A.D., Camargo Mendoza, J.E., Awad García, C.E., Vergara Vela, E.P.: Tuberculosis diagnosis support analysis for precarious health information systems. Comput. Meth. Prog. Biomed. **157**, 11–17 (2018). ISSN 0169-2607
2. BBVAAPIMarket. Django: guía rápida para desarrollar páginas web con este framework (2016)
3. Chapman, A.L.N., Darton, T.C., Foster, R.A.: Managing and monitoring tuberculosis using web-based tools in combination with traditional approaches. Clin. Epidemiol. **5**, 465 (2013)
4. Developer.mozilla.org. Introducción django (2018)
5. Docs.python.org. 1. Introduccin (2017)
6. González-Martín, J., et al.: Documento de consenso sobre diagnóstico, tratamiento y prevención de la tuberculosis. Archivos de Bronconeumología **46**(5), 255–274 (2010)
7. Nadol, P., Stinson, K.W., Coggin, W., Naicker, M., Wells, C.D., Miller, B., Nelson, L.J.: Electronic tuberculosis surveillance systems: a tool for managing today's TB programs. Int. J. Tuberc. Lung Dis. **12**(3), S8–S16 (2008)
8. PostgreSQL. What is postgresql (2015)
9. Raschka, S.: Python Machine Learning. Packt Publishing Ltd., Birmingham (2015)
10. Vranken, R., et al.: Use of a computerized tuberculosis register for automated generation of case finding, sputum conversion, and treatment outcome reports. Int. J. Tuberc. Lung Dis. **6**, 111–120 (2002)

Enabling Semantic Interoperability of Disease Surveillance Data in Health Information Exchange Systems for Community Health Workers

Nikodemus Angula and Nomusa Dlodlo[✉]

Department of Informatics, Namibia University of Science and Technology,
Windhoek, Namibia
chcangula@gmail.com, ndlodlo@nust.na

Abstract. The Integrating the Healthcare Enterprise (IHE) advocates for the integration of distributed and heterogeneous health information systems. This is achieved through the development of standards that specify protocols through which the integrated systems can communicate as profiles. In Namibia, healthcare services are extended to communities through community health workers (CHW). Most CHW are sent to the field to educate and raise awareness of diseases in the communities. However, there is no platform for them to communicate the disease surveillance information to the regional and Head offices in real-time. The IHE, through its Information Technology Infrastructure Technical Framework Volume 2b Transaction B provides a Cross-Gateway Patient Discovery (XCPD) profile that can support the means to locate communities which hold patient-relevant health data as well as the translation of patient identifiers across communities that hold similar patient data. The XCPD profile can be adapted to support communication between the CHW, the DHIS-2 in the Ministry of Health and Social Services (MoHSS) and silo HIS in the regional hospitals, for them to share and also to exchange information within a health information exchange ecosystem. At the present moment, the DHIS-2 and the silo health information systems work in isolation simply because these HIS are heterogeneous, they are not interfaced and also not distributed. The study sought to develop a framework to enable the semantic interoperability of the DHIS-2, silo systems and CHWs for data semantic interoperability so that they can exchange disease-surveillance information.

Keywords: Community health workers · Disease surveillance
Health standards · Semantic interoperability · Systems integration

1 Introduction

In the Namibian health domain, the DHIS-2 and silo health information systems are not interlinked in order to share and exchange disease surveillance data for health programmes across various departments of the Ministry of Health and Social Services and the public hospitals in Namibia. At the present moment, the DHIS-2 and the silo health information systems work in isolation because of the fact that the silo systems are not

H. Florez et al. (Eds.): ICAI 2018, CCIS 942, pp. 119–130, 2018.
https://doi.org/10.1007/978-3-030-01535-0_9

interfaced. This also includes community health workers who are sent out in the field in the various communities to educate the citizens and also to collect disease surveillance data. These community health workers cannot communicate the data that is collected in real-time to the relevant authorities through automated means since their HIS are not interlinked to the DHS-2 and the other silo systems that are in operation. The Namibia health sectors therefore lack a semantic interoperability framework for community health workers to assist them as a form of guidance for them to collect disease surveillance data from the 14 different regions of Namibia from which they operate, to the Head Office and Regional Offices of the Ministry of Health and Social Services (MoHSS). Despite the MOHSS' efforts in the deployment of community health workers in the regions to educate and deliver health services to the communities in Namibia, the community health workers are the ones who gather disease surveillance information, which is time consuming. As a result, the government spends more money to cater for the community health workers who operate in the 14 regions of Namibia (CDC global health strategy 2012–2015). It is noted that Namibia's health domain does not have a framework that acts as guide to aggregate disease surveillance data to help the community health workers when collecting disease surveillance information in the 14 regions across the country. Thus there is a need to have a semantic interoperability framework that would enable a community health worker in the Namibian health domain of the MOHSS and public hospitals in Namibia to exchange and communicate disease surveillance information. National Policy on Community Based Health Care Draft (2007), states that a community health worker is a member of the community who works on a volunteering basis or is remunerated by the community or society that 'he/she provides services to. The community health worker is trained in basic health care by health professionals. The IHE is a health standard that enables the interoperability of HIS within the health domain (Integrating the Healthcare Enterprise, 2014). It allows access to and sharing of health information electronically, thereby improving speed, quality and security of patient data. In the Namibian context, however, there is a need to have systems in place that can support health workers as they exchange information from their remote locations. Therefore, there is a need to have a standard way in which health information from community workers can be exchanged with the DHIS-2 and silo systems. This paper proposes this through the adaptation of the Cross-Community Patient Discovery (XCPD).

2 Problem Statement

The community health workers in the Namibian health domain are experiencing challenges of communicating disease surveillance information on time to the relevant health facilities across the country. The community health workers in the Namibian health environment do not have a framework that guides them as to how to communicate disease surveillance information to the health decision-makers in real-time. The Centre for Disease Control (CDC) agency, as the custodian of disease surveillance information, coordinates and facilitates the collection and communication of non-communicable and communicable disease information. The CDC faces the challenge of exchanging disease surveillance information to other regions in Namibia. As a result, community health workers are usually deployed in the 14 regions in Namibia to gather disease surveillance information. The process of access to information is long, for instance taking a month or more for the data to be transferred from one entity to the other (CDC 2013). The current method that is used to collect data is that the community health workers are normally sent into the field to inspect the situation of non-communicable and communicable diseases that occur in the region, and then these communality health workers compile reports on specific issues of disease occurrence. This is time consuming as the information has to be sent to the head office in Windhoek where strategic decisions are taken and implemented (CDC global health strategy 2012–2015). The community health workers in the Namibian health domain struggle when they are in the field because they find themselves in deeply remote areas where the telecommunications network is limited. As a result, the present research was motivated from this noted challenge to develop a semantic interoperability framework as a solution or improvement to this current problem that experienced by the community health workers in Namibia when collecting disease surveillance data in the regions. WHO (2008) states that surveillance is an activity that has to be done for those conditions and diseases that are might be deemed as critical and has public health significance. It is useful to have a catalogue of diseases and syndromes that are in the national health information system (HIS) to enable planning and routine management, yet also noteworthy is that owing to financial and human resources limitations this might prove to be extensive for effective and useful surveillance of diseases. Therefore, depending on the objectives of the system, priority diseases for surveillance should be identified and reviewed regularly to ensure that they remain relevant and important. There are no Health Level Seven (HL7) standards for community health workers to be supported in a standardised manner. In general, there are research efforts that standardise communications among healthcare workers.

2.1 Preliminaries or Basic Concepts

2.2 Community Health Workers

Many professional organisations have defined what a *community health worker* actually is. The American Public Health Association (APHA)'s Community Health Worker Section (2009) regards a CHW as: "Community Health Workers (CHWs) are frontline public health workers who are trusted members of and/or have an unusually close understanding of the community served. This trusting relationship enables CHWs to serve as a liaison/link/intermediary between health/social services and the community to facilitate access to services and improve the quality and cultural competence of service delivery. CHWs also build individual and community capacity by increasing health knowledge and self-sufficiency through a range of activities such as outreach, community education, informal counseling, social support and advocacy." In addition, Bhutta (2010) provides WHO's definition as: "CHWs should be members of the communities where they work, should be selected by the communities, should be answerable to the communities for their activities, should be supported by the health system but not necessarily a part of its organization, and have shorter training than professional workers" (Bhutta 2010).

2.3 Health Information Exchange

HIE is there to provide means of accessing and retrieving information about a patient by users that are authorized to do so, with the goal of providing patient care that is effective, safe, efficient and timely manner. The creation of formal organisations in some regions and states has been done for the provision of technology, support and governance of HIE efforts. These formal organisations are called Health Information Organisations (HIOs) or Regional Health Information Organisations (RHIOs). The formation of HIEs is through having a group of stakeholders that are from specific locality or region that aim for the facilitation of the electronic exchange of information that is health-related with the aim of enhancing healthcare for a specific population. Therefore the HIE helps with the provision of capabilities of the organisations that are participants to share health information in a safe and secure manner with providers who are authorized to work for the improvement and expedited delivery of processes pertaining to clinical decision-making. Notable is that HIE is not necessarily an information system that operates a single organisation, neither is it something that operates in one directional flow of information. A real HIE is one where there is an involvement a multi-directional flow of information in electronic form between providers which hospitals, labs, clinics, physicians) as well as some administrative or clinical information sources which are provided by health planners, consumers, and employers, which are inclusive of local, state and or national organisations. Moreover, HIMSS further points that the electronic movement of health-related information among organisations that are disparate in accordance with nationally recognized standards has to be in a manner that is both authorized and secure. The first and foremost purpose of HIE is that of facilitating the exchange of health information that is relevant for the support of patient care coordination, as a way to ensure quality patient care outcomes and in this way it demonstrates meaningful use of such information. Warholak and Hincapie (2014) posit that Health Information Exchange (HIE) implies the sharing of clinical and administrative data beyond the confines of various healthcare institutions, as well as data repositories, and other groups (these might include patients, providers, payers and such other players) in accordance to standards that are recognized nationally.

2.4 Disease Surveillance

The Namibian Centre for Disease Control and Prevention (CDC) posits that disease surveillance is an "ongoing systematic and continuous collection, analysis and interpretation of health data often designed to detect the appearance of specific diseases allowing epidemiologists to follow in time and space the health status and some risk factors associated with diseases for a given population, for use in the planning, implementation, and evaluation of disease control measures" (CDC 1999). Moreover, The European Centre for Disease Prevention and Control (2008–2013) stipulates that "a more coordinated approach to surveillance will improve the regional comparability of data, reduce the complexity in surveillance across Europe, allow to tackle surveillance in a synergistic way, avoid duplication of work, provide better quality public health evidence in the long term, thanks to more relevant and reliable data, make it easier to strengthen the national surveillance systems, most likely be economically more efficient and sustainable, allow easier access to, and use of the data and enhancing the detection and monitoring of international outbreaks". The Centre for Global Health (2011), proffers that "both communicable and non-communicable diseases remain among the leading causes of death, illness, and disability in African communities." In that vein, it can be argued that with the availability of surveillance information, such diseases, conditions, and events can be detected and investigated in a timely manner and thereby enabling the support of an effective public health response. In the year 1998, the World Health Organization Africa Regional Office established the Integrated Disease Surveillance and Response (IDSR). This is a strategy that is meant to strengthen the availability and as well as the use of surveillance and laboratory data that is meant to detect, reporting, investigate, confirm, and respond to well-known and generally other priority diseases that are preventable, including any other public health events.

3 Related Work

3.1 Systems Integration and Interoperability

Roberts (2004), articulates that "integrated systems improve the quality of information, and thereby the quality of decisions by eliminating error-prone redundant data entry". Furthermore, through data sharing amongst systems, this integration enables the improvements in the timeous access to information, and this is an important factor at some places like the justice decisions centres (for example when there is a need to set). Furthermore, integration allows critical information to be shared without regarding time or space constraints since as multiple users are able to simultaneously access the same set of records from different locations throughout the day. Through integration there is a substantial improvement with regards to the reliability and consistency of information, and this allows for immediate access to information by those who have to make key decisions. However, for the occurrence of systems integration to be possible, they must be interoperable. Hasselbring (2000) posits that "in many application areas, data is distributed over a multitude of heterogeneous, often autonomous information systems, and an exchange of data among them is not easy". The IEEE Computer Society defines interoperability as "the ability of two or more systems or components to exchange information and to use the little information that has been exchanged". Achieving interoperability in this context can be considered as two problems that need to be solved:

• Technical interoperability: the reliable delivery of data from one system to the next
• Semantic interoperability: ensuring that each system can understand the information received from others through aligning data models.

3.2 Interoperability of Health Information Systems

Health Information and Management Systems Society (HIMSS) define interoperability as "the extent to which systems and devices can exchange data, and interpret the shared data" (HIMSS.org 2014). The three levels of health information technology interoperability can be identified as: (i) foundational; (ii) structural; and (iii) semantic. Foundational interoperability enables the exchange of data from one information technology system to be received by another systems and this does not require the ability for the receiving information technology system to interpret the data. Structural interoperability defines the message format standards of data it moves from one system to another such that its meaning is unaltered and preserved. Semantic interoperability enables two or more systems to exchange information and the ability to use the information that has been exchanged.

One of the defining characteristics of Healthcare Information Systems (HIS) is that they are data intensive. The major challenge with data intensive systems is interoperability. The adoption of Health Level Seven messaging standard (HL7) (Health Level Seven 2018) is for defining a common message structuring scheme for message exchange between medical information systems, and the Integrating the Healthcare Enterprise (IHE) (Sinha 2012). It is an important step in enabling the interoperability of HISs. The ability of HIS to speak the same language and recognise the formats, structure and care codes in their communication is a critical component in determining the success of interoperability initiatives and the ability to improve care levels.

3.3   Health Level Seven

Integrated systems are a necessity to allow doctors to be connected with each other, during the transfer of care (HIMSS 2012). Moreover, doctors also need to be connected with other health departments such as pharmacy so as to reduce harmful errors; on the other hand hospitals need to be connected to each other for medical records transfers. The Health Level Seven (HL7) international was founded in 1987, and has members in 55 countries. It is a not-for-profit, ANSI-accredited standards-developing organisation. HL7 is dedicated to providing a framework and related standards for the exchange, integration, sharing and retrieval of electronic health information that supports clinical practice and management, as well as the delivery and evaluation of health services.

"Level Seven" is the highest level of the International Organisation for Standardisation (ISO) communications model for Open systems Interconnection (OSI). It exists at the application level. The application level defines the data to be exchanged, the timing of the interchange, and also communicating certain errors to the application. This level supports functions such as security checks, participant identification, availability checks, exchange mechanisms negotiations, and most importantly, data exchange structuring.

The mission of HL7 is to provide standards to enable interoperability so as to achieve:

- Improved delivery of care
- Optimisation of workflow
- Reduction in ambiguity
- Enhancement of knowledge transfer

4   Results

4.1   The IHE-Profile: Cross-Community Patient Discovery (XCPD)

The Cross-Community Patient Discovery (XCPD) was identified in this research as the closest profile that suits current challenges experienced by Community health workers in the Namibian health environment. It is used in this as a support to locate communities that hold patient relevant health data and also in the translation of patient identifiers across communities holding the same patient's data (ITI) Technical Framework (2014) (Fig. 1).

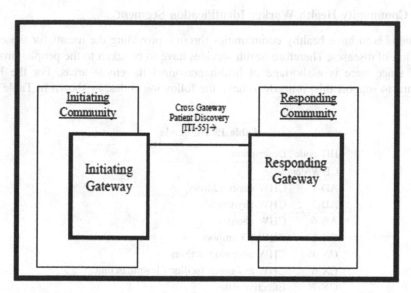

Fig. 1. The community health workers profile adapted from cross-community patient discovery (XCPD) (IHE_ITI_TF_Vol1)

4.2   Initiating Gateway

The Gateway is a server that acts as an entry for a local network when it is in communication with other networks. The purpose of the Initiating Gateway is to carry outgoing messages. These messages have to be synchronous in real-time. The communication supported by the Gateway consists of software/hardware which is in the form of a router that connects a network to another. The software is uploaded onto the Gateway. The security features of the network are also uploaded onto the Gateway. From a data perspective, controls are put on the gateway on what incoming or outgoing data is allowable on the network, or what data is acceptable. When it comes to health data, privacy is of vital importance. Only certain systems or networks can access health data that is exchanged between the CHW and the DHIS-2 and any other silo HIS.

4.3   Responding Gateway

The responding gateway is meant to support all incoming inter-community health workers. Therefore, XCPD utilize this actor to receive the Cross-Gateway Patient Discovery [ITI-55]. The Responding Gateway supports Asynchronous Web Services Exchange on all transactions that are implemented. This allows the Initiating Gateway to choose the better of the two messaging formats (synchronous or asynchronous) that fits the needs of the workflow. The support for Asynchronous Web Services 6400 Exchange allows for workflows which scale to large numbers of communities because it can handle latency and scale more efficiently.

4.4   Community Health Worker Identification Segment

The focus is to have healthy communities through providing the means for the early detection of diseases. Therefore health services have to be taken to the people through CHW since there is a shortage of health personnel in remote areas. For the HL7 standard to support this, it needs to have the following codes, as shown in Table 1:

Table 1. HL7 code

Hl7 code	Description
CHW details	
AD-1	CHW street address
AD-3	CHW city/town
AD-6	CHW country
CX-1	CHW ID number
CX-4	CHW assigning authority
CX-6	CHW assigning facility - hospital/clinic
CX-7	Effective date
CX-8	Expiry date
CX-9	Assigning jurisdiction/region
CX-10	Assigning agency or department
Disease details	
DT	Disease report Date
DTM	Disease report Date time
DTN	Disease type and type ID
ED-1	Source of disease
MSG-1	Disease code
NM	Number of community members affected
TM	Disease time

An extract from the message header is structured as follows in Table 2:

Table 2. Message header extract: Adapted from Health Level Seven technical report

Sequence	Length	Code	Element name
1	1	ST	Field separator
2	4	ST	Encoding characters
3	18	HD	Sending application
4	18	HD	Sending facility
5	18	HD	Receiving application
6	18	HD	Receiving facility
7	26	TS	Date/Time of message

4.5 Architecture for CHW Sourced Information

As shown in Fig. 2, the community health worker or crowd source user can use a desktop or mobile device to report back disease surveillance occurring in the 14 regions in Namibia in real-time and the crowd source user or community health workers can request disease surveillance information from the DHIS.

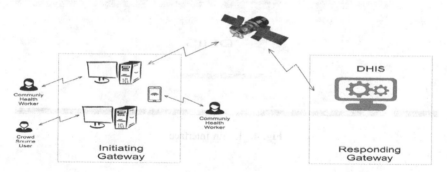

Fig. 2. Community health worker or crowd source user Architecture

4.6 Architecture for the Interlink Protocol

As shown in Fig. 3, the architecture demonstrates different hospital in Namibia with silo systems. Therefore these hospitals can organize their health data in a JSON format and then JSON will transmit this data into information which health professional can use for fast decision making within the Namibian health environment.

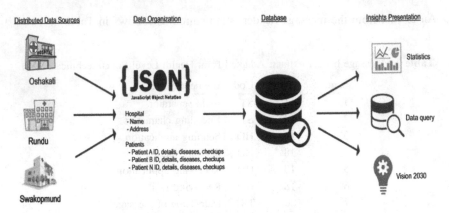

Fig. 3. Architecture of the interlink protocol

5 The Demonstrator

The user can view all the patients that are recorded in the country's HIS (see Fig. 4) or also view patient details per hospital or institution (see Fig. 5).

Fig. 4. Login interface

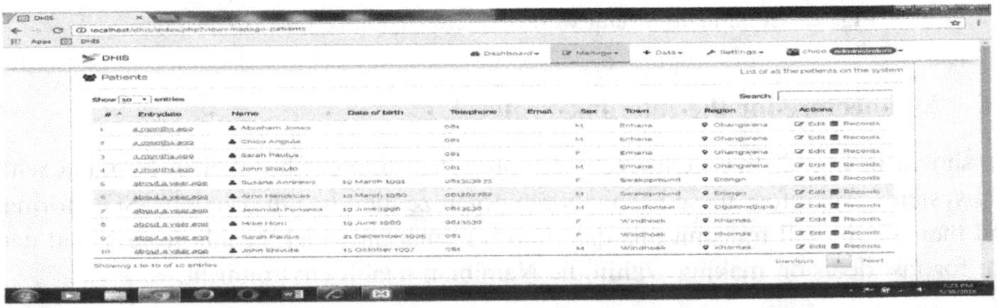

Fig. 5. Patients recorded on the system

6   Business Benefits

Over a long period, the MoHSS has been experiencing challenges associated with timely access to disease surveillance information, not only from the CDC, but also from the regional offices and equally from the sub-regional offices and also from CHW. The length of time to access information can range from as little as a month to more. This simply means that the methods followed in communicating disease surveillance information do not support prompt decision making. As things stand in the health sector now, disease surveillance data is obtained only from official sources and not from unofficial sources. These methods of communication encompass emails and telephone calls, which are technologies that do not support real-time. It is for this reason that this research proposes ways for enabling CHW to effectively communicate disease surveillance data to the other HIS. The information from the CHW should be enabled to integrate with the heterogeneous information systems. This is where HL7 interoperability standards come into play. The XCPD profile was selected from the HL7 standards as the closest to suiting the integration of disease surveillance information from CHW with the HIS. The framework for CHW interoperability would make it easier to collect disease surveillance information. The CDC supports the MOHSS to conduct disease surveillance activities, and to monitor and evaluate such activities. The study used the CHW from remote regions of Namibia to capture disease surveillance data and to communicate it in real-time to the relevant authorities/HIS for decision making. The problem in the Namibian health sector is that there is a plethora of silo HIS that generate a lot of data which cannot be integrated for efficient decision-making due to the fact that these silo systems do not communicate with each other. Almost all public hospitals in Namibia host an HIS of one form or the other, but sharing the data they produce with other hospitals and with the MOHSS is curtailed because of a lack of interoperability. Namibia is yet to adopt these standards hence the motivation for this research.

6.1   Conclusions

The study developed a framework for interoperability of HIS for disease surveillance data from CHW through adopting the HL7 standards. For proof of concept, this research developed a prototype to demonstrate how disease surveillance data can be integrated. The Namibian health domain sends community health workers in the 14 regions to educate the community on health programmes or to make the community aware of particular outbreaks of communicable and non-communicable disease. The study therefore developed a semantic interoperability framework adopting HL7 standards.

Appendix

ACRONYMS/ABBREVIATIONS

MoHSS-Ministry of health and social services
CHW-Community health worker
CDC-The Centre for Disease control
HL7-Health level seven
EHRs-Electronic Health records
XCPD-Cross-community patient discovery

References

Bhutta, Z.A., Lassi, Z.S., Pariyo, G., Huicho, L.: Global experience of community health workers for delivery of health related millennium development goals: a systematic review, country case studies, and recommendations for integration into national health systems. Global Health Workforce Alliance, vol. 1, pp. 249–261 (2010). http://www.who.int/workforcealliance/knowledge/publications/alliance/Global_CHW_web.pdf. Accessed 2 Nov 2015
CDC Global Health Strategy (2012–2015). Centers for Disease Control and Prevention Global Health Strategy. https://www.cdc.gov/globalhealth/strategy/pdf/cdc-globalhealthstrategy.pdf
CDC in Namibia. https://www.cdc.gov/globalhealth/countries/namibia/pdf/namibia.pdf
CDC (2013). CDC in Namibia
Centers for Disease Control and Prevention (CDC) (1999). Promoting the use of Standard Methods and Procedures in the management of Transboundary Animal Diseases
Centre for global health (2011). Integrated disease surveillance and response (IDSR)
European Centre for disease prevention and control (2008–2013). Surveillance of communicable diseases in the European Union long-term strategy
Hasselbring, W.: Information system integration (2000). https://www.researchgate.net/publication/220419996
Integrating the Healthcare Enterprise (2014). IHE IT Infrastructure (ITI) Technical Framework, vol. 1 (ITI TF-1) Integration Profiles
National Policy on Community Based Health Care Draft, 1 November 2007
Roberts, D.J.: Integration in the context of justice information systems: a common understanding (2004)
Warholak, T.L., Hincapie, L.: The impact of health information exchange on health outcomes. Appl. Clin. Inform. 2(4), 499–507 (2014)
World Health Organization (2008). Essential environmental health standards in health care, Geneva 27, Switzerland

Enabling the Medical Applications Engine

Fernando Yepes Calderon[1](✉), Nolan Rea[1],
and J. Gordon McComb[1,2]

[1] Children's Hospital Los Angeles, Neurosurgery,
1300 N. Vermont Avenue, Los Angeles, CA, USA
fernandoyepesc@gmail.com
[2] Keck School of Medicine, University of Southern California,
1975 Zonal Avenue, Los Angeles, CA, USA

Abstract. The advent of imaging methods in medicine has yielded new diagnosing dynamics inside hospitals. Since imaging allows the inspection with few or no intrusiveness, there is a remarked intention in producing medical verdicts from the radiology data by implementing computational algorithms and, therefore preclude the use of the long-lasting analytics that involve manual segmentation or often painful procedures such as histology. Currently, troves of medical-imaging data are stored in the picture archiving and communication system (PACS) – the standard imaging database –. The massive storage is initially created and maintained obeying to the legal regulations, but the resulting repository holds unbeatable conditions to apply artificial intelligence and derive conclusions from hidden patterns, a new mechanism never envisaged before. However, the same regulations that enabled the creation of the medical imaging repository have precluded the quantifications from images stored in PACS.

This paper presents a strategy that empowers PACS so that analytical procedures can run without violating confidentiality policies or creating security breaches. The platform supports unlimited analytical procedures, and, as a prof of concept, the problem of accurately measuring the maximum head circumference in pediatrics is solved and presented.

Keywords: PACS · Medical imaging · Clinical research

1 Introduction

The use of the picture archiving and communication system (PACS) has worldwide spread within hospitals and clinics [23]. This system keeps the coherency among the continuously growing imaging database that is currently the diagnosis core of radiology units. The PACS replaced the old filming system by profiting of the transmission control and internet protocols (TCP/IP), which are widely used even for exigent tasks as video streaming, real-time reporting or conferencing. In the conception of the system, data-security and coherent availability are pillars; therefore, analytical capabilities are the weakest part of the platform, despite the need was firstly envisaged in 2000 [1,2].

© Springer Nature Switzerland AG 2018
H. Florez et al. (Eds.): ICAI 2018, CCIS 942, pp. 131–143, 2018.
https://doi.org/10.1007/978-3-030-01535-0_10

1.1   PACS Commercial Scope

PACS comes in different levels of commitment, ranging from free of license packages to software-as-a-service implementations provided by prestigious companies such as Siemens, Fuji, LG, Bruker among others. Since the imaging transport and management are critical for clinicians, PACS platforms are frequently hired to renowned companies that have started a race to empower their systems with utilities aiming to have commercial advantages. In general, having a prestigious provider assures usability and robustness, but very often, the hospital's administrations start struggling when changing the provider. Although the core of PACS is the same, the methods in the higher layers and the mechanisms that interact with final users are proprietary and different for each maker. The providers are reluctant to share or make their methods compatible among companies because that would fade their commercial advantages.

1.2   Attempts to Provide PACS with Analytics

Developers have proposed different approaches to assert quantifications within PACS. Those solutions start from completely replacing the actual system [16], until a full scheme of back-end and front-end plugs-ins as explained in [2]. The idea proposed in [16], despite well designed to support the desired flexibility obviates the fact that PACS was already adopted at 76% of the hospitals in the US by 2008 [23]; therefore, a total replacement would be a remote option to consider for hospital administrators. Regarding the classification done by [2], there exists plug-in like packages that target PACS processing capabilities in very specific scopes such as [18], others empowering team interactivity like in [19] and traffic alleviation [21] among others. Despite these tools are launched with free BSD licenses are unknown for clinicians and hospital administrators. In addition, in their marketing strategies, concepts such as everywhere availability, java-script remote interactivity, displaying in portable devices are recurrently claimed, underestimating the confidentiality and security policies that are the core of PACS.

1.3   Confidentiality and Regulation

Market conditioning being the most visible drawback for PACS development is not the most prejudicial for further advancement. Consider that radiology departments are currently handling the imaging of all other units inside hospitals and consequently, speeding diagnosis with accuracy is in high demand to overcome the natural overheat [20]. The word accuracy here is vague because the verdicts are interpretations done upon qualitative insights, but more striking is the fact that verdicts might not be repeatable even when obtained by the same operator on the same sample [12,24]. To venture into the needed deterministic world, clinicians should quantify and, since PACS has not been conceived for this purpose, the images need to be downloaded and put into software that is out of the clinical pipeline. If this activity is done without Institutional Review Board

(IRB) [13] consent, the people involved and the institution will be violating the law. The strong regulations materialized in health insurance portability and accountability act (HIPAA), preclude the use of the needed and possibly existing algorithms. Under current regulations, confidentiality precedes any other need, and consequently, the images are not available for quantifying purposes unless permissions have been granted. The timing to process an IRB even in the scenario of dealing with retrospective data, overpasses that of the clinical needs, condemning the automatic approaches to research purposes [13].

1.4   Clinical Research and Programmatic Tools

Hospitals, when possible, employ individuals to perform research and some of those colleagues are working in the field of clinical imaging research. Their outcomes often go beyond the scientific contribution manifested in papers. These researchers are capable of quantifying events underlying in the images using programmatic tools. As the quantifications are obtained with numerical computations, the results may or not be accurate, but they will always be repeatable. Instrument designers know that repeatability is the first goal; once achieved, the accuracy is reached by tunning the device [7]. The concept of repeatability is tempting to physicians by itself, and recently, with the advent of the artificial intelligence (AI), it seems like all the needed components are in place. The new algorithms can be developed using programming frameworks that allow a natural pass between prototyping and compiling for production purposes – like Python –, and the AI can automatically extract information from images saved in PACS without opening security breaches.

1.5   Purpose of the Current Development

As explained in Sect. 1.1, PACS providers have developed proprietary platforms with no compatibility with versions supported by other makers. In this paper, we present a solution conceived inside a hospital that acknowledges the needs of all authors and legal regulations as well. The presented platform solves the problem of being locked to a specific provider. Moreover, we provide a proof of concept running on the vehicle that automatically calculates the maximum head's circumference (MHC) in babies undergoing MRI to discard head growing abnormalities. A wrongly estimated value for the MHC misleads diagnosis and treatment, that is why there exists a complete guide to performing the measurement [17]. Factors such as the constant movement of the patient and incorrect positioning of the tape induce errors in the manual reading. As the popularity of MRI increases and the associated costs drop down, the pediatric units are less prone to let the patients go without, at least, one scanning session. The automatic maximum head circumference estimator (AMHCE) obtained from the images is accurate and repeatable.

2   Materials and Methods

2.1   The PACS Vehicle

The network at the hosting institution can be conceptualized as it is shown in Fig. 1.

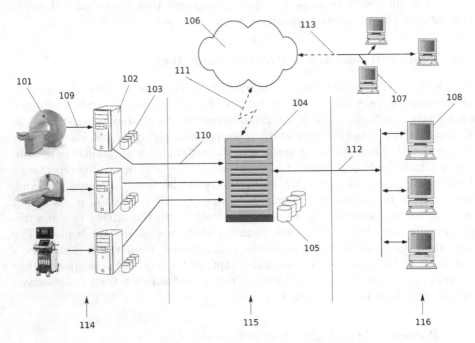

Fig. 1. Default PACS network. The PACS runs on a client-server architecture sharing DICOM messages among stations.

The medical images inside hospitals reside in one of two environments. The acquisition machines *[114]* or the PACS system *[115]*. Once in the PACS, the data is made available for visualization through the viewers in environment *[116]*. The acquisition systems *[101]* temporarily store the files in their respectively associated terminals *[102]* that holds a local database *[103]*. The data flow *[109]*, is primarily raw data in native graphical formats such as JPG, TIFF, and PNG that is subsequently dicomized. The PACS only receives information holding digital imaging and communications in medicine (DICOM) headers [9], formerly called dicomized data. Every piece of information in the flow *[110]* is dicomized, and once it hits the PACS *[104]*, the DICOM fields are read to create an entry profile in the database *[105]*. When the information has been profiled in the PACS, it is ready to be queried and visualized by the local clients *[108]*. Remote clients *[107]*, when authorized by the administrator, can also visualize the data. The data flow *[112]* holds compressed/encrypted DICOM information that needs to be expanded/decrypted in the client's terminals *[108]* before the visualizers can render any information. Authorized clinicians can see the data in their viewports, but they do not have access to the data at a bit level. This viewing-access is granted throughout a graphical user interface. Data flow *[111]* despite inherently available in TCP/IP networks through the cloud *[106]* – known as the Internet –, is generally deactivated in PACS due to security reasons, rendering data flow *[113]* void.

The PACS administrator may prevent the use of external scripts, but it will be unlikely to restrict the routine functions of the client consoles citing operational or technical inconveniences. This fact is of high relevance to grant vendor independence.

The current strategy pivots around empowering a client *[108]* in the network so it can communicate with the PACS and produce bit-level transactions. This empowered client –namely the processing application server (PAS)– generates a new pattern of communications with the PACS and other viewports as well. The automation in the PAS is done using Pythonic gadgets that boost the filtering power of the common Query/Retrieve (Q/R) scheme defined to implement digital imaging and communications in medicine DICOM transactions. The PAS solves the problem of coherently transporting the data and having it available for extracting qualitative insights.

Once the PAS-PACS interactivity is established, the following design aspects are considered.

Query/Retrieve Optimized Filtering. The Q/R actions in the PACS environment are performed through the Dicom Message Service Element DIMSE-C Services (like C-Find and C-Move), where there is always a Service Class User (SCU) at one end and a Service Class Provider (SCP) at the other [4]. For the querying, the SCU is always a client (local terminal), while in a retrieving function, the SCP is a client, that in turn forces the PACS to act as the SCU. This last operation points to role swapping rarely used in the hospital setting but is highly relevant to this application. Regarding the Q/R functions, the design requirements are:

- The C-Find method to produce only small transactions that are optimized to target specific instances within studies.
- The C-Move method that enables image transportation must be selective and ideally should allow sending information back to PACS.
- Since the analytical information is not required in real-time, the strategy involves the optimization of the best time to transfer [22].

Restrictions on Produced Information and Reports. Almost any kind of data can be using the standard internet protocol implementation, and the PACS platform exerts this flexibility if the data is wrapped in DICOM headers. In general, DICOM is very inefficient regarding space, but highly efficient when moving large amounts of data in a shared media. This transporting protocol allows flexibility although, the following considerations must be applied to avoid traffic overload issues:

- The PAS must present its results in economic formats.
- The PAS can move reports backward to the PACS, but this will be restricted to only dicomized-pdf reports.
- The PAS receives compressed DICOM files, then uncompress these files and then packs them into Nifti format; facilitating the processing and anonymizing the data.
- The PAS may allow enhanced visualization linked to the proper study through the use of permalinks [5]. As the display port in PAS is web-based, economic formats are mandatory.

Adding Interactivity with the Produced Analytical Data. Since PACS prioritizes data security and availability, it remains limited in its display features. Opening 3D capabilities and interactivity with the generated data is just the beginning of an enriched scheme of functionality that is non-existent at present. To this end, the following specifications are highly desired:

- The system to provide client-side interactivity through Javascript language; thus operations are mostly executed in the viewports (local terminals) reducing server interactivity and consequently, traffic overload.
- 3D visualization is also provided by using economic formats such as the stereolithography (STL) [15].

2.2   Proof of Concept. Measuring the MHC

Clinical Data. Images of eight randomly selected children were chosen to feed the automatic maximum head circumference estimator (AMHCE). Previously, the children underwent the standard head circumference measurement with a metric cloth tape, so the automatic process has a manual counterpart to estimate its accuracy. The clinical images have different acquisition parameters as those are chosen each time to favor patient comfort. The acquisition parameters for each patient are registered in Table 1.

The Method. Refer to Fig. 2 and its blocks when the acronyms "B-No" appear. In BI, the volumes are extracted from the PACS using the vehicle presented in Sects. 3.1 and 3.2. The images need to undergo processing – BII – to eliminate encryption, be uncompressed and set in a unified format different from DICOM. Next, the nypype [8] module of python is invoked to use an interface to FLS [11] – BIII – where the function bet2 is applied with the parameters to generate the surfaces –BIV–. From the outcome yield in BIV, the masks corresponding to the out-skin and in-skull segments are selected to continue the process. Here the pipeline is bifurcated. Branch A is intended to find the right location for MHC measurement that must go above the eyebrow level – BVIa and VIIa–. Meanwhile, branch B detects the edges –BIb– by subtracting to the original image, an eroded version of itself, and counts –BVIIb– the number of pixels composing the outer edge of the skull. Finally, The edge length is calculated as the product of the number of pixels in BIIb and the pixel's length in the direction of propagation.

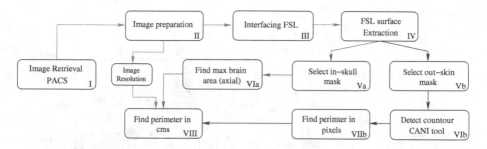

Fig. 2. Pipeline for the automatic MHC extraction. The depicted process returns the perimeter of MHC slice. However, this method can return the perimeter of the whole set of slices composing the head and several other measurements unfeasible by physical means in alive subjects.

3 Results

3.1 New PACS Architecture

The arrangement in Fig. 3 shows the inclusion of PAS *[202]* and its database *[203]* in the hospital local network. Note how the PAS is connected to the network as any other client. Although, the PAS has been equipped with boosted querying capabilities.

The PAS acquires the information using the same querying mechanisms utilized by any other authorized client on the network; however, unlike other clients, the PAS has access to the data at a bit-level; therefore, it is image-processing capable. The PAS can perform associative queries and retrieve data in a bulk manner. The PAS is transparent to PACS administrators while its specifications enable the creation of innovative clinical and research-derived applications. With the PAS in the network, new data flows *[204]* and *[205]* are created. Data flow *[204]* is mainly used for loading the new analytical tools and for associating clinical studies or instances with analytical procedures. Data flow *[205]* is kept optional but if activated would provide to remote clients, the same services that local clients producing data flow *[204]* have.

3.2 PACS - PAS Interaction

When one of the local terminals in the network becomes a PAS, a new set of interactions is enabled. Figure 4conceptualizes the associations and new capabilities. The left side corresponds to clients-PAS interactions and the PAS procedures. The horizontal column defines the set of messages interchanged between the PAS and PACS.

In the proposed architecture Fig. 4, a regular curse of execution requires physicians to associate the imaging studies to the procedures using the configuration interface residing in PAS and accessible to authenticated clinicians throughout the hypertext transfer protocol (HTTP). The studies are filtered in

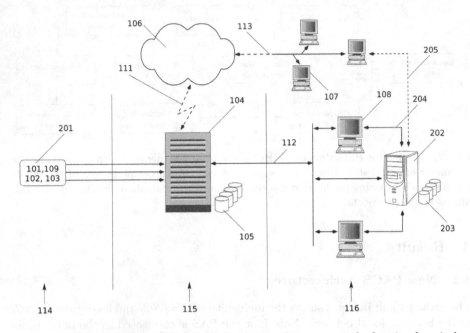

Fig. 3. The PAS [202,203] is part of the data architecture at the hosting hospital

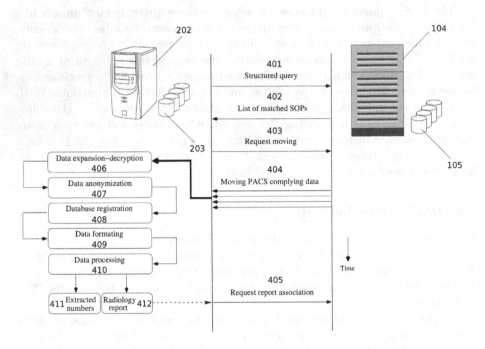

Fig. 4. PAS interactions and workflow in the enhanced PACS system

a wide range of possibilities, flexibility not enabled in the commonly used PACS viewers.

The PAS builds a DICOM complying query [401] obeying the directives given by the user in the configuration interface. The PACS responds with the SOPs that point to the required data [402]. Next, the PAS delivers a request for transfer [403], and the PACS starts transferring the requested information [404].

The PAS also schedules this moving task in the low usage periods of the network that are dynamically defined by ping-tests.

When the data transfer from the PACS to the PAS is complete, the PAS proceeds to decrypt and expand [406], anonymize [407] and register the data in the PAS database [408]. All these steps also assert formatting in a lighter format (Nifti, analyze).

After formatting, the data is ready to be treated by the selected quantifying algorithm [410].

The results of the quantifying algorithm are used to produce the radiology report [412] that is sent back to the PACS [405].

3.3   The Maximun Head Circunference Estimator (MHCE)

The Table 1, compares the MHC values obtaines by hand (current standard of care) and the one obtained on the images and using the automation conceptualized in Fig. 2.

Table 1. Comparison between manually and automatic obtained MHC using correction factors.

Serial	Res	MHCE		Difference
		Manual	Automatic	
1	$0.58 \times 0.58 \times 5.00$	57.1 ± 0.1	57.6 ± 0.6	-0.5 ± 0.6
2	$0.41 \times 0.41 \times 4.00$	44.8 ± 0.1	43.9 ± 0.5	0.9 ± 0.5
3	$0.58 \times 0.58 \times 5.00$	49.0 ± 0.1	49.6 ± 0.6	-0.6 ± 0.6
4	$0.85 \times 0.85 \times 3.99$	48.5 ± 0.1	49.0 ± 0.6	-0.5 ± 0.6
5	$0.46 \times 0.46 \times 4.99$	57.1 ± 0.1	56.4 ± 0.6	0.7 ± 0.6
6	$0.57 \times 0.57 \times 4.99$	54.6 ± 0.1	53.9 ± 0.6	0.7 ± 0.6
7	$0.79 \times 0.79 \times 4.99$	56.0 ± 0.1	55.5 ± 0.6	0.5 ± 0.6
8	$0.57 \times 0.57 \times 4.00$	42.2 ± 0.1	42.2 ± 0.5	0.0 ± 0.5

3.4   Linking the PACS Vehicle and Further Developments

Once the PACS vehicle is established, one needs a mechanism to populate the system with analytical procedures to enable the medical applications engine in medicine. After all the effort done within the vehicle, it would be uncompleted without the possibility of adding more analytical procedures. In this implementation, we have decided to conceive the linkage between the vehicle and any third party development through the JSON specification provided in Listing 1.1.

```
1  [
2    {
3      owner :[
4        {
5          pname: 'Jon Smith',
6          pemail: 'jsmith@_____'
7        }
8      ],
9      tstamp: '1528126994',
10     inputstudies: '4036656, 4876598, 4327869, 6564932',
11     imgtype: 'MRI',
12     input_img_dir:'hp_fyc:imready/fyepes_/01_Raw/',
13     ip_request: '192.168.1.134',
14     output_img_dir: 'hp_fyc:/fyepes_/03_Nifti/',
15     out_report_type: 'pdf, xls',
16     output_report_path: 'hp_fyc:/fyepes_/04_Report/',
17     code_location: hp_fyc:proc/amhce.py
18     analytics_by: 'AMHCE',
19     developer: 'f_____@_____ , g_____@_____'
20   }
21 ]
```

Listing 1.1. Json file produced by the PACS vehicle linking the AMHCE. This file is mandatory in any development regardless of the platform used and allows the PAS to control the data flow within the implementation.

This file is automatically created by the PACS vehicle. It is initially intended to define the paths where the information needed is located and also where the results are going to be saved. Some of the information carried on here is created by the system using the timestamp of the request (line 9) and the profile of the requesting physician lines (5,6); here, the timestamps itself creates unique paths per request. Some other information such as the type of the input (line 12) and outgoing-files' extensions (line 15) is found in the specification of the software – that are requested as mandatory to the developers.

4 Discussion

Technological instruments that assist clinicians are hard to implement due to the intense regulation that varies from country to country. However, independently of the country, is the growing demand for services to radiology departments that inevitably forces the implementation of technology to speed up the diagnosing processes. The concept of a highly technological scenario analytically capable is not new; according to Huang et al. [10], during the infancy and puberty of PACS, the objectives were framed by format standardization and modality integration. The same author states that the PACS is currently in its adolescence and highlights the imaging informatics as the developing core for the current state of the system.

The displayed development has been implemented in an institution that fully complies with the HIPAA regulations; therefore, its usability in less legally critical environments is granted.

Our solution has been conceived to utilize the existing PACS implementation, profiting the connectivity protocols that are standard on the internet and therefore, are fully compatible up to the transport level – refer to the OSI model – assuring independence among PACS providers. In addition to making the images available at a bit-level without violating current confidentially policies, we propose a framework that allows researchers to test innovations and validate their models with medical data.

There is, however, a restriction that arises from legal clauses. As law protects confidential information of the patients, the created algorithms are compelled to be fully automatic rendering manual and semi-automatic assessments futile. That explains why an initially easy task such as the MHC, requires a relatively high effort of instrumentation when implemented inside hospitals.

Regarding the clinical necessity that inspired the proof of concept explained in this paper, there exists a reluctance to use automatic measurements due to the low-resolution hold by clinical images. Fortunately for the head circumference calculations, the images used are axial, so we profit of the high in-plane resolution often used, which is in cents of micrometers.

In MRI, acquisition time is saved in the Z-axes where lengths of 4 and 5 mm are common. The massive displacement in the Z-axes may mislead the location of the MHC. However, this large values in imaging dimensions correspond to a small fraction of the error that a human operator may induce in the positioning of the metric tape.

As for the perimeter measuring strategy, it is derived from the ultra-fast hardware implementation proposed by Benkrid and Crookes [3]. The results yielded by the algorithm are within the accepted range of tolerance when compared with those yielded by the standard of care.

The Nellhaus curves were proposed in 1968 and since they are of commonly used in the pediatric units. Other studies reproducing the Nellhaus chart have been presented from 1987 to 2000 [6,25], including digital files provided by the WHO [17]. More recently, automatic methods with sophisticated approaches such as [14] have been proposed. Unfortunately, the implementation of these kinds of technological advances is precluded by the PACS policies. In contrast, our implementation is PACS compatible and thus, ready to use effortlessly by clinicians.

5   Conclusions

A significant amount of research-derived solutions are daily presented to the medical research community. Not all of these solutions involve clinical data mostly because the production of this data obey to clinical necessities and, as the field is highly qualitative, the concept of standardized procedures is not met during acquisition. As a consequence, the images are generated with few uniformizations. Clinical researchers have been venturing this field with innovative strategies to quantify from this data, but they lack access to the data in the amount it is required to generalize solutions and also easiness of translation from prototypes to massively use of algorithms within their commonly used tools.

The presented development overcomes all these drawbacks, providing a clear path for both, having access to the images at a bit level and enabling an interfacing mechanism that assists the transfer of knowledge to useful tools, as it has been done with the AMHCE algorithm. Validations of the AMHCE can be appreciated in the videos posted in www.fernandoyepesc.com. Further work involve the creation of a bank of algorithms and a robust automation scheme that allows administrator to setup the system so the physicians receive the analytical reports in their console with only a click of the mouse.

References

1. Bellon, E., Feron, M., Deprez, T., Reynders, R., den Bosch, B.V.: Trends in PACS architecture. Eur. J. Radiol. **78**, 199–204 (2011)
2. Bellon, E., et al.: Incorporating novel image processing methods in a hospital-wide PACS. Int. Congress Ser. **1281**, 1016– 1021 (2005). https://doi.org/10.1016/j.ics.2005.03.210, www.ics-elsevier.com
3. Benkrid, K., Crookes, D., Benkrid, A.: Design and FPGA implementation of a perimeter estimator. In: Proceedings of the Irish Machine Vision and Image Processing Conference, pp. 51–57 (2000)
4. Bidgood, W.D., Horh, S.T., Prior, F.W., VanSyckle, D.E.: Understanding and using DICOM, the data interchange standard for biomedical imaging. J. Am. Med. Inform. Assoc. **4**, 199–212 (1997)
5. Blood, R.: How bloggin software reshapes the online commnunity. Commun. ACM **14**, 53–55 (2004)
6. Rollins, J.D., Collins, J.S., Holden, K.R.: United states head circumference growth reference charts birth to 21 years. J. Pediatr. **156**(6), 907–13 (2010)
7. Reinstein, D.Z., Archer, T.J., Silverman, R.H., Coleman, D.J.: Accuracy, repeatability, and reproducibility of artemis very high-frequency digital ultrasound arc-scan lateral dimension measurements. J. Cataract. Refract. Surg. **32**(11), 1799–1802 (2006). https://doi.org/10.1016/j.jcrs.2006.07.017
8. Gorgolewski, K., et al.: Nipype: a flexible, lightweight and extensible neuroimaging data processing framework in python. Front. Neuroinform. **5** (2011). https://doi.org/10.3389/fninf.2011.00013, http://dx.doi.org/10.3389/fninf.2011.00013
9. Gueld, M.O., et al.: Quality of DICOM header information for image categorization. In: Proceedings of SPIE, Medical Imaging, vol. 4685 (2002)
10. Huang, H.K.: Short history of PACS. Part I: USA. Eur. J. Radiol. **78**(2), 163 – 176 (2011). https://doi.org/10.1016/j.ejrad.2010.05.007, http://dx.doi.org/10.1016/j.ejrad.2010.05.007
11. Jenkinson, M., Beckmann, C., Behrens, T., Woolrich, M., Smith, S.: FSL. Neuroimage **62**, 782–90 (2012)

12. Chamberlain, J., Rogers, P., Price, J.L., Ginks, S., Nathan, B.E., Burn, I.: Validity of clinical examination and mammography as screening tests for breast cancer. The Lancet **306**(7943), 1026–1030 (1975). https://doi.org/10.1016/S0140-6736(75)90304-9

13. Dickersin, K., Min, Y.I., Meinert, C.L.: Factors influencing publication of research results follow-up of applications submitted to two institutional review boards. JAMA **267**(3) (1992). https://doi.org/jama.1992.03480030052036

14. Li, J., et al.: Automatic fetal head circumference measurement in ultrasound using random forest and fast ellipse fitting. IEEE J. Biomed. Health Inform. **22**(1), 215–223 (2017)

15. Ma, D., Lin, F., Chua, C.K.: Rapid prototyping applications in medicine. Part 2: STL file generation and case studies. Int. J. Adv. Manuf. Technol. **18**, 118–127 (2001)

16. Mahmoudi, S.E., et al.: Web-based interactive 2D/3D medical image processing and visualization software. Comput. Methods Programs Biomed. **98**(2), 172 – 182 (2009). https://doi.org/10.1016/j.cmpb.2009.11.012, http://dx.doi.org/10.1016/j.cmpb.2009.11.012

17. de Onis, M.: WHO Child Growth Standards. Methods and Development. No. 978 92 4 154718 5, World Health Organization (2009). http://www.who.int/childgrowth/standards/velocity/tr3_velocity_report.pdf?ua=1

18. Perez, F., et al.: RADStation3G: a platform for cardiovascular image analysis integrating PACS, 3D+t visualization and grid computing. Comput. Methods Programs Biomed. **110**(3), 399–410 (2012). https://doi.org/10.1016/j.cmpb.2012.12.002, http://dx.doi.org/10.1016/j.cmpb.2012.12.002

19. Qiao, L., et al.: Medical high-resolution image sharing and electronic whiteboard system: a pure web-based system for accessing and discussing lossless original images in telemedicine. Comput. Methods Programs Biomed. **121**(2), 77–91 (2015). https://doi.org/10.1016/j.cmpb.2015.05.010, http://dx.doi.org/10.1016/j.cmpb.2015.05.010

20. European Society of Radiology 2009: The future role of radiology in healthcare. Insights Imaging **1**(1), 2–11 (2010). https://doi.org/10.1007/s13244-009-0007-x

21. Ratiba, O., Rosset, A.: Can PACS benefit from general consumer communication-tools? Int. Congress Ser. **1281**, 948–953 (2005). https://doi.org/10.1016/j.ics.2005.03.344, www.ics-elsevier.com

22. Rodola, G.: Psutil package: a cross-platform library for retrieving information on running processes and system utilization (2016). https://pypi.python.org/pypi/psutil

23. Tieche, M., Gump, J., Rieck, M.E., Schneider., A.: This white paper explores the decade of PACS technology, changes, growth in numbers of vendors, and installations in hospitals in the United States. The Dorenfest Institute (2010)

24. Tollard, E., Darsaut, T., Bing, F., Guilbert, F., Gevry, F., Raymond, J.: Outcomes of endovascular treatments of aneurysms: observer variability and implications for interpreting case series and planning randomized trials. Am. J. Neuroradiol. **33**(4) (2012). https://doi.org/10.3174/ajnr.A2848

25. Villar, J., et al., for the International Fetal, for the 21st Century (INTERGROWTH-21st), N.G.C.: International standards for newborn weight and length and head circumference by gestational age and sex the newborn and cross-sectional study and of the intergrowth-21st project. Lancet **384**, 857–68 (2014)

Use of Virtual Reality Using Render Semi-realistic as an Alternative Medium for the Treatment of Phobias. Case Study: Arachnophobia

Jonathan Almeida[✉], David Suárez[✉], Freddy Tapia[✉], and Graciela Guerrero[✉]

Departamento de Ciencias de la Computación,
Universidad de Las Fuerzas Armadas ESPE, 171-5-231B Sangolquí, Ecuador
{jsalmeidal, dasurem, fmtapia, rgguerrero}@espe.edu.ec

Abstract. The design of virtual scenarios and organic models, through the use of virtual reality with the inclusion of photorealism, with all these components can develop a process of handling reactions to phobias that generates an immersive experience similar to reality, obtaining as a result an alternative treatment to arachnophobia, this contribution of help can be partial or total, since it will depend on the time of use. To verify the states of improvement in the users that are submitted to the test of the application, guidelines will be provided to continue the research using a set of technological tools for the area of phobia treatment, as well as the connection of virtual reality in other branches of medicine.

Keywords: Arachnophobia · Virtual reality · Photorealism · Phobia Treatment

1 Introduction

Anxiety and fear are concentrated emotional experiences that fulfill critical functions by organizing necessary survival responses [1]. Although affective systems that work properly offer responses that are adaptive, excessive trepidation is restrictive and may be a sign of unregulated anxiety. Affective dysregulation, including anxiety disorders, specific phobias, as well as panic disorder and post-traumatic stress disorder (PTSD), can cause significant disruptions in daily life. Repeated and early exposure to stress in people with a particular genetic disposition can lead to the development of anxiety [2]. Excessive arousal and deprivation can influence the affective system and can induce changes in the emotional circuits of the brain that can contribute to psychopathology related to stress [3]. According to Rothbaum et al. [4], a good amount of research has shown that exposure therapy is effective in reducing negative affective symptoms. In the study by Lange et al. [5] it has been found that in vivo exposure therapy has a higher efficacy compared to imaginal exposure, especially in the treatment of specific phobias. Exposure to emotional situations and prolonged testing results in the regular activation of brain metabolism in areas of the brain associated with the inhibition of maladaptive associative processes [6].

© Springer Nature Switzerland AG 2018
H. Florez et al. (Eds.): ICAI 2018, CCIS 942, pp. 144–154, 2018.
https://doi.org/10.1007/978-3-030-01535-0_11

To execute a therapy of exposure to a phobia can be done through the use of virtual reality, in which users can interact with a simulation within a virtual environment generated by a computer, however, this virtual simulation must possess the characteristic of be immersive, such as: updating the virtual environment in a natural way to the movement of the head and/or the movement of the user's body. When a user is immersed in a virtual environment, he can be systematically exposed to specific feared stimuli within a relevant context, and this is in accordance with the model of emotional processing that sustains the fear network that is activated by confrontation with threatening stimuli [7]. Virtual Reality is characterized by the illusion of participation in a synthetic environment than external observation of such an environment. Virtual reality exposure therapy on affective outcomes has emerged more and more in the last 10 years, as virtual reality systems have become less expensive, more available and generally more usable. A possible problem to interpret and reconcile the findings about the nature and scope of the affective changes resulting from exposure therapy with virtual reality is that several factors besides exposure to virtual reality can be associated with these changes, being factors such as demographic data such as age, sex, ethnicity, etc.

Regarding the related work, there are proposals such as Shiban et al. [8], who perform scenarios with four types of spiders (of different colors) for patients with arachnophobia, the results were successful in reducing the fear or phobia of arachnids in the short and long term of the environments. As an improved feature, the proposed work is emphasized in the test of two types of spiders that are distinguished by their size and not by their color. Another similar related work is that developed by Miloff et al. [9], Who carried out a scenario of exposure to users in a traditional scenario. From this work, it was decided to generate 4 scenarios.

In the work developed by Diemer et al. [10], they perform an analysis of phobias from a psychological perspective with the use of tests to patients. As an additional feature, it has been decided to perform the test and measure the values with the heart rate of each patient.

The research work developed is structured under the following sections: (i) Introduction, a description is made of what exists, the objective and the proposal of what is intended. (ii) The methodology applied for the technical development is exposed, this methodology is based on the creation of the virtual scenario, the selection and modeling of the phobia object (spiders) and the implementation of the scenarios in the Oculus Rift Glasses. (iii) In the third section, the evaluation of the proposed case of the study is carried out, the sessions carried out, the proposed scenarios are exposed, and the analysis of the results obtained from the experiences carried out is presented. (iv) Finally, in section four, the conclusions and recommendations obtained after carrying out the development and evaluation of the case study are presented.

2 Applied Method

2.1 Virtual Scenarios

For the present case study, the virtual scenario has been developed with Blender open source software, through the use of textures with a semi-realistic effect, providing a

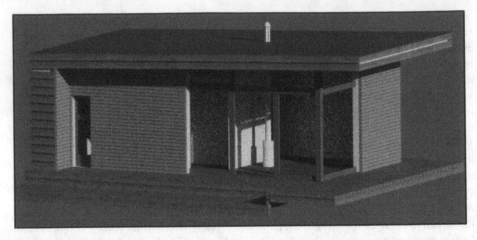

Fig. 1. Creation of the virtual image with textures and shadows as a contribution to immersion.

feeling much closer to reality. In Fig. 1 the graphic has textures in the model, which with the contrast of light offered by the platform provides a sense of natural reality.

2.2   Creation of the 3D Spider Model

For the modeling of the 3D spider, the ZBrush software was used, for which two specific species of spiders most feared and known in the world were considered, according to Clark [8] and Davey [9] respectively: the American black widow (Latrodectus mactans) (see Fig. 2). and the tarantula (Lycosa Tarantula) (see Fig. 3).

Through the use of images and videos corresponding to the structure of the body of these arachnids, they were modeled. For the rendering part, the Autodesk Maya

Fig. 2. Realistic photo image of the American black widow (Latrodectus Mactans)

Fig. 3. Realistic photo image of Tarantula (Lycosa Tarantula)

software was used, which allowed to generate patterns of movement and textures that imply the semi-realistic representation.

2.3   Implementation

The implementation was made with the Unity tool, with which the 3D model was structured, the style and functionality of the created scenarios. Thus, the Unity environment took advantage of its range of tools, including the Unity DayDream instrument that allows creating virtual reality for devices that support this technology, in the case of this case study, the device to use are the Oculus Rift glasses.

The scenarios were created with a route that each spider will follow, since the naturalness of the spider's approach to the test subject and the subsequent reaction it will have with this reagent (the spider) depend on it.

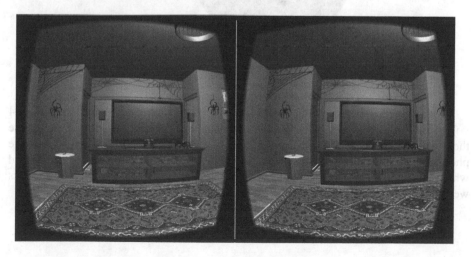

Fig. 4. Virtual Reality Scenario

Another aspect that has been taken into account in the creation of three dimensional scenarios is the inclusion of sound, this will provide a state of tranquility, but as you advance in the experience, this will change to improve immersion in the virtual environment.

In the development of the virtual environment (see Fig. 4), semi-realism has been a brand in the design of virtual reality. For the development of the application, it is one of the central axes. The application of light and shadow within the Unity and Blender platform offers that feeling of reality and immersion for the user.

3 Evaluation and Results

To evaluate the application developed for Oculus Rift glasses, initially 14 volunteers participated. The research study used for the present pre-experimental type work [10] that contains the following characteristics: (i) case study design (ii) selection of a pretest/posttest design group and (iii) static group style cut study (crossover).

For the correct obtaining of data of the present study case, a previous survey was carried out to obtain qualitative information of the type of reaction that the person may have within the proposed system.

The questions of the surveys are the following

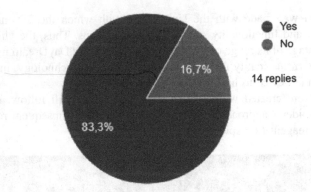

Fig. 5. Do you have any kind of fear or phobia, specifically spiders?

Regarding the first question (see Fig. 5), it was determined that among the 14 volunteers, only 10 will be those who will participate with the application of alternative therapy with virtual reality, because of the 14 volunteers, only 10 seemed to have phobias with spiders, after a test with a phobia specialist. These people were asked which of the two spider models felt the greatest fear, to which the following results were obtained (see Fig. 6):

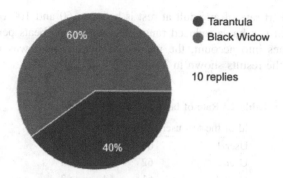

Fig. 6. What kind of arachnids are the ones that scare you the most?

Once the models that frighten the 10 people are established, a controlled environment was established in which users would be willing to be evaluated (see Table 1):

Table 1. Summary of the virtual reality therapy preference data for each tested user

Therapy	Black widow	Tarantula
Therapy of photos and videos	1	2
Static arachnids in the virtual environment	1	1
Arachnids moving in distant environment	1	3
Arachnids moving in a close environment	1	0

In Table 1, it is determined that among the 10 volunteers that are part of the tests, there are 3 people who will only be subjected to the tests through the sample of images and videos, of which there are two people who prefer to observe the tarantula, while one prefers to observe the black widow spider. There are two people who have preferred to observe the spiders using the static model, each one decided by the models of each of the two types of spiders. In the case of the model about the distant movement of the spiders, there are 3 people who have selected the model of the tarantula, while only one person has decided on the black widow spider. Finally, for the close movement model, a person has been decided by the type of black widow spider

In the case of the participants, the tests were carried out in the environment of their preference, taking into account the different tolerance specifications that can be accepted. The heart rate of the test subject was checked to confirm his level of stress through heart beats when evaluated in a virtual environment where the arachnid can be presented at any time.

The measurement of the heart rate of each person was done through a software called Samsung Health, for this, previously a heart rhythm test was performed with a volunteer nurse who has the necessary instruments and the results thrown between the nurse and the application were accurate, in addition the use of the application allows the ease of taking samples at any place and time. The heart rate of people was measured in three fundamental stages of the tests: before, during and after.

The normal heart rate of an adult at rest is between 60 and 100 beats per minute (ppm). A person at rest has a reduced range between 60–76 beats per minute (ppm). Taking these values into account, the respective measurement was made. The data collected yielded the results shown in Table 2:

Table 2. Rate of beats per minute of the test user

Id of the test user	Before	During	After
User 1	61	65	63
User 2	62	73	64
User 3	61	64	62
User 4	61	66	62
User 5	63	65	61
User 6	60	69	63
User 7	62	67	64
User 8	62	66	63
User 9	60	65	62
User 10	61	64	62

After evaluating each scenario model, the highest difference indices in relation to the number of palpitations per minute of the heart, the following scenarios were obtained as relevant for each test user (see Table 3):

Table 3. Environments exposed to each user

Id of the test user	Type of environment model
User 1	Therapy of photos and videos
User 2	Arachnids moving in a close environment
User 3	Therapy of photos and videos
User 4	Arachnids moving in a close environment
User 5	Arachnids moving in a close environment
User 6	Arachnids moving in distant environment
User 7	Arachnids moving in distant environment
User 8	Arachnids moving in a close environment
User 9	Arachnids moving in a close environment
User 10	Therapy of photos and videos

In relation to the models of scenarios and the number of heart beats per minute, it can be observed that the closer the user is to the object to which he has phobia, the subject of the test will begin to alter and increase the heartbeat. In this way, it can be seen that such an increase in the beats per minute of the subjects is an indicator that the person really felt immersed within this system, since the measurement of the heart beats per minute of the person in the process. The evaluation indicates that her stress level increased an average of 9.4% to what the user presented at the time of "before" the heartbeat.

Considering tables two and three, three scenarios were carried out:

- Scenario 1: Three test users performed the model of photo and video therapy.
- Scenario 2: Five test users performed the model of arachnid therapy with close movements.
- Scenario 3: Two Five test users performed the model of arachnid therapy with distant movements.

To obtain results of the therapy, 4 sessions lasting 30 min each were carried out, in which the following results were obtained for each scenario (see Tables 4, 5 and 6):

Table 4. Results after the fourth session of scenario 1.

Id of the test user	Before	During	After
User 1	62	63	61
User 3	60	62	61
User 10	60	61	59

Table 5. Results after the fourth session of scenario 2.

Id of the test user	Before	During	After
User 2	60	63	61
User 4	61	64	62
User 5	63	82	69
User 8	60	63	59
User 9	60	63	61

Table 6. Results after the fourth session of scenario 3.

Id of the test user	Before	During	After
User 6	60	63	60
User 7	62	63	61

If a comparison of the palpitations per minute of the heart of the user of the test is made, in the first session each user has an average difference of 6,8 beats between "before and during" and an average of 4,6 beats between "during and after" of exposure to virtual reality phobia therapy. While, after executing the fourth session, results are obtained of 2,2 beats between "before and during" and an average of 2,3 beats between the "during and after" exposure to phobia therapy with virtual reality.

Table 7. Average results of the first evaluation session of each test user

Id of the test user	Before	Difference Before-During	During	Difference During-After	After
User 1	61	4	65	2	63
User 2	62	11	73	9	64
User 3	61	3	64	2	62
User 4	61	5	66	4	62
User 5	63	19	82	13	69
User 6	60	9	69	6	63
User 7	62	5	67	3	64
User 8	62	4	66	3	63
User 9	60	5	65	2	63
User 10	61	3	64	2	62
	Average Before-During	6,8	Average During-After	4,6	

Table 8. Average results of the fourth evaluation session of each test user

Id of the test user	Before	Difference Before-During	During	Difference During-After	After
User 1	62	1	63	2	61
User 2	60	3	63	2	61
User 3	60	2	62	1	61
User 4	61	3	64	2	62
User 5	63	2	65	4	61
User 6	60	3	63	3	60
User 7	62	1	63	2	61
User 8	60	3	63	4	59
User 9	60	3	63	1	62
User 10	60	1	61	2	59
	Average Before-During	2,2	Average During-After	2,3	

As can be seen in Tables 7 and 8 respectively, the difference in the average palpitations per minute of the heart of the users in the "before-during" phase there is a difference of 4.6 less pulsations after the execution of the therapy using virtual reality environments. While in the phase "during - after" there is an average difference of 2.3 pulsations per minute. Indicating that the user's exposure to virtual reality therapy scenarios can be used as an alternative therapy to arachnophobia.

4 Conclusions

For the process of creation of the scenarios, it is necessary to take into account the environment of the real scenarios that it is intended to generate, the 3D perspectives and the high-level 3D computer graphics, in which special attention should be paid to the textures and its details in 3D modeling, as well as its relationship with the lighting of the environment, all this so that the user's immersion in a virtual world is total.

In the case of the use of virtual reality exposure therapies, it has shown that users have a very intense sense of immersion, especially when using semi-realistic techniques in the representation of the virtual world.

It is important to emphasize that being a pre-experiment of the proposal, it is necessary for future work to take a sample with a representative number of users, in order to affirm that this research work is used as an alternative method for arachnophobia.

From the results shown in the previous section, it can be determined that virtual reality can be used as an alternative means to cure phobias, in this particular case for arachnophobia. For which you can use techniques such as realistic photo rendering, to improve the user experience and to make more inclusive the patient with the environment in which the object of phobia is controlled. In addition, there must be a record of the person to whom this type of treatment is proposed. This antecedent will belong to the level that the patient can tolerate for the exposure of some type of representation to the phobia that is being treated within this type of systems. In this way, it correctly manages the patient's introduction into the system and there is no risk of worsening this type of fear.

It should be noted that, with the proper guidance of an expert, this technique can be combined with those that are used more frequently (OST: One Session Treatment), in order to have a complete improvement in the user with respect to their respective phobia, given that by using a virtual reality system, the patient would be introduced in a small contact with the object that produces the phobia, so when it is the right time to have direct contact with that object, the patient can react from a good way.

References

1. Fendt, M., Fanselow, M.: The neuroanatomical and neurochemical basis of conditioned fear. Neurosci. Biobehav. Rev. 23(5), 743–760 (1999)
2. Heim, C., Nemeroff, C.: The impact of early adverse experiences on brain systems involved in the pathophysiology of anxiety and affective disorders. Biol. Psychiatry 46(11), 1509–1522 (1999)
3. Davidson, R., Jackson, D., Kalin, N.: Emotion, plasticity, context, and regulation: perspectives from affective neuroscience. Psychol. Bull. 126(6), 890–909 (2000)
4. Rothbaum, B., Schwartz, A.: Exposure therapy for posttraumatic stress disorder. Am. J. Psychother. 56(1), 59–75 (2002)
5. Lange, A., Rietdijk, D., Hudcovicova, M., Van de Ven, J., Schrieken, B., Emmelkamp, P.: Interapy: a controlled randomized trial of the standardized treatment of posttraumatic stress through the internet. J. Consult. Clin. Psychol. 71(5), 901–909 (2003)

6. Schwartz, J.: Neuroanatomical aspects of cognitive-behavioural therapy response in obsessive-compulsive disorder. An evolving perspective on brain and behaviour. Br. J. Psychiatry Suppl. **35**, 38–44 (1998)

7. Foa, E., Kozak, M.: Emotional processing of fear: exposure to corrective information. Psychol. Bull. **99**(1), 20–35 (1986)

8. Clark, R.: The Safety and efficacy of antivenin Latrodectus mactans. J. Toxicol. Clin. Toxicol. **39**(2), 125–127 (2001)

9. Davey, G.: The disgusting spider: the role of disease and illness in the perpetuation of fear of spiders. Soc. Anim. **2**(1), 17–25 (1994)

10. Kirk, R.E.: Experimental design. In: The Blackwell Encyclopedia of Sociology. American Cancer Society (2015)

IT Architectures

A Security Based Reference Architecture for Cyber-Physical Systems

Shafiq ur Rehman$^{(\boxtimes)}$, Andrea Iannella, and Volker Gruhn

Institute of Software Technology,
University of Duisburg-Essen, 45127 Essen, Germany
shafiq.rehman@paluno.uni-due.de

Abstract. Today we live in a world full of digital content. Digitalization is growing and the use of cyber-physical systems too. A cyber-physical systems (CPS) is a system that integrates both physical and virtual capabilities which communicates via a network. Attributes of CPSs includes real-time, fault-tolerance, security, safety, scalability, reliability, distributed, adaptability and heterogeneity. Hence, security for CPS is very crucial due to the nature of CPS and the interaction with the physical world. Therefore, the use of effective security mechanisms is crucial. Moreover, we have to ensure that we build these systems in a way that they meet the CPS specific requirements and to adapt the security mechanism accordingly, since the security threats of CPSs differ from classical software. This paper analyzes the security threats of cyber-physical systems, presents countermeasure to these threats and propose a security based reference architecture for cyber-physical systems. Furthermore, the architecture is applied on a case study of smart home to validate the proposed architecture. The proposed security based reference architecture is a good start to focus on this important aspect of security for CPS and great contribution to the research community.

Keywords: Security · Threats · Security requirements · Architecture
Cyber-physical systems (CPS)

1 Introduction

A cyber-physical system (CPS) is a system that integrates both virtual and physical capabilities according to the system environment [1]. A CPS therefore consists of a physical entity also referred to as physical space or physical component and of a cyber-entity also referred to as cyber space or cyber component. Each physical component has cyber capabilities and they can be controlled by the system [2]. The cyber space is basically a simulation-model of the physical space. This means that the cyber entity can virtually replicate the exact behavior of the physical machine. In a CPS the virtual world of information integrates seamlessly with the real world. These systems can interact with humans and the physical environment through the use of sensors, actuators or smart devices. According to [4, 5, 14] a CPS usually composed of three layers that includes application layer, networking layer and physical layer.

© Springer Nature Switzerland AG 2018
H. Florez et al. (Eds.): ICAI 2018, CCIS 942, pp. 157–169, 2018.
https://doi.org/10.1007/978-3-030-01535-0_12

The environments of cyber-physical systems become more and more complex and therefore their security issues grow in complexity. Since human can interact with the physical space from the cyber space, this physical space can be taken over or corrupted by evil entities. For instance, an attacker who is able to access critical data of a medical CPS or even perform an operation which can lead to severe damage to the health of patient. Therefore, we have to make sure that a CPS is dependable, safe, secure, and efficient and performs in real-time environment [2]. Furthermore, we also have to ensure that architectures or frameworks for CPS support these requirements. In the CPS environment there are several security challenges that need to be taken into account. One of these security issues is the authentication of users and sensors that are used in that CPS environment. For this purpose, we use logins, e.g. passwords, for websites to authenticate a user in the internet. Internet browsers use protocols like Transport Layer Security (TLS) to authenticate a website.

Adopted secure technologies that are used in the distributed environment, not necessarily work well in a CPS environment too. Therefore, security of the CPS environment should be taken into account regarding the authentication of a sensor device which leads to new challenge. Little or even no attention has been given to sensor, hardware, network, and third party elements of cyber-physical systems [23]. The physical layer consists of sensors and actuators that sense and change the physical world. This physical layer is also prone to attacks. There are multiple malicious software tools known that perform attacks on CPSs like Stuxnet and CarShark [6]. Currently there are very few reference architectures for cyber-physical systems [24–26]. Most of them do not go much into detail and just provide an abstract overview of what countermeasures are needed to compensate security challenges. For developers of CPS, it is helpful to have a reference architecture in order to make the secure system. Our proposed security based reference architecture provides a template solution and support to analyze the security threats for CPS.

2 Security Threats in Cyber-Physical Systems

CPSs consist of a physical and a cyber-component. These different subsystems are often referred to as perception layer or physical layer for the physical component, network layer or transportation layer for the network between the perception layer and the system, and application layer for the logical system [9, 10]. These terms are used to describe the respective components in this paper. Each of these layers has a specific purpose. The perception layer gathers all information from the physical world through sensors and performs actions in the physical world through actuators. The transportation layer provides a data transmission infrastructure between the perception layer and the application layer. The main task of application layers' is to manage data that is collected by the sensors and provides services like servers, cloud computing, databases, human interfaces or mobile devices [2, 3, 10]. Because of the different purposes of the layers and the technologies they are using each of these layers have specific security threats that need to be taken into account when developing a secure architecture.

In order to develop a proper secure architecture, the security threats of CPS should be clarified. Security plays an important role in the CPS environment that's why it is important to understand the specific security issues for the CPS environment. Even though a lot of the security issues that exists in CPS also exist in other well-known systems like embedded systems. However, the security issues in CPS are more complex and different from traditional software and cannot exactly be solved as others systems. There are mainly four security goals: integrity, availability, confidentiality and authenticity [5–8]. These security goals do not only specifically apply to CPSs but to software systems in general.

A. Integrity is the opposite of corruption. Integrity refers to data being consistent from when it was recorded exactly as intended upon retrieval. This means a system should ensure that data cannot unintendedly be altered or deleted as a result of storage, processing, malicious intents, unexpected hardware failures or human errors [5].
B. Availability means that the system and its services are available when needed [6].
C. Confidentiality means that the system is capable to prevent not authorized entities to disclose information [7]. Confidentiality is usually achieved by encryption techniques.
D. Authenticity means that data, transactions and communications are authentic. For example, a medical system retrieves data from a blood pressure sensor the system must ensure that this sensor node is actually the one it claims to be and not a sensor added by an attacker which could result in fake data [8].

3 Countermeasures to Security Threats

Security threats of cyber-physical system can either be caused by an attack that origins from inside the system or from an attack that origins from outside the system. Attacks that are typically performed from outside the system are Denial-of-Service/Distributed Denial-of-Service/Distributed Denial-of-Service (DoS/DDoS), traffic analysis, data tampering, data intercept man-in-the-middle, unauthorized access etc. Most attacks from outside the system can be prevented by secure communications using encryption and authentication [8]. Most important threats and their countermeasures of CPS are listed in Table 1.

Table 1. Threats and countermeasures

Perception layer threats	Countermeasures
Eavesdropping	Encryption [3, 4, 12, 13]
Node compromising	Monitoring of nodes [12], intrusion detection [2]
Data tampering	Data authentication [12]
DoS	Detection and prevention [2], authorization [14], payment for network resources [15], strong authentication and identification of traffic [15]

(continued)

Table 1. (*continued*)

Perception layer threats	Countermeasures
Jamming	Frequency hopping [12]
Replay attack	Message authentication code (MAC) [3, 12], authentication [13]
Exhaustion attacks	Rate limitation (time slots for transmission) [12, 16]
Network Layer Threats	**Countermeasures**
DDoS	Detection and prevention [2]
Man-in-the-Middle Attack	Authentication [13, 17]
Routing attack	Message authentication code (MAC) [12, 16], timestamps [16]
Sinkhole attack	Authentication [12], secure routing protocol [11, 12]
Black Hole Attack	Authentication [12], key management [4]
Selective forwarding	Authentication [12], key management [4]
HELLO flooding	Authentication [8, 12], key management [4], prevent based on signal strength [18]
Sybil attack	Authentication [12], key management [4, 8, 12, 19]
Wormhole attack	Authentication [12], key management [4], packet leashes [19]
Traffic analysis	Randomize communications [12], mask channel by sending dummy traffic
Application Layer Threats	**Countermeasures**
Leakage of privacy data	Encryption [12]
Malicious code	Antivirus Software [4], good maintaining and configuration of operating systems and applications [4]
Unauthorized access	Authentication [20, 21], Access Control [11], key management [17, 21]
SQL injection	SQL Detection and prevention techniques [20, 22]

4   Proposed Security Based Reference Architecture

The proposed security architecture covers all three layers of CPSs namely application layer, network layer and perception layer. The perception layer includes security measures to perception nodes. This includes data encryption and integrity, node authentication and secure routing for the perception layer. For the network layer security measures include access network security, data encryption and integrity. Security measures for the application layer include service security, access control and privacy (Fig. 1).

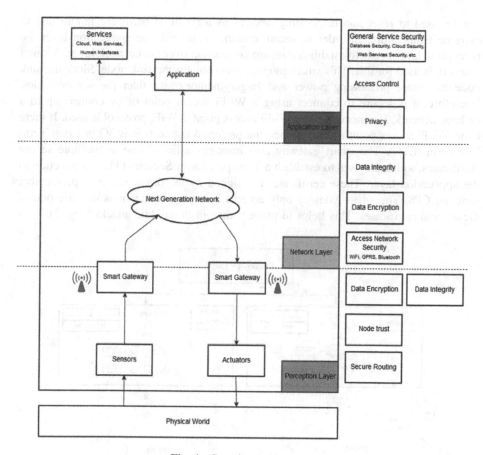

Fig. 1. Security architecture

4.1 Perception Layer

There are several techniques to handle perception layer. It can be used here like key pre-distribution schemes or Secure Personal Identification Number (SPINS). Message Authentication Codes (MAC) and timestamps are also needed in order to provide data integrity. Key pre-distribution makes sure that nodes get keys prior to the deployment. Which key pre-distribution algorithm to use depends on the security requirements and on the size of the sensor network. For small networks it is suitable to distribute (n − 1) keys for every node such that every node holds a key to every other node in the network. If the security requirements are not high, a network key for all nodes can also be used. If a compromised node is detected, the according key in the key rings of nodes should be discarded. Data encryption is provided by using the shared keys. Nodes can either use these keys for symmetric encryption or generate new keys using the already available keys to securely exchange them. Since encryption does not prevent traffic analysis there is also the need of either masking channels by sending dummy traffic or randomize communications between nodes [12]. According to [11] watchdog timers can be used to reset non responding devices as a result of hardware failure due to extreme temperature. In order to secure communicate with the application layer the perception layer needs to establish a secure connection over the network layer. A smart gateway is used for this. This smart gateway incorporates the sink node. Since the sink node has more processing power and larger memory size than the sensor nodes. Therefore, it is secure to connect using a Wi-Fi access point or by connecting to a cellular network. If connecting to a Wi-Fi access point, a WiFi protocol is used. If there is no Wi-Fi access point available, then the preferred connection is 3G or Long Term Evolution (LTE). The smart gateway also manages a list of one or multiple secure certificates, which are used to establish a Transport Layer Security (TLS) connection to the application layer. These certificates are signed by the organization or person that runs the CPS. The smart gateway only accepts incoming connections that use one of these valid certificates. This helps to prevent man-in-the-middle attacks (Fig. 2).

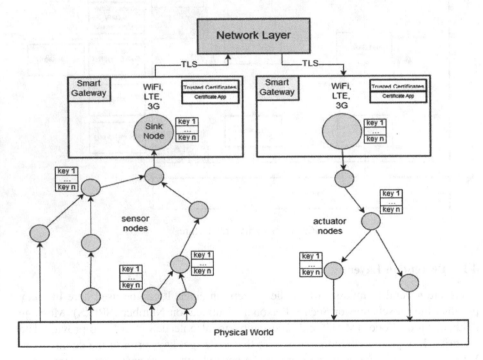

Fig. 2. Perception layer of the proposed architecture

4.2   Network Layer

Security in the network layer is done by using a secure TLS 1.2 connection between the perception layer and the application layer. The application and the smart gateways in the perception layer uses one or more trusted certificates which ensure that they are communicate with either the application or with one of the smart gateways. TLS also ensures data security. A cipher suite that can be used for this TLS connection is TLS_ECDHE_RSA_WITH_AES_128_GCM_SHA256.

4.3   Application Layer

The application layer also includes external services like data centers, clouds for additional storage or processing. The application uses a database to store user information for authentication and authorization. A user can interact with the application using a login via human interfaces like web applications, or mobile applications. This connection should use HTTPS and in addition TLS as a security measure. This helps to prevent data leakage, man-in-the-middle attacks and other security threats related to data authenticity, integrity and confidentiality. The login consists usually username and password that is saved into the database in order to verify the identity of the user. To further improve security, salt and hash is used to store the user passwords. Salt helps to prevent rainbow table attacks and hashing usually prevents an attacker that has read only rights on the database. To verify a user, the following steps could be assumed.

1. Receive username and password from user client.
2. Find username in database.
3. Get the salt from database and compute password hash using salt and received password.
4. Compare this result with the hash stored in the database.
5. If the hashes match, the user is granted to access.

If the user has a legitimate identity, then user is able to access data or services. In order to communicate with the perception layer over the internet, the application manages a list of one or multiple certificates. Certificates help to prevent man-in-the-middle attacks. It builds a secure TLS connection to the smart gateways of the perception layer. To improve security, it is important to use up-to-date operating systems, virus detection software, a firewall and a well maintained system configuration (Fig. 3).

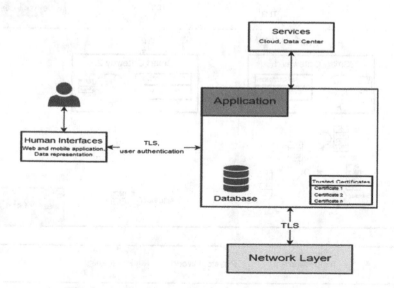

Fig. 3. Application layer of the proposed architecture

5 Case Study

Smart home plays a vital part in daily life routine to regulate home appliances. From any distance, users can control home devices from laptops, iPhone, iPod or other smart phone. Sensors and actuators are significant parts for smart home technology. Security threats are major issue while adopting the home automation system in cyber-physical as attackers don't need to travel to targeted homes, they can approach virtually to attack smart homes easily [27]. This case study for a cyber-physical system represents a smart home environment as shown in Fig. 4. A sensor network is used to monitor the temperature in a room. The user can communicate with the application using a PC or a smartphone. An actuator can manipulate the heating in that room.

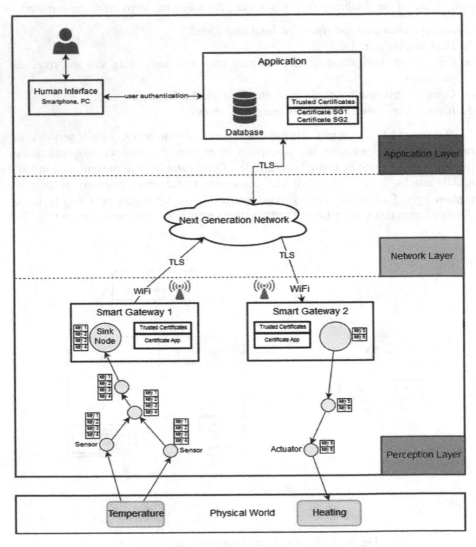

Fig. 4. Secure smart home

5.1   Securing the Smart Home Using the Reference Architecture

During the setup phase of the system the user has to create an account or user so that the system knows that he is an authorized person. This is done using a username and a password. Both username and password are stored in a database of the system. The password must fit specific security requirements. It must be at least 8 characters long and must contain at least one letter and a number. The password is further stored using salt and hash. Therefore, the salt must also be stored in the database. Further a key pre-distribution scheme is used in the setup phase in order to distribute the keys to the sensor nodes and actuators. For this case study link keys are pre-distributed between the nodes because the system does only consist of a small sensor network. Another alternative is to simply use a network key since a smart home environment is not unattended and therefore it is unlikely that sensor nodes are being captured physically. This will prevent of adding fake nodes to the system since the nodes already share a secret with each other. Certificates are also used to prevent man-in-the-middle attacks. One certificate is used for each smart gateway and one for the application.

After this setup phase the user is able to communicate with the system using a PC or smart device over a secure TLS connection. The user can access the system using the credentials of an authorized user. Since the user knows his credentials he is able to login legitimately with his account and has access to different application features. This access control prevents an outside attacker to log into the system illegitimately. The TLS connection also prevents the attacker from man-in-the-middle attacks. The user configures the system such that the smart home system maintains a temperature of 20 °C in the living room. The sensor nodes measure the temperature in the living room and send the collected data to the smart gateway 1 by encrypting the messages using the pre-distributed keys. The sensor nodes also add a MAC to the message to guarantee data integrity. The encryption additionally prevents eavesdropping. The smart gateway 1 builds a secure connection to a WiFi access point using WPA2 in order to get access to the network layer. It then communicates with the application using a secure TLS connection and sends the received data to the application. The temperature is above the configured value and the system decides to turn down the heating. This is done using a secure TLS connection to the Smart Gateway 2. The smart gateway 2 then communicates with the actuator using the encryption keys and MAC. The actuator turns the heating down.

5.2   Threats

Using reference architecture, we have successfully identified the very important threats and these threats helps to secure the smart home. However, they are different types of threats that affect this system if there are no security measures but here we explained the most important ones. Data could be leaked because of wireless transmission between sensor nodes and actuator nodes. Another threat is that an attacker is able to insert a fake node into the network. With this node the attacker would be able to start different type of attacks from inside the network like sinkhole attacks, data tampering, selective forwarding and black hole attacks. The attacker would also be able to log into the system if there is no user authentication and then manipulate it. Because of the wireless connection an attacker would also be able to start man-in-the-middle attacks, data analysis, jamming, and eavesdropping in network communication.

5.3 Security Requirements

Requirements are needs and conditions to fulfill for a project or an architecture. Requirements are helpful because they represent a list of features, conditions and restrictions of a system and once written down it is easier for developers to implement all functionalities of the system. While considering the conditions and restrictions since they are listed in a structured manner. When all requirements are implemented, the developers know that they do not forget to implement any functionality. Therefore, this list can also be used to check if all relevant security requirements are implemented. Using these security requirements, it is then possible to distinguish which counter-measures are applicable for the proposed security architecture.

The following list contains the relevant security requirements for smart home system. Every requirement in this list starts with R (Requirement) followed by a number which is incremented for every requirement in the same hierarchy.

R-1: The system shall ensure to be available all the time.

    R-1.1: Services that the system provides shall always be available, despite of any malfunctioning.

        R-1.1.1: The system shall avoid any single points of failure at smart home devices.

        R-1.1.2: The system shall adjust itself to node failures of home devices.

R-2: Perception Layer of Smart Home

    R-2.1: Security technologies in perception layer shall be lightweight.

        R-2.1.1: Technologies shall be able to run on hardware with limited computing power.

        R-2.1.2: Technologies shall be able to run on hardware with limited memory.

        R-2.1.3: Technologies shall have low power consumption.

    R-2.2: Perception Nodes

        R-2.2.1: Nodes shall ensure authenticity.

            R-2.2.1.1: Nodes communicating with each other shall ensure to communicate with a legitimate node.

            R-2.2.1.2: Nodes shall be able to detect integrity of messages.

                R-2.2.1.2.1: Nodes shall discard altered messages.

                R-2.2.1.2.2: Messages from unauthorized nodes shall be rejected.

    R-2.3: Perception Network of Smart Home

        R-2.3.1: The perception network shall ensure secure routing.

R-2.3.2: Data transmitted between nodes shall not be able to leak.

R-2.3.3: Information send between nodes shall not be able to disclose to unauthorized parties.

R-3: Network Layer of Smart Home

R-3.1: The system shall ensure message integrity

R-3.1.1: Data send through the network shall be persistent

R-3.1.2: The system shall be able to detect tampered messages.

R-3.2: The system shall be able to establish secure connections between perception layer and application layer

R-3.2.1: Information send through the network shall not be able to disclose to unauthorized parties.

R-3.2.2: Smart Gateway shall be able to build up wireless connections

R-3.2.2.1: The sink nodes shall support WiFi, 3G, LTE

R-4: Application Layer of Smart Home

R-4.1: Information stored in the system shall not be able to disclose to unauthorized parties.

R-4.2: The system shall protect user's privacy.

R-4.2.1: The system shall keep sensitive information concealed to everyone.

R-4.2.2: The system shall store user passwords in a secure manner.

R-4.2.2.1: The system shall only access, use or send sensitive information through the network if it is necessary for the systems purposes.

R-4.3: The system shall ensure that the entities are the one they claim to be.

R-4.4: The system shall ensure that only authorized entities are able to access services.

6 Conclusion

Cyber-physical systems have additional security requirements in comparison to traditional systems. This results due to the inclusion of sensor networks and actuators which are also referred to as the perception layer. The perception layer consists of low cost devices that have limited computation power and small storage. They are deployed in unattended environments. Due to these circumstances security differs from traditional systems. Attacker can get easy access to these devices that make them prone to be compromised and due to the fact that they have limited resources and energy they cannot run resource intense security measures. Still there is a lack of reference architectures that focus on security. Therefore, this paper proposes a secure reference architecture for cyber-physical systems by analyzing the security threats and providing countermeasure to them. The proposed architecture uses lightweight key management algorithms to protect the authentication of sensor networks. Moreover, it uses symmetric key encryption, MAC and timestamps to protect communication between the nodes. In order to communicate with the application layer, a secure TLS 1.2 connection is used from the smart gateway to the application. To prevent man-in-the-middle attacks, certificates are used. The application layer supports user authentication and access control using a database and user logins. All communication is done using secure TLS connections. This prevents threats like eavesdropping, man-in-the-middle and unauthorized access to the system. Finally, the proposed architecture is applied to a case study to verify it. In conclusion it can be said that there are still no effective security schemes that protect the perception layer from severe large scale attacks. Probability based key pre-distribution schemes can also only guarantee that an attacker is not able to compromise a system by given probability.

Acknowledgment. This work has been supported by the European Community through project CPS.HUB NRW, EFRE Nr. 0-4000-17.

References

1. Rehman, S., Gruhn, V.: Security requirements engineering (SRE) framework for cyber-physical systems (CPS): SRE for CPS. In: New Trends in Intelligent Software Methodologies, Tools and Techniques: Proceedings of the 16th International Conference SoMeT_17, vol. 297, p. 153. IOS Press (2017)
2. Dong, P., Han, Y., Guo, X., Xie, F.: A systematic review of studies on cyber physical system security. Int. J. Secur. Appl. **9**(1), 155–164 (2015)
3. Jing, Q., Vasilakos, A.V., Wan, J., Lu, J., Qui, D.: Security of the internet of things: perspectives and challenges. Wirel. Netw. **20**, 2481 (2014). Springer
4. Gao, Y.: Analysis of security threats and vulnerability for cyber-physical systems. IEEE (2013)
5. Rehman, S., Gruhn, V.: An effective security requirements engineering framework for cyber-physical systems (2018). Int. J. Inf. Commun. Technol. Special issue Cyber-Physical Systems: Data Processing and Communication Architectures **6**(3) (ISSN: 2227-7080; ESCI-WoS index)
6. Wang, E.K., Ye, Y., Xu, X., Yiu, S.M., Hui, L.C.K., Chow, K.P.: Security issues and challenges for cyber physical system. IEEE (2010)
7. Fischer, K., Geßner, J.: Security architecture elements for IoT enabled automation networks. IEEE (2012)
8. Karlof, C., Wagner, D.: Secure routing in wireless sensor networks: attacks and countermeasures. Elsevier (2003)
9. Zhao, K., Ge, L.: A Survey on the Internet of Things Security. IEEE (2014). https://doi.org/10.1109/CIS.2013.145
10. Callaway, E.H.: Wireless Sensor Networks Architectures and Protocols. Auerbach Publications, New York (2003)
11. Chen, D., Chang, G., Jin, L., Ren, X., Li, J., Li, F.: A novel secure architecture for the Internet of Things. IEEE (2011)
12. Di Pietro, R., Guarino, S., Verde, N.V., Domingo-Ferrer, J.: Security in wireless ad-hoc networks – a survey. Comput. Commun. **51**, 1–20 (2014)

13. Kim, K.-W., Hian, Y.-H., Min, S.-G.: An authentication and key management mechanism for resource constrained devices in IEEE 802.11-based IoT Access Networks. https://doi.org/10.3390/s17102170

14. Mendez, D., Papapanagiotou, I., Yang, B.: Internet of Things: survey on security and privacy (2017). https://arxiv.org/pdf/1707.01879.pdf. Accessed 21 Dec 2017

15. Pathan, A.-S.K., Lee, H.-.W., Hong, C.S.: Security in wireless sensor networks: issues and challenges. IEEE (2006)

16. Wang, Y., Attebury, G., Ramamurthy, B.: A survey of security issues in wireless sensor networks. IEEE (2006)

17. IEEE: IEEE Standard for Low-Rate Wireless Networks (2015)

18. Singh, V., Jain, S., Singhai, J.: Hello flood attack and its countermeasures in wireless sensor networks. Int. J. Comput. Sci. 7(3), 23 (2010)

19. Hu, Y.-C., Perrig, A., Johnson, D.B.: Packet leashes: a defense against wormhole attacks in wireless networks. IEEE (2003)

20. Qian, J., Xu, H., Li, P.: A novel secure architecture for the Internet of Things. IEEE (2016)

21. Jia, X., Feng, Q., Ma, C.: An efficient anti-collision protocol for RFID tag identification. IEEE (2010)

22. Halfond, W.G.J., Viegas, J., Orso, A.: A classification of SQL injection attacks and countermeasures. IEEE (2006)

23. Rehman, S., Gruhn, V.: An effective security requirements engineering framework for cyber-physical systems. Int. J. Inf. Commun. Technol. 6(3) (2018). Special issue Cyber-Physical Systems: Data Processing and Communication Architectures (ISSN: 2227-7080; ESCI-WoS index)

24. Tan, Y., Goddard, S., Perez, L.C.: A prototype architecture for cyber-physical systems. ACM Sigbed Rev. 5(1), 26 (2008)

25. Kellerman, C.: Reference architecture for cyber-physical systems (2016). https://www.nist.gov/programs-projects/reference-architecture-cyber-physical-systems

26. Weyrich, M., Ebert, C.: Reference architectures for the internet of things. IEEE Softw. 33(1), 112–116 (2016)

27. Rehman, S., Gruhn, V.: An approach to secure smart homes in Cyber-physical systems/Internet-of-things. In: The Fifth IEEE International Conference on Software Defined Systems (SDS-2018) (2018)

An Effective Wireless Media Access Controls Architecture for Content Delivery Networks

Ayegba Alfa Abraham[1], Abubakar Adinoyi Sadiku[1],
Sanjay Misra[2(✉)], Adewole Adewumi[2], Ravin Ahuja[3],
Robertas Damasevicius[4], and Rytis Maskeliunas[4]

[1] Kogi State College of Education, Ankpa, Nigeria
abrahamsalfa@gmail.com
[2] Covenant University, Otta, Nigeria
{sanjay.misra,wole.adewumi}@covenantuniversity.edu.ng
[3] University of Delhi, Delhi, India
ravinahujadce@gmail.com
[4] Kaunas University of Technology, Kaunas, Lithuania
{robertas.damasevicius,rytis.maskeliunas}@ktu.lt

Abstract. A number of solutions were advanced for problems of delays and overcrowdings of networks such as caches and proxies. The purpose of caches and proxies was to bring information closer to the users by serving user requests as if there were originating servers. Later, other challenges evolved as a consequence of caches and proxies for the Internet content distribution and services. Web caches are situated between Web servers (or originating servers) and clients in order to fulfils HTTP propagated requests instead of the servers. The distinct features of Web caches is storage of copies of objected requested lately which are used quickly fulfils the requests without the need to transfer object from the distant original server. Though, caches can be classified into browser cache, client-side cache and server-side cache. Nowadays, several CDNs (such as Akamai and DigitalIsland) are faced with imminent storage congestion and management. This paper offered best media access controls architecture for the CDNs for improved quality of service, integrity and content sharing.

Keywords: ICD · Networks · MAC · CDN · Web · Internet
Caching · Protocol

1 Introduction

Internets are built by linking local networks by means of special computer software called gateway [1]. Several communications channels (such as telephone lines, optical fibres, radio and satellite links) establish interconnection through specialized gateways in order to facilitate information delivery and exchanges. This is achieved by the use machine unique addresses. Thereafter, Internet protocol (IP) is software that control and specifies the way machines gateways route information from the sending computer to receiving computer. Similarly, the functions of Transmission Control Protocol (TCP) are to enable the entire process of communication to be complete, and initiate

© Springer Nature Switzerland AG 2018
H. Florez et al. (Eds.): ICAI 2018, CCIS 942, pp. 170–182, 2018.
https://doi.org/10.1007/978-3-030-01535-0_13

retransmission in event of misses [1]. One of the primitive network model deployed is the basic Internet, which is a client-server based architecture. The client-server network model is made up of groups of servers containing processed information and services to be retrieved by clients upon their request [2].

The unprecedented advancements in Internet technology generated a corresponding high traffic and increase in the amount of content expected to be provided. Studies have revealed that traffic carried on Internet and amount of video propagated presently is very alarming and expected to grow in the coming years [3]. Again, the growing traffic size gave rise to consolidated content sources such as bigger Content Delivery Networks (CDNs) and Internet Service Providers (ISPs) with higher dimensions [4]. Akamai technology is one common CDN that has been deployed on wireless and wired networks which encompasses several thousands of content of contribution servers globally to serve or deliver content to the closest clients. The benefits include reduction of client latencies, server load and network traffics. But, this technology is short in the required performance due to low coverage, cost ineffectiveness, reconfiguration, deployment, installation and maintenance [5, 6].

Recently, there are quests to develop reliable networks access protocols to enhance communication and applications processes automation of CDNs such as (Akamai technology) [5, 7]. Media Access Controls (MACs) offer certain potentials for network-based content distribution services such as concurrent accesses and multi-users of shared medium of communication, effective channel utilization, lesser interferences and low collision. In particular, majority of CDNs such as Akamai rely on wired or wireless networks backbone to operate effectively. However, the present network architectures deployed support multiusers access channels and allocation of channels to the proxy cache server as against to the origin/source server [8]. In this paper, a new CDNs architecture is proposed using wireless local area network (WLAN) MACs for effective content and service delivery. The remaining portion of this paper is subdivided into Sect. 2 (literature review), Sect. 3 (methodology), Sect. 4 (presentation of results), and Sect. 5 (conclusion).

2 Literature Review

Content delivery manages the total Web server utilization through distribution of content. Web caching is one solution responsible for transmitting the requests/queries of users to the most suitable caches in any networks arrangement. The role of MAC protocol in typical wireless network is to govern the operations to benefit subscribers (users) and network at large [9]. In the recent times, scholars are focussing efforts at advancing solutions that explore the effectiveness of MAC utilities (such as IEEE 802.11 and 802.16 standards) for Internet Content Delivery services [6, 9].

2.1 Cloud Information Distribution Technologies

The level of prominence obtained by Internet in lives of people the world over is well connected to the capabilities of acquiring information regardless of location and time. These advancements in Internet have come along with several issues such as congestion of network links and delays experienced by users in retrieving information (downloads). Caches and proxies were put in networks links to minimize delays generated by networks and bring information nearer to the users; thereby serving users' requests as if there were originating servers [10].

(i) *World Wide Web* is the communication revolution initiated by Microsoft Internet Explorer and Netscape. These applications enable users access the network easily and retrieve desired information. To accomplish this, users engages services of agent (or browser) display queried information; offer several configuration and direction-finding tools. In the layout of WWW, the information is presented in the form of Web page or a group of web objects such as HTML, JPEG image, GIF image, JAVA applet, audio and video clip. The Uniform Resource Locators (URLs) of objects are referenced by the base HTML page. Web applications uses communication protocol called Hypertext Transfer Protocol (HTTP), which set the rules governing the exchange between server and users (clients) during webpage transfer [2, 10]. The HTTP is an application layer protocol depending on transport layer protocol called the Transport Control Protocol. A client running HTTP begins connection to server using server's IP address (realized from server's URL). HTTP makes use of persistent and non-persistent TCP connection between servers and clients whose intention was to minimized delays arising from three-way handshake for multiple TCP connection step [2, 10].

(ii) *Internet Caching*: This The motivation for Internet (or Web caching) came about because of the unprecedented need for the Internet services and connections. These increased the load carrying capacity of the network, server overcrowding and enormous traffic delays. Consequently, the quest to decrease the latency and traffic overcrowding of Internet led to the development of Web caches. Web caches are situated between Web servers (or originating servers) and clients in order to fulfils HTTP propagated requests instead of the servers [10]. The distinct features of Web caches includes storage facilities for copies of objected requested recently. Caches decreases time to responds to supplied requests by utilizing nearest server against originating servers. The network overloading is reduced because of the fact that every popular object is requested from the original server once throughout the lifecycle of the object. Subsequent requests for the same object are satisfied by the cache server. This method assists content providers to deliver content to users rapidly without high-speed Internet connectivity [2, 10].

(iii) *Collaborative and Hierarchical Caching:* Several web caches situated at different location in the Internet potentially to collaborate and enhance network's performance. Cache servers can be placed in a network to serve different levels such as HTTP requests sent to local and national caches. When the objects requested are not found at the local cache, the request is redirected to the Internet Service Provider (ISP) backbone at national cache to be satisfied. Otherwise, the HTTP requests are sent to the originating server when objects are not found at the national cache. The hierarchical caching architecture depicts higher number of users, requests floods and increased rate of transactions. The processes of objects/information exchanges are facilitated by HTTP and Internet Caching Protocol (ICP). The benefits include: support for discovering and retrieving of files from neighbouring caches, hierarchical proxies caches collaborate to limit traffic supplied to the Internet backbone. The inter-cache communications protocols cause serious overhead for large-scale proxies' implementation. In cache miss cases, multicasting mechanism of proxy cache is used to discover content of neighbouring caches which is expensive to actualize.

iv) *Content Distribution Networks:* Content providers (or ISPs) can adopt the technique of distributing the content to caches situated throughout the entire network. Presently, a number of content providers build their personalized caches or out-source their caching services to popular provider such as Akamai, Mirror Image and DigitalIsland [10]. Content Distribution Networks (CDNs) was a solution to the high traffic and greater business opportunities offered by Internet. CDNs architectures have various caches with large storage and bandwidth infrastructure distributed geographical locations. There is a central server and content access points that superintends the state of the network links and cache servers [2]. The distinguishing factor of the CDNs is the ability of client's requests to be redirected to proxy caches; and occasionally redirects clients to central server based on real-time information over states of caches as illustrated in Fig. 1.

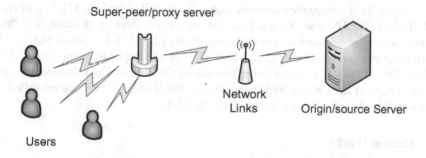

Fig. 1. Akamai CDNs architecture.

From Fig. 1, the Akamai technology based CDNs exhibits a client-server model; though, peer-to-peer network model is a currently deployed for content delivery network architecture enabling clients to act as servers.

(v) *Peer-to-Peer Networks:* The paradigm for solving the issues arising from client-server model for content distribution is the peer-to-peer network, which all content receivers (or nodes) perform the function of content providers collaborating in the content distribution [11]. Nodes have dual functions called peers, in sharp divergence from the client-server relationship. The peers independently form network connection for the purpose of contributing bandwidth and computing resources for the content distribution. Interestingly, peer-to-peer architecture presents a potential for building scalable, more fault-tolerable and faster CDNs [11, 12].

The structured peer-to-peer network architecture requires a central server to keep the location information of all content in the common distribution network such as Napster. The unstructured peer-to-peer network architecture has no centralized server, but requires each node to keep the information of all the content locations within the local network such as Gnutella [10]. Other architectures exist for multiple clients multiple servers, private network, restricted file sharing and other functions [11]. At the moment, peer-to-peer network architecture has been valuable for fixed Internet; many applications are being developed for mobile scenarios [12].

2.2 Local Area Networks Media Access Controls

In the Open Systems Interconnection (OSI) model, the data link layer serves as an important sub-layer because it contains data communication protocol called the medium access control (MAC). Medium access controls (MACs) are responsible for addressing functions and channel access control method for different network stations contending for inadequate transmission medium. The IEEE 802 standards that support Distributed Coordination Function (DCF) and Point Coordination Function (PCF) have emerged as leading standards today [5, 13, 14].

The DCF is fit for asynchronous data broadcast, whereas, the PCF is widely held to be developed for time-bounded services such as voice and video [16, 17]. In particular, IEEE 802.11 WLAN was designed to run on mobile devices through broadband wireless access applications at homes or enterprises [8, 15]. It has paved the way for newer standards such as 802.11a, 802.11e, 802.11n and the latest being 802.11-2012 [8, 16]. The IEEE 802.11e task force introduced the Hybrid Coordination Function (HCF) to support the QoS as improvement over the IEEE 802.11 standard called the Enhanced Distributed Channel Access (EDCA) [16].

2.3 Related Works

In an improvised setup, the DCF is the cardinal entry configuration of the IEEE 802.11 MAC that embraces the carrier sense multiple accesses with collision avoidance (CSMA/CA) approach. Nonetheless, this entry configuration is unsupportive of special categories of traffic requiring prioritization such as real-time; the single first-in-first-out (FIFO) broadcast queue is utilized on 802.11 MAC on the basis of channel states either engaged by traffic broadcast or shiftless [18].

Hybrid MAC procedure is based on contention and contention-free settings to surmount the issues of scalability and packet collision. This is attained by setting aside time slots contention period and nodes transmit data in the period of slot time apportioned during period of contention-free. Also, the distinguishing attributes of hybrid MAC procedure include: reservation of time slots and preservation of all nodes information on reservation table. Collision of controls occurrences was only possible when details of nearby nodes are not contained on the similar reservation table [17].

Again, [19] advanced an algorithm known as scalable QoS (SQ) MAC protocol. This is a modest multimedia traffic QoS in Wireless Sensor Networks (WSNs) which is effective for minimizing end-to-end delay and multimedia streaming content broadcast scalability. SQ outweighed the IEEE 802.15.4 and IEEE 802.11e EDCF and MACs protocols. SQ offered reservation recovery method for the end-to-end delay problems [19].

QoS is the capacity to provide guarantee of resource in a network and the underlying needs of wireless centred applications [20]. The study of [20] attempted to propose panacea to the clear-cut issue of dearth of inadequate bandwidth in WLANs with thrifty QoS for diverse classes of time sensitive applications. This is accomplished by classifying the MAC layer service into station based and queue-based configurations; in so doing fashioning finite state machine transition system for PCF and DCF.

The study in [23] proposed the super-distribution of digital content. Super-distribution allows a peer to redistribute legally obtained content to other peers that can access the content by purchasing the licenses. The clearinghouse gives the distributing peer some monetary or (social credit) as licenses are bought by other peers, which is combination of peer-to-peer network and Digital Right Management. According to [23], super-distribution is beneficial to the peers (profit-making and individual) usages. However, the peers are always willing to share content created by self-efforts. This means that the incentives for peers to super-distribute are largely social and profit-making purposes. A digital content super-distribution system is depicted in Fig. 2.

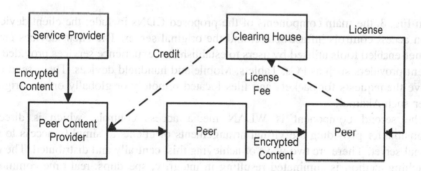

Fig. 2. Super-distribution network for digital content [12].

The common feature of ICN techniques is the control and usage of information. Though, they are unable to process ever increasing computing needs and managing large scale content implementation.

3   Methodology

Previously, [23] utilised web caching approach to increase the efficiency and latency of content transmitted through the networks. In this paper, the web caching approach is replaced by Media Access Controls infrastructure to enable clients contact the original server directly without the need to route through the superpeers and local ISP. This approach offers a virtual configuration of the wireless network access medium into central and distributed arrangements. At the client side, the HTTP protocol is used to deliver the content to clients. At the server-side, the MAC protocol is used to enable the client device establish connection to the original server warehousing the content of interests through the queries and requests. The structure of proposed CDNs is illustrated in Fig. 3.

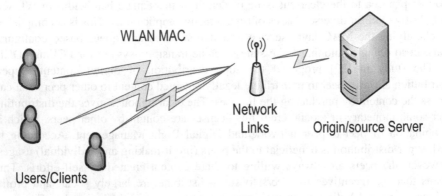

Fig. 3. Architecture of proposed MAC based CDN.

In Fig. 3, the main components of the proposed CDNs include: the client devices, media access controls infrastructure, and the original server. The client devices entail Internet-enabled tools utilised by users to establish and experience services provided by content providers such as PCs, Tablets, Mobile and handheld devices. These send and receive the requests for packets and files located remotely or globally on the original server such Akamai.

The second component is WLAN media access controls, which is directly responsible for providing the virtual arrangements of clients to simplify access to the original server. There are two ways of achieving this, centrally and distributed. The use of caching method is eliminated resulting in integrity, speedups, real-time communication, increased traffic, concurrent and multi-users functionalities. The last major component is the original server. This is used to store, maintain and serve content of diverse forms such as text, audio, stream, pictures and voices services. The rate of accessibility and availability of contents are maintained. The HTTP and MAC protocols collaborate to offer effective file sharing and communication between diverse clients and origin content server.

The proposed wireless MACs based CDN was experimented using OPNET 14.5 Modeller to investigate two MAC protocols deployed in CDNs environment whose parameters are presented in Table 1. The process is performed severally on the distinct components of the setups in order to validate the proposed CDNs architecture using selected WLAN MACs. OPNET modeller is used to conduct validating activities such as analysis of flow, NetDoctor validation, analysis of failure impact, and discrete event simulation. This paper deployed event-based simulator to provide a detailed outcomes for an extended times runs. More so, it gives analysis of links loads, explicit traffic control, and conversation pair traffic.

The experimentation stages begin with modelling of input, processes and outputs through understanding and assessing of problem stated. The next stage specifies parameters formats and standards such as routers, servers and layout of WLAN situation. Thereafter, the input stage gives the simulator the needed for different scenarios modelled such as traffics. The desired outputs are realized after processing of inputs. The evaluation stage verifies results as to have conformed to the set objectives for solving the problem. The stop/final stage terminates the simulation runs or reviews the network parameters to give the desired results.

Table 1. Experimental parameters.

Item	Values
MAC	HCF, PCF
Network type	WLANs
Client nodes	25
Evaluation	Load, delays
Traffic type	HTTP, FTP
Duration	150 s
Node speed	20 m/s

The application module design of the experimental setup is used to define the evaluation parameters such as email, file transfer protocol, and HTTP. The description of the evaluation metrics is as follows:

(i) *Media access end-to-end delay:* The delay in media access is determined as at the time the packet secures the MAC layer connection before it is eventually pass on the wireless channel. Often, the average channel access delay is calculated to allow for maximal tolerance for most real-time applications, after which the data is discarded. It expected that a MAC protocol gives smaller delays for real-time processes.

(ii) *Throughput:* This reveals the level of utilization and access of network medium and channels by all the workstations. It provides information on the QoS schemes and service differentiation priorities in the both WLAN MAC protocols. It is important that, MAC protocols to build well-organized service controls to solve inadequate bandwidth problems of wireless networks.

(iii) *Network load capacity:* The load contributed by each node to network medium is estimated. It shows the WLAN MAC protocol for content delivery services because it gives the propensity of the network medium for extended loading as well as the matching effects on number of nodes and load propagation.

4   Presentation of Results

This paper investigated the performance of MACs (central and distributed) protocols deployed in CDNs architecture as an innovation over caching technology proposed by [22]. To achieve this, three CDNs situations were experimented including (a) end-to-end packets delay and, (b) throughput (3) network load. Consequently, CDNs setups were uniformly composed of 1 server, 1 Wireless router, 25 nodes and 1 Access Point. Similarly, WLAN MAC protocols selected include: central MAC scheme (PCF) and distributed MAC scheme (HCF).

4.1   CDNs Packets Delays

In this setup, the end-to-end packet delays between the original content server and client devices when requests for file download are initiated. The central and distributed MACs were deployed for a 50 node WLAN as illustrated in Fig. 4.

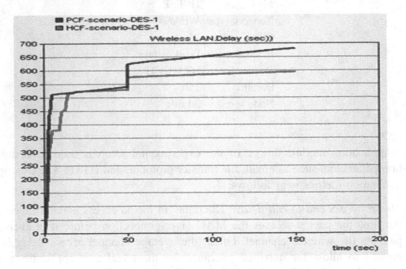

Fig. 4. CDNs delays measured for distributed and central MACs.

The first setup showed that the distributed MACs (HCF) protocols outweighed those of central (PCF) protocol on the basis of end-to-end delays as Fig. 3. The distributed MACs offered significantly smaller network delays by 46.51% to 53.49%. This implies that CDNs can effectively control loads on the network in a manner to reduce congestions and speedy delivery of contents and requests propagated by client nodes in WLAN situation with distributed MACs.

4.2   CDNs Network Load

In the second setup, the Network load of the proposed CDNs with 50 clients capacity connected concurrently to the original content server were measured for the distributed and central MACs implemented accordingly as shown in Fig. 5.

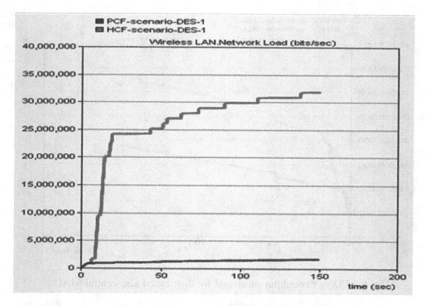

Fig. 5. CDNs Network load measured for distributed and central MACs.

The second setup, central (PCF) protocol contributes relatively smaller Network load rate of 31.91% against 68.09% for distributed (HCF) protocol as shown in Fig. 4. In CDNs environment, there is the demand for high traffic load which is supported by distributed MACs. Distributed MACs is best suitable for CDNs because; it allows access to content for numerous client nodes at the same time, increased the number of packets exchanges at a specific time and low contention/collision rates. This paper discovered that the rate of contention is higher for central MACs due to common Access Point and control. These stand in way of networks load amount established on the network medium at a particular time, which is unattractive to content delivery networks.

4.3   CDNs Throughput

In the third setup, the throughput of the proposed CDNs with 50 clients capacity connected concurrently to the original content server were measured for the distributed and central MACs implemented accordingly as shown in Fig. 6. In this last setup, central (PCF) protocol contributes relatively smaller throughput degree of 35.85% against 64.15% for distributed (HCF) protocol as shown in Fig. 6. In CDNs situation, there is the need for high packets to be returned as matching high requests which is supported by distributed MACs.

This is the converse of delays outcomes presented in Fig. 4. Therefore, distributed MACs are most reliable for implementing CDNs because the number of clients' requests is matched with replies from the original or source server.

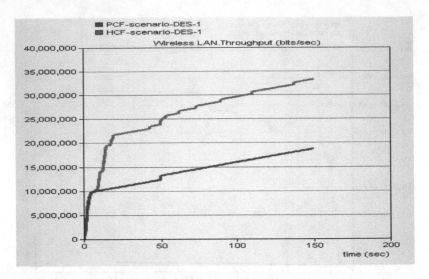

Fig. 6. CDNs throughput measured for distributed and central MACs.

The summary of the results obtained from three experimental setups of WLANs MACs in CDNs are presented in Table 2.

Table 2. Performance of WLANs MACs for CDNs compared.

Parameter	Distributed MACs (%)	Central MACs (%)
Packets Delays	46.51	53.49
Network load	31.91	68.09
Throughput	35.85	64.15

From Table 2, it is discovered that for central MACs schemes due to the high rate of contention, and common Access Point and control. These stand in way of its effectiveness in building networks for the purpose of content distribution and delivery services. The distributed MACs enable clients to reach the origin/source servers without passing through proxy/cache servers in a more efficient ways. The overheads and imminent storage problems, out-dated contents, connection failures and scalability [23] are minimized with MACs network infrastructure in CDNs.

5   Conclusion

The reason behind the innovations of content distribution is to discover the most suitable location existing between the originating/source and client whenever contents demanded. The need to deliver content through the Web and file storage methods in large scale filing systems gave rise to CDNs solutions. The CDNs introduced the concept of Web access and user-centric control of the network. The use of special incentives to reduce complexity of the network involved distribution network controls and efficient allotment of the available resources on the network.

The paper explored the possibility of using MACs such as DCF schemes to allow clients interconnect directly to the original/source Server rather than routing through super-peers, local ISP, and proxy cache servers. The other benefits include: speed, control of traffic, management of clients' requests/queries and improved service. Again, the impending storage shortages of servers, out-dated contents, concurrent multiple accesses of clients to services, minimal packets losses, reduced collision due to requests/traffics, and increased exchanges. Two categories of WLAN MACs schemes were experimented.

The outcomes revealed that the roles of distributed MACs were analogous to web caching approach except for easy of deployment, integrity of information, speed, traffic controls and effective content delivery. Again, distributed WLAN MACs provided best performance and support against central WLAN MAC for implementation in CDNs.

References

1. Vinton, C.: Fascinating Facts about the Invention of the Internet (1973). http://www. ideafinder.com/history/inventions/internet.htm
2. Zhang, N.: Internet Content Delivery as a Two-Sided Market. Unpublished Master of Science Engineering Thesis, Department of Communications and Networking, Aalto University (2010)
3. Cisco.: Cisco Visual Networking Index: Forecast and Methodology, 2009–2014 (2010)
4. Labovitz, C., Iekel-Johnson, S., McPherson, D., Oberheide, J., Jahanian, F., Karir, M.: ATLAS internet observatory 2009 annual report. In: Presentation at 47th North American Network Operators' Group Conference (2009)
5. Snickars, C.: Design of a wirelessHART simulator for studying delay compensation in networked control systems. Unpublished M.Sc. Thesis, KTH Electrical Engineering, Stockholm, Sweden, pp. 1–120 (2008)
6. Amar, N.M., Deepak, A., Shashwat, S., Vineet, S.: Performance evaluation of mobile ad-hoc network (MANET) routing protocols GRP, DSR and AODV based on packet size. Int. J. Eng. Sci. Technol. 4(6), 2849–2852 (2012)
7. Rajaraman, R.: Wireless Networks. Pearson Eduction, North Asia Ltd., Hong Kong (2007)
8. Gupta, J.S., Grewal, G.S.: Performance evaluation of IEEE 802.11 MAC layer in supporting delay sensitive services. Int. J. Wirel. Mob. Netw. 10, 42–53 (2010)
9. Al-mefleh, H.: Design and analysis of MAC protocols for wireless networks. A Ph.D. Thesis, Department of Computer Engineering, Iowa State University, Ames, USA, pp. 1–130 (2009)
10. Kang, H.J.: Secure and Robust Overlay Content Distribution. Unpublished Ph.D. Thesis, Department of Computer Networking, University of Minnesota, USA (2010)
11. Hughes, J., Lang, K.R., Vragov, R.: An analytical framework for evaluating peer-to-peer business models. Electron. Commer. Res. Appl. 7(1), 105–118 (2007)
12. Karikoski, J.O.: Scenarios and System Dynamics of Mobile Peer-to-Peer Content Distribution. A M.Sc. Thesis, Department of Communications and Networking, Helsinki University of Technology, Helsinki (2009)
13. Puschita, E., Palade, T., Pitic, R.: Wireless LAN medium access techniques QoS perspective. In: Signals, Circuits and Systems, pp. 267–270 (2005)

14. Kaur, M.: Performance evaluation of MAC protocols in VANETs. Int. J. Eng. Res. Appl. **2** (1), 93–98 (2012)
15. Harpreet, S.C., Ansari, M.I.H., Ashish, K., Prashant, S.V.: A survey of transmission C.P over mobile ad-hoc networks. Int. J. Sci. Technol. Res. **1**(4), 146–150 (2012)
16. Kim, B.S., Kim, S.W., Fang, Y., Wong, T.F.: Two-step multipolling MAC protocol for wireless LANs. IEEE J. Sel. Areas Commun. **23**(6), 1277–1286 (2005)
17. Bianchi, G., Tinnirello, I., Scalia, L.: Understanding 802.11e contention-based Prioritization mechanisms and their coexistence with legacy 802.11 stations. Institute of Electrical Electronic Engineers Network., vol. 6, pp. 28–34 (2005)
18. Ahmed, M., Fadeel, G.A., Ibrahim, I.: Differentiation between different traffic categories using multi-level of priority in DCF-WLAN. In: Advanced International Conference on Telecommunications, vol. 6, pp. 263–268 (2010)
19. On, J., Jeon, H., Lee, J.: A scalable MAC protocol supporting simple multimedia traffic QoS in WSNs. Int. J. Distrib. Sens. Netw. **495127**, 1–11 (2011)
20. Puthal, D.K.: Quality of Service Provisioning with modified IEEE 802.11 MAC Protocol. Unpublished M.Tech Thesis, Department of Computer Science and Engineering, National Institute of Technology Rourkela, Orissa, India, pp. 1–106 (2008)
21. Schmidt, A.U.: On the superdistribution of digital goods. In: Proceedings of 2008. Third International Conference on Communications and Networking in China, Hangzhou (2008)
22. Kostamo, I.N., Kassinen, O., Koskela, T., Ylianttila, M.: Analysis of concept and incentives for digital content superdistribution. In: 6th Conference on Telecommunication Techno-Economics, Helsinki, Finland, pp. 1–6 (2007)
23. Alfa, A.A., Ogwueleka, F.N., Dogo, E.N., Sanjay, M.A.: Hybrid web caching design model for internet-content delivery. Covenant. J. Inform. Commun. Technol. **4**(2), 34–47 (2016)

Automating Information Security Risk Assessment for IT Services

Sandra Rueda(✉) and Oscar Avila

Computing and Systems Engineering Department, School of Engineering,
Universidad de los Andes, K 1E 19A 40, Bogota, Colombia
{sarueda,oj.avila}@uniandes.edu.co

Abstract. Information Security (IS) Risk Assessment is a main part of risk analysis; it helps organizations make decisions to protect their Information Technology (IT) services and underlying IT assets from potentially adverse events. How to do assessment in this context, however, is not a well defined task. Some approaches provide guidelines but leave analysts to define how to implement them, leading to different mechanisms to identify input data, different procedures to process those inputs, and different results as a consequence. To address this problem, we present a semiautomatic procedure, based on data systematically obtained from modern IT Service Management (ITSM) tools used by IT staff to handle IT services' assets and configurations. We argue that these tools handle actual data that may be used to collect inputs for a IS risk assessment procedure, thus reducing subjective values. We evaluated the procedure in a real case study and found that our approach actually reduces variability of some results. We also identified areas that must be addressed in future work.

Keywords: IT risk evaluation · Configuration management system
Configuration item · Service security

1 Introduction

Risk analysis nowadays is a common practice that helps companies understand their own business processes, identify the risks of those processes, and decide about the better options to manage their risks. Since most companies rely on Information Technology (IT) services to support their business processes, Information Security (IS) risk assessment is a main part of risk analysis.

Different well-known standards, like National Institute of Standards and Technology (NIST) SP800-30 [25] and ISO 27005 [20] propose the same set of general steps to perform IS risk assessment: (1) identify threats, (2) identify vulnerabilities, (3) establish likelihood of an adverse event to occur, (4) quantify impact, and (5) compute risk. Standards also give guidelines to perform these steps but leave analysts to decide by themselves how to actually implement them. As a consequence, different analysts end up implementing different operational procedures, leading to different results even for the same system.

© Springer Nature Switzerland AG 2018
H. Florez et al. (Eds.): ICAI 2018, CCIS 942, pp. 183–197, 2018.
https://doi.org/10.1007/978-3-030-01535-0_14

Different researchers have studied particular implementations of IS risk assessment and have found two main problems: how to select and collect input data necessary to perform risk assessment, and how to process such input data [5,18]. To identify inputs, security analysts use different sources, including well known databases, logs, local and public statistics, and judgments from experts. However, there is no actual methodology to systematically select relevant inputs, from the available sources, for a particular organization. As a consequence results may vary; if an analyst were to repeat selection and collection of input data, results could be different. To process data, security analysts define their own IS assessment procedures. Nevertheless, some definitions in these procedures are ambiguous, leading to the problem already mentioned: if an analyst were to repeat an assessment procedure, results would be different.

The problem is that input selection, as well as the steps of the analysis itself, may change from analyst to analyst leading to different results for the same system. Analysts may consider different criteria, enlist experts with different views, build different interpretations of one standard, or follow different analysis principles, thus arriving to different results. Furthermore, since there is not an automatic or semiautomatic tool to support these steps, and decisions are not documented, it is difficult to repeat a given analysis to check the results. Additionally, a manual analysis has response times that may not be adequate.

To deal with this situation, our approach to assess IS risk for IT services includes two stages. In the first stage, we analyze the steps of IS risk assessment in order to identify parts that may be automated. To this end, we evaluate the relevance of using Information Technology Service Management (ITSM) tools and vulnerability databases to automate input data selection and collection, and IS recommendations such as NIST [25] and the Open Web Application Security Project (OWASP) [22] to discuss how to structure and execute each step in the assessment. In the second stage, we operationalize IS risk assessment by proposing a semi-automatic procedure that uses the concepts and tools identified in the analysis carried out in the previous stage.

This paper is structured as follows: Sect. 2 presents previous work. Section 3 presents our proposal to partially automate IS risk assessment. Section 4 presents a case study. Finally, Sect. 5 concludes and outlines future work.

2   Related Work

Previous works have identified the problems associated to the absence of well defined procedures to perform IS risk assessment and have proposed various solutions. We classified those works in two main groups: proposals to select relevant input data and proposals to process data.

Proposals to select relevant input data. The works that address input selection mainly focus on methods to handle differences that arise from working with experts. For example, an administrator may enlist several experts to study a particular IT system and establish its vulnerabilities and the experts may end with different results for the very same system. The works in this category evaluate different techniques as fuzzy logic, multi-attribute analysis and analytic hierarchy process (AHP).

Proposals based on the first technique [2, 10, 14] use principles from fuzzy logic to handle differences among several experts, they take different values for a given variable and compute the best option (the most likely) for it. The second technique, multi-attribute analysis, applies statistical methods to establish the relative importance of a given variable in a set of variables. In IS risk assessment, multi-attribute analysis is used to identify what kind of security events can represent a higher threat for a company; each kind of event is a variable to be considered, experts assign impact to each threat, and multi-attribute analysis computes what threats have higher impacts [11]. Finally, the AHP technique may be used to handle different opinions from several experts. The difference with multi-attribute analysis is that AHP uses group consensus instead of statistics. Therefore, AHP is used in IS risk assessment to decide what variable is more relevant, by creating consensus between the opinions of several experts [16].

Proposals to process data. The second group includes proposals to model reasoning behind implemented procedures. This approach aims at modelling and registering the phases an administrator follows to perform IS risk assessment, leading to a procedure that may be repeated.

Authors in [9] propose an assessment procedure based on three knowledge bases: one stores company assets; including physical spaces, hardware, software, and management; the second one identifies vulnerabilities and establishes their relationships with the assets, and the last one identifies threats and relationships between threats and vulnerabilities. The proposal defines formulas to automatically compute relevant values. Authors in [5] propose an assessment procedure based on a security ontology that includes relevant elements, like infrastructure and personnel, their attributes and relationships. The ontology serves as a framework that can be instantiated by IT administrators with the elements of a specific IT infrastructure.

These proposals and our proposal share some goals, we all want to model and register the decision procedure. Our proposal also looks for options to reduce human intervention and as a consequence the variability in the results. We argue that the process of IS risk assessment can be improved by automating input data collection from reliable sources in order to not only depend on knowledge from experts. To this end, our proposal identifies specific data sources and defines a procedure to use them.

3   Proposal: Semiautomatic Information Security Risk Assessment

This section presents our proposal to automate some steps of an IS risk assessment. The main idea behind this proposal is using Information Technology Service Management (ITSM) tools that IT administrators are currently using to collect and store information about actual infrastructure elements and their configurations for a particular organization. We want to use the information stored by these tools as inputs of the assessment, more specifically, the selection of relevant security-related data from available data sources. First, we briefly explain the steps of IS risk assessment, and then we evaluate step by step what parts of risk assessment may be automated and how to do so. Finally, we describe our implementation.

The main steps of IS security risk assessment, according to well-known standards [20,25] are: (1) Identification of threats. A threat is any event that may adversely affect an organization. Threats may be human, structural or natural (generated by resources within organization control or natural disasters respectively). (2) Identification of vulnerabilities. A vulnerability is a weakness in procedures or system configurations that may contribute to materialize a threat. (3) Quantification of likelihood of adverse events to happen. This value measures how the presence of vulnerabilities and other elements may contribute to materialize a threat. (4) Quantification of impact. This value represents the damage to the organization if a threat materializes. (5) Risk Assessment. A risk level is the combination of likelihood and impact. Adverse events with high impact and high likelihood of happening should be the first ones to be addressed.

Some parts of step 1 may be automated, however, we left that issue as future work. Steps 2 to 5 may be partially automated by using information stored by ITSM tools and other available data sources and IS recommendations to structure and execute each step. Below, we identified the parts that may be automated and describe how to do it.

3.1   Identification of Vulnerabilities

We propose using two available data sources: vulnerability databases and information from ITSM tools, to partially automate this step.

(1) Vulnerability Data Bases. Available vulnerability databases, like the Common Vulnerabilities and Exposures (CVE) [4] and the NIST National Vulnerabilities Database (NVD) [23], store known vulnerabilities and their characteristics and are free to the public. CVE and NVD databases use a standard set of attributes to describe vulnerabilities thus providing a valuable data source to automate queries and security tasks, like the ones we are interested in.

Standard vulnerability attributes are: product names, as defined by the Common Platform Enumeration (CPE) Dictionary [24], and the features defined by the Common Vulnerability Scoring System (CVSS) [7].

CPE is a 'Structured naming scheme for information technology systems, software, and packages. Based upon the generic syntax for Uniform Resource Identifiers (URI), CPE includes a formal name format, a method for checking names against a system, and a description format for binding text and tests to a name.' [24]

CVSS 'provides a way to capture the principal characteristics of a vulnerability and produce a numerical score reflecting its severity.' [7] There are two CVSS versions, 2.0 and 3.0, in use. CVSS 2.0 includes the following features [15]:

- Access vector. A feature to indicate the means of access to exploit a vulnerability, it has three possible values: local, adjacent network, and network.
- Access complexity. It represents the knowledge and resources required to exploit a vulnerability, after having gained access to a system. It has three possible values: high, medium and low.
- Authentication. A feature to indicate the number of times a malicious agent must authenticate, it has three possible values: multiple, single and none.
- Score. A number computed with base on all the CVSS features, that represents the severity of a vulnerability.

CVSS 3.0 [8] has slightly different features, like Privileges required and User interaction. Figure 1 shows snippets of a vulnerability from the NVD database with CVSS 2.0 features. Our approach is based on CVSS 2.0, because we worked with NVD files that use this version. Updating the procedure requires establishing what CVSS 3.0 features must be used to compute the needed values, in the same way that we describe throughout this section, and changing the implementation accordingly.

(2) Information Technology Service Management (ITSM) Tools. To ease management, business processes are typically divided into a set of structured activities that follow a logical sequence in order to reach an objective. Each of the activities of a business process can be supported by one or more IT services. An IT service is an abstract representation of IT, processes and people, brought together to generate value to organizations and their customers. To manage IT services, administrators use ITSM tools.

```
<vuln:vulnerable-software-list>
  <vuln:product>cpe:/a:microsoft:edge</vuln:product>
</vuln:vulnerable-software-list>

...
<vuln:cvss>
  <cvss:base_metrics>
    <cvss:score>6.8</cvss:score>
    <cvss:access-vector>NETWORK</cvss:access-vector>
    <cvss:access-complexity>MEDIUM</cvss:access-complexity>
    <cvss:authentication>NONE</cvss:authentication>
    <cvss:confidentiality-impact>PARTIAL</cvss:confidentiality-
        impact>
    <cvss:integrity-impact>PARTIAL</cvss:integrity-impact>
    <cvss:availability-impact>PARTIAL</cvss:availability-impact>
    <cvss:source>http://nvd.nist.gov</cvss:source>
    <cvss:generated-on-datetime>2017-01-11T09:49:58.903-05:00</cvss:
        generated-on-datetime>
  </cvss:base_metrics>
</vuln:cvss>
...
<vuln:summary>Microsoft Edge allows remote attackers to bypass the
    Same Origin Policy via vectors involving the about:blank URL and
    data: URLs, aka "Microsoft Edge Elevation of Privilege
    Vulnerability."</vuln:summary>
</entry>
```

Fig. 1. Snippets of a vulnerability from the NVD database. This record uses CVSS 2.0 features.

ITSM tools are applications and databases for collecting, storing, managing, updating, analyzing and presenting all the knowledge, information and data that IT staff will need to understand its IT resources and capabilities. One of the most used ITSM tools is the Configuration Management System (CMS) that includes functionality for the registration, support and management of IT services' configuration items (CIs) and their relationships. A CI is an IT component or asset that needs to be managed in order to deliver an IT service. These components typically are other IT services, hardware, software, buildings, people and formal documentation such as process documentation and service level agreements. Every CI in the configuration hierarchy of a service has attributes that describe it. For instance, a CI like a server has location, operating system and manufacturer attributes, and a CI like a database management system has developer and version attributes. In addition, most of the CMSs allow adding personalized attributes, to a CI or to a family of CIs, in order to characterize additional aspects that were not originally anticipated such as business impact in case of failure, which is of interest to calculate risk. Figure 2 illustrates this kind of representation.

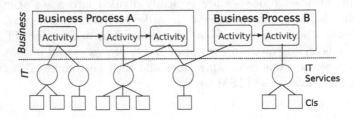

Fig. 2. Processes are divided into activities to ease management. Each activity is supported by one or more IT services, and IT Services consist of configuration items (CIs), like assets or other IT services.

We use information from vulnerability and CMS databases to automatically identify the list of potential vulnerabilities for a particular IT service. Our approach to automate this task has two main parts: identification of CIs, and identification of their known vulnerabilities. In the first part, we query the CMS to generate the list of CIs associated to the IT service of interest and their attributes. In the second part, for each CI in the list we check whether there are matches in the vulnerability database or not. The final result is the list of known vulnerabilities for the actual components that support a service.

3.2 Quantification of Likelihood

To estimate likelihood we combined NIST [25] and OWASP [22] recommendations. Likelihood estimation involves various factors grouped in three categories: characteristics of the human threat sources, predisposing conditions, and organizational susceptibility [22,25]. Below we discuss how to compute values for these factors.

Characteristics of Human Threat Sources. OWASP [22] defines four factors to measure the intention and ability of human threat sources: (1) skill level, a measure of the skills that potential attackers have; (2) motive, how motivated an attacker may be; (3) opportunity, the kind of the resources an attacker needs to exploit a vulnerability; and (4) size, a measurement of how large is the group of potential attackers.

We handle these factors as follows. First, we must ask analysts to manually estimate skill level and motive because, as previously said, we are not addressing how to automate threat identification. Second, we moved opportunity to the following category, *Predisposing Conditions*, because it matches the concept of ease of exploit in that category. Finally, we use two features from a standard vulnerability entry: CVSS Access-vector and CVSS Authentication, to estimate size. As mentioned in the previous section, the CVSS Access-vector has three possible values: Local, Adjacent Network, and Network [15]; to compute size, we assume that Local access implies a lower number of potential threat agents or attackers than network access. CVSS Authentication has three possible values: Multiple, Single, and None [15]; we assume that Multiple implies a lower number of potential threat agents than None.

Predisposing Conditions. This category measures how difficult it is to find and exploit a vulnerability. OWASP defines four factors in this class: (1) ease of discovery, it measures how easy is to find a vulnerability that may be exploited; (2) ease of exploit, it measures what resources are required to exploit a vulnerability that is already known; (3) awareness, it measures how well known is a vulnerability; and (4) intrusion detection, it establishes whether there are controls in place to detect intrusions to the system and counteract them.

We handle these factors as follows. First, we estimate ease of discovery based on number of identified vulnerabilities. This number represents the number of different weak entry points an attacker may use. Thus, the higher the number of vulnerabilities the easier to find a weak entry point. Second, we consider that ease of exploit matches the concept of opportunity and we use CVSS Access-complexity to compute this value. CVSS Access-complexity has three possible values, related to the level of knowledge and resources needed to exploit a vulnerability: High, Medium, and Low; we assume that a higher complexity implies a lower opportunity. Third, we estimate awareness as HIGH because we are using a public database, and as a consequence all of these vulnerabilities are of public knowledge. We cannot estimate anything regarding vulnerabilities that have not been reported, and we left improvements on methods to estimate this factor as future work. Finally, we consider that intrusion detection belongs to the following category, organizational susceptibility, and handle it there.

Organizational Susceptibility. This category reflects whether an organization has deployed security controls that may detect and counteract an attacker. In this case we ask analysts to manually establish if the controls in the list of critical security controls [3, 21] are deployed in their organizations. The lower the number of implemented controls the higher the susceptibility of the organization and, in turn, the higher the likelihood of an attack. Examples of critical controls are:

inventory of authorized devices, inventory of authorized software, and management of secure configurations. The first one means management of all network devices to only allow access to those explicitly authorized [21], the second one means software management to only allow installation and execution of vetted software [21], and the last one means defining secure configuration for all devices in the organization and having a procedure to control changes [21].

3.3 Quantification of Impact

Impact, as used in this research work, refers to the negative business consequences that follow from a security incident or realized risk. Even though some of such consequences can be easily expressed in terms of money, others can be difficult to quantify because of their nature. The exact scope of potential business losses has not been addressed as a primary subject in prior research. However, some works have considered the nature of business losses in more detail as a secondary task when formulating questionnaires or checklists to IT managers. Typical business losses that prior research has associated with systems risks are: [17]: Operative business losses (additional labour, material or capital cost), Lost revenues due to problems in operative or customer service processes, Opportunity losses or costs resulting from wrong management decisions, Competitive losses resulting from theft of confidential information, Business losses resulting from theft of money or goods, Company image losses: losses resulting from negative media exposure, Shareholder losses: negative impact on company's share price, Losses resulting from legal processes and punishments against the company, IT losses: lost value of IT assets or significant unbudgeted IT costs.

Different works propose different procedures to quantify impact. For instance, [1] proposes a set of 25 indicators to quantify impact, including monetary losses and adverse impact on reputation. It requires experts to manually assign weight and values to the indicators, and applies an analytic hierarchy process (AHP) to consolidate the results. Another proposal [11] uses other factors, like decreased profit, loss of customers, decreased productivity, and data recovery lost. Similarly, this proposal requires experts to manually define preferences, applies a multi-attribute analysis technique to select the criteria that are more important, and uses those criteria to compute impact. The mentioned works depend on expert's judgments to weight factors and accumulate knowledge and do not explicitly consider the relationships between IT services, infrastructure components and the business processes that they support.

However, some recent works state that security analysis should be aligned to business processes and goals [12,13,19]. In this sense, one of the most used techniques to this purpose is the business impact analysis (BIA). BIA includes the identification of relevant business processes, and the potential loss to the organization in case of an incident on the IT services that support those processes. To help practitioners use BIA results, modern ITSM tools, such as CMS, handle information about the criticality of the IT services and their CIs as well as the relationships among these services and business processes. We propose using this information to automatically get the level of impact in case of incident. Indeed, the higher the criticality of an IT service, the higher the impact on the business processes that it supports. In this sense, our proposal and [6,13] are close, as we all consider the relevance of business processes, and compute potential impact based on the related services' relevance or criticality.

Since there are methods to compute impact, like the ones previously mentioned, and the results are stored in the ITSM tools, such as CMS, we propose to automate the collection of impact values for a given IT service and its corresponding CIs by extracting data from these tools.

3.4   Automating Value Generation

This section presents an overview of the procedure to generate the values required to compute risk, based on the ideas presented in the previous sections.

(1) Identification of Vulnerabilities. This step includes two activities:

(1.1) Generation of IT components. We query the CMS DB to generate the list of CIs associated to the IT service of interest. The list includes operating systems and applications, and their characteristics.

(1.2) Identification of known vulnerabilities. For each element in the list, we query the vulnerability DB to generate the list of potential vulnerabilities. The result is the list of known vulnerabilities for the actual CIs of a given IT service.

(2) Quantification of Likelihood.

(2.1) Skill level of threat agents. We ask an administrator to manually assign value to this factor. The possible values are HIGH, people with knowledge and experience in penetration testing; MEDIUM, people with advanced skills regarding computers; and LOW, regular users. In all cases we translate qualitative values to quantitative values by dividing the 0–1 interval into subintervals of the same size. Thus, HIGH, MEDIUM and LOW are internally represented as 1, 0.66 and 0.33 respectively.

(2.2) Motive of threat agents. We also ask an administrator to manually assign value to this factor. The possible values are HIGH, MEDIUM, and LOW which correspond to High reward, possible reward, and no reward as defined by OWASP [22].

(2.3) Size of the groups of threat agents. We process the list of vulnerabilities identified in the previous step as follows: (i) for each vulnerability in the list we extract CVSS Access-vector and CVSS Authentication. (ii) we translate qualitative values of Access-vector and authentication values to numerical values (as previously said we distribute a 0–1 interval into subintervals of the same size). (iii) For each vulnerability we multiply the two numerical values. (iv) Finally, we compute the average of the values generated for all the vulnerabilities resulting in a number within the 0–1 range.

(2.4) Ease of discovery of vulnerabilities. For each IT component, we divide the number of vulnerabilities identified for that component by the vulnerabilities identified for the entire IT service of interest.

(2.5) Ease of exploitation of vulnerabilities. We process the list of identified vulnerabilities as follows: (i) for each vulnerability in the list we extract the value for the CVSS Access-complexity feature. (ii) we translate the qualitative values for this feature to a numerical value. (iii) we compute the average of the values generated in (ii).

(2.6) Awareness of vulnerabilitites. We process the list of vulnerabilities and determine the level of awareness for them. Possible values for this factor are HIGH, MEDIUM and LOW depending on how well known the vulnerabilities are. However, since we are working with a public DB of vulnerabilities, we initially assign HIGH to this factor. Nevertheless, if an administrator can identify particular vulnerabilities for his system, the value may be lower as these new vulnerabilities are not necessarily known by potential attackers. As before, we translate the qualitative values of this feature to a numerical value.

(2.7) Deployed security controls. We present the list of critical security controls and ask the administrator which ones are deployed in the organization. We compute the percentage of deployed security controls and subtract that percentage from 1; the higher the percentage of deployed security controls the lower the likelihood of a security incident.

(3) Quantification of Impact. As previously stated, new ITSM tools such as CMS provide the possibility of adding or creating specific attributes to register how critical a CI is or its impact in case of an incident. The possible values for this attribute are normally HIGH, MEDIUM and LOW, depending on previous impact analysis. We translate qualitative values into numerical values.

(4) Computing Risk. We follow the common way of computing information security risk as Likelihood vs. Impact. Table 1 summarizes the list of criteria we use to compute likelihood and impact. We consider seven factors, grouped in three categories, to compute likelihood: Skill, Motive, Size, Ease of Discovery, Ease of Exploit, Awareness, and Deployed Security Controls. Column Generation shows whether those values must be manually assigned (M) or may be automatically generated (A). The last column shows used data sources.

4   Case Study

The case study concerns the internal IT department of a South-American company that manages their IT services and infrastructure by using IT service management best practices and tools. The organization uses a CMS to manage information about IT services and CIs related to the underlying IT infrastructure that supports these services. We focus on one of the services: the Administrative Information System (AIS). This service partially supports one of the core business processes of the company and provides information to external customers as well as to internal ones that belong to other departments in the same company.

Table 1. Criteria used to evaluate Risk grouped in factors. Values may be (H)IGH, (M)EDIUM and (L)OW. Generation may be (M)anual or (A)utomated.

Step	Factor category	Factor	CVSS metric	Values	Generation	Data source
Likelihood	Human threat sources	Skill		H, M, L	M	Admin
		Motive		H, M, L	M	Admin
		Size	Access-vector	Network, Adjacent, Local	A	NVD
			Authentication	None, Single, Multiple	A	NVD
	Predisposing conditions	Ease of discovery		0–1	A	NVD
		Ease of exploit	Access-complexity	H, M, L	A	NVD
		Awareness		HIGH	A	
	Organizational susceptibility	Deployed security controls		0–1	M	NVD
Impact		Criticality or CI impact		H, M, L	A	ITSM tool

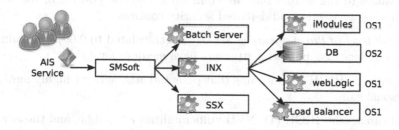

Fig. 3. Administrative Information System (AIS) and its CIs, all are related to an Operating System (OS)

AIS is supported by SMSoft, a software application, while SMSoft consists of three software components (see Fig. 3): (i) A batch server for data loading; (ii) INX, a component to support administrative tasks; (iii) SSX, a component to support regular tasks, like online information queries for external customers. To ease understanding of our approach (by reducing complexity), we only focus on the CIs related to the INX software component (see Fig. 3): (i) Production environment database. It stores company's data. (ii) iModules allowing the company to carry out 'email marketing' and publication of events. (iii) WebLogic server. Web application server that runs the INX application. (iv) Load balancer.

We evaluated the proposal with the following results:

(1) Generation of the list of applications and operating systems. We used the CMS user interface to query the records that store CI information

(e.g. information of applications and operating systems). Although the current interface is manual, we are developing scripts to directly query the CMS DB via its API.

(2) Identification of known vulnerabilities. For each IT component in the generated list we checked the NVD database of reported vulnerabilities. We generated thus a list of vulnerabilities that includes: 46 vulnerabilities for the production environment database, 24 for the webLogic application server, 1 for the operating system (OS1) of the iModules, webLogic and Load Balancer servers, and 12 for the operating system (OS2) of the production database. We did not find any records for SMSoft and their modules; they are applications of specific purpose and are not widely used. We set the search patterns to look for records between January 2015 and June 2017.

The main problem with these searches was that application names, stored in the CMS, are not standard thus we had to manually adjust the search patterns. We believe this problem may be solved by establishing a standard procedure to assign names, like CPE. Another limitation is that the database of vulnerabilities only includes reported vulnerabilities and we did not find reports for products that are not so commonly used. This issue must be solved, one option is supporting manual addition of vulnerabilities to the generated list.

(3) Quantification of likelihood. We first asked an administrator to manually assign values to the factors that are common for all components of the service: skill, motive, awareness and deployed security controls.

(3.1) Skill level of threat agents = MEDIUM (translated to 0.66). The administrator considers that potential attackers have medium level skills.

(3.2) Motive = HIGH (1), meaning that potential attackers are highly motivated by personal gain.

(3.3) Awareness = HIGH (1). NVD vulnerabilities are public, and the administrator did not identify new vulnerabilities for the studied IT service.

(3.4) Deployed Security Controls = 0.35. The organization has implemented 13 of the 20 selected controls. Thus, this factor contributes $(1 - 0.65)$ to likelihood.

Then, we estimated size, ease of discovery, and ease of exploit for each component of the CIs (Database, App, OS1 and OS2). Table 2 summarizes the results for these factors.

(3.5) Size. This is the average value of (Access-Vector * Authentication) over all vulnerabilities for one component. As an example, we present the procedure for OS2: (1) We extract the value of Access-Vector and Authentication for each of the 12 vulnerabilities of OS2. Access-vector: (NETWORK, NETWORK, LOCAL, NETWORK, NETWORK, NETWORK, LOCAL, NETWORK, NETWORK, NETWORK, ADJACENT-NETWORK, LOCAL) and Authentication: (NONE, NONE, NONE, NONE, NONE, NONE, NONE, NONE, NONE, NONE, SINGLE-INSTANCE, NONE). (2) We translate Access-vector quality values to (1, 1, 0.33, 1, 1, 1, 0.33, 1, 1, 1, 0.66, 0.33) and Authentication quality

values to $(1, 1, 1, 1, 1, 1, 1, 1, 1, 1, 0.66, 1)$. (3) We multiply the two numerical values for each vulnerability and obtain: $(1, 1, 0.33\ 1, 1, 1, 0.33, 1, 1, 1, 0.4356, 0.33)$. (4) Finally, we compute the average of the values generated for all the vulnerabilities and obtain: 0.785466 which is rounded to 0.79.

(3.6) Ease of discovery. To assign value to this aspect, OWASP [22] proposes considering whether there are scanners that can automatically look for a given vulnerability. We are planning, on future work, to develop mechanisms to search this information. Meanwhile, we estimate the percentage of responsibility of a given component. To do so, we first compute the total number of vulnerabilities for the components under study: $46+24+1+12 = 83$ and we use this value to compute the percentage per component. For example, we found 46 reported vulnerabilities for the production environment database giving a value of $46/83=0.55$ for this component. Considering the number of database reported vulnerabilities, it may be easier for an attacker to find an entry point to this CI than to the others that are being studied.

(3.7) Ease of exploit. This is the average value of (Access-Complexity) over all vulnerabilities for one component. For example, for OS2, we extract the value of Access-Complexity for its 12 vulnerabilities: (MEDIUM, LOW, LOW, LOW, MEDIUM, LOW, MEDIUM, MEDIUM, LOW, MEDIUM, LOW, LOW) which is translated to $(0.66, 1, 1, 1, 0.66, 1, 0.66, 0.66, 1, 0.66, 1, 1)$. Then, we compute the average of the values, getting 0.8583 which is rounded to 0.86. As showed in Table 2, the production database, webLogic application and OS2 have high values in this factor. This means that, considering the low levels of access complexity required to access those components, an attacker would need a low level of resources to exploit their vulnerabilities, giving an attacker a high opportunity.

Table 2. These factors are computed for each component of a given service: Size of threats, ease of discovery and ease of exploit.

	Size of threats	E. of discovery	E. of exploit	Likelihood
DB	0.61	$46/83 = 0.55$	0.9	0.27
WebLogic app	0.98	$24/83 = 0.28$	0.85	0.27
OS1	0.33	$1/83 = 0.01$	0.66	0.21
OS2	0.79	$12/83 = 0.14$	0.86	0.25

We used previous values to compute likelihood per component. We compute the average of the six factors that can increase likelihood: skill, motive, size, ease of discovery and exploit, and awareness. We then multiply the resulting average by the value of deployed security controls; this one may decrease likelihood. Table 2 presents results per component. To compute likelihood for a CI with several subcomponents, we would need to model those components as a series or parallel system. Then, based on the model and individual likelihoods, we could compute the overall likelihood of the CI. We mapped values back to a qualitative value (LOW: 0–0.33, MEDIUM: 0.34–0.66, and HIGH: 0.67–1). Thus, the set of analyzed CIs have a LOW likelihood that an adverse event occurs, mainly because of the security controls deployed by the IT department of the company. *(4) Generate impact.* The IT administrator assigned HIGH to the criticality of the service associated to the analyzed CIs (the service supports a core business process). We extracted the criticality from the CMS DB and assigned it to each component.

(5) Compute risk. The final result for the set of evaluated CIs is LOW likelihood vs. HIGH impact.

5 Conclusions and Future Work

This work presents an approach to systematically select and collect input data, from information stored by ITSM tools and available vulnerability databases, to perform IS risk analysis. We identified several advantages of our approach: it may be run as many times as wanted, results will be consistent as they are based on objective sources, and there will be evidence regarding the logic applied to obtain those results. In future work we may integrate additional data from other tools; we could use inventory tools, for instance, to look for deployed security controls.

We found that integrating information from two very different sources, like ITMS tools and Vulnerabilities databases, is not so difficult if we count with standards like structured naming schemes (CPE). However, current implementations do not necessarily use those standards, this is one of the main limitations to completely automate vulnerability searches.

Some experts argue that vulnerability databases, like NVD, are not precise enough. However, their data is result of the work of several experts, it is also public and checked by various interested third parties, and may be updated when required. Thus, we considered these databases as objective sources.

This work may be improved in several ways. We want to analyze threat identification to find the tasks that may be automated in this step. We also need to extend likelihood analysis; we have automated some parts, but we still have manually assigned values. Also, we want to handle different levels of vulnerability awareness as our current proposal only considers vulnerabilities from public databases.

References

1. Anikin, I.: Information security risk assessment and management in computer networks. In: International Siberian Conference on Control and Communications (2015)
2. Anikin, I., Emaletdinova, L.Y.: Information security risk management in computer networks based on fuzzy logic and cost/benefit ratio estimation. In: Proceedings of the 8th International Conference on Security of Information and Networks, SIN 2015, Sochi, Russia, pp. 8–11. ACM (2015). ISBN 978-1-4503-3453-2
3. Center for Internet Security. CIS Controls. https://www.cisecurity.org/controls/

4. MITRE Corporation: CVE Common Vulnerabilities and Exposures (2017). http://cve.mitre.org
5. Ekelhart, A., et al.: Security ontologies: improving quantitative risk analysis. In: 40th Annual Hawaii International Conference on System Sciences, HICSS 2007, p. 156a. IEEE (2007)
6. Eom, J.-H., et al.: Risk assessment method based on business process oriented asset evaluation for information system security. In: Proceedings of the 7th International Conference on Computational Science, ICCS 2007, pp. 1024–1031. Springer, Heidelberg (2007). ISBN 978-3-540-72587-9
7. FIRST Organization: Common Vulnerability Scoring System SIG. https://www.first.org/cvss
8. FIRST Organization: Common Vulnerability Scoring System v3.0 Specification Document. 3.0. FIRST Organization Inc
9. Guan, J.-Z., et al.: Knowledge-based information security risk assessment method. J. China Univ. Posts Telecommun. **20**(3), 60–63 (2013)
10. de Gusmão, A.P.H.: Information security risk analysis model using fuzzy decision theory. Int. J. Inf. Manage. **36**(1), 25–34 (2016)
11. Je, Y.-M., You, Y.-Y., Na, K.-S.: Information security evaluation using multi-attribute threat index. Wireless Pers. Commun. **89**(3), 913–925 (2016)
12. Karabey, B., Baykal, N.: Attack tree based information security risk assessment method integrating enterprise objectives with vulnerabilities. Int. Arab J. Inf. Technol. **10**(3), 297–304 (2013)
13. Khanmohammadi, K., Houmb, S.H.: Business process-based information security risk assessment. In: Fourth International Conference on Network and System Security (2010)
14. Korchenko, O., et al.: Increment order of linguistic variables method in information security risk assessment. In: International Scientific-Practical Conference Problems of Infocommunications Science and Technology (2015)
15. Mell, P., Scarfone, K., Romanosky, S.: A Complete Guide to the Common Vulnerability Scoring System Version 2.0
16. Sajko, M., Hadjine, N., Pesut, D.: Multi-criteria model for evaluation of information security risk assessment methods and tools. In: International Convention on Information and Communication Technology, Electronics and Microelectronics (2010)
17. Salmela, H.: Analysing business losses caused by information systems risk: a business process analysis approach, pp. 180–216 (2016). cited By 0
18. Shameli-Sendi, A., Aghababaei-Barzegar, R., Cheriet, M.: Taxonomy of information security risk assessment (ISRA). Comput. Secur. **57**, 14–30 (2016)
19. Sherwood, J., Clark, A., Lynas, D.: Architecture, Enterprise Security (2009)
20. International Organization for Standardization: ISO 27005. Information Security Risk Management (2011)
21. Symantec. Internet Security Threat Report. Techical report Symantec (2016)
22. The OpenWeb Application Security Project. OWASP Risk Rating Methodology. http://www.owasp.org
23. U.S. National Institute of Standards and Technology - NIST. National Vulnerability Database. http://nvd.nist.gov
24. U.S. National Institute of Standards and Technology - NIST. Official Common Platform Enumeration (CPE). https://nvd.nist.gov/products/cpe
25. U.S. National Institute of Standards and Technology - NIST. SP 800–30. Guide for Conducting Risk Assessments (2012)

Smart-Solar Irrigation System (SMIS) for Sustainable Agriculture

Olusola Abayomi-Alli[1], Modupe Odusami[1], Daniel Ojinaka[1],
Olamilekan Shobayo[1], Sanjay Misra[1(✉)], Robertas Damasevicius[2],
and Rytis Maskeliunas[2]

[1] Department of Electrical and Information Engineering,
Covenant University, Ota, Nigeria
{olusola.abayomi-alli,modupe.odusami,
olamilekan.shobayo,
sanjay.misra}@covenantuniversity.edu.ng
[2] Kanus University of Technology, Kaunas, Lithuania
{robertas.damasevicius,rytis.maskeliunas}@ktu.lt

Abstract. This study seeks to develop an automated solar-powered irrigation system. This will provide a cost-effective solution to the traditional irrigation method. This project is aimed at designing a system that harnesses solar energy for smart irrigation and allows for more efficient way to conserve water on the farmland. The system developed is portable and is designed to be adaptable to existing water system. The system incorporates wireless communication technology established using NRF module. For easy operations, the system can be controlled via an Android app-enabled with Bluetooth network. The user experience allows selection of either manual control for scheduled irrigation or automatic control using wireless sensors.

1 Introduction

Agriculture is the foundation of Africa's economy and the major source of food in any nation, therefore, improving this sector plays a crucial role in building sustainable systems and growing any economy. Around 70% of Africans are rural dwellers and are mostly of the poor populace which depends majorly on agribusiness to maintain sustainability and employment. Agribusiness is the principal wellspring for sustenance for 60–70% of the populace in sub-Sahara Africa. This sector is confronted with several difficulties making it hard to meet its main role of nourishing the country [1].

The increasing growth of the global population with over 7 billion individuals and an estimated increase of 9.6 billion by the year 2050 [2] shows that there is a need to double generation and production within a discreetly brief time. This will be essential in achieving the Sustainable Development Goal (SDG) 1 and 2, "NO POVERTY" and "ZERO HUNGER". There is a need to change the traditional agricultural practice in order to meet the rising demands of food security thus contributing effectively to the reduction of poverty and hunger in the economy.

Recently, 90% of food production in sub-Saharan comes from small-scale farmers, cultivating on an exact piece of the 70% of arable land accessible, depending on rainfall

© Springer Nature Switzerland AG 2018
H. Florez et al. (Eds.): ICAI 2018, CCIS 942, pp. 198–212, 2018.
https://doi.org/10.1007/978-3-030-01535-0_15

as opposed to irrigation [3]. Agriculture practice in Africa is faced with numerous challenges some of which includes:

1. Poor Power Supply to Farms
2. Poor Irrigation, Fertilization and Drainage System
3. Poor Transportation Network
4. Limited access to funds
5. Poor Farm Mechanization

These challenges have made agricultural practice frustrating for the farmer and also contributed to the poor turn-out in large-scale farming. This study, however, focuses on automated irrigation system with a clean and affordable power supply which is a major factor associated with large-scale farming in Africa.

Automating Irrigation system is an intelligent or artificial application of water for effective agriculture and cultivation production. This condition is essential for insufficient rainfall with its focus on supplying satisfactory quantity of water at the right time for improving growth and development of farm produce. In agricultural irrigation, the effects of the applied amount of water, the timing of irrigation and water utilization are particularly important. With the increasing water requirements in irrigation systems, there is a need for an automated water system with scheduling features to save about 80% of the water thus, improving water efficiency and agricultural productivity in general particularly under conditions of water scarcity [4]. The rest of the paper is divided into sections where: Sect. 2 gave a comprehensive description of the literature review and Sect. 3 gave a detailed methodology. The system implementation and testing is discussed in Sect. 4 and the conclusion and future recommendation is summarized in Sect. 5.

2 Literature Review

The major limitations in sustainable agricultural development and advancement in the sub-Saharan include the crude way in farm practices and production, low efficiency and poor technological adaptation. Thus, current headway is the need for a system that makes the agricultural process simpler and stress-free for farmers thereby increasing the annual/seasonal production through creating an agro-driven environment. Several works has been done by researchers globally, in developing a smart irrigation controller system.

2.1 Related Work

Various methodologies have been adapted to implement most of the smart irrigation systems over the years. This technology includes the use of wireless communications, weighing lysimeter technique, SCADA systems for supervisory and Artificial Neural Network (ANN).

2.2 Irrigation System Based on Wireless Communication Technologies

This section describes the various types of wireless communication protocols and its standards that are being adopted in agriculture varying from Zigbee wireless protocol, Bluetooth, Wifi, GPRS, etc. The fast advancement of wireless communication and embedded micro-sensing electromechanical systems (MEMS) technologies has made wireless sensor networks (WSN) possible.

[5] designed an autonomous solar-powered irrigation system using GPRS, Zigbee, and Radio connectivity. The system designed to consist of two major units; the wireless sensor units and the wireless information unit linked together using radio transceivers. The wireless sensor is configured using ZigBee technology and firms the sensors, a microcontroller, and power sources. Several wireless sensors can be utilized in-field to configure a distributed sensor network for the automated irrigation system. [6] presented a soil moisture sensor to estimate the soil volumetric water content. The sensor is based on the soils dielectric constant also known as soil bulk permittivity. In his design, the temperature of the soil was measured using LM35 wrapped-in. The temperature and the soil moisture level measured are read using an Arduino Uno and the analog values are converted appropriately and the result is displayed on the LCD while it is also sent to the control room located few distances away from the farmland sent wirelessly using Bluetooth technology.

[7] proposed an automated wireless watering system which has a user-friendly interface to notify with information regarding the system status. The system was designed to enable the user with the option of operating it manually or automatic and also provides a data history of the activities of the system. [8] proposed a wireless sensor technology to automate the Indian agricultural systems. The proposed system was able to control several data such as Humidity, Soil Moisture, and Soil pH using the wireless sensor nodes which serve as inputs to the Peripheral Interface Controller (PIC). These data are continuously monitored by the controller and a GSM modem was incorporated to send SMS to the farmer. The summary of the cons and pros of wireless communication technology is depicted in Table 1.

Table 1. Pros and cons of a wireless communication technology.

Wireless communication technologies	
Pros	Cons
1. Enables remote monitoring and control by User or farmer	This is a major barrier to implementing IOT enabled irrigation because it tends to increase the cost by acquiring internet services
2. Enables collecting, storing and sharing of data through web servers for agricultural improvements	
3. Mobile Application and GSM communication are easily integrated with the system and enable instant notification of system operations	

2.3 Irrigation System Based on Weighing Lysimeter Technique

A lysimeter is a device used in agronomy to measure the volume of incoming water (rainfall and irrigation) and water coming out (drainage, evapotranspiration) of a container containing an isolated mass of soil [9]. [9] designed an irrigation system based on a weighing lysimeter for potted plants. The system consist of a triangular platform that supports the pot rests on three load cells located at their vertices and are used to measure the weight. In order to measure the irrigation water, a high-precision low-range flow meter was required. [4] developed a prototype smart watering system for small potted plants. The system consists of a microcontroller (ATmega328), moisture and temperature sensors, water pump and the servo engine. The pros and cons of the lysimeter techniques are represented in Table 2.

Table 2. Pros and Cons of weighing Lysimeter technique.

Weighing Lysimeter	
Pros	Cons
1. Accurate crop evapotranspiration data is gathered	Complex and not cost effective
2. Efficient in irrigation timing and drainage use	Limited to potted crops only and requires a lot of precision
	Implementation on large scale farming is difficult

2.4 Irrigation System Based on SCADA Software

Supervisory Control and Data Acquisition (SCADA) is a PC framework for the gathering and examination of real-time information [10]. This utilizes a focal framework that examines and controls the entire configuration of other systems, which is stretched over distances of long range. [10] developed and implemented a solar-powered irrigation system using SCADA software. The parameters used are the soil moisture condition, suns position, water level condition, etc. The pros and cons are listed in Table 3.

Table 3. Pros and Cons of SCADA softwares.

SCADA	
Pros	Cons
1. SCADA systems are good software's for supervision and monitoring and processes real-time data	SCADA systems are expensive and difficult to implement on a small scale farms

2.5 Irrigation System Based on Artificial Neural Network

Recently, "Machine to Machine (M2 M) and ANN" communications is getting more attention, the capacity of information transfer among gadgets to servers or Cloud through core networks enables ANN systems to learn fast. ANN control systems can be utilized to accomplish the definitive point of water management on farmland [11]. [12] proposed the application of ANN controllers using MATLAB for irrigation purposes. The parameter used in the proposed study is based on natural temperature and water content in the soil. The experiment was demonstrated using environmental conditions, evapotranspiration and the kind of crop. However, the measure of water required for the water system is assessed and related outcomes were evaluated. [13] developed an intelligent IOT based Automated Irrigation system where sensor information relating to soil dampness and temperature gathered and likewise, kNN arrangement machine learning calculation sent for analyzing the sensor information for expectation towards flooding the soil with water. This is a completely automated with devices communicating with the other and apply the intelligence in irrigation. This has been created utilizing minimal cost embedded systems like Arduino Uno, Raspberry Pi3.

Considering the existing work on automating irrigation system there are needs for a more enhance Agric-support system with efficient power, cost-effective and functional system in rural areas and beyond. Table 4 shows the overview of related study based on automatic irrigation system.

3   Design Methodology

This section gives a detailed description of the proposed system design and its specification. Considering the cost of manpower, cost of powering a pumping machine, and cost of effectively monitoring of an irrigation process within a large expanse of farmland, there is a need for a smart irrigation system. The Solar Smart Irrigation System (SMIS) is designed to specific requirements. These requirements are categorized as follows;

1. Hardware requirements
2. Software requirements

3.1   Hardware Requirement

This stage is divided into two main parts namely the central control unit and the sensor units. The central control unit act as the brain of the entire system and its major role is to coordinate and manage the activities of the different parts of the system which include the solar panel, battery, microcontroller (ATmega328), solenoid valve and the float channels. While the sensory units consist of the soil moisture sensor for gathering data about the soil moisture content and send feedback to the central control unit automatically. Wireless communication was established between the central control unit and the sensory part using near radio frequency (NRF4L). Each of the sensor unit and the central control unit is designed to have an independent solar power supply built with the system. The block diagram of the system is shown in Fig. 1.

Table 4. Overview of related works.

Author	Power			Micro-contoller			GSM	GPRS	SCADA	Webserver	Operation mode		Sensor types			
	AC	DC	Solar DC	Arduino	Other	Zigbee					Automatic	Manual	Moisture sensors	Humidity sensor	PH sensors	Temperature sensors
[14]	*			*						*	*		*	*		*
[15]		*	*		*					*	*	*	*		*	*
[4]		*		*				*			*		*			*
[10]			*		*						*		*			
[16]	*		*		*		*	*			*	*	*			*
[17]			*	*	*		*		*		*		*			
[18]			*								*		*			
[19]		*		*	*					*	*		*			
[20]			*	*						*	*		*			
[21]		*			*	*				*	*					
[9]				*							*		*			
[6]	*	*		*							*		*			*

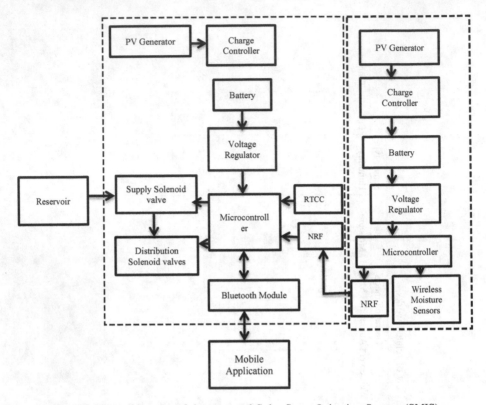

Fig. 1. The architecture of the proposed Solar Smart Irrigation System (SMIS)

In a bid to design a portable and compact irrigation system, the design of the water flow was considered to be built and housed within the main controller. The flow of water is channeled from the reservoir or storage tank to the inlet of the controller where the actuators are placed. This system is designed to have two outlets for each sensory unit as shown in Fig. 2.

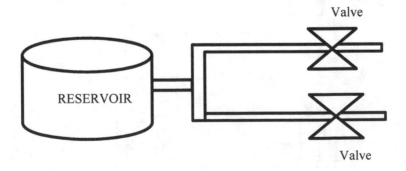

Fig. 2. Schematics Piping Channels of the proposed system

3.2   Software Requirement

The SMIS was designed to enable the user operates the system manually from a control room using Bluetooth technology. The mobile application is built to function on Android Operating System. The choice of Bluetooth network as a communication link between the mobile application and the hardware device is based on the power consumption, cheaper and less complexity when compared with ZigBee or Wi-Fi technology. The flexibility of the proposed system allows users to decide the mode of the system operation and it, however, allows interoperability of mode operations from automatic or manual. The flowchart diagram for the proposed SMIS system is depicted in Fig. 3 and the algorithm for the mobile application is shown in Algorithm 1.

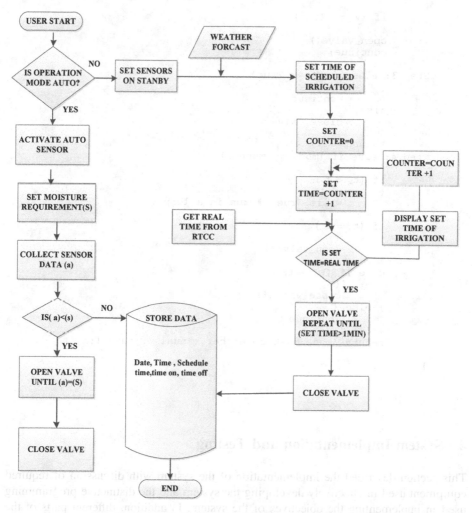

Fig. 3. The flow diagram for the Proposed SMIS system

Algorithm 1. Algorithm for the Mobile Application

```
    Input { procedure (mode): auto, manual sensor data 'data', soil
moisture threshold       s, current time t_c, time on t_o, set time t_s}
Output: {open valve V_o, closed valve V_c }
Start
    Step 1: if (mode == auto)
    {
            activate_sensory_unit()
            while True: # run in a loop
            data = sensor_data();
    Step 2: if (data < s)
    {
            if (V_c == True)
            {
            open_valve()
            continue;
            }
    Step 3: else if (V_o == True)
            {
                    continue
            else{
                    close_valve
                    }
            }
    Step 4: else if (mode == manual)
            {
            if (t_o== t_s)
            {
                    while True: # run in a loop
            }
            if (t_c== t_o)
            {
                    open_valve()
            }
            else if (tC > tS)
                    {
                    close_valve()
            } else {
                    Continue
            }else {
            return 'mode must be either manual or auto !!'
            }
    }
End;
```

4   System Implementation and Testing

This section described the implementation of the system with discussion of required equipment used in effectively developing the system and the distinctive programming used in implementing the objectives of the system. In addition, different parts of the system were examined and tested in order to ensure that the proposed system plays up to its required capacity.

4.1 Hardware Implementation

The hardware implementation consists of the following engineering practical steps which include the circuit Boarding Process, PCB Design, Soldering of Components, and Packaging.

Circuit Boarding Process: The control unit and the sensing unit were simulated on a bread board to ascertain the workability of all components before the system is completed. During the course of bread boarding, copper jumper cables were us to establish connections between components and the Arduino microcontroller. The soil moisture sensor connected to the wireless transmission link was also simulated. 5 V power supply from the USB was used in the simulation process.

PCB Design: Printed Circuit Board (PCB) is cards made for connecting modern electronics components together. It represents the electrical schematics in the physical implementation. However when partitioning the PCB layout, the component positioning is very important. Components are grouped into logical functional blocks. The PCB layout of this system was properly designed using Proteus software.

Soldering of Components: After the boarding process is completed and the PCB design is ready, the components were placed on the PCB pad and soldered on the traces to establish a permanent connection as shown in Fig. 4.

Packaging: The Control Unit part of the system was packaged using plastic casing with the solar panel mounted on it. In packaging the system some design consideration was taking into account to ensure smooth operation of the system. The solar panel was properly positioned on the top layer of the casing. The inlet and outlet piping system were properly sealed and aligned to avoid water leakage. The sensory unit was packaged in a plastic casing fitted with a cylindrical pipe to enable the soil moisture sensor to penetrate the soil as depicted in Fig. 5. The Figs. 6 and 7 shows the snapshot of control unit and the sensory unit.

Fig. 4. The soldered components of the control unit

Fig. 5. The packaging of the Control Unit

Fig. 6. The Control Unit   **Fig. 7.** The Sensory Unit

4.2   SMIS Mobile Application Implementation

The Android mobile application was developed using React Native. React Native is a JavaScript framework for building native mobile applications. It allows for large amounts of inbuilt components like camera, GPS, and APIs. React Native has the native ability just like normal Android Java, Native Mobile and is faster.

Other JavaScript packages are used to implement this project together with React Native. These are a subset of libraries that enables some special features. For the implementation of the Bluetooth communication, react native – Ble-Plx was deployed. Geo Location API is deployed to get to the location of the system. Open Weather API was also deployed to get the real-time weather of the location. Figure 8 shows the screenshot of the SMIS mobile application.

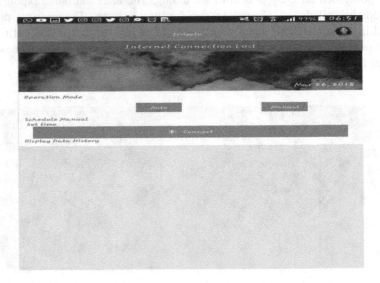

Fig. 8. Screenshot of SMIS mobile application

4.3   Testing

In this section, different tests were conducted to monitor and verify the operations and performance of the developed system. The key tests conducted in this project are:

1. Unit Testing
2. Integration Testing
3. System Testing

Unit Testing: The system developed consists of different components and two (2) major subsystem which was coupled together to obtain the whole system. Tests on units independent of one another were carried out such as the resistance and capacitance values before circuit connections. The solar panel was tested in order to ensure that it provides the necessary voltage and current supply when it is connected to charge the battery. The transistors, capacitors, and resistors were also tested in order to ensure that they were functioning properly. The NRF and Bluetooth module were individually tested to ensure functionality and connection from varying range. The power supply unit of each subsystem consists of 5 V solar panel connected to charge the storage battery of 3.7 V. The test was carried out using millimeters to take the readings of the solar panel and the battery to ascertain how much voltage is stored and how long it takes to be fully charged. The control unit consists of the microcontroller, solenoid valve, the Bluetooth module and the NRF receiver for communication with the sensor unit. The sensory unit consists of the soil moisture sensor and the NRF transmitter. Each unit was tested to ensure compatibility and functionality within the subsystem.

Integration Testing: The interaction between separate subsystems of the project was evaluated using the integration testing including the user application software. Table 5 shows the various voltage levels obtained at different outputs of the system. The expected values obtained during the system design and the practical values obtained during the implementation of the project are also compared.

Table 5. Test results of the system power efficiency.

S/N	Outputs/Inputs	Expected values	Practical values
1	Battery Output at full charge	7.4 V	7.8 V
2	Input at the Solenoid Valve	3.3 V	3.8 V
3	Input at microcontroller	5 V	5 V
4	Input at NRF module	3.3 V	3.5 V
5	Input at Bluetooth module	3.3 V	3.6 V

System Testing: The full operation of the system was tested from the user's experience using the mobile application developed for control of the systems full operation. The complete system was tested for correct operation by applying the system to irrigate different soil samples. Figure 9, shows the amount of time the system took to irrigate different soil samples in different initial states.

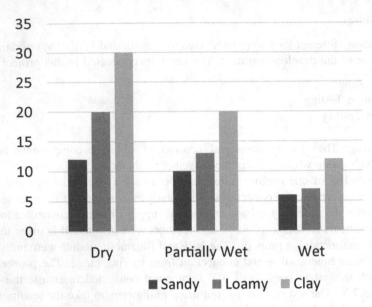

Fig. 9. Graph of irrigation time against soil samples.

The result from Fig. 9 shows the time taken for the different soil sample in a one-square meter container to get irrigated in the three (3) initial states. It can be deduced from the graph that the system was able to irrigate a effectively a dry soil, sample for the soil type: sandy soil, loamy and clay soil at 12 s, 20 s and 30 s respectively. While irrigating a partial wet soil for sandy, loamy and clay gave a 10 s, 13 s, and 20 s respectively. The time taken to irrigate a wet soil sample for sandy, loamy and clay are 6 s, 7 s, and 12 s respectively.

5 Conclusion

The climatic changes in sub-Sahara Africa nations has made sustainable agriculture quite challenging due to the harsh sun radiation, scarcity of water which is completely up to individual's water generation. These factors however, have been coined towards the development of a smart solar irrigation system with the aim of addressing the challenges of power consumption and water management for sustainable agriculture in the sub-Sahara Africa. The system incorporates solar panels as its power source which enables the system to work effectively without the need of an AC source. Water management is achieved by the timely operations of the solenoid valve controlled by the microcontroller. The experimental result shows effectiveness of the proposed system with the practical values being so close to the expected result. In conclusion, the efficiency of the system guarantees that only the right amount of water need is supplied to the farmland and it can operate both automatically and manually for scheduled irrigation. Further study is to enhance the system over the internet using advanced mobile application.

References

1. Nwaiwu, I.U.O., Ohajianya, D.O., Orebiyi, J.S., Eze, C.C., Ibekwe, U.C.: Determinants of agricultural sustainability in Southeast Nigeria - the climate change Debacle. Glob. J. Agric. Res. **I**, 1–13 (2013)
2. Katariya, S.S.: Automation in agriculture. Int. J. Recent. Sci. Res. **6**(6), 4453–4456 (2015)
3. Ezekiel, A.A., Olarinde, L.O., Ojedokun, I.K., Adeleke, O.A., Ogunniyi, L.T.: Effect of irrigation and drought on agricultural productivity in Kwara State, Nigeria. Advances Agric. Botanics **4**(1), 6–9 (2012)
4. Darshna, S., Sangavi, T., Mohan, S., Soundharya, A., Desikan, S.: Smart irrigation system. IOSR J. Electron. Commun. Eng. **10**(3), 32–36 (2015)
5. Gutiérrez, J., Villa-Medina, F.J., Nieto-Garibay, A., Porta-Gándara, M.Á.: Automated irrigation system using a wireless sensor network and GPRS Module. IEEE Trans. Instrum. Meas. **63**(1), 0018–9456 (2014)
6. Ale, D.T., Ogunti, E.O., Daniela, O.: Development of a smart irrigation system. Int. J. Sci. Eng. Investig. **4**(45), 27–30 (2015)
7. Kestikar, C.A., Bhavsar, R.M.: Automated Wireless Watering System (AWWS). Int. J. Appl. Inf. Syst. (IJAIS) **2**(3), 40–46 (2012)
8. Saleemmaleekh, A., Sudhakar, K.N.: Real-time monitoring of agricultural activities using wireless sensor network. Int. J. Sci. Res. (IJSR) **4**(5), 2843–2846 (2015)
9. Jiménez-Carvajal, C., Ruiz-Peñalver, L., Vera-Repullo, J.A., Jiménez-Buendía, M., Antolino-Merino, A., Molina-Martínez, J.M.: Weighing lysimetric system for the determination of the water balance during irrigation in potted plants. Agric. Water Manag. **183**, 78–85 (2016)
10. Abdelkarim, A.I., Sami Eusuf, M.M.R., Salami, M.J.E., Aibinu, A.M., Eusuf, M.A.: Development of solar powered irrigation system. In: 5th International Conference on Mechatronics (ICOM 2013) (2013)
11. Prisilla, L., Rooban, P., Arockiam, L.: A novel method for water irrigation system for paddy fields using ANN. IJCSN **1**(2), 1–5 (2012)
12. Umair, S.M., Usman, R.: Automation of irrigation system using ANN based controller. Int. J. Electr. Comput. Sci. **10**(2), 41–47 (2010)
13. Shekhar, Y., Dagur, E., Mishra, S.: Intelligent IoT based automated irrigation system. Int. J. Appl. Eng. Res. **12**(18), 7306–7320 (2017)
14. Parameswaran, G., Sivaprasath, K.: Arduino based smart drip irrigation system using Internet of Things. Int. J. Eng. Sci. Comput. **VI**(5), 5518–5522 (2016)
15. Gupta, A., Krishna, V., Gupta, S., Aggarwal, J.: Android-based solar powered automatic irrigation system. Indian J. Sci. Technol. **IX**(47), 0974–6846 (2016)
16. Uddin, J., Taslim Reza, S.M., Newaz, Q., Uddin, J., Islam, T., Kim, J-M.: Automated irrigation system using solar power. In: 7th International Conference on Electrical and Computer Engineering, Dhaka, Bangladesh (2012)
17. Kansara, K., Zaveri, V., Shah, S., Delwadkar, S., Jani, K.: Sensor-based automated irrigation system with IOT: a technical review. Int. J. Comput. Sci. Inf. Technol. **VI**(6), 5331–5333 (2015)
18. Poyen, E.F., Dutta, B., Manna, S., Pal, A., Ghosh, A.K., Bandhopadhyay, R.: Automated irrigation with sun tracking solar cell and moisture sensor. In: International Conference on Innovative Engineering Technologies (ICIET 2014), Bangkok (Thailand) (2014)
19. Geoffrey, G., de Dieu, M.J., Pierre, N.J.: Design of automatic irrigation system for small farmers in Rwanda. Agric. Sci. **6**, 291–294 (2015)

20. Nagarajapandian, M., Ram Prasanth, U., Selva Kumar, S., Tamil Selvan, S.: Automatic irrigation system on sensing soil moisture content. Int. J. Innov. Res. Electr. Electron. Instrum. Control. Eng. **3**(1), 96–98 (2015)
21. Kabalci, Y., Kabalci, E., Canbaz, R., Calpbinici, A.: Design and implementation of a solar plant and irrigation system with remote monitoring and remote control infrastructures. Sol. Energy **139**, 506–517 (2016)

Learning Management Systems

Applying the Flipped Classroom Model Using a VLE for Foreign Languages Learning

Oscar Mendez and Hector Florez(✉) (iD)

Universidad Distrital Francisco Jose de Caldas, Bogotá, Colombia
oscfrayle@gmail.com, haflorezf@udistrital.edu.co

Abstract. Currently, there are different trends in terms of education. Some of these trends require the support of information technologies. For example, since some years ago, the flipped classroom educational model has been presented, which is a strategy that reverses the traditional learning model through instructional content developed by students. Flipped classroom is directly related to blended learning, which is a methodology that combines the traditional classroom learning environment with the use of online digital material. Moreover, blended learning requires both students and teachers, who communicate in presence and virtual manners. This paper presents a Virtual Learning Environment (VLE) as a technological tool for the development of learning activities and language teaching with the flipped classroom model in the blended learning education program. This VLE allows highlighting the importance of monitoring and feedback to the student from the collected data. Likewise, the VLE allows highlighting the importance of the teacher as the main actor behind the operation of the software. Finally, the VLE articulates the methodological proposal allowing the virtual work and the classroom class.

Keywords: Flipped classroom · Blended learning
Virtual Learning Environment (VLE)
Educational performance indicators

1 Introduction

The incorporation of Information and Communication Technologies (ICT) in classrooms highlights the need for a new definition of roles, especially for students and professors [14]. The inclusion of new instruments and technologies in the classroom suggests a new way to develop processes that foster students autonomy as well as propose a transformation of traditional classroom to diversification, extension, and integration of physical and virtual environments. In addition, it promotes the development and use of emerging teaching models such as flipped classroom [11].

© Springer Nature Switzerland AG 2018
H. Florez et al. (Eds.): ICAI 2018, CCIS 942, pp. 215–227, 2018.
https://doi.org/10.1007/978-3-030-01535-0_16

Several auto regulatory processes by students are focused on time management, physical environments, and activities planning to achieve the expected learning goals [5,9]. Then, these processes become the main problems to tackle in this study. It is important to mention that these processes differ from the ideal conditions for applying information technologies in learning and teaching processes.

Regardless of the educational model, learning is the result of student activities. Thus, the professor's role is focused on generating the conditions that increase the probabilities of obtaining a desired performance [8]. Then, the development of a Virtual Learning Environment (VLE) becomes very important because it focuses on generating the necessary conditions to facilitate the development of student activities, facilitating permanent monitoring and feedback of activities outside the physical classroom by professors.

Likewise, it is important to understand that ICTs constitute new conversations, aesthetics, narratives, and relational links between all participants in learning and teaching processes [13]. For this reason, in this paper, we present a VLE as the techno-pedagogical materialization in a process of learning-teaching for languages, based on ICT and supported by the flipped classroom model.

The paper is structured as follows. Section 2 presents the designed pedagogical model. Section 3 presents the proposed Virtual Learning Environment approach based on the designed pedagogical model. Section 4 illustrates the results of the work. Finally, Sect. 5 concludes the paper.

2   Pedagogical Model

The pedagogical model has been designed for a languages institute; nevertheless, it can be extended to be used in other learning domains. It is focused on the problem-based learning model [4]. The model proposes a work structure, for students interaction based on the flipped classroom model and blended learning education program. In addition, the model is supported by a Virtual Learning Environment (VLE) as technological tool for mediating the teaching-learning activities.

2.1   VLE Structure

The pedagogical model is based on academic courses that attend the following main characteristics [3]:

1. The academic program for learning languages is made up of four academic levels. Each academic level is divided by four academic modules. Each academic module is composed by three units.
2. The academic program has been designed to be completed in twelve months. Each academic level has been designed for three months. Each academic module has been designed for one month. Finally, each unit lasts one week. The distribution of time for the academic program is presented in Fig. 1.

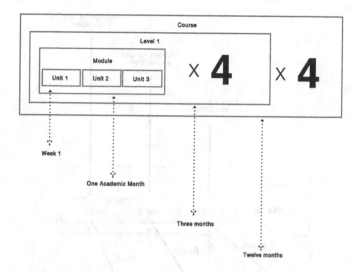

Fig. 1. Time distribution.

3. The workflow for modules and units regarding time defines the agenda structure, which indicates the students' activities that include the students' interactions with the VLE and the classes that the students must attend in physical
   classrooms. Figure 2 presents the course structure, which defines the workflow
   of students and teachers. It is important to highlight that the workflow is
   defined by standards of Flipped classroom model and Bloom Model [14].
4. Since it is a blended learning approach, in the first session students are
   informed about their role and their agenda for using the VLE and for attend-
   ing the classes in the physical classroom.
5. The VLE defines the necessary components for articulating the virtual and
   classes in physical classrooms based on a method that allows doing monitoring, control, and feedback of the students' activities, as well as, the
   direct instructions presented through Virtual Learning Objects (VLO) such
   as classes video simulated. The activities are documented in rubrics, which
   are evaluated by the professors [1].

The method presented in the model of Fig. 3 relates the required components for running this study. This is a bottom up model ans has the following
components.

– **Direct Instruction**. This component is used for the design of videos made
  by professors, since such videos are used by students as framework for each
  topic. With this in mind, students take these videos as guideline for learning
  desired topics.
– **Instructional Design**. This component presents a framework and template
  for developing the elements of the VLE. It also defines how content is distributed and how instructions are defined

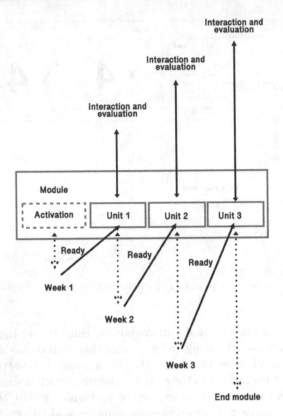

Fig. 2. Course structure.

- **Flipped Learning and Flipped Class.** These components seeks to engage previous components with the components related to the disciplinary area represented by the doted line box in the model. It suggests a framework that adopts other methodologies to develop an integral workflow.
- **Disciplinary Area.** It is the doted line box which proposes decouple the model to the disciplinary area (e.g., *Communicative approach*). It means that the disciplinary area and its corresponding model may be replaced in other projects.
- **Follow Up.** This component allows tracing the virtual and in site work made by students. The VLE includes registries regarding all activities such as: video watching, content reading, platform usage, etc. This trace is base on data such as dates, geographic location, frequency of use, navigation flow, etc.
- **Evaluation.** Based on this component, professors have a tracing binnacle of the in site class. In addition, this component allows planning classes for evaluations students individually and by groups in order to determine the autonomous progress fostering the evolution of the class activities.

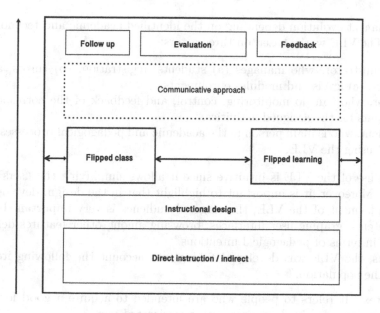

Fig. 3. Method for the VLE.

– **Feedback**. This component is used by professors and students. It is enriched using the VLE data. Based on this, the VLE offers students strategies to go on in the development of activities in order to achieve the academic goals.

3 Proposed VLE Approach

For the technological development, it was very important to inquire conceptually about existing techniques and applications that allow managing courses, modules and units accordingly to the proposed pedagogical design. In this way, Wang et al., [16] offer an holistic perspective regarding blended learning education program aligned to the flipped classroom model. Based on this, we were able to define the necessary technologies to be designed and developed in this work.

It is suitable to highlight that the development of technological tools for application purposes in teaching and learning require a defined contextualization, which implies the characterization of the goals in terms of the disciplinary area in the social context in which the teaching-learning activities are developed.

As a result, the VLE is a software application developed in Django[1], MySQL[2], MongoDB[3], and Angular[4], which is executed in the cloud computing [10]. It is important to mention that this is still in progress; then, all components are

---

[1] https://www.djangoproject.com/.
[2] https://www.mysql.com/.
[3] https://www.mongodb.com/.
[4] https://angular.io/.

in permanent evolution depending on the identified academic and technological needs. The VLE works based on three actors:

1. Administrator, who manages (a) students' registration, (b) tutors' assignments, (c) levels and modules enrollments.
2. Tutor, who can do monitoring, control, and feedback of the corresponding students for the assigned activities.
3. Student, who is main person in the academic and pedagogical processes developed using the VLE.

The use of the VLE is intuitive since it allows simplifying the users' interactions. Moreover, it is important to highlight that in the design, development, and deployment of the VLE, the targeted audience is very important because the contents, graphic user interfaces, browsing among other features define he success in terms of pedagogical intentions.

Thus, the VLE was developed taking into account the following items to define the population.

– Context. It refers to people who are intended to acquire a good level of a foreign language in short time with a moderated cost.
– Accessibility. It refers to audience that use to browse internet using mobiles, tablets, laptops, and desktops.
– Geographical location. Since the VLE works based on the flipped classroom and the blended learning education program, people must attend easily the venue of the languages institute.

3.1 Development Process

In the flipped classroom context, it is necessary that the student organizes its time to perform academic activities such as assignments, reviews, as well as, to watch pre-recorded classes, and to access online tutorials. This suggests the decentralization of academic activities allowing students creating their own personal learning environment, where they are able to discover the diversity of tools that technology offers in order to complement their knowledge acquisition processes [15].

For these activities, the VLE provides an agenda module, where proposed activities and contents are distributed over week showing daily progress. Figure 4 presents the VLE agenda highlighting the following items:

1. Assignments highlighted in red
2. Sessions with the tutor highlighted in blue

Once the student knows the content distribution regarding the time, the VLE provides the content organized by courses, where each course is organized by modules and classified by levels. Said contents are sequentially activated based on the progress of the student. Figure 5 presents the academic content organized by modules.

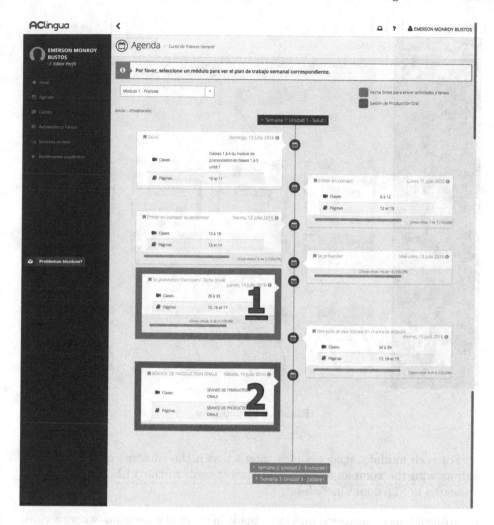

Fig. 4. VLE Agenda.

The agenda module is one of the most important because it allows professors to suggest learning strategies regarding time and space. Also, it gives the opportunity to manage the time that students must invest out of the classroom in order to take advantage of the in site classes making use of the new information learned from the VLE. With this in mind, based on [5], the characteristics of an auto regulated student are the capacity to star several processes such as cognitive, meta-cognitive, affective, and motivational. Nevertheless, [5] suggest that time management and activities planning are the most common problems in this learning method.

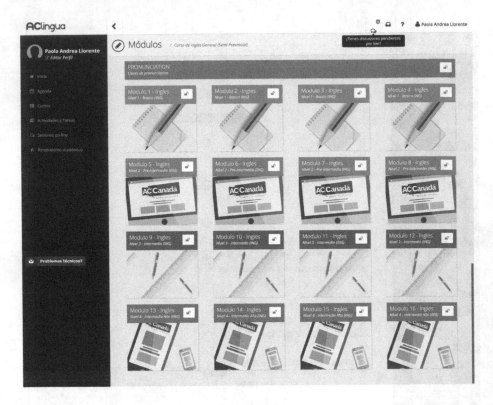

Fig. 5. VLE modules.

For each module, students may interact with the contents of the course as well as with the communications and tracing tools of the VLE. This service is presented in Fig. 6 and includes:

1. Notifications of answered questions made in every class session, where a video is considered a class session [12].
2. Additional content such as pdf documents, audio files, or file to download.
3. Component to browse between modules of the active course. The main contents in the VLE are video classes that allows students to play them several times [12].
4. Presentation of a class session (the VLE includes board and book class sessions) allowing tracing the students interaction with the course contents.
5. Classification by units of the video simulated classes with the corresponding progress stamp, as well as the amount of visualizations done by the student [12].
6. Services menu of the content
7. Component to make questions to tutors or students about the class, in order to simulate some actions or behaviors in the physical classroom.
8. Report of the viewed video classes.

Fig. 6. VLE interaction services.

The VLE allows students to solve questions about proposed topics in real time, storing the information of the activity for posterior analyses by the tutors. For this, a component presented in Fig. 7, which was built based on the framework *Big Blue Button*[5], has the following elements:

1. List of connected student in the online tutorial.
2. Blackboard where the tutor can load presentations or pdf files, as well as write the answers of the corresponding questions.
3. Online chat.

The VLE also includes a component that allows students visualizing the tracking and control activities done by the tutor an the VLE. The main idea is to keep students well informed regarding their activities progress. In addition, it allows tutors to access and observe this information in order to know the students commitment. It helps tutor to prepare contents and strategies for classes in the

---

[5] https://bigbluebutton.org/.

Fig. 7. VLE Online Tutor.

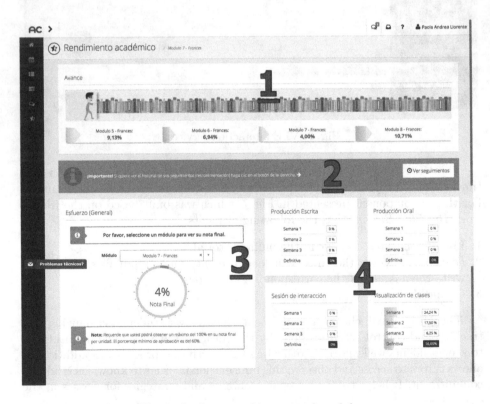

Fig. 8. Students tracking control module.

physical classroom. Figure 8 presents this module. The module has the following parts:

1. Report of the completed modules of the course.
2. Detailed feedback of the activities done by students. This feedback is done by tutors.
3. Historical report of students' academic processes by course and module.
4. Weekly tracking generated while students interact with the VLE through activities such as: submitting homework, watching tutor's videos, chatting with tutors, among others.

This module foregrounds the importance that represents collecting the data of activities done by languages students and tutors through the VLE. This allows making decisions in terms of the impact, pros, and cons focused on the model and its technological components improvement [7].

4   Results

The Common European Framework suggests a minimum time dedication to achieve the necessary skills, when learning a foreign language. Nevertheless, when the learning process is done in a big city, students need to invest a high economic and time cost just moving to the languages academy. It usually impacts directly in the students desertion and low academic performance. In addition, when classes in physical room are 100%, usually there is not detailed tracking of the activities of all students [2].

Based on the explained above, several pedagogic and technological strategies where evaluated in order to strengthen the learning process specifically for languages and to overcome the desertion problem. Then, the VLE based on the blended learning education program and the flipped classroom model allowed reducing the time in the physical classroom and promoting more active students. In addition, the VLE provided tutors technological tools to track the students progress.

The VLE offered student to take the activities in the desired place and time, which also promotes the autonomous work. It is important to highlight that the VLE and the flipped classroom model helped to separate in different environments the superior order skills, which are those skills developed by students in the physical classroom with the inferior order skills, which are those skill developed by students as autonomous work using the VLE.

The tutor is a fundamental part in the development of the academic activity managed by technology. In this way, the tutors team stimulate the pedagogic intention articulating the virtual activities with the activities done in the physical classroom through the flipped classroom model.

Contrasting with other similar studies [6], the role of the technology in this work is fundamental in terms of the motivation and academic performance of students. In addition, the technology allows improving the tutors behavior regarding tracing and comprehension of the activities developed by students out of the physical classroom.

5   Conclusions

The implementation of the VLE posed the question: is it necessary to develop the VLE or is it better using an existing VLE and modifying it?. The answer is based on the experience and background acquired on implementing systems like moodle, chamilo, blackboard, and opendex [1]. Based on this, It is necessary to understand the context in order to know how learning activities are done in order to achieve the pedagogical objectives. This is really important to obtain efficient tools for these tasks. With this in mind, it is necessary to highlight that a pedagogic context not always is focused on just in the existence of students and professors. Academic activity transcends beyond making evident the need of interpreting and integrating the diversity of social contexts as well as the configuration and characterization of components such as managerial, logistics, technological, economical, politics, and cultural that act directly in the academic activity in terms of learning and teaching.

The sum of students' activities defined the scope of the proposed learning goals; thus, the teacher responsibility is oriented to the conditions for getting those activities as ideal as possible [8]. It means, not all existing systems or tools can give a definitive solution to a particular problem. In such cases, it is necessary to create new tools in order to provide solutions that match the developments of the proposed academic activity.

The VLE developed allowed applying properly the flipped classroom learning model because the VLE generated the possibility to built different kinds of contents useful to students in their learning process. Moreover, the blended learning education program was articulated properly to the flipped classroom model through the VLE allowing permanent communication between tutors and in both the virtual and physical contexts.

Based on the VLE, it was possible to make evident the students progress giving as result better language learning processes. Then, as future work, the VLE will be applied in other areas such as basic sciences in order to measure the model in other contexts. In this way, we want to identify the knowledge areas in which this learning model might be applicable.

References

1. Arshavskiy, M.: Instructional Design for ELearning: Essential guide to creating successful eLearning courses. CreateSpace Independent Publishing Platform (2013)
2. Baepler, P., Walker, J., Driessen, M.: It's not about seat time: blending, flipping, and efficiency in active learning classrooms. Comput. Educ. **78**, 227–236 (2014)
3. Basal, A.: The implementation of a flipped classroom in foreign language teaching. Turk. Online J. Distance Educ. **16**(4), 28–37 (2015)
4. Dabbagh, N.: Pedagogical models for e-learning: a theory-based design framework. In: International Journal of Technology in Teaching and Learning (2005)

5. Davis, D., Chen, G., van der Zee, T., Hauff, C., Houben, G.-J.: Retrieval practice and study planning in MOOCs: exploring classroom-based self-regulated learning strategies at scale. In: Verbert, K., Sharples, M., Klobučar, T. (eds.) EC-TEL 2016. LNCS, vol. 9891, pp. 57–71. Springer, Cham (2016). https://doi.org/10.1007/978-3-319-45153-4_5

6. Evseeva, A., Solozhenko, A.: Use of flipped classroom technology in language learning. Procedia - Soc. Behav. Sci. **206**, 205–209 (2015)

7. Hung, H.T.: Flipping the classroom for english language learners to foster active learning. Comput. Assist. Lang. Learn. **28**(1), 81–96 (2015)

8. Joyce, B., Weil, M., Calhoun, E.: Models of Teaching. Georgia Southern University (2003)

9. Kizilcec, R.F., Pérez-Sanagustín, M., Maldonado, J.J.: Self-regulated learning strategies predict learner behavior and goal attainment in massive open online courses. Comput. Educ. **104**, 18–33 (2017)

10. McLaughlin, J.E., et al.: The flipped classroom: a course redesign to foster learning and engagement in a health professions school. Acad. Med. **89**(2), 236–243 (2014)

11. Ozdamli, F., Asiksoy, G.: Flipped classroom approach. World J. Educ. Technol. Curr. Issues **8**(2), 98–105 (2016)

12. Raths, D.: Nine video tips for a better flipped classroom. Educ. Dig. **79**(6), 15 (2014)

13. Severin, E.: Enfoques estratégicos sobre las tics en educación en américa latina y el caribe. Santiago de Chile: Organización de las Naciones Unidas para la Educación la Ciencia y la Cultura (2013)

14. Tourón, J., Santiago, R., Díez, A.: The Flipped Classroom: Cómo convertir la escuela en un espacio de aprendizaje. Grupo Océano (2014)

15. Wallace, A.: Social learning platforms and the flipped classroom. In: Second International Conference on e-Learning and e-Technologies in Education (ICEEE) 2013, pp. 198–200. IEEE (2013)

16. Wang, X.H., Wang, J.P., Wen, F.J., Wang, J., Tao, J.Q.: Exploration and practice of blended teaching model based flipped classroom and SPOC in higher university. J. Educ. Pract. **7**(10), 99–104 (2016)

An Educational Math Game for High School Students in Sub-Saharan Africa

Damilola Oyesiku[1], Adewole Adewumi[1], Sanjay Misra[1(✉)],
Ravin Ahuja[2], Robertas Damasevicius[3], and Rytis Maskeliunas[3]

[1] Covenant University, Ota, Nigeria
{damilola.oyesiku, wole.adewumi,
sanjay.misra}@covenantuniversity.edu.ng
[2] University of Delhi, Delhi, India
[3] Kanus University of Technology, Kaunas, Lithuania
{robertas.damasevicius, rytis.maskeliunas}@ktu.lt

Abstract. The concept of educational games is to aid students in understanding various subjects in an interactive and engaging environment. Subjects like mathematics have continued to pose a challenge to many secondary school students in developing countries like Nigeria as seen from recent low performance in the Senior Secondary Certificate Examination (SSCE). Lack of interest is one of the key factors that contribute to the low performance hence there is need for a system that can help to improve student's interest in mathematics and subsequently their rate of success. The goal of this study is thus to develop an educational game software to help stimulate students' interest in mathematics and to also help them in understanding and improving their performance in the subject. The game was created by leveraging on the Unity game engine platform and the programming language used for development was C#.

Keywords: Education software · High school · Math game
Sub-Saharan Africa

1 Introduction

Research proves that one of the best ways to learn transpires not when students are idly seated and passively listening to a lecture, but when they are engaged in a form of active learning [1]. The educational process these days leverages on constantly changing technology [2, 35]. The most common development in technology that tends to affect education the most are games [3]. Educational games are designed to teach people about different cultures or historical events, increase knowledge on certain subjects [34], strengthen development and promote the learning of a certain skill as they play [4]. For example, games like chess were used to learn and develop strategies of war [5].

Gaming has not only modified the way learning takes place, but it teaches different valuable skills of its own [6]. Today's computer games have attention-grabbing characteristics which challenge the normal traditional learning/educational system [7]. Hence, such games create opportunities for changes that can help to advance the

© Springer Nature Switzerland AG 2018
H. Florez et al. (Eds.): ICAI 2018, CCIS 942, pp. 228–238, 2018.
https://doi.org/10.1007/978-3-030-01535-0_17

educational system [2]. The conventional approach to learning where students sit to receive lectures and tutorials is no longer adequate as it provides a one-way learning environment [8]. These days, students prefer to have a more self-paced learning approach [9]. With the new learning pedagogy and teaching techniques, most universities are beginning to embrace the idea of having a student-centered learning approach [10]. The most suitable tools for this are computer games because they fit in the student-centered learning approach [11]. Computer games are not just for entertainment, they are capable of providing a substantial self-learning environment for students [12]. For instance, in simulation, the gamer or learner is given full control of the gameplay. As a result, it is suitable to apply to the education context. Based on this circumstance, a simulation environment can be created for students to practice particular skills or techniques [12].

In 2002, there were several areas where professors began to make use of computer simulations, such as Physics, Chemistry, Oscillations and Electronics [13]. The idea was to incorporate carrying out virtual experiments based on real experiments on modern personal computers rather than the traditional experiments. These applications helped students to learn and understand the theories behind different chemical reactions and test natural occurrences by introducing different parameters as numbers and variables in a safe environment.

Computer games have also been widely applied in the learning process of the education field due to the increase of computer use in the market [14]. By using computer games as a learning tool, it assists in aiding the students learning and improving understanding. This is because an educational game provides the much-needed interaction context for a student. Students can interact with the game and immediately get feedback or response. Today, most learning centres, ranging from primary school to universities, are fully equipped with the necessary computer facilities, hence this gives reason to think about how to fully utilize them [15]. Using computers as learning and teaching tools is one of the best approaches [12].

Recently, math games, as a specific subdomain of STEM (Science, Technology, Engineering and Mathematics) educational games, have received significant attention from the research community [16]. Although the average man needs some knowledge of mathematics to go about his daily activities, students tend to find the subject quite challenging especially in developing countries like Nigeria. The performance in this subject is quite low especially in the SSCE (Senior Secondary Certificate Examination) and NECO (National Examination Council) written by students in Nigeria. Between the year 2000 and 2011 the average percentage of students that passed this subject (A1–C6) was 40.38% [18, 19]. This means a greater percentage failed the subject which causes them to change from careers that could have benefitted them and the country for the better [17]. Lack of interest is a key factor that contributes to the high failure rate in mathematics hence there is need for a system that can help to improve student's interest in mathematics and subsequently their rate of success [20, 21].

The goal of this study is thus to develop an educational game to help stimulate students' interest in mathematics and to also help them in understanding and improving their performance in the subject. The rest of this study is outlined as follows: Section two reviews existing educational games in order to gather requirements for a new game. In section three, the analysis and design of the proposed mathematics educational gaming system is presented. Section four discusses the system implementation while section five compares the newly developed system to existing ones. Section six concludes the paper with recommendations for further studies.

2 Related Works

The earliest game that was used for educational purposes was developed in 1967 by Seymour Papert and Wally Fuerzeig called 'Logo' [22]. Logo blended mathematics and programming by allowing users to program a mall cursor called a 'turtle', to move and draw lines through series of codes. By 1970, schools began to implement it to teach young students. This section gives a review of existing educational mathematics games. They include; Math Apocalypse, Sudoku, the X detectives, Math millionaire, Ratio stadium and Math apprentice.

Math Apocalypse is a mathematical game that was developed by Esteban Gallardo [23–25]. It is suited for students within the age of 13 and below. This game was designed to help students develop their multiplication, addition, subtraction and division skills. The idea was to use their mathematical skills to fight off an alien invasion by solving the presented problems. It was developed as an online game as well as an android application. In order to play it online, a user would require Adobe flash player. Users are given the opportunity to select the level of difficulty which ranges from 1 to 9 with 1 being the least difficult and 9 being the most difficult.

Sudoku is another math-based game that has been around for many years and was originally called Number Place [26]. It caught on first in Japan, where number puzzles were more dominant. The game comprises of a 9×9 grid with numbers. In order to play the game, the player would rely on the use of logic. Some benefits of the game include the fact that it (i) improves the memory of the player (ii) stimulates the mind (iii) increases the ability to concentrate and (iv) keeps the brain active. This game has been developed on different platforms including the web and on mobile devices.

The X detectives is an online math-based game that teaches students to help a detective solve cases using mathematics [27, 28]. Students navigate through the various buildings using a car controlled by the arrow keys. The student while playing applies some mathematical techniques in solving problems that involve symmetry, translations, rotations, algebraic puzzles, integers and functions as well as graphs while justifying the solutions. The game consists of four buildings; the Gadget Shop, X detective Headquarters, Transformation room, and the Function Factory. The player visits each building and attempts the activities there and once done, more buildings are unlocked to begin assisting Kai the spy guy with his mission to find Agent X.

Math millionaire tests a student's knowledge of mathematics with a series of questions [29]. It follows the same design as the popular game show, 'Who wants to be a Millionaire', but focuses solely on mathematics. It has three lifelines; ask the audience, phone a friend and 50:50. If a player is unsure after using the lifelines s/he can walk away thus ending the game. The game helps reinforce mathematics in an entertaining way. It also captures the attention of students who feel restless or tired. In addition, it helps increase students understanding and memory.

Ratio stadium is a racing game developed by Arcademics, which can be single or multiplayer [30]. It allows students to race each other while matching equivalent ratios. The speed of player's bike is determined by how fast s/he can answer the ratio problems. It teaches students to simplify fractions and identify equivalent ratios.

Math Apprentice is a game that teaches students how mathematics is used in every day careers [31]. It helps students answer the lingering question in mathematics that is 'When will we ever use this in real life?'. In the game students intern at any one of eight different companies in a growing metropolis. An employee greets them and explains the mathematics behind the job then they are presented with specific problems to solve or explore the math concepts on their own. The main aim of this game is to connect mathematics to real world careers and introduce students to more advanced mathematical ideas.

3 Methodology

From the studies reviewed in the previous section, it is clear that math-based games should have a clear focus. In other words, the game should be designed to aid in the understanding some specific mathematical concepts. The games should also target

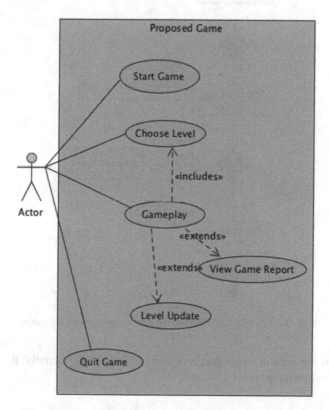

Fig. 1. Use case diagram for proposed math-based game

specific platforms that are readily accessible to the intended audience. The proposed game was modelled using a number of unified modelling language (UML) diagrams. This includes the use case diagram which shows the various interactions of the user with the system; the activity diagram which shows the flow of activities in the game; the class diagram which shows the various entities that make up the game and the interaction between them. Figure 1 depicts the use case diagram which consists of one actor – the player and six use cases namely: gameplay, choose level, level update, start game, quit game and view game report.

Figure 2 shows the activity diagram for the proposed game. From the diagram, when a user starts up the game, s/he can choose the level to start playing based on competence. Once a level is selected, the game will proceed until the player wins or loses. If the player wins, s/he proceeds to the next level otherwise they would have to repeat the level as depicted in the diagram.

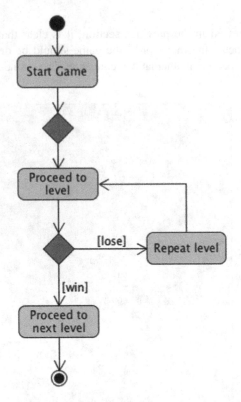

Fig. 2. Activity diagram for the proposed math-based game

Figure 3 is the class diagram that comprises of five entities namely: the main menu, the levels – and pause game.

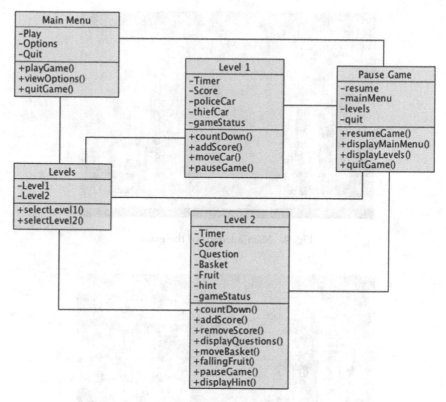

Fig. 3. Class diagram for the proposed math-based game

4   System Implementation

For the development of the game, the Unity game engine platform was leveraged, and the programming language used for development was C#. In this section, the game interfaces are shown and explained in detail.

The first interface that a user comes across when the game is started is depicted in Fig. 4. It shows three options that can be selected by the user. Play option starts the game play. Options allows the user to adjust the game settings such as the level of the difficulty of the game or the level to play while quit ends the game.

Suppose a user selects the Options from Fig. 4, s/he will be taken to the Levels interface which shows the various levels of the game similar to the X detectives game. This is depicted in Fig. 5.

Each level in the game teaches a different concept. However, until the user completes the first two levels s/he cannot proceed to the next levels. In level 1, basic mathematical concepts required to master surds are presented in an interesting scenario. The player is a police officer chasing a bunch of thieves who have just robbed a bank. The objective of the game in this level is to catch the thieves by outrunning them with the police vehicle. To achieve this feat, the player is required to respond to questions

Fig. 4. Main interface of the game

Fig. 5. Levels interface of the proposed game

that pop up from time to time so to increase the acceleration of the police car. If the police car is able to outrun the vehicle used by the robbers before the time elapses, then the player wins the game else s/he may have to try again. Level 1 is depicted in Fig. 6.

Level 2 teaches surds. It is done using a hospital cafeteria setting. The objective of this level is for the user to catch the right fruit that solves the given question. This is based on the six rules of surds. The level begins with an introductory interface where the objective of the level is explained as depicted in Fig. 7.

Once a user clicks proceed, the game begins with the display of a question, the user's score and the countdown timer. Once the timer is up the game ends but if the user catches the right fruits for the question (representing the sequence of steps to solving the question) then they advance to the next question. An explanation on how to proceed is shown when the user presses the hint button as shown in Fig. 8.

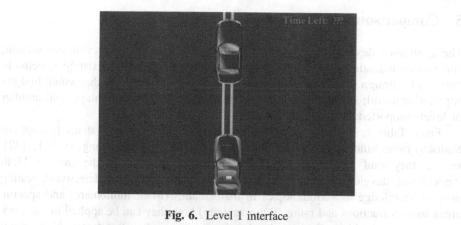

Fig. 6. Level 1 interface

Fig. 7. Level 2 introduction

Fig. 8. Level 2 in progress

5 Comparison and Discussion

The application developed in this study is work in progress. However, in this section, comparison is made between the newly proposed system and the existing systems in terms of the design rationale; deployment platform(s); the age range that would find the application useful; whether or not the application is single or multiplayer and number of levels supported.

From Table 1, it can be observed that most of the existing systems (except for Sudoku) target kindergarten to middle school students in the age range of 5–13 [32]. Hence, they tend to focus on building arithmetic skills as in the case of Math Apocalypse, developing forensic skills through mathematics (X detectives), testing general knowledge of various topics in mathematics (Math millionaire) and specific areas such as fractions and ratios (Ratio stadium) how they can be applied in the work place (Math apprentice). On the other hand, our proposed system targets high school students (14–18 years of age) especially those in sub-Saharan Africa who take part in the SSCE examinations to qualify to advance to institutions of higher learning.

Table 1. Comparison of proposed game with existing games

	Math Apocalypse	Sudoku	X detectives	Math millionaire	Ratio stadium	Math apprentice	Proposed system
Design rationale	Develop arithmetic skills in students	Enhance logical thinking in students	Develop forensic skills using mathematics	Test students' broad knowledge of math	Teaches students to simplify fractions and identify equivalent ratios	Teaches mathematics for the workplace	To stimulate interest in high school maths
Deployment platform(s)	Online, mobile	Online, mobile	Online	Online	Online	Online	mobile
Age range	5–13	All ages	5–13	5–13	5–11	5–13	14–18
Single or Multiplayer	Both	Both	Single	Single	Both	Single	Single
Levels supported	9 levels	N/A	They are unlocked progressively	N/A	N/A	8 levels to be covered	Levels unlocked progressively

Also, unlike the existing games that tend to be deployed as mostly online games, the proposed system is mobile based considering the proliferation of mobile devices among high school students in sub-Saharan Africa [33]. At the moment, the game is single player and the levels are unlocked progressively similar to the X detectives game.

6 Conclusion

Math-based games are still being looked into as a new aid to teaching. In this study the topics focused on are those that most students tend to have issues with. The game is designed to assist students in understanding the basics of these difficult topics. Hopefully with more improvements more steps can be given to the levels and more levels can also be added thereby expanding the range of topics student can learn. The game was developed by leveraging the Unity game engine platform and so can be deployed to a wide range of media including game consoles, the web and of course mobile devices hence its viability. For future work, we intend to carry out empirical studies to compare the performance of students who use the game with those who do not and how it impacts on their performance in secondary school mathematics examinations being taken in Nigeria.

Acknowledgments. We acknowledge the support and sponsorship provided by Covenant University through the Centre for Research, Innovation and Discovery (CUCRID).

References

1. Ellis, R.A.: Qualitatively different university student experiences of inquiry: associations among approaches to inquiry, technologies and perceptions of the learning environment. Act. Learn. High Educ. **17**, 13–23 (2016)
2. Collins, A., Halverson, R.: Rethinking Education in the Age of Technology: The Digital Revolution and Schooling in America. Teachers College Press, New York (2018)
3. Hamari, J., Shernoff, D.J., Rowe, E., Coller, B., Asbell-Clarke, J., Edwards, T.: Challenging games help students learn: an empirical study on engagement, flow and immersion in game-based learning. Comput. Hum. Behav. **54**, 170–179 (2016)
4. Koehler, M.J., Mishra, P.: Introducing TPCK. In: Herring, M.C., Mishra, P., Koehler, M. J. (eds.) Handbook of Technological Pedagogical Content Knowledge (TPCK) for Educators, pp. 13–40. Routledge, New York (2014)
5. Thompson, J.M.: Defining the abstract. Game Puzzle Des. **1**, 83–86 (2015)
6. Kalelioğlu, F.: A new way of teaching programming skills to K-12 students: Code.org. Comput. Hum. Behav. **52**, 200–210 (2015)
7. Özpinar, İ., Gökçe, S., Yenmez, A.A.: Effects of digital storytelling in mathematics instruction on academic achievement and examination of teacher-student opinions on the process. J. Educ. Train. Stud. **5**, 137–149 (2017)
8. Butt, A.: Student views on the use of a flipped classroom approach: evidence from Australia. Bus. Educ. Accredit. **6**, 33 (2014)
9. Kolb, D.A.: Experiential Learning: Experience as the Source of Learning and Development. FT Press, Hertfordshire (2014)
10. Robinson, S., Neergaard, H., Tanggaard, L., Krueger, N.F.: New horizons in entrepreneurship education: from teacher-led to student-centered learning. Educ.+Train. **58**, 661–683 (2016)
11. Hwang, G.J., Chiu, L.Y., Chen, C.H.: A contextual game-based learning approach to improving students' inquiry-based learning performance in social studies courses. Comput. Educ. **81**, 13–25 (2015)
12. Seng, W.Y., Yatim, M.H.M.: Computer game as learning and teaching tool for object oriented programming in higher education institution. Procedia Soc. Behav. Sci. **123**, 215–224 (2014)
13. Dumitrache, A., Almăşan, B.: Educative valences of using educational games in virtual classrooms. Procedia Soc. Behav. Sci. **142**, 769–773 (2014)
14. Hamari, J.: Do badges increase user activity? A field experiment on the effects of gamification. Comput. Hum. Behav. **71**, 469–478 (2017)
15. Korenova, L.: What to use for mathematics in high school: PC, tablet or graphing calculator? Int. J. Tech. Math. Educ. **22**, 59 (2015)

16. Derboven, J., Zaman, B., Geerts, D., De Grooff, D.: Playing educational math games at home: the Monkey Tales case. Entertain. Comput. **16**, 1–14 (2016)
17. Kuku, O.O., Alade, O.M.: Impact of frequency of testing on study habit and achievement in mathematics among secondary school students in Ogun State, Nigeria. J. Educ. Res. Pract. **7**, 1–18 (2017)
18. Kayode, G.M., Ayodele, J.B.: Impacts of teachers' time management on secondary school students' academic performance in Ekiti State, Nigeria. Int. J. Second. Educ. **3**, 1–7 (2015)
19. Yahya, S.A.: Leadership styles, types and students' academic achievement in Nigeria. Doctoral dissertation, Universiti Tun Hussein Onn Malaysia (2015)
20. Wang, J.J., Odic, D., Halberda, J., Feigenson, L.: Changing the precision of preschoolers' approximate number system representations changes their symbolic math performance. J. Exp. Child Psychol. **147**, 82–99 (2016)
21. Rozek, C.S., Svoboda, R.C., Harackiewicz, J.M., Hulleman, C.S., Hyde, J.S.: Utility-value intervention with parents increases students' STEM preparation and career pursuit. Proc. Natl. Acad. Sci. **114**, 909–914 (2017)
22. Kahn, K.: A half-century perspective on Computational Thinking. Tecnologias, Sociedade e Conhecimento **4**, 23–42 (2017)
23. Karaali, G.: Can zombies do math. In: Mind in mathematics, pp. 126–139 (2015)
24. Teixeira, R.: DO THE MATH!: magical data restoration. Math Horizons **24**, 12–14 (2017)
25. de Menconça, J.P.A., Ferreira, L.R.N., Teixeira, L.D.M.D.V., Sato, F.: Modeling our survival in a zombie apocalypse. arXiv preprint arXiv:1802.10443 (2018)
26. Samide, M.J., Wilson, A.M.: Games, games, games; playing to engage with chemistry concepts. Chem. Educ. **19**, 167–170 (2014)
27. Shelton, B.E., Parlin, M.A.: Teaching math to deaf/Hard-of-Hearing (DHH) children using mobile games: outcomes with student and teacher perspectives. Int. J. Mob. Blended Learn. **8**, 1–17 (2016)
28. Shaw, J.M.: The curious transformation of boy to computer. M/C J. **19**, 1–3 (2016)
29. Molino, P., Lops, P., Semeraro, G., de Gemmis, M., Basile, P.: Playing with knowledge: a virtual player for "Who Wants to Be a Millionaire?" that leverages question answering techniques. Artif. Intell. **222**, 157–181 (2015)
30. Kim, G.B.: The Effect of E-Based Virtual Manipulative on Third-Grade Elementary Students' Algebraic Thinking in Math Education. California State University, Long Beach (2017)
31. Turner, P.E., Johnston, E., Kebritchi, M., Evans, S., Heflich, D.A.: Influence of online computer games on the academic achievement of nontraditional undergraduate students. Cogent Educ. **5**, 1437671 (2018)
32. Maher, C.A., Sullivan, P., Gasteiger, H., Lee, S.J.: Topic study group No. 45: knowledge in/for teaching mathematics at primary level. In: Kaiser, G. (ed.) Proceedings of the 13th International Congress on Mathematical Education, pp. 585–587. Springer, Cham (2017). https://doi.org/10.1007/978-3-319-62597-3_72
33. Porter, G., et al.: Mobile Phones and education in Sub-Saharan Africa: from youth practice to public policy. J. Int. Dev. **28**, 22–39 (2016)
34. Omoregbe, N.A., Azeta, A.A., Adewumi, A.O., Omotoso, O.O.: Design and implementation of a yoruba language mobile tutor. In: Proceedings of 6th International Conference on Education and New Learning Technologies, pp. 3942–3947 (2014)
35. Azeta, A.A., Omoregbe, N.A., Misra, S., Adewumi, A., Olokunde, T.O.: Adapted cloudlet for mobile distance learning: design, prototype and evaluation. In: Proceedings of the 7th International Conference on Applications of Digital Information and Web Technologies, pp. 220–228 (2016)

Selecting Attributes for Inclusion
in an Educational Recommender System
Using the Multi-attribute Utility Theory

Munyaradzi Maravanyika and Nomusa Dlodlo[✉]

Namibia University of Science and Technology,
13 Storch Street, Box 13388, Windhoek, Namibia
mmaravanyika@gmail.com, ndlodlo@gmail.com

Abstract. In linear e-Learning management systems, also referred to as
Learning Management Systems (LMS), content is presented to the learners in
the same way irrespective of their different learning styles, educational, social
and historical background, their interests and learning abilities. In education
recommender-based adaptive systems, learning is personalized and differentiated, taking into consideration the students' different attributes. Adaptivity is
automatic adjustment of the content provided to learners to suit their individual
attributes. Personalisation is the ability to provide content and services that are
tailored to individuals based on knowledge about their preferences and behavior.
This research applies pedagogical foundations of teaching and learning in
identifying learner attributes to go into an educational recommender-based
adaptive system. Through a literature review, 40 attributes of personalized/
differentiated learning were identified. A user-centric approach was adopted to
prioritise the attributes in order to identify the 10 top attributes. This was done
by using the Multi-Attribute Utility Theory (MAUT). The 40 attributes of
personalised learning initially fed into questionnaires for students. From a
population of 1203 students from a higher education college called EDU-REC,
for the purpose of this research and to preserve anonymity of the college, a
sample of 200 students was purposively selected for the research on the basis of
their familiarity with the college's eLearning system, and 103 students
responded to the questionnaire representing a response rate of 52%. From the
responses of the students, the following top ten (10) attributes were identified for
inclusion in an educational recommender platform: culture, emotional/mental
state, socialisation, motivation, learning preferences, prior knowledge, educational background, learning/cognitive style, and navigation and learning goals.

1 Introduction

The advances in technology over the last two decades have resulted in tremendous
changes in education in general and distance/online learning in particular. These
changes have been driven by increased use of mobile technologies as well as the
internet in order to enhance learning, a concept that is commonly referred to as
Technology Enhanced Learning (TEL). According to (Goodyear and Retalis 2010),
TEL is using technology to help other people learn. With the use of these technologies

© Springer Nature Switzerland AG 2018
H. Florez et al. (Eds.): ICAI 2018, CCIS 942, pp. 239–252, 2018.
https://doi.org/10.1007/978-3-030-01535-0_18

having gained widespread acceptance in educational circles, the focus has shifted to the affordances that the technologies promise. One such area that is gaining attention from the research community is personalisation or differentiation of teaching and learning and how this may result in improvements in the quality of teaching and learning. The term differentiated/personalised teaching refers to teaching in an e-learning environment that focuses on academic achievement of each individual student, taking into account their educational, historical and social backgrounds while at the same time taking into consideration the learner's interests and learning ability (Prain et al. 2013).

Of particular concern has been the ad-hoc nature in which these technologies have been designed, resulting in the current state of affairs where contradictory results have been reported. This study focuses on what attributes one such technology, an Educational Recommender Systems (ERS) may be designed and implemented for more effective results. A recommender systems is an information filtering system that seeks to predict the preferences a user would give to an item and an adaptive recommender system responds to unexpected changes (Etaati and Sundaram 2014). ERS on the other hand is the adoption of recommender systems to teaching and learning systems (Santos and Boticario 2012).

This research explores the identification of attributes for implementing a differentiated e-learning approach for learners with different learning competencies. The purpose of this research is to identify attributes to go into a framework on education recommender systems using Multi-Attribute Utility Theory (MAUT).

2 Background and Motivation

Instructional materials and/or learning experiences greatly influence how the learning process takes place within different individuals (Pajores 1992). The process of learning can either be delivered through face-to-face contact, standalone computers, or through networked computers that run web-based e-learning systems which can be accessed from any place and at any time. E-learning usually takes place through either a synchronous or an asynchronous mode. Asynchronous e-learning systems enables students to undertake studies at their own time and pace, whereas in synchronous e-Learning systems, all students who are registered for a particular course will access the same e-learning materials at the same time (Hilt and Wellman 1997). Although in asynchronous e-learning systems students are theoretically able to move at their own pace; in practice, the sequencing of the material is done under the assumption that all the learners' levels of understanding and absorption of the learning material will equally be the same (Wirth and Perkins 2005).

It is important to solve personalisation and adaptive teaching and learning problems in LMS. Linear learning platforms (LLP) continue to be developed, thereby exposing learners to the same learning experiences at the same time. For learners engaged in self-study online distance learning, this may result in material being presented at either too high or too low cognitive levels. These linear systems' non-differentiated and non-adaptive approach to e-Learning has been identified as a possible cause for "cognitive disorientation" in e-Learners engaged in self-studying, that is, with minimum support from the instructor. This may result in either frustration or boredom among learners leading to higher drop-out rates and lower achievement of educational outcomes for those students engaged in self-study e-Learning when compared to other modes of distance study.

Adaptivity is defined in Graf and List (2005) as the automatic adjustment of the learning content to suit an individual learner's needs (Graf and List, 2005). In this research, an adaptive framework is a structure that enables an e-learning system to provide content that is at an appropriate cognitive level for each particular learner without compromising on the need to achieve pedagogical goals that are common to all students. Adaptivity may be a single point, that is, results of a diagnostic test are used to determine adaptation, or it may be continuous adaptation, where continuous data mining is used to provide real-time adaptation (Brown et al. 2005). The term differentiated teaching is used to refer to teaching in an e-learning environment that focuses on academic achievement of each individual student, taking into account their educational, historical and social backgrounds while at the same time taking into consideration the learner's interests and learning ability (Gynther 2016). According to (Boticario and Santos 2007), existing adaptive learning management systems have reported modest improvements due to the under-specification of design criteria and the ad-hoc nature of the design process. In addition, in the educational arena, the nature of the models built for recommender systems have given little consideration to educational theory. In particular, the role distance learning theory as well as other behavioural theories that may have an impact on educational recommender systems has not been given prominence by research communities.

This research explores the modelling of attributes for an integrated framework for implementing a differentiated e-learning approach for learners with different learning competencies.

3 Problem Overview

In the process of personalization in e-learning, content and services that are tailored to individuals based on knowledge about their preferences and behaviour. To create more effective personalization services, the system developed should be able to understand not only what people like, but why they like it, which calls for a more sophisticated understanding of the user. However, as things stand, there is still a challenge when it comes to the determination of which user attributes need to be acquired in order to provide effective recommendations. In education, this complexity is more pronounced in that the potential attributes that have to be included in any recommender system are many. This has resulted in educational systems designers being confounded by the available choice, thus calling for a mechanism of evaluating the alternatives that are available.

The characteristics of differentiated teaching and learning, that is, personalisation and the ability to cater for individual differences have the potential to transform the teaching and learning environment. Educational Recommender Systems (ERS) are one of the possible ways personalised content may be made available to learners, while at the same time being able to cater for their differences in attributes such as learning styles and background knowledge among others. ERS, in addition, have the potential to address some of the pedagogical concerns that educators have.

In addition, although recommender-system based adaptive LMS have the potential to cater for individual differences in terms of adapting to individual learners' needs by adapting the learning environment to different contexts of use, offering such a learning experience that meets learners' individual needs in a complex environment such as online distance education is a huge task. Not only do learners exhibit a wide range of individual differences in learning needs, but also, their needs are not static, but are dynamically changing as learners progress with their learning. As such, static profiles or one-time determination of personalisation needs can be grossly inadequate. Therefore the design of recommender-system based adaptive LMS is taking place in an environment of multiple attributes. The application of decision theories such as Multiple Attribute Utility Theory (MAUT) and Multi-Criteria Decision Making (MCDM) to choose the attributes to be modelled by the recommender system is relevant.

In summary, even though the field of recommender-system based adaptive LMS technology promises great potential for the transformation of online distance learning, there are still concerns in achieving effective learning environments when applying these technologies. These challenges include:

(a) Pedagogical challenge, that is, the challenges of understanding and applying sound pedagogical principles in the design of recommender-system-based adaptive LMS for effective learning in online distance environments.
(b) Diversity challenge in term which are in the form of individual differences in learning needs, that is, the wide range of attributes available for the designer to choose from

   • Limited exploration of social dimension of ERS in order provide not only personalized learning but also to provide collaborative support
   • Learner engagement challenge, in that, there is limited learner involvement in the design of adaptive learning systems, which is a crucial component in achieving effective learning

Due to the focus on internal learner context with little focus on instructor context, institutional/national development goals and social context, which promises great potential in enhancing learner engagement in online distance learning has not been explored.

Essentially, there is a need for an efficient approach that will be able to benefit from systems that have are not narrow in scope and are able to accommodate the complexity in modelling student knowledge and understanding. Such an approach should tap into the full potential recommender-based adaptive LMS offer with the aim of satisfying learner needs, is based on sound pedagogical principles and involves the learners and instructors in the design process. The current setup where predominantly linear learning platforms that do not adequately accommodate learners with different backgrounds and abilities thereby exposing learners to the same learning experiences at the same time needs to be revamped. These systems are possibly causing "cognitive disorientation", which has been identified as a factor causing higher drop-out rates and lower achievement of educational outcomes for those students engaged in self-study e-learning when compared to other modes of distance study (Knewton 2015), (Yu et al. 2010).

4 Multi-attribute Decision Analysis Theory

The theory that guides this research is the Multiple Criteria Decision Analysis (MCDA) (Greco 2005). This theory has emerged in the field of Decision Theory as a way of dealing with multidimensional problems. The MCDA provides a way for decision makers to evaluate a varied range of alternatives based on multiple attributes or criteria. MCDA, thus will be useful in this research for evaluating the multiple competing perspectives in order to come up with the features of a recommender system that are derived from research. The MCDA framework enables the viewing of a designer of an Educational Recommender System as decision maker in a Decision Process where several attributes have to be chosen for inclusion in the recommender system under design. MCDA aims at assisting a decision maker in dealing with the difficulties associated with seeking compromise between conflicting interests and goals, and represented by "multiple criteria". The weights of criteria or rather, attributes, have a very important role in the decision making process. Therefore, it is crucial to determine how the weights of the attributes are going to be determined. MAUT is an application of MCDA. Multi-attribute utility function represents the preferences under conditions of uncertainty about results of any potential choice or under conditions of uncertainty (Serin 2013).

5 Research Aims and Objectives

The aim is to determine personalisation criteria for real-time dynamic adoption by applying the MAUT to address the diversity of attribute challenges.

The objectives are:

- Explore the concepts of multi-criteria decision-making (MCDM)/MAUT
- Select and apply an MCDM/MAUT approach to selection of learner attributes for inclusion in the adaptive educational recommender framework

6 Methodology

This research applies pedagogical foundations of teaching and learning when designing educational recommender systems. A case study of a higher education institution called ED-RECOM for the purposes of this research. The research paradigm is interpretive. The methodology is qualitative. The guiding theory is MAUT.

Through a literature review, 40 attributes of personalized learning were identified. A user-centric approach was adopted to prioritise the attributes in order to identify the 10 top attributes to go in as personalized learning framework components. This was done by using the MAUT. The 40 attributes of personalised learning initially fed into questionnaires for students and lecturers. From a population of 1203 students from the college called EDU-REC, a sample of 200 students was purposively selected for the research on the basis of their familiarity with the college's eLearning system, 103 students responded to the questionnaire representing a response rate of 52%. From the responses of the students, the following top ten (10) attributes were identified for inclusion in the platform: culture, emotional/mental state, socialisation, motivation, learning preferences, prior knowledge, educational background, learning/cognitive style, and navigation and learning goals.

7 Results and Discussions

The evaluation tool used in this research for both lecturers and students considered a number of factors that can be classified under effectively engaging students, effective assessment practices, effective management of workload, building an effective knowledge and skills gradient, create an effective design and production process, make study experience seamless, create an effective induction, enhance students' social integration, enhance students' academic integration.

In the questionnaire, the learners and lecturers had to rate the factors that had been identified from literature on a scale of 1 to 7. A score of 1 indicates that the learners were of the opinion that EDU-REC was not doing very well in this aspect while a rating of 7 indicates that EDU-REC is doing well. The factors were then clustered. Cluster 1 represented an aggregate of factors 1–3, where the students felt the need to provide more services on the LMS. Cluster 2 was for the factor 4, which represented neutral. Cluster 3 represented an aggregate of factors 5–7, where the students were satisfied with the services received on the LMS. For the purpose of inclusion of a factor into the top 10, it must have been rated lowly, that is, the aggregate of ratings 1, 2 and 3. A rating of 4 is regarded as a neutral rating, meaning that the learners are undecided. On the other hand, aggregate of factors 5, 6 and 7 indicates that the learners are satisfied with the service offered within the EDU-REC's LMS. Therefore, these the factors will not be considered in the final framework. To select an attribute cluster 1 is compared against cluster 3 totals. If cluster 1 is greater than cluster 3, then that factor is included in the list.

The simple ranking method described above has some shortcomings in that outliers can influence the outcome of the rank. As a result, in order to improve the selection of factors, the Rank Order Centroid (ROC) technique in the MUAT was employed. ROC penalises the undesirable elements and gives more weight to the desirable elements. According to (Roberts and Goodwin 2002), ROC is given by:

$$w_i(ROC) = 1/n \sum_{j=1}^{n} 1/j, \ i = 1, \ldots, n$$

ROC weights are given in the Table 1 below:
In our case, our rank was from 1 up to 7 hence the following weights were used:

Table 1. ROC weights

Rank	Weight
1	0.3704
2	0.2276
3	0.1561
4	0.1085
5	0.0728
6	0.0442
7	0.0204

The only condition for ROC is that the total weight is one. All factors ranked 1 are multiplied by 0.3704. From the opinion of one factor, for instance, you add the weights per individual who ranked that factor. For example, if factor Rank 1 had 16 respondents. This is multiplied by 0.3704 to gives 5.9264. Rank 2 had 11 respondents, giving an aggregate value of 2.5036, etc. The total for factor 1 was determined to be 14.6829. Finally, the totals for all the factors are arranged in numerical order from highest to lowest. Using this method, the top 10 highest factors are chosen to be modelled in the proposed framework. In selecting the factors, the following criteria is used (Table 2).

Table 2. Rank aggregates

Rank aggregate	Meaning
1–3	Not satisfied with current LMS
4	Neutral
5–7	Satisfied with current LMS

The results of the analyses are as follows:

Factor 1: Consider my Learning/Cognitive Style in e-Learning Design

For consideration of the students' learning/cognitive styles in e-learning design, 15.5% ranked it 1, 10.7% ranked it 2, 12.6% ranked it 3, 21.4% ranked it 4, 14.6% ranked it 5, 8.7% ranked it 6 and 16.5% ranked it 7. This means 39.8% were not satisfied (ranking 1–3), 21.4% were neutral (ranking of 4) and 38.8% were satisfied (ranking of 5–7). Rank 4, which represents a neutral sentiment, is the highest. This may possibly be attributed to lack of awareness among learners about what cognitive/learning style represents. 16.5% in Rank 7 represents the percentage of learners who are of the opinion that their learning styles are being met within the current LMS at EDU-REC. The percentage of respondents who are satisfied (39.8%) is evenly balanced with the percentage of respondents who are dissatisfied (38.8%). Such a scenario may be attributed to the diversity of implementation of e-learning by lecturers, with some lecturers making use of advanced LMS features while others may be at the preliminary level of implementation where they only use the LMS as an information repository, to store content and course outlines.

Factor 2: Consider my Culture in e-Learning Design

For consideration of the student's culture in e-learning design, 30.1% ranked it 1, 18.4% ranked it 2, 15.5% ranked it 3, 14.6% ranked it 4, 9.7% ranked it 5, 9.6% gave ranked it 6 and 1.7% ranked it 7. This means 64.0% were not satisfied (ranking 1–3), 14.6% were neutral (ranking of 4) and 21.4% were satisfied (ranking of 5–7). Some of the attributes of culture include language and the actual teaching and learning content. The high number of respondents who feel that the current LMS is not meeting their cultural needs may be attributed to recommended textbook content such as case studies, etc. that is put on e-learning platform without being customised to take into account the local context. The figure for neutral is 14.6% while 21.4% are satisfied with the cultural component, possibly because of a closer alignment of their culture with the English language used in teaching and learning.

Factor 3: Consider my Emotional and Mental State

For consideration of the student's emotional and mental state in e-learning design, 33.1% ranked it 1, 12.6% ranked it 2, 12.6% ranked it 3, 17.5% ranked it 4, 10.7% ranked it 5, 7.8% ranked it 6 and 4.9% ranked it 7. This means 58.5% were not satisfied (ranking 1–3), 17.5% were neutral (ranking of 4) and 23.5% were satisfied (ranking of 5–7). The current predominant feeling is that the respondents' emotional and mental state is not being adequately addressed by the LMS. This could possibly be attributed to a number of respondents feeling that the e-learning environment is de-personalised or possibly that there is little affective support. The respondents were transitioning from high school and this could prove to be a challenge for some learners.

Factor 4: Consider my Intrinsic and Extrinsic Motivation

For consideration of the student's intrinsic and extrinsic motivation in e-learning design, 14.6% ranked it 1, 17.5% ranked it 2, 16.5% ranked it 3, 17.5% ranked it 4, 12.6% ranked it 5, 12.6% ranked it 6 and 7.8% ranked it 7. This means 48.6% were not satisfied (ranking 1–3), 17.5% were neutral (ranking of 4) and 33.5% were satisfied (ranking of 5–7). Intrinsic motivation is a type of motivation that comes from within internal factors of an individual while extrinsic motivation comes from external sources. Examples of extrinsic motivation include support structures from the lecturer as well as student centred methodologies that focus on teaching learners how to learn. 48.5% of the learners feel that more needs to be done in terms of motivating learners on the e-learning platform. 33% are of the opinion that the motivation levels within the EDU-REC's e-learning platform are appropriate. The majority of the students are transitioning from high school to tertiary education. This may require the creation of a support buffer in e-learning before they are allowed to be on their own.

Factor 5: Consider my Prior-Knowledge, Aptitude and Educational Background

For consideration of the student's prior knowledge, aptitude and educational background in e-learning design, 18.4% ranked it 1, 10.7% ranked it 2, 13.6% ranked it 3, 14.6% ranked it 4, 8.7% ranked it 5, 13.6% ranked it and 20.4% ranked it 7. This means 42.7% were not satisfied (ranking 1–3), 14.6% were neutral (ranking of 4) and

42.7% were satisfied (ranking of 5–7). The totals for the learners who feel satisfied is equivalent to those who were dissatisfied at 42.7%. Further work is necessary to determine if entry requirements at EDU-REC may have anything to do with the 42.7% who feel that the e-learning platform is not accommodating their prior knowledge. It is also possible that in face-to-face interaction, the lecturer is able to adjust to the needs of particular students, which may not be possible with a non-adaptive LMS. This is supported by literature which highlights the pitfalls of presenting learners with the same content at the same time, and expecting learners to move at the same pace. Another possibility that may need further investigation is the background of computer studies at high school level or whether the learners are encountering computer science related subjects only at tertiary level.

Factor 6: Consider my Learning Goals in Learning Design
For consideration of the student's learning goals in e-learning design, 16.5% ranked it 1, 9.7% ranked it 2, 10.7% ranked it 3, 14.6% ranked it 4, 9.7% ranked it 5, 17.5% ranked it 6 and 21.4% ranked it 7. This means 36.9% were not satisfied (ranking 1–3), 14.6% were neutral (ranking of 4) and 48.5% were satisfied (ranking of 5–7). 48.5% of the learners are satisfied with the consideration that is given to learning goals in the LMS compared to 36.99% who feel their learning goals are not being considered. This could be attributed to the fact that even on the e-learning platforms, the learning goals are clearly outlined in the course outline. However, as factor 5 has highlighted, the learners are coming to the teaching-learning environment with different background knowledge, and thus they may have different learning goals, which may need to be adaptively considered within the e-learning platform. Learning goals are what the students what they want to achieve by the end of the course.

Factor 7: Consider my Learning Preferences
For consideration of the student's learning preferences in e-learning design, 14.6% ranked it 1, 17.5% ranked it 2, 16.5% ranked it 3, 17.5% ranked it 4, 12.6% ranked it 5, 12.6% ranked it 6 and 7.8% ranked it 7. This means 48.6% were not satisfied (ranking 1–3), 17.5% were neutral (ranking of 4) and 33.5% were satisfied (ranking of 5–7). The majority of the learners (48.6%) consider the LMS as providing material not tailored to their learning preferences, against 33.5% who profess the LMS is tailored to their learning preferences. This finding could be supported by literature which indicates that learners have different learning styles. It is possible the material does not differentiate according to learning preferences but may still meet the needs of a particular group of students.

Factor 8: E-learning Platform Should Provide me with Personalised Suggestion of Relevant Content
For consideration of the student's expectation of the eLearning platform to provide personalised suggestion of relevant content, 14.6% ranked it 1, 6.8% ranked it 2, 7.8% ranked it 3, 17.5% ranked it 4, 15.5% ranked it 5, 17.5% ranked it 6 and 20.5% ranked it 7. This means 29.2% were not satisfied (ranking 1–3), 17.5% were neutral (ranking of 4) and 53.4% were satisfied (ranking of 5–7). A surprising finding of this research is that 53.4% of the learners do not want the LMS to provide them with personalised content. Most educational recommender systems are constructed based on a direct

translation from e-commerce, whose main focus is providing relevant items. This finding seems to bolster the assertion that we cannot implement recommender algorithms and frameworks in education in the same way they have been implemented in e-commerce and travel and tourism.

Factor 9: E-learning Platform Should Provide me with Strategies for More Effective Learning

For consideration of the student's expectation for the e-learning platform to provide with strategies for more effective learning, 6.8% gave it a ranking of 1, 10.7% ranked it 2, 9.7% ranked it 3, 15.5% ranked it 4, 11.7% ranked it 5, 22.2% ranked it 6 and 23.3% ranked it 7. This means 26.2% were not satisfied (ranking 1–3), 14.6% were neutral (ranking of 4) and 58.3% were satisfied (ranking of 5–7). The research seems to suggest that the learners are comfortable with their learning strategies and do not feel the need to have suggestions on how best to study. This could be a result of teenage attitude. It could also mean that a majority of the learners are performing very well and thus do not see strategies as a hindrance to their studies. This assertion may need to be further examined from performance data of the target population.

Factor 10: E-learning Platform Should Provide me Appropriate Learning Guidance

For consideration of the student's culture in e-learning design, 6.8% ranked it 1, 6.8% ranked it 2, 5.8% ranked it 3, 15.5% ranked it 4, 15.5% ranked it 5, 17.5% ranked it 6 and 31.1% ranked it 7. This means 19.4% were not satisfied (ranking 1–3), 15.5% were neutral (ranking of 4) and 64.1% were satisfied (ranking of 5–7). The majority of the learners (64.1%) are currently satisfied with the level of learning guidance they are receiving on the e-learning platform. On close examination, it appears as if the implementation of e-learning is a blended-learning model. Thus, it is possible that the learners are receiving guidance from the lecturers where appropriate. It may also be speculated that the learners have high background skills in terms of computer literacy from prior studies and orientation actives and may thus feel comfortable with accessing content on e-learning platform.

Factor 11: E-learning Platform Should Provide me with Appropriate Learning Feedback

For consideration of the student's expectation that the eLearning platform should provide them with appropriate learning feedback, 6.8% ranked it 1, 6.7% ranked it 2, 12.6% ranked it 3, 10.7% ranked it 4, 14.6% ranked it 5, 15.5% ranked it 6 and 30.1% ranked it 7. This means 28.2% were not satisfied (ranking 1–3), 10.7% were neutral (ranking of 4) and 60.2% were satisfied (ranking of 5–7). A total of 28.2% of the learners are not satisfied with the level of feedback they are receiving on the e-learning platform compared to 60.2% who are satisfied. Again, the blended learning approach may account for this result because lecturers are available to provide feedback to learners when needed. At EDU-REC, e-learning is mostly used to complement face-to-face learning. Even the distance learners have some contact sessions so the level of support from the lecturers is higher than in a purely e-learning/distance mode of learning.

Factor 12: I Like the Pacing of Learning Material not to be too Fast or too Slow but to Match my Needs

For consideration of the student's expectation that they like the pacing of the learning material not to be too fast or too slow but to match their needs, 10.7% ranked it 1, 12.6% ranked it 2, 13.6% ranked it 3, 15.5% ranked it 4, 12.6% ranked it 5, 16.5% ranked it 6 and 18.4% ranked it 7. This means 36.9% were not satisfied (ranking 1–3), 15.5% were neutral (ranking of 4) and 47.6% were satisfied (ranking of 5–7). 36.9% of the respondents expressed having found the pacing of the e-learning material either too slow or too fast, while 47.6% found the material paced appropriately. What is curious about the 36.9% percent is that eLearning is supposed to allow learners to move at their own pace. Therefore, it might be necessary to investigate why over a third of the learners found the material either paced too fast or too slow. One possible reason that could have something to do with the regularity of posting content and requirements on when responses are required. This would especially apply for graded labs and assessments.

Factor 13: I Would like to Receive Personalised Remediation Decisions and Guidelines

For consideration of the students' expectations that they would like to receive personalised remediation decisions and guidelines, 16.5% ranked it 1, 12.6% ranked it 2, 14.6% ranked it 3, 20.4% ranked it 4, 11.7% ranked it 5, 10.7% ranked it 6 and 12.6% ranked it 7. This means 43.7% were not satisfied (ranking 1–3), 20.4% were neutral (ranking of 4) and 35.0% were satisfied (ranking of 5–7). More learners, representing 43.7% of the respondents, compared to 35% of the respondents would like to receive personalised remediation. Personalised remediation provides the learners with more opportunities to interact with the lecturer. This finding seems to support the need for a recommendation system to suggest remediation exercises based on results of assessments carried out by learners.

Factor 14: I Would Like to Receive Exercises Appropriate to my Academic Level

For consideration of the students' expectations to receive exercises appropriate to their academic levels, 10.7% ranked it 1, 5.8% ranked it 2, 7.8% ranked it 3, 11.7% ranked it 4, 12.6% ranked it 5, 22.3% ranked it 6 and 28.2% ranked it 7. This means 24.3% were not satisfied (ranking 1–3), 11.7% were neutral (ranking of 4) and 63.1% were satisfied (ranking of 5–7). This question is close to the previous question. It is therefore not surprising that only 24.3% feel that the exercises they are receiving are not appropriate to their level. Again, an investigation into entry requirements and practices would be helpful to shed more light on the specific learners who are finding it difficult to cope with university exercises. In addition, this is a task that may be handled by a recommender system in an e-learning environment to provide additional support to the learners.

Factor 15: I Value Interaction with Other Learners Studying Similar Courses to Myself

For consideration of the student's valuing of interaction with other learners studying similar courses to themselves, 13.6% ranked it 1, 4.9% ranked it 2, 10.7% ranked it 3,

15.5% ranked it 4, 18.4% ranked it 5, 13.6% ranked it 6 and 23.3% ranked it 7. This means 29.1% were not satisfied (ranking 1–3), 15.5% were neutral (ranking of 4) and 55.3% were satisfied (ranking of 5–7). In general, there is a high satisfaction rate with the LMS in terms of interaction among learners (55.3%). As alluded to earlier, this may be attributed in part to the blended learning approach where the learners participate in group assignments as well as discussions. However, even 29.1% still feel interaction is inadequate. This may also be due to the diversity in implementation of e-learning collaborative feature such as wikis and discussion forums. Some lecturers may possibly be at an advanced stage of interaction while others are still adopting the platform and have not made use of the features.

Factor 16: I Value Receiving Information on Learning Tools that can Make my Learning More Effective

For consideration of the students' expectations to receive information on learning tools that can make their learning more effective, 6.8% gave it a ranking of 1, 5.8% gave it a ranking of 2, 10.7% gave it a ranking of 3, 10.7% gave it a ranking of 4, 9.7% gave it a ranking of 5, 19.4% gave it a ranking of 6 and 36.9% gave it a ranking of 7. This means 23.3% were not satisfied (ranking 1–3), 10.7% were neutral (ranking of 4) and 66.0% were satisfied (ranking of 5–7). Almost two-thirds (66%) of the respondents are of opinion that they are receiving the tools they need for effective learning. This result is not surprising given that the learners are generally satisfied with the content they are receiving.

Factor 17: I Value Receiving Information on Learning Resources that can make my Learning more Effective

For consideration of the student's valuing of receiving information on learning resources that can make their learning more effective, 5.8% ranked it 1, 1.9% ranked it 2, 7.8% ranked it 3, 9.7% ranked it 4, 17.5% ranked it 5, 17.5% ranked it 6 and 39.8% ranked it 7. This means 15.5% were not satisfied (ranking 1–3), 9.7% were neutral (ranking of 4) and 74.8% were satisfied (ranking of 5–7). Nearly three quarters of the respondents at 74.8% are satisfied with the learning resources they are receiving versus the 15.5% who are not satisfied. The resources include course outlines, notes and links to additional resources.

Factor 18: I Enjoy Socialising with Other Learners and Other People Online

For consideration of the students' enjoyment of socialising with other learners and other people online, 35.9% ranked it 1, 8.7% ranked it 2, 11.7% ranked it 3, 15.5% ranked it 4, 5.8% ranked it 5, 8.7% ranked it 6 and 13.6% ranked it 7. This means 56.3% were not satisfied (ranking 1–3), 9.7% were neutral (ranking of 4) and 28.2% were satisfied (ranking of 5–7). Unlike issues dealing with receiving content, 56.3% of the respondents want more socialisation and are of the opinion that the LMS is not social enough compared to 28.2% who professed that they are satisfied.

8 Conclusions from the Learners' Questionnaire

The results of the study suggest that the learners are generally satisfied with content and the learning resources they are receiving. However, they professed that they need more support in terms of socio-cultural and affective elements of learning. According to these results, it would be more appropriate to design a social recommender system that takes into account psychographic factors in the user profile. The top ten factors that are to be considered in the model are: Culture, Emotional/mental state (Psychographic factors), Socialisation, Motivation, Learning preferences, Prior-knowledge, aptitude and educational background, Learning/Cognitive style, Navigation (technical), and Learning goals. The recommender system will not recommend content but will focus on the social factors. In other words, the recommender system will only play a supportive role.

References

Boticario, J., Santos, O.: An open IMS-based user modelling approach for developing adaptive learning management systems. J. Interact. Media Educ. (2007). http://jime.open.ac.uk/2007/02

Brown, E., Cristea, A., Stewart, C., Brailsford, B.: Patterns in authoring of adaptive educational hypermedia: a taxonomy of learning styles. J. Educ. Technol. Soc. **8**(3), 77–90 (2005)

Etaati, L., Sundaram, D.: Adaptive tourist recommendation system: conceptual frameworks and implementations. Vietnam J. Comput. Sci. **5**(2), 95–107 (2014)

Goodyear, P., Retalis, S. (eds.): Technology-Enhanced Learning. Sense Publishers, New York (2010)

Graf, S., List, B.: An evaluation of open source e-Learning platforms stressing adaptation issues. In: 5th IEEE International Conference on Adavnced Learning Technologies ICALT 2005, pp. 163–165 (2005)

Greco, S.: Multiple Criteria Decision Analysis. Springer, New York (2005). https://doi.org/10.1007/b100605

Gynther, K.: Design frameowrk for an adaption MOOC Enhanced by bleneded learning: supplementary training and personalised learning for teacher professional development. Electron. J. e-Learn. **14**(1), 15–30 (2016)

Hilt, S., Wellman, B.: Asynchronous learning networks as a virtual classroom. Commun. ACM **40**(9), 44–49 (1997)

Pajores, M.: Teachers' beliefs and educational research: cleaning up messy construct. Rev. Educ. Res. **62**(3), 307–332 (1992)

Prain, V., et al.: Personalised learning: lessons to be learnt. Br. Edu. Res. J. **39**(4), 654–676 (2013)

Roberts, R., Goodwin, P.: Weight approximations in multi-attribute decision models. J. Multi-criteria Decis. Anal. **11**(6), 291–303 (2002)

Santos, O., Boticario, J. (eds.): Education recommender systems and technologies: policies and challenges. IGI Global, USA (2012)

Sarin, R.K.: Multi-attribute utility theory. In: Gass, S.I., Fu, M.C. (eds.) Encyclopedia of Operations Research and Management Science, pp. 1004–1006. Springer, Boston (2013). https://doi.org/10.1007/978-1-4419-1153-7

Wilson, K., Nichols, Z.: The knewton platform: a general purpose adaptive learning infrastructure (2015). http://www.knewton.com

Wirth, K., Perkins, D.: Knowledge surveys: an indispensable course design and assessment tool. Innovations in the Scholarship of Teaching and Learning (2005)

Yu, C., Jannasch-Pennel, A., Digangi, S., Kaprolet, C.: A data mining approach for identifying predictors of student retention from sophomore to junior year. J. Data Sci. **8**(2), 307–325 (2010)

Mobile Information Processing Systems

Android Malware Detection: A Survey

Modupe Odusami[1], Olusola Abayomi-Alli[1], Sanjay Misra[1(✉)],
Olamilekan Shobayo[1], Robertas Damasevicius[2],
and Rytis Maskeliunas[2]

[1] Department of Electrical and Information Engineering,
Covenant University, Ota, Nigeria
{modupe.odusami,olusola.abayomi-alli,sanjay.misra,
Olamilekan.sobayo}@covenantuniversity.edu.ng
[2] Kanus University of Technology, Kaunas, Lithuania
{robertas.damasevicius,rytis.maskeliunas}@ktu.lt

Abstract. In the world today, smartphones are evolving every day and with this evolution, security becomes a big issue. Security is an important aspect of the human existence and in a world, with inadequate security, it becomes an issue for the safety of the smartphone users. One of the biggest security threats to smartphones is the issue of malware. The study carried out a survey on malware detection techniques towards identifying gaps, and to provide the basis for improving and effective measure for unknown android malware. The results showed that machine learning is a more promising approach with higher detection accuracy. Upcoming researchers should look into deep learning approach with the use of a large dataset in order to achieve a better accuracy.

1 Introduction

The mobile device has undeniably become a new growing trend in this modern age as many internet applications have migrated their products, accessibility, and applications to this platform for improved productivity and interoperability. The growth of mobile devices is driving a circumvolution change in our information security [1]. However, the growth of mobile device has increased the associated threat some of which are: SMS spam threat [2], phishing, malware, license to kill spyware, etc. Android Operating System (OS) platform has become the fastest growing mobile OS based on its open nature thus making it the most preferred OS for many consumers and developers [3]. This OS has, however, allowed the operations of several thousand of applications from different market hence easy users' functionality [4]. The advantages of Android OS over other mobile Operating System include the following: it runs very powerful applications, it is very flexible and friendly as it allows users to make their choice of applications [5]. Android phones have been an attraction to several illegitimate operations because of its popularity and increasing openness. An attacker can easily incorporate its own code into the code of a normal application. Hence, malware infiltrating the android application is growing at a dangerous rate and under this situation, security of the devices and the assets these devices allow access to is very crucial [6]. To address this security issue, researchers have established several methods

H. Florez et al. (Eds.): ICAI 2018, CCIS 942, pp. 255–266, 2018.
https://doi.org/10.1007/978-3-030-01535-0_19

for the detection of Android malware to prevent Android devices against security breaches. Numerous approaches with diverse aims and objectives had been widely utilized in bringing out their strengths and weaknesses. Evaluation of the techniques is done based on true positive, true negative, false positive, false negative, precision, accuracy, f-score etc. The aim of this study is to see the trend in Android malware detection and suggests an improved method by reviewing, categorizing and comparing existing works.

Malicious operations are often referred to as the accessing of users private information by stealing, spying and displaying of the undesirable advertisement [6]. The umbrella term for these malicious operations is Malware. Malware is derived from malicious software and it is often referred to as software program that consciously possesses the deep attributes of malicious attackers and characterizes by its malicious aim [7]. Different types of Malware are shown in Fig. 1 based on their diverse purposes and ways of penetration.

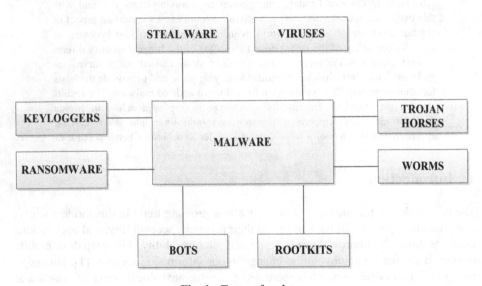

Fig. 1. Types of malware

The remaining part of the study is sectioned as ensues: Sect. 2 details related work. Section 3 gives the result and discussion. The study concludes in Sect. 4.

2   Existing Android Malware Detection Methods

Several works have been carried out by researchers in detecting android malware detection. This section discusses various approaches that had been used in literature.

2.1   Static Analysis Approach

Most of the applications are not analyzed at runtime. Distinct signatures can be achieved by unknown applications through obfuscation and encryption hence static methods are not effective for the identification of unknown malware.

Authors in [8] proposed a method that detects and classifies android malware using static analysis with the combination of the attacker information. The effectiveness of Android malware detection is improved by integrating the attacker's information as a feature and categorizes illegitimate applications into homogeneous classes. The system could recognize malware with 98% exactness. The general drawback of the model is overcome by adding dynamic analysis functionality. Faruki et al. [9] employed a syntactic foot-printing techniques using variable length signatures to classify an app as malware or benign. Results showed 60% accuracy. Song et al. [10] proposed an integrated static framework using a filtering technique consisting of four layers to identify and evaluate mobile malware on android of nearly 99% accuracy. Sun et al. [11] presented an approach that interfaces static logic- structures and dynamic runtime information to detect android malware. Behavior similarity is used for the classification of malware. Results showed that the approach is easy to implement and has low computational overhead.

Authors in [12] presented Permission based malware detection system using machine learning classifiers on the behavioral patterns to consequently distinguish for inconspicuous applications conceivably unsafe conduct in view of the blend of permission they require. The result showed over 94% accuracy. Wu et al. [13] proposed a novel approach using permission and API. The requested information is extracted from each application manifest file and classifier into the normal app or malicious app using K nearest neighbor. The model achieved 97.87% accuracy.

Talha et al. [14] presented a permission-based Android malware detection consisting of three components namely central server, android client and signature database using static analysis to categorize the android application as normal or harmful. The experimental results showed 88% accuracy. Sato et al. [15] employed a lightweight technique to detect Android malware by analyzing strictly the manifest.xml file. The extracted information from the manifest.xml is compared with the keyword lists and the cost of analysis is low. The results also showed an accuracy of 90%. Ping et al. [16] presented the use of contrasting permission patterns to show the differences between illegitimate and normal applications. Experimental results showed 94.38% accuracy.

Description of the static approach methods are basically signature based, and permission based. In signature based approach, the impressions of known malware families are generated and stored in a database as a model. An unknown app is compared with any existing app and if the similarity score exceed the set threshold, it is termed a malware [9]. Although the signature based method does not have false positive detection but it is unable to effectively detect new unknown malware. Permission based approach utilized both the server side and client side for the authentication of apps instances. The behavior of application instances are categorized as either normal or malicious at the server side [12]. Some of the permissions based method include: Read_ External_ Storage permission which enables an application to read from the External storage, the Write_ External_ Storage permission enables an application write to the external storage. There is low false positive rate in permission based method as compared to signature based method [12].

2.2 Dynamic Analysis Approach

Dynamic analysis can identify application behavior at run time and it is mostly done in a sandbox environment.

Authors in [17] studied the boot sequence of system calls deeply based on pattern recognition to detect malware in android. The result showed 95.8% accuracy. Shankar et al. [18] designed a runtime malware detection using honeypot based detection environment to find intent and session malware. The results showed 96% accuracy. Chaba et al. [6] presented an approach that observes the dynamic behavior of applications based on system call logs. System call logs of each application observed are used to build a dataset which classifies the application as malicious or normal. The dataset is tested on Naïve Bayes, Random forest, and Stochastic gradient descent with 93.75%, 93.84%, 95.5% accuracy respectively. In [19] a novel multi-level approach based on behavior is used to identify android malware using system call sequences as malware behavior. It aims is to detect and stop any malware at runtime. Although the accuracy of detection is very high, the performance rate is very low. Authors in [20] presented an Android application sandbox to find doubtful behavior in Android applications by statically and dynamically evaluating the app. This can improve the scholastic anti-virus applications usable for the Android OS.

Anomaly behavior method and the use of system calls log are widely utilized in dynamic analysis approach. Anomaly behavior based is the detection of patterns in a particular dataset which do not correspond to a deep – rooted licit behavior. Although this method is able to effectively detect unknown apps but false positive rate is high. System calls log is a method in which a program request being serviced from the basic operating system's kernel [5]. Malicious detection is carried out at the kernel level at high detection accuracy with few false positive rates.

2.3 Machine Learning Approach

Authors in [21] proposed a machine learning – based approach to identify malware using dynamic analysis to extract a feature of system functions. J48 decision tree and Naïve Bayesian are used to train and test classifiers. Results showed that in the detection of malware Android applications, the classification accuracy 90% with low false positive. In [22], a novel model consisting of dynamic and static analysis, machine learning, and the local and remote host is used to identify android malicious operations. Malware detection accuracy is high because of better efficiency in terms of storage consumption and power. The model detects malware application with 99% accuracy.

Authors in [23] employed back propagation Neural Network to identify illegitimate applications based on application system call sequence. A static Markov Chain is a replica of the system call sequence and the transitions probabilities from one system call to another in illegitimate applications are different from normal Applications. The results showed a F-score of 0.982773.

Yerima et al. [24] employed a technique that uses ensemble learning for detection of Android malware. This approach prompt zero-day malware detection as there is no need for feature selection hence provides robustness and resilence to code obfuscation. The results showed detection accuracy of 97%.

Yuan et al. [25] proposed an approach using Deep Learning to identify malware in Android phone. Deep learning is a new aspect of machine learning research whose application in artificial intelligence is increasing tremendously and it has also inspired a large number of victorious applications in speech and image recognition. Datasets greater than 200 features were extracted from both static analysis and dynamic analysis of each Android applications, and deep learning mechanism is used to group the illegitimate apps from normal apps. The model achieved an accuracy of 96.60% indicating that deep learning method is far more proper than some other machine learning methods. However, it was not deployed for the online android malware detection system. Authors in [26] proposed a deep learning technique for malware process detection involving two stage Deep Neural Networks. Features are extracted using trained Recurrent Neural Network and classification of feature images are achieved by using convolutional neural network. Although, best result was achieved with the techniques but it was not fully utilized due to small dataset usage.

Hasegawa and Iyatomi [27] proposed a light-weight Android malware detection method in which a small portion of the Android application package file of the target is analyzed using one-dimensional convolutional neural work. Results showed that illegitimate applications can be identified with an accuracy of 97%. The model captured some of the major features but they are not confirmed since APK is a compressed file. Authors in [28] proposed an approach using Artificial Immunity based on detector set artificial immune system (MAIS) for the discovery of illegitimate applications in mobile computing devices based on the data flows in Android apps. Results showed 93.33% accuracy with reduced false negative rates (FNR). However, the false negative rate remained high. In [29]; Hidden Markov Model (HMM) with the combination of structural entropy is used for the detection of Android malware. The Statistical pattern analysis algorithm that uses a length of the observed sequence, the number of definite observation symbols, observation sequence, state transition probability matrix, and initial state distribution matrix is employed for the detection of the malicious codes. The result showed that the accuracy of malware families' recognition is very high but can be improved by using a larger number of datasets. Li and Jin [30] presented an approach to identify Android Malware Detection based on Feature Codes. As the feature vector, both Function call and system call are evaluated and extracted from the malicious sample library. This will be exposed to training and classification upon machine learning and data mining algorithm, hence a feature library and a detection model is created. By using the feature vectors of codes from the Android applications, the system developed proved that it can efficiently uncover the unknown malicious Applications of android with high accuracy and low false positive rate.

Traditional machine learning method such as back propagation neural network is very shallow and hence could only train with small dataset which reduced the accuracy of detection. The conventional method often called deep learning utilized several layers of neural network is able to train with large dataset which improved the accuracy of detection.

A comprehensive comparative study of the existing techniques used in the detection of Android malware explained above is presented in Table 1.

Table 1. Android malware detection techniques.

Approach	Author	Description of method	Strengths	Weakness
Static analysis	[8]	Signature based	React efficiently to Android malware threats	High false negative
	[9]	Signature based	Detect unknown malware	Generate false positive
	[10]	Filtering	The degree of correctness is high	Resist latest malicious application
	[11]	Signature generation	Low computational overhead, the false positive rate is zero	It intercepts binders call and system calls
	[12]	Permission-based	Detect unknown malware	High false positive
	[13]	Permission and Application Programming Interface (API) based	Low cost of deployment	Cannot correctly detect Android malware
	[14]	Permission-based	Detect well-known malware	Contain some external dependencies
	[15]	Permission-based	Analyze manifest files to detect malware	Inadequate for detecting adware samples
	[16]	Contrasting Permission pattern	Error is minimal	The interval of the contrasting pattern is very wide
Dynamic Analysis	[17]	Boot sequence	Good compliments	High false negative
	[18]	Honey pot	Detect intent and session hijacking malware	Cannot detect root exploits and scripts malware
	[6]	System calls log	Detect unknown malware with minimal processing time	
	[19]	Anomaly behavior monitoring	High efficacy with low overhead	Low performance and energy overhead
	[20]	System call logs	Run Android applications in an isolated environment	

(continued)

Table 1. (*continued*)

Approach	Author	Description of method	Strengths	Weakness
Machine learning	[21]	Hybrid	Capture instantaneous attacks	Slightly lower True Positive Rate (TPR)
	[22]	Hybrid	It consumes low resources	Performance is reduced due to communication dependent on the server
	[23]	Back propagation Neural network	Achieves 0.982773 F-score	The number of the states of Markov chains quite large
	[24]	Ensemble learning	Detection with low false positive	Large feature space is required
	[25]	Deep learning (Deep Belief neural network)	Detects illegitimate applications with 96.7% accuracy	Unrealistic dynamic analysis of malicious may evade the detection system.
	[26]	Recurrent Neural Network and Convolutional Neural Network		
	[27]	Deep learning (Convolutional Neural Network)	A malicious application can be identified with an accuracy of 96–97%	Features captured were not confirmed.
	[28]	Artificial Immunity	High False negative rate	Inadequate dataset for experimentation
	[29]	Hidden Markov Model	Identify malicious applications with a precision of 0.96	The verification of the technique is done on a large dataset
	[30]	Feature vector	Detect the unknown malware effectively	Insufficient behavior features

3 Results and Discussion

This section gives various results that were gathered from the survey with respect to approaches used to detect android malware. From Table 1, the approaches can broadly be classified into static analysis approach, Dynamic analysis approach, and Machine learning. The detection accuracy for each of the review papers is analyzed as shown in Figs. 2, 3 and 4.

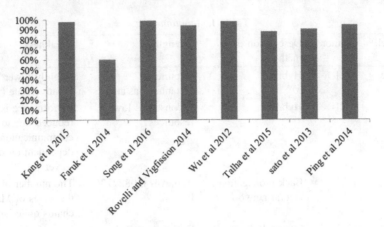

Fig. 2. Detection accuracy for static analysis

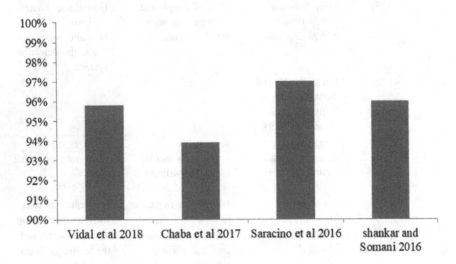

Fig. 3. Detection accuracy for dynamic analysis

All of the three categories of Android Malware techniques have shown promising techniques as shown in Figs. 1, 2 and 3 above. The accuracy of machine learning techniques is of close merging to each other and they are closer to 100% accuracy than other techniques. From Fig. 3, the study that shows highest accuracy used a hybrid method of machine learning. Deep learning method also shows a higher accuracy because it highly learned other relevant features for training. The accuracy of most of the methods is affected by the total number of Data sets used. Table 2 indicates the number of datasets used in each of the review papers and their sources.

In Table 2 authors in [24] employed the largest dataset. The malware dataset was obtained from AMD dataset (24,553 malware) and Android Drebin project dataset (5,560). Normal application dataset was obtained from Appsap and pk pure.the dataset was divided into two in which 5000 were taken from both malware dataset, and 2000

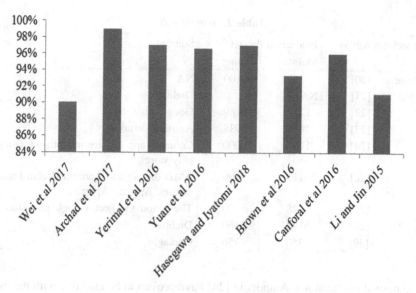

Fig. 4. Detection accuracy for machine learning

Table 2. Total number of Datasets used in each of the review papers and their sources

Approach	Author	Evaluation dataset		Source
		Malware	Bening	
Static analysis	[7]	4,554	51,179	Virus share, contagio mobile, malware.lu, Google play store
	[8]	3309	15993	The genome project, Google play store
	[9]	4006	100	security service provider, Google play store
	[10]	3723	500	The genome project, droid analytics, contagio minidup
	[12]	238	1500	Contagio, Google play store
	[13]	6909	1853	Drebin, Genome project, Google play store
	[14]	130	235	the designated website, Google play store
	[15]	1260	1227	slideme, panndaapp, Google play store
Dynamic analysis	[16]	2850	2850	Genome, Drebin,
	[18]	705	10000	Genome, chjneze app store, virus total detected app, Google app store, Amazon app store and Samsung app store.Baidu app store,
	[5]	Not specified	Not specified	The data set was created
	[18]	2,784	NA	Genome, Contagio mobile, virus share
	[19]	NA	NA	NA

(continued)

Table 2. (*continued*)

Approach	Author	Evaluation dataset		Source
		Malware	Bening	
Machine learning	[20]	100	100	NA
	[21]	NA	NA	Drebin
	[22]	1227	1189	Google play store
	[23]	2925	3938	Antivirus vendor
	[24]	1760	20000	Contagio app set, genome project, Google play store
	[26]	30113	2000	AMD dataset and Android Drebin Project dataset. Appsap, Apkpure
	[27]	28	30	The genome project, Google play store
	[28]	6192	5560	Drebin
	[29]	350	750	Contagio

for the normal applications. Authors in [24] have proven to be effective with the use of more dataset than other methods. Although in the study [20], the total number of the dataset was not specified, the result showed very high detection accuracy with the use of Drebin dataset. Drebin dataset helps classifier to provide high detection rate because malicious applications and normal applications are scattered in a manner that it bypasses the overfitting of the classifier [20]

4 Conclusion and Future Work

In this study, a survey was conducted by considering existing techniques and their accuracy based on the dataset used in the literature. The study indicates a promising approach to Android malware detection. Machine learning showed a better approach with higher detection accuracy than other approaches most especially the hybrid based. Therefore researchers need to look into the development of an improved mechanism in the area of machine learning by exploring more of the deep learning techniques in the detection of Android malware and training the model with large datasets for fully utilization of the model.

Acknowledgments. We acknowledge the support and sponsorship provided by Covenant University through the Centre for Research, Innovation, and Discovery (CUCRID).

References

1. Akinboro, S.A., Omotosho, A., Odusami, M.O.: An improved model for securing ambient home network against spoofing attack. Int. J. Comput. Netw. Inf. Secur. **10**(2), 20 (2018)
2. Onashoga, A.S., Abayomi-Alli, O.O., Sodiya, A.S., Ojo, D.A.: An adaptive and collaborative server-Side SMS spam filtering scheme using AIS. Inf. Secur. J. Glob. Perspect. **24**(4–6), 133–145 (2015)

3. Singh, R.: An overview of android operating system and its security. Int. J. Eng. Res. Appl. **4** (2), 519–521 (2014)

4. Arp, D., Spreitzenbarth, M., Hubner, M., Gascon, H., Rieck, K., Siemens, C.E.R.T.: DREBIN: effective and explainable detection of android malware in your pocket. In: NDSS, vol. 14, pp. 23–26, Febrauary 2014

5. Gandhewar, N., Sheikh, R.: Google Android: An emerging software platform for mobile devices. Int. J. Comput. Sci. Eng. **1**(1), 12–17 (2010)

6. Chaba, S., Kumar, R., Pant, R., Dave, M.: Malware Detection Approach for Android systems Using System Call Logs (2017). arXiv preprint arXiv:1709.08805

7. Ye, Y., Li, T., Adjeroh, D., Iyengar, S.S.: A survey on malware detection using data mining techniques. ACM Comput. Surv. (CSUR) **50**(3), 41 (2017)

8. Kang, H., Jang, J.W., Mohaisen, A., Kim, H.K.: Detecting and classifying android malware using static analysis along with creator information. Int. J. Distrib. Sens. Netw. **11**(6), 479174 (2015)

9. Faruki, P., Laxmi, V., Bharmal, A., Gaur, M.S., Ganmoor, V.: AndroSimilar: robust signature for detecting variants of Android malware. J. Inf. Secur. Appl. **22**, 66–80 (2015)

10. Song, J., Han, C., Wang, K., Zhao, J., Ranjan, R., Wang, L.: An integrated static detection and analysis framework for Android. Pervasive Mob. Comput. **32**, 15–25 (2016)

11. Sun, M., Li, X., Lui, J.C., Ma, R.T., Liang, Z.: Monet: a user-oriented behavior-based malware variants detection system for Android. IEEE Trans. Inf. Forensics Secur. **12**(5), 1103–1112 (2017)

12. Rovelli, Paolo, Vigfússon, Ýmir: PMDS: permission-based malware detection system. In: Prakash, Atul, Shyamasundar, Rudrapatna (eds.) ICISS 2014. LNCS, vol. 8880, pp. 338–357. Springer, Cham (2014). https://doi.org/10.1007/978-3-319-13841-1_19

13. Wu, D.J., Mao, C.H., Wei, T.E., Lee, H.M. and Wu, K.P.: DroidMat: android malware detection through manifest and API calls tracing. In: 2012 Seventh Asia Joint Conference on Information Security (Asia JCIS), pp. 62–69. IEEE, August 2012

14. Talha, K.A., Alper, D.I., Aydin, C.: APK Auditor: permission-based Android malware detection system. Digit. Investig. **13**, 1–14 (2015)

15. Sato, R., Chiba, D., Goto, S.: Detecting Android malware by analyzing manifest files. Proc. Asia Pac. Adv. Netw. **36**(23–31), 17 (2013)

16. Ping, X., Xiaofeng, W., Wenjia, N., Tianqing, Z., Gang, L.: Android malware detection with contrasting permission patterns. China Commun. **11**(8), 1–14 (2014)

17. Vidal, J.M., Monge, M.A.S., Villalba, L.J.G.: A novel pattern recognition system for detecting Android malware by analyzing suspicious boot sequences. Knowl. Based Syst. **150**, 198–217 (2018)

18. Shankar, V.G., Somani, G.: Anti-Hijack: runtime detection of malware initiated hijacking in Android. Procedia Comput. Sci. **78**, 587–594 (2016)

19. Saracino, A., Sgandurra, D., Dini, G., Martinelli, F.: Madam: Effective and efficient behavior-based android malware detection and prevention. IEEE Trans. Dependable Secur. Comput. **15**(1), 83–97 (2016)

20. Bläsing, T., Batyuk, L., Schmidt, A.D., Camtepe, S.A., Albayrak, S.: An android application sandbox system for suspicious software detection. In: 2010 5th International Conference on Malicious and Unwanted Software (MALWARE), pp. 55–62. IEEE, October 2010

21. Wei, L., Luo, W., Weng, J., Zhong, Y., Zhang, X., Yan, Z.: Machine learning-based malicious application detection of Android. IEEE Access **5**, 25591–25601 (2017)

22. Arshad, S., Shah, M.A., Wahid, A., Mehmood, A., Song, H., Yu, H.: SAMADroid: a novel 3-level hybrid malware detection model for android operating system. IEEE Access **6**, 4321–4339 (2018)

23. Xiao, X., Wang, Z., Li, Q., Xia, S., Jiang, Y.: Back-propagation neural network on Markov chains from system call sequences: a new approach for detecting Android malware with system call sequences. IET Inf. Secur. **11**(1), 8–15 (2016)
24. Yerima, S.Y., Sezer, S., Muttik, I.: High accuracy android malware detection using ensemble learning. IET Inf. Secur. **9**(6), 313–320 (2015)
25. Yuan, Z., Lu, Y., Xue, Y.: Droiddetector: Android malware characterization and detection using deep learning. Tsinghua Sci. Technol. **21**(1), 114–123 (2016)
26. Tobiyama, S., Yamaguchi, Y., Shimada, H., Ikuse, T., Yagi, T.: Malware detection with deep neural network using process behavior. In: 2016 IEEE 40th Annual Computer Software and Applications Conference (COMPSAC), vol. 2, pp. 577–582, June 2016
27. Hasegawa, C., Iyatomi, H.: One-dimensional convolutional neural networks for Android malware detection. In: 2018 IEEE 14th International Colloquium on Signal Processing & Its Applications (CSPA), pp. 99–102. IEEE, March 2018
28. Brown, J., Anwar, M., Dozier, G.: Detection of mobile malware: an artificial immunity approach. In: 2016 IEEE Security and Privacy Workshops (SPW), pp. 74–80. IEEE, May 2016
29. Canfora, G., Mercaldo, F., Visaggio, C.A.: An HMM and structural entropy based detector for android malware: an empirical study. Comput. Secur. **61**, 1–18 (2016)
30. Li, Y., Jin, Z.: An Android malware detection method based on feature codes. In: 4th International Conference on Mechatronics, Materials, Chemistry and Computer Engineering (2015)

Architectural Approaches for Phonemes Recognition Systems

Luis Wanumen and Hector Florez(✉) (iD)

Universidad Distrital Francisco Jose de Caldas, Bogotá, Colombia
{lwanumen,haflorezf}@udistrital.edu.co

Abstract. Based on the literature, it is possible to build voice recognition systems by using voice synthesizers and voice command controls. In addition, phonemes recognition can be made by implementing algorithms already created for this kinds of tasks. Nevertheless, phonemes recognition might generate some errors, when the implementation of such algorithms is unsuitable. Then, the possibility to perform phonemes recognition based on open source APIs arises. In the work presented in this paper, we used open source APIs for voice commands recognition. Thus, we propose an architecture that allows the construction of a system for phonemes recognition and voice synthesizers. The results have been implemented and validated in order to illustrate the reliability of the proposed architecture.

Keywords: Voice recognition · Software architecture
Phonemes recognition

1 Introduction

The process of phonemes recognition is also called process of voice recognition and is related to all technologies and techniques required to transform voice signals to their corresponding word sequences [1]. Improving the ways for voice processing allows improving the applications based on this technology such as applications with voice dialogues, calls routing, interactive voice answering, voice dictation, voice document transcription, learning systems based on audio content, voice-based searching, and interactive mobile applications based on voice recognition [2].

Nowadays, it is necessary that voice recognition algorithms keep working in hostile acoustic environments, basically because nowadays acoustic environments are full of noise and different audio signals [3]. In addition, there are several factors that affect the way in which voice is recognized such as voice volume, language, or even the distance between the microphone and the person. Consequently, different algorithms are required depending the mentioned factors [4].

Software applications for voice recognition are very useful in knowledge management based on pronunciation [5], systems for home automation [6], systems

© Springer Nature Switzerland AG 2018
H. Florez et al. (Eds.): ICAI 2018, CCIS 942, pp. 267–279, 2018.
https://doi.org/10.1007/978-3-030-01535-0_20

for language therapy [7], recognizing and diagnosing of illness based on phonemes pronunciation [8], detection of emotional state [9], people recognition [10], among other important contexts.

On of the most novelty application for voice recognition systems and in particular phonemes recognition systems is the non supervised learning for infants [11]. This motivated the development of a project for phonemes recognition. However, to achieve the systems, it was necessary to study the effectiveness and efficiency of some architectonic alternatives for the development of the system.

On the one hand, the selection of the architecture of the system is based on the possibility to use the selected architecture in any other system for voice recognition [12]. On the other hand, the focus of the architectonic proposal is based on the discovery of those architectural elements that allows establishing a framework, which is very important in software engineering, since it provides contributions, when domain specific projects are developed [13].

This paper presents two proposed architectures that allow phonemes recognition pronounced by a person. The first architecture is focused on voice commands recognition, while the second architecture is focused on voice synthesizers. Such architectures are suitable to be implemented in mobile devices that use Android a operating system.

The paper is structured as follows: Sect. 2 presents the background of phonemes recognition, Sect. 3 presents the proposed architecture, Sect. 4 illustrates the approach developed using the architecture, Sect. 5 reports the results, Sect. 7 proposes some ideas as future work, and finally Sect. 6 concludes the paper.

2   Phonemes Recognition

There are a lot of options for phonemes recognition. However, it is important to state in which scenarios and circumstances the use of APIs is useful. The options to achieve voice recognition are related to the implementation of algorithms in a device or a computer cluster [14]. however, the amount of exiting algorithms is very long and each algorithm is useful in one specific context [15]; then, it is necessary to analyze the aim of the phonemes recognition process.

For the specific case of phoneme recognition, its aim is to recognize just one word each time that the algorithm is run, based on a voice has associated one characteristic vector that encapsulates information about such voice [16]. Thus, it is possible to compare two voices just comparing their corresponding characteristic vectors [17].

Comparing the characteristic vectors of voices previously stored against a characteristic vector of a new voice is a complex computer-based process when the amount of stored voices is large; however, it is the best solution for a small amount of stored voices.

In the case of this work, which is focused on phonemes recognition, the user pronounces a letter and the system must discover the corresponding letter. Thus, Table 1 presents the list of characteristic vectors used in this work.

Table 1. Phonemes list [18]

Phoneme	Features
/a/	Vocal phoneme with maximum opening
/B/	Bilabial sonorous obstructive phoneme
/c/	Palatal phoneme
/D/	Coronal-alveolar sonorous obstructive phoneme
/e/	Palatal vowel phoneme with half opening
/f/	Lip-dental fricative phoneme
/G/	Obstructive phoneme sonorous
/i/	Vocal palatal phoneme with minimal opening
/j/	Flaring velar phoneme
/k/	Deaf occlusive phoneme
/l/	Lateral phoneme
/m/	Lip nasal phoneme
/n/	Nasal phoneme
/o/	Vocal phoneme velar with half opening
/p/	Occlusive phoneme
/r/	Simple vibrant phoneme
/s/	Alveolar fricative phoneme
/t/	Occlusive phoneme
/u/	Vocal velar with minimum opening
/y/	Palatal sonorous phoneme

There are some architectures that can match for phonemes recognition using APIs; nevertheless, this work is focused on an architecture proposal based on free APIs of voice synthesizers, which has been tested trough a software prototype. In addition, its results were taken by running the system several times using different phonemes types.

3   Proposed Architectures

We present two top-down architectures, which are focused on the description of the elements that must be available, when developers are intended to implement a software application for phonetic recognition of each syllable pronounced by a human being.

3.1   Architecture Based on Voice Command Control APIs

In this section, we present the proposed architecture for phonemes recognition based on the use of APIs for voice command control. The proposed architecture is presented in Fig. 1.

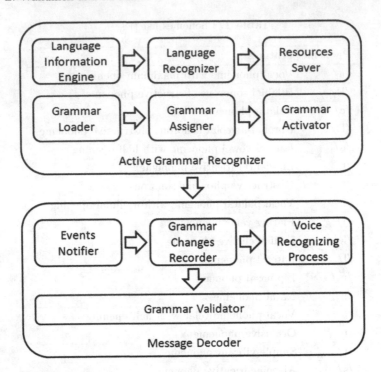

Fig. 1. Architecture based on voice command control.

Different voice command control APIs can be used following the presented architecture. However, in this work, we have used the *Java Speech API (JSAPI)*[1]. *JSAPI* is an extension of the platform Java, which based on its developers it can be used to extend the functionality of an application independent of the provider.

The architecture has the subsystems: *active grammar recognizer* and *message decoder*. The *active grammar recognizer* subsystem has the following components:

1. **Language Information Engine.** Languages models are an essential component in the context of the application for voice recognition [19]. One way to implement language models in voice recognition systems is through the creation of an engine for the local language. Thus, using the class `Locale` from the package `java.util` of the *Java Development Kit (JDK)*[2], it is possible to instantiate an object (e.g., *emd*) from the class `EngineModeDesc` for recognizing the local device language by using the following code line.

```
EngineModeDesc emd = new EngineModeDesc(Locale.ROOT)
```

---

[1] http://jsapi.sourceforge.net/.
[2] http://www.oracle.com/technetwork/java/javase/overview/index.html.

In addition, it is possible to use the class `EngineProperties` to add certain language properties to the instantiated object (e.g., *emd*). Furthermore, the class `EngineStateError` can be used to manage an control the corresponding exceptions.

2. **Language Recognizer.** This subsystem is in charge of creating a voice recognizer. It is done by using *JSAPI*. Thus, it is possible to create a recognizer through the classes `Central` and `Recognizer`, which are part of the package `javax.speech.recognition`, which allows this operation from objects of the class `EngineModeDesc`. The following code line presents the creation of the recognizer.

```
Recognizer recognizer = Central.createRecognizer(emd)
```

3. **Resources Saver.** This subsystem works in a similar way that the garbage collector of Java, which is able to make a verification of resources that are not available and objects that has lost their context. With this in mind, this system is able to free memory. This is very important to be implemented in a voice recognition system because based on this functionalities, it is possible to have available resources when the application is running in a mobile device. The following code line allows the functionality described for this subsystem based on *JSAPI*.

```
recognizer.allocate()
```

Then, this code line set free the resources associated to the object *recognizer* leaving it ready to receive a new grammar file. If before executing the code line, a grammar file was already assigned, the system eliminates it and a new grammar file needs to be assigned.

4. **Grammar Loader.** This is a subsystem in charge of finding and loading in memory the information from a file, which describes the grammar to be interpreted for a desired application. In this case, the grammar loader works with the standard *Java Speech Grammar Format (JSGF)*[3], which is a format developed by *SUN Microsystems* that allows making grammar textual representations to be used in speech recognition systems. Indeed, some technologies such as *XHTML+Voice*[4] adopt the style and conventions of Java through the technology *JSFG* and thus, *SUN Microsystems* allows developers to adopt notations of traditional grammars. It is important to mention that the classes of Java included in the package `java.io` are required to read files and they are completely compatible to be used with the *recognizer*. The basic structure of a file based on the *JSFG* specification is presented in the following code lines.

```
#JSGF V1.0;
grammar commands;
public < commands > = send | turn off | turn on;
```

---

[3] https://www.w3.org/TR/2000/NOTE-jsgf-20000605/.
[4] https://www.w3.org/TR/xhtml+voice/.

In addition, another formats have been created based on the *JSFG* standard; for instance, the format *Speech Recognition Grammar Specification (SRGS)*[5]. For the architecture presented in this work, we assume that there is a file named *grammar.txt*, which has the grammar information in *JSGF* format. This file is loaded by using the class `FileReader` that is contained in the package `java.io`. The following code line loads the grammar file.

```
FileReader grammar = new FileReader("grammar.txt")
```

Another functions of this subsystem are related to the exception handling and grammar file validation in order to ensure that the grammar is well formed and coherent regarding the specification *JSGF*.

5. **Grammar Assigner**. It is necessary to assign to the *recognizer* the grammar file loaded by the previous subsystem. The following code line makes this assignment by using the class `RuleGrammar` which is part of the *JSAPI*.

```
RuleGrammar ruleGrammar = recognizer.loadJSGF(grammar)
```

6. **Grammar Activator**. Based on the object *ruleGrammar* it is necessary to activate the grammar. In this case, it is done with the following code line.

```
ruleGrammar.setEnabled(true)
```

There are some other ways to activate the grammar; nevertheless, they are required when there are problems of configuration or compatibility. In such cases, it is necessary ti include certain grammar rules using the *JSGF* language.

3.2   Architecture Based on Voice Synthesizers APIs

In this section, we present the proposed architecture for phonemes recognition based on the use of APIs for voice synthesizers. Figure 2 presents the proposed architecture.

The architecture is made up of the following subsystems:

1. **Voice Recorder.** It is used by users and aims to record the voice that is intended to be recognized.
2. **Voice Generator.** It uses APIs for voice synthesizers generating several voices. For each voice, this subsystem modifies its acoustic properties such as voice intensity, nasal resonance, and tone. The speed of the voice is not modified in this subsystem in order to avoid unnecessary complexity in the implementation. In addition, since the phonetic properties are randomly modified, the behavior of the produced voice signals are different.

---

[5] https://www.w3.org/TR/speech-grammar/.

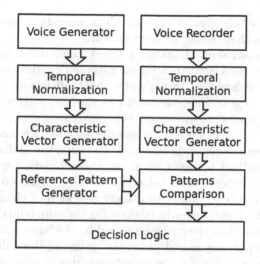

Fig. 2. Proposed architecture.

3. **Temporal Normalization.** It is based on lineal transformations in the time axis in order to generate voices that can be compared to other voices. It is important to mention that there are another techniques to make this transformations such as dynamic transformations, which take into account the voice speed. However, when the voice speed is constant, lineal transformations are good enough for this subsystem.

4. **Characteristic Vector Generator.** It generates an spectral representation for each basic unit of voice delivering vectors with finite values. In the literature, the set of these vectors is known as *Code Book*. The aim of this subsystem is to reduce the rate of information delivered to the next subsystem. Thus, let a voice signal sampled to KHz and its amplitude is coded to 32 bits; the, the rate of information delivered to the next subsystem is 512 Kbps (i.e., 16 KHz × 32 bits). Nevertheless, this subsystem generates cepstrals with dimension $Q = 10$ and using 120 frames per second as frames rate. Then, the rate of information delivered to the next subsystem is 38.4 Kbps (i.e., 120 × 10 × 32 bits). Thus, this subsystem reduces the information from 512 Kbps to 38.4 Kbps obtaining a reduction around 75% in the amount of information delivered to the next subsystem.

5. **Reference Pattern Generator.** First of all, this subsystem can be achieve by using: (a) casual training, (b) robust training, and (c) training by clustering. The casual training was discarded due to the project uses several versions of each word to build the reference pattern and this training just offers support when there is a unique version of each word. The robust training offers support when there are different versions of one word; however, it does not offer support when speakers are different. The training by clustering offers support for several version and different speakers; thus, it is proper for this kind of work. It is important to mention that for the set of voices generated

using the voice synthesizer, it is required to generate a reference pattern for one set of voices that belong to just one word.

6. **Patterns Comparison.** It makes a direct comparison between the characteristic vector associated to a signal gathered by the voice recorder (i.e., the signal that is intended to recognize) with all possible patterns learned in the training stage. Thus, the result is the one with more similarity. In the case of the characteristic vector generator, we use cepstrals coefficients, which implies that we can use euclidean distance in such comparisons. Before applying euclidean distance, in this work we tested the Mahalanobis distance; however, this method is useful when the characteristic vector is not homogeneous, but the experimental behaviour of the recognition is homogeneous; then, this distance is no proper to classify this kind of phonemes.

7. **Decision Logic.** It can make decisions using the minimum distance classifier. This classifier associate the gathered sound by the voice recording subsystem with one of the previous stored phonemes gathered through the voice generator subsystem and classifies the sound matching it with one of the training sounds.

4   Approach for Phonemes Recognition

We have designed and developed a mobile application for phonemes recognition called *FonoUD* based on the architectures presented in the previous section. The developed approach corresponds to a mobile application implemented using the platform Android 5.0 Lollipop. It has an user interface with the following options:

– **Phonemes capturing.** It deploys a sound recorder in order to provide users a mechanism to record a desired phoneme. The recorded sounds are stored in the MicroSD or Transflash memory of the mobile device. The extension of the file is Waveform Audio File (WAV). The recorder allows users to play the recorded audio in order to verify that it was correctly stored. It is important to mention that users must pronounce slowly and clearly in order to allow the application to differentiate each pronounced letter. Figure 3 presents a screenshot of this service

– **Phonemes analysis.** It allows analyzing the recorded audio files. The results of the analysis process is also stored in the MicroSD o Transflash memory of the mobile device. In this process, WAV files are decoded using an API for voice synthesizer. Thus, for decoding phonemes, it is necessary to divide the word in various sections and for each section a temporal file is created. Finally, the algorithm is applied to each part of the original audio. If the resultant parts were to small, it is possible that one part has the same consonant or vowel several times; then, it is necessary to eliminate the repeated adjacent letters in order to obtain the final word. Users can play the result in order to agree or disagree.

– **Analysis Results.** Using this option, users can review the results of the analysis process.

Fig. 3. *FonoUD* recording service.

The result of the sound file is store in a SQLLite database in the mobile device; then, it can be played again even if the application is restarted. Once the processing is finished, the user can return to the main menu and select the option *Analyze through voice command control*. With this service, the user can check the results of the voice recognition analysis for a desired sound file. Figure 4a presents a screenshot of the analysis processing, while Fig. 4b presents a screenshot with the results of the service to analyze sound files in which on top of the screenshot there is a multimedia navigation control in order to select and play a desired sound file previously captured.

In Fig. 4b the file analyzed is *voice03.wav* and has been interpreted by the application as the word *universidad*. In this case, the user might agree or disagree the result of the analysis.

5   Results Validation

In order to validate the architectures, which has been proved through the application presented in the previous section, we have selected 40 people, who have recorded the word *cebolla* in order to test the application. Based on the corresponding sound files, we executed the voice recognition subsystem of both proposed architectures.

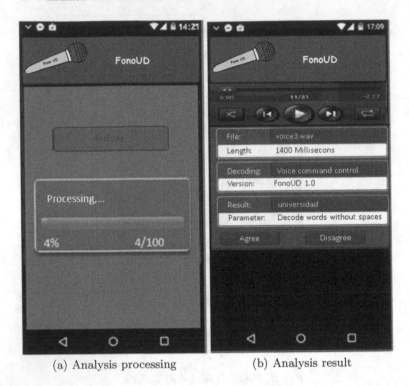

(a) Analysis processing   (b) Analysis result

Fig. 4. *FonoUD* analysis service

The system was executed again obtaining the same results of the first execution. The system was executed three more times for a total of five times and each time the results were the same. This test allowed us to conclude that a word is interpreted in the same way, when the sound is the same and is pronounced by the same person with the same speed.

In addition, in this test we appreciate that despite the word is the same, since it was pronounced by different people, the system can provide different results. It means that there are possible factors such as strength, intensity, speed, tone that can alter the result. Moreover, the results indicate that 27 sound files were correctly interpreted and 13 were incorrectly interpreted. Thus, the system has an effectiveness of *67.5%*.

The same procedure was done using the voice command control architecture for the words: *television, universidad, facultad, ingenieria,* and *articulo.* These words were pronounced by the same people. The results of analyzing the sound files are presented in Table 2.

Once again, the same procedure was done using the voice sinthesizer architecture for the words: *reconocimiento, voces, universidad, pluralismo,* and *refineria.* These words were pronounced by the same people. The results of analyzing the sound files are presented in Table 3.

Table 2. Analysis results with different words

Words	Correctly classified	Incorrectly classified	Success rate	Failure rate
Cebolla	27	13	67.5%	32.5%
Television	26	14	65.0%	35.0%
Universidad	26	14	65.0%	35.0%
Facultad	24	16	60.0%	40.0%
Ingenieria	27	13	67.5%	32.5%
Articulo	30	10	75.0%	25.0%

Table 3. Analysis results

Words	Correctly classified	Incorrectly classified	Success rate	Failure rate
Reconocimiento	28	12	70.0%	30.0%
Voces	32	8	80.0%	20.0%
Universidad	26	14	65.0%	35.0%
Pluralismo	24	16	60.0%	40.0%
Refineria	27	13	67.5%	32.5%

Based on the results, we can observe that the classification of correct words is stable. Thus, we can conclude that the way in which certain people speak impacts negatively the phoneme recognition system. In addition, making a detailed analysis about people who pronounced one word were not recognized correctly by the system, it is very likely that the system do not recognize further words pronounced by said people.

We analyzed each case and we could observe that the not recognized words were pronounced faster that the words correctly recognized by the system. Thus, the right pronunciation is necessary in order to be correctly recognized. For instance, some people use to pronounce very fast; as consequence, they omit consonants especially at the end of the words. Finally, we can state that the performance of both architectures are good enough and very similar.

6 Future Work

We propose the following ideas as future work:

- Extend the architectures taking into account different frameworks in order to enable the architectures to work with other mobile technologies such as iPhone or iPod.
- Extend the architecture in order to use further APIs for voice recognition in order to improve the rate of success.
- Study the technological reasons in which the system does not provide a correct recognition.

7 Conclusions

Since any phoneme captured by the voice recorder service is classified in one of the phonemes previously obtained, when such phoneme is not part of the phonemes of the system, the system provides the most similar phoneme. It means that the system is very useful, when it is known in advance what phonemes are going to be pronounced.

It is necessary to pronounce correctly the words without omitting consonants in order to achieve a good interpretation of the words by the system

There is a trend of the system to interpret correctly words pronounced by certain people. It means that the tone, volume, strength among others characteristics affect the way in which the system works.

It is necessary to study other APIs that include another kinds of sounds because it is possible that the tones of the voices of the system are very different to the tones used for the development of the voice command control API used in this work. Then, it will produce sounds that is unlikely to be recognized by the system.

There are two ways for phonemes recognition. The former consists in allowing users to pronounce one word and the system identifies the corresponding word. The latter consists in knowing which word in a list users are going to pronounce. For this, it is possible to use APIs for voice command control and voice synthesizers that generate the list of words in order to calculate the characteristic vector of each word that can be compared to the voice pronounced initially. Based on the comparisons, it is possible to know which word was pronounced.

The proposed architecture is useful for systems such as: systems for orders processing where the amount of orders are low, systems to search context-specific words (e.g., erotic words), and systems used to verify whether or not users have pronounced specific words.

The proposed architecture is not useful in the following cases: systems for voice dictation, systems for voice translation, systems for teaching based on the students voice, robotics systems that receive orders to perform desired behaviour.

References

1. Huang, X., Acero, A., Hon, H.W., Reddy, R.: Spoken Language Processing: A Guide To Theory, Algorithm, and System Development, vol. 95. Prentice hall PTR, Upper Saddle River (2001)
2. He, X., Deng, L.: Speech-centric information processing: an optimization-oriented approach. Proc. IEEE **101**(5), 1116–1135 (2013)
3. Deng, L., et al.: Distributed speech processing in mipad's multimodal user interface. IEEE Trans. Speech Audio Process. **10**(8), 605–619 (2002)
4. Kumatani, K., McDonough, J., Raj, B.: Microphone array processing for distant speech recognition: from close-talking microphones to far-field sensors. IEEE Signal Process. Mag. **29**(6), 127–140 (2012)
5. Zhang, B., Gan, Y., Song, Y., Tang, B.: Application of pronunciation knowledge on phoneme recognition by LSTM neural network. In: 2016 23rd International Conference on Pattern Recognition (ICPR), pp. 2906–2911. IEEE (2016)

6. Karan, G., Kumar, D., Pai, K., Manikandan, J.: Design of a phoneme based voice controlled home automation system. In: 2017 IEEE International Conference on Consumer Electronics-Asia (ICCE-Asia), pp. 31–35. IEEE (2017)
7. Grossinho, A., Guimaraes, I., Magalhaes, J., Cavaco, S.: Robust phoneme recognition for a speech therapy environment. In: 2016 IEEE International Conference on Serious Games and Applications for Health (SeGAH), pp. 1–7. IEEE (2016)
8. Jahan, M., Khan, M.: Sub-vocal phoneme-based EMG pattern recognition and its application in diagnosis. In: 2015 Annual IEEE India Conference (INDICON), pp. 1–4. IEEE (2015)
9. Wu, T., Yang, Y., Wu, Z., Li, D.: Masc: a speech corpus in mandarin for emotion analysis and affective speaker recognition. In: IEEE Odyssey 2006: The Speaker and Language Recognition Workshop, pp. 1–5. IEEE (2006)
10. Ichino, M., Sakano, H., Komatsu, N.: Text-indicated speaker recognition using kernel mutual subspace method. In: 10th International Conference on Control, Automation, Robotics and Vision, ICARCV 2008, 957–961. IEEE (2008)
11. Miyuki, Y., Hagiwara, Y., Taniguchi, T.: Unsupervised learning for spoken word production based on simultaneous word and phoneme discovery without transcribed data. In: 2017 Joint IEEE International Conference on Development and Learning and Epigenetic Robotics (ICDL-EpiRob), pp. 156–163. IEEE (2017)
12. Kharchenko, O., Raichev, I., Bodnarchuk, I., Zagorodna, N.: Optimization of software architecture selection for the system under design and reengineering. In: 2018 14th International Conference on Advanced Trends in Radioelecrtronics, Telecommunications and Computer Engineering (TCSET), pp. 1245–1248. IEEE (2018)
13. Hochgeschwender, N., Biggs, G., Voos, H.: A reference architecture for deploying component-based robot software and comparison with existing tools. In: 2018 Second IEEE International Conference on Robotic Computing (IRC), pp. 121–128. IEEE (2018)
14. Deng, L., O'Shaughnessy, D.: Speech Processing: A Dynamic and Optimization-Oriented Approach. CRC Press (2003)
15. Acero, A.: Acoustical and Environmental Robustness in Automatic Speech Recognition, vol. 201. Springer Science & Business Media (2012)
16. Kolossa, D., Haeb-Umbach, R. (eds.): Robust Speech Recognition of Uncertain or Missing Data: Theory and Applications. Springer Science & Business Media, Heidelberg (2011). https://doi.org/10.1007/978-3-642-21317-5
17. Deng, L.: Front-end, back-end, and hybrid techniques for noise-robust speech recognition. In: Kolossa, D., Häb-Umbach, R. (eds.) Robust Speech Recognition of Uncertain or Missing Data, pp. 67–99. Springer, Heidelberg (2011). https://doi.org/10.1007/978-3-642-21317-5_4
18. Hualde, J.I.: The Sounds of Spanish with Audio CD. Cambridge University Press (2005)
19. Dziadzio, S., Nabożny, A., Smywiński-Pohl, A., Ziółko, B.: Comparison of language models trained on written texts and speech transcripts in the context of automatic speech recognition. In: 2015 Federated Conference on Computer Science and Information Systems (FedCSIS), pp. 193–197. IEEE (2015)

Towards a Framework for the Adoption of Mobile Information Communication Technology Dynamic Capabilities for Namibian Small and Medium Enterprises

Albertina Sumaili[✉], Nomusa Dlodlo, and Jude Osakwe

Namibia University of Science and Technology,
P. Bag 13388, Windhoek, Namibia
sumailia@telecom.na, ndlodlo@gmail.com,
jdosakwe@yahoo.com

Abstract. A company's ability to be mobile is the capability to transact any-time, anywhere, Mobile information and communication technologies (ICT) ability to transform businesses is attributed to the dynamic capabilities (DCs) of ICT. In response to changing technologies and as a means to gain profits, organizations use DC, which is a catalyst of the business ability to design and adjust resources. As such DCs effect is also felt on resource base affording the organization competitive advantage. In this qualitative Namibian case study, the DCs of mobile ICT were closely analyzed as a means to investigate the usage of DCs of mobile ICT by Namibian Small and Medium Enterprises (SME), and how it can enhance SME transformation and strategies used for its adoption. The analysis of this study was conducted using the Theory of Dynamic Capabilities. For this study 40 SMEs were identified by means of convenience sampling and one employee per SME by means of purposive sampling. The collection of data was primarily through interviews and ques-tionnaires subsequently the data was coded. The results showed that although some SMEs in Namibia use technology, there is still a significant number that is oblivious to the advantages that DCs of mobile ICT can offer. The researcher therefore recommends that governing bodies of Namibian SMEs enforce poli-cies that facilitate the adoption of mobile ICT and sponsor local SMEs as conduit for economic advancement; that owners of SMEs adopt mobile ICT as a means to gain competitive advantage; that SMEs with existing mobile ICT infrastructure should look into ways of adopting diverse DCs of mobile ICT thus creating a better environment for faster service delivery; that SMEs should adopt the culture of ICT training to enable employees to effectively use mobile ICT; that in order to reduce software costs SMEs should opt for open source appli-cations; and that as means to gain visibility and increase customer base SMEs should make use of mobile technology to market their services and products.

Keywords: Information and communication technology (ICT)
Mobile ICT · Dynamic capabilities · Small and medium enterprises

© Springer Nature Switzerland AG 2018
H. Florez et al. (Eds.): ICAI 2018, CCIS 942, pp. 280–291, 2018.
https://doi.org/10.1007/978-3-030-01535-0_21

1 Introduction

Within the ICT dynamic area, all kinds of applications can be found. SMEs can benefit by adopting this dynamism. The rebirth of ICT has been propelled by mobile ICT; a development that has transformed businesses and processes. This rebirth has triggered a modern technology evolution [1]. What characterizes the dynamic capability of mobile ICT is the changing nature of ICT applications that brings great benefits to businesses. The constant changes in emerging technology personifies ICT as dynamic. Therefore, if businesses want to use cutting edge technology they must move along with emerging changes. This is mainly because mobile ICT dynamic capabilities (DC) increases customer satisfaction, breaks business borders, makes business more appealing, increases business throughput, etc. Adopting mobile ICT allows an enterprise to transact anywhere and anytime outside the confined business premises. Businesses can transform from the ancient ways of transaction to more innovative ways by using dynamic capabilities of mobile applications. More often than not, SME activities have a high level of flexibility. These activities require an enabler. In this case, mobility comes in handy. [2] conducted a survey and came to the conclusion that in most countries, SME mobility is on the priority list. The report also established that a good number of managers spend much time on the go rather than being in offices. Some managers are fully convinced that the use of laptops does simplify their work. It is also established that it is the desire of some of the business owners to deploy more ICT facilities as time progress [2]. Over the years, employee mobility has been re-evaluated and allocated mobile devices and mobile applications to achieve better communication as they are on the move as well as transact on the fly. According to [3], "the benefits of developing mobile business could potentially include enhanced throughput, competence, client relations, employee satisfaction and reduced mobile security costs. However, business mobility success is only possible when there is a strategic mobility plan in place" [4]. In recent years, the adoption of mobile ICT has seen a rapid growth, more so in SMEs. This then calls for researches to establish best practices and the details involved that can be beneficial such as availability, reachability, portability, localization and accessibility [1]. Mobile ICT has alarming areas like evasion of incompatible technologies and cost effectiveness [5]. This research is an analysis of the capability of mobile ICT to transform SMEs in Namibia.

2 Literature Review

The literature review section covers the following: mobility, mobile enterprise, mobile adoption of ICTs, Namibian SMEs and mobile ICT and the Theory of Dynamic Capabilities.

2.1 Mobility

Enterprise mobility, has become a common phenomenon lately and most enterprises can no longer ignore it. During the course of this study, mobility is defined as: mobile technology and wireless computing advancement, it includes business advancement, communication and teamwork [6]. The rapid growth of ICT has brought about diffi-culties as enterprises try to keep up-to-date with ICT hardware or software and constant upgrade is no longer a choice. At the end, such upgrades result in a more useful and popular capability [7]. [8], said that mobile ICT includes but is not restricted to net-works consisting of users, hardware, wireless networks, user interfaces and software. The ubiquity of mobility components is explained by academics as "an always avail-able" [1, 2], They further stated that "the widespread use of communication tech-nologies (mobile and wireless) namely 3G and 4G, Radio Frequency Identification (RFID) and wireless local area networks (WLAN) promoted the growth and sale of innumerable applications and services". Consolidation and the rise of mobile tech-nology has made this achievement possible, which has led to a massive adoption of mobile ICT [8, 9]. Furthermore, the leap in drastic change in storage space and price drop of mobile devices has contributed to making these devices common and acces-sible thus, enabling new business creation and marketing prospects [9].

2.2 Mobile Enterprise

For the sake of this study, a mobile enterprise "refers to a firm whose business func-tions and applications have been transformed through the use of wireless mobile devices to transact and interact with the market" [10]. The characteristics of a mobile enterprise are much more than assigning laptops to employees to be able work remotely. In the mobility arena, laptops do not contribute more than half the mobility aspect of an enterprise [11]. The leveraging of mobile technology is greatly facilitated by wireless data transmission that enables the employees to remotely access company information. This is also what determines the enterprise mobility [10].

2.3 Mobile Adoption in ICTs

Constant access to information has become a necessity to meet customer demands, as employees become so dependent on the use of mobile devices, be it company devices or Bring-Your-Own-Device (BYOD) which are their main sources of technology. Both can offer greater productivity and instant access to business resources anywhere any-time [12]. Ideally, the core of mobility adoption is to propel business growth by creating innovative business applications. This is referred to as dynamism and a highly competitive environment [6]. Researchers are of different opinions, as some suggest that competitive gain is sustained in such a dynamic environment [14, 15]. Continuous upgrading is considered to be the best way as opposed to retaining the same resources for competitive advantage [16]. The use of dynamic environments is not sufficient for upholding the capability assets, products, brand name but rather the incorporation of innovative methods and replacement of obsolete resources on a continuous basis [15].

2.4 Namibian SMEs and Mobile ICT

The role of mobile ICT in the SME sector of Namibia is very vital. It provide the medium for communication and also drives technology enhancement. The Namibian economic sector has made major strides in its advancement, thanks to a number of emerging SMEs [17]. It goes without saying that the various SMEs that have arisen in the past years are inundated with the plethora of technology which most of them cannot afford to adopt due to financial constraints. The same financial constraints have seen a good number of these SMEs vanish [18]. The fierce fight for survival among SMEs therefore requires strategic plans in order to make it. One of these major strategies that Namibian SMEs ought to adopt is that of mobile ICT adoption. [19] affirms that there is a low adoption rate. Therefore, in order for Namibian SMEs to function to their full potential, much work still lies ahead [20–23]. As outlined by [24], the adoption of mobile ICT by SMEs was initially greatly impacted by the lack of infrastructure, business processes, skills and organization norms and behaviours. However, these same factors kept being revised and soon SMEs realised the benefits of mobile ICT adoption.

2.5 Underpinning Theory of Dynamic Capabilities

For the sake of this study the Theory of Dynamic Capabilities is used as the basis for collection of field data and the process of data analysis. Dynamic capabilities theory is a theory used by various academics and companies to gain competitive advantage [25].

[26] Elaborated on the idea of capabilities as being a firm's ability to assemble resources in a performance-stimulating manner and ICT competencies as knowledge, know-how, and skills. Albeit, ICT capabilities are defined as the firm's ability to perform ICT driven tasks [27].

3 Aim and Objectives of This Research

This study aims to investigate the DCs of mobile ICT towards its adoption in Namibian SMEs. The objectives of this research therefore are:

- To investigate usage pattern of Dynamic Capabilities of Mobile ICT by Namibian SMEs.
- To investigate how Dynamic Capabilities of mobile ICT can enhance SME transformation in Namibia.
- To recommend strategies for the adoption of Dynamic Capabilities of mobile ICT in Namibian SMEs.

The main research question is, "How can the DCs of mobile ICT be adopted in Namibian SMEs?" The sub questions of the research are:

- What is the usage pattern of Dynamic Capabilities of Mobile ICT in Namibian SMEs?
- How can the Dynamic Capabilities of mobile ICT enhance SME transformation in Namibia?
- What strategies can be recommended for the adoption of the Dynamic Capabilities of mobile ICT in Namibian SME?

4 Methodology

The paradigm of this research is interpretive. The research approach is qualitative. The theoretical perspective used is interpretivist. The nature of study was exploratory in a case study research setting. The Namibian Ministry of industrialization and trade classifies SMEs according to the number of employees which must be a maximum of one hundred (100) and/or a maximum turnover of ten million N$. This mean that the number of employees may range from one to one hundred and the required turnover may not exceed ten million [30]. A convenience sampling technique was used to identify the SMEs for this study. SMEs were selected based on proximity and accessibility. Furthermore, a purposive sampling technique was used to select the participants. These participants were selected by choosing those that are acquainted with the knowledge of the research in question. Thus, the participants selected ranged from Operation Managers, Chief Executive Officers, to managers and engineers. Data collection methods included questionnaires and interviews. The data was coded. The Theory of Dynamic Capabilities was used as the basis for data collection as well as the data analysis process.

5 Findings

5.1 Demographics of Participant Sample

The use of ICT technologies in the Namibian SME sector is high. 95% of SMEs surveyed use mobile phones; 87.5% use mobile Internet; 90% use mobile email; 55% use mobile calendars; 60% host mobile websites; 47.5% use web applications; 57.5% use instant messaging; 87.5% support wireless networks; 80% use laptops; 20% use PDA (personal digital assistant); 22.5% use tablets; 10% use cloud computing; 0% use RFID; 20% use mobile application and 22.5% use Bring-Your-Own-Devices. This is a clear indication that a high percentage of SMEs use mobile email and that there is a high level of mobility within Namibian SMEs, although there are some mobile capabilities that are not very common such as cloud computing and mobile applications. Most companies do not have the BYOD policy as depicted in the 22.5% response.

5.2 Strategic Benefits

While 67.5% of the SMEs asserted that they gained strategic benefits from mobility, 82.5% said that they gain informational benefits, 85% said that they gained transactional benefits, 65% said that they gain Enterprise transformation benefits and 65% gain Business values of ICT. The term "mobility" is more than simply the use of mobile technology. It embraces concepts such as transformation of business processes as means to maximize the benefits of mobile ICT. To that 64.1% said their enterprise is mobile while only 35.9% said no. This shows that most SMEs do not gain benefits from mobility, and others gain competitive advantage or enterprise transformation benefits.

5.3   Training

The question on the re-evaluation and reorientation of activities to gain advantage from mobile ICT, yielded 62.5% yes and 37.5% said no. The number of SMEs saying no is still high, which implies that a high number of SMEs have no re-evaluation procedures in place. 86.8% of the SMEs said yes to an increase in teamwork through mobility while 13.2% said no. 73.7% of the SMEs responded that they are well trained in the use of mobile ICTs while 26.3% said they are not. This shows that there is a training culture in Namibian SMEs. The question is to what extent. However, 75% stated that training is a priority and 25% said that training is not a priority in their companies. This negative drop in the numbers shows that training is not a priority in all departments of the SMEs according to [32].

5.4   DCs for Communication

From the following percentages, it is clearly evident that communication is highly affected by technology in most SMEs, and they all use various modes of technology to communicate with the relevant stakeholders 69.2% of SMEs said that technology is very important for the purpose of communication, while 30.8% said that technology is relatively important for the purpose of communication.

90% of the sample agreed that mobility contributed to the openness of communication and 10% disagreed. The primary methods of communication and collaboration with customers and suppliers are that 92.5% use email, 65% use telephone, 10% use messaging, 50% use face-to-face mode, 2.5% use newspapers and 2.5% use website, 5% use social media and 2.5% use video conferencing. On the importance of mobile technology for the purpose of communicating with the customer and suppliers, 75% said that technology is important while 25% said that technology is not that important for the purpose of communicating with customers. 85% of the SMEs said that communication has encouraged convenience partnerships while 15% said that it has not. ICT has become one of the pillars of information dissemination and communication it avails infra-structure and diverse technologies [33].

5.5   Integrating Mobile Technology into Strategic Planning

It is important to embrace innovative ways of working with technologies and techniques to deliver new services [34]. The following percentages show that Namibian SMEs have made some sort of efforts to integrate mobile planning to organization strategic goals strategic plan. This can be attributed to the fact that 69.2% of SMEs said that they have made efforts to integrate mobile planning to the overall company strategies and 30.8% said that no efforts were made. 43.2% of SMEs agreed to not having a vision regarding mobility while 56.8% have some sort of vision toward mobility. Only 23.1% of the SMEs' top management have a neutral perspective towards mobile ICT while 74.4% fully support mobile ICT, while 2.6% do not support mobile ICT totally. This is a clear indication that most SMEs have no plan/strategy for mobile adoption except the bigger SMEs, yet the majority of SMEs management does support the use of ICT.

These percentages show that overall, management have little motivation in investing in mobile ICT. 7.7% have no management motivation to invest in mobile ICT, 15.4% of the SMEs have low motivation towards mobile ICT investments, while 30.8% have a medium motivation and 46.2% have high motivation.42.5% said that management have high influence on mobile ICT adoption, 40% said that top management has a medium influence on the success of mobile ICT deployment, 17.5% said low influence.

5.6   ICTs for Marketing

Most SMEs desire visibility. Therefore a high percentage of them use mobile technology for marketing their products. While 77.5% of SMEs use mobile technology for marketing, 22.5% indicated they do not use mobile technology for marketing.

5.7   ICT Support

SMEs have different approaches to obtaining ICT support [35, 36]. The low justification of mobile ICT use forces management to be foreign to the concept of using strategic ICT partnerships or investing in procedures to acquire new technology. While 42.5% of the SMEs said that they do not outsource ICT services, 57.5% said that they outsource. Strategic alliances with diverse stakeholders to support companies are only seen in 30% of the SMEs while the remaining 70% do not have strategic alliances. 55% of the SMEs deploy standard mobile ICT solutions, 50% use tailored solutions. The research also shows that 67.5% of SMEs have no standard procedures for acquiring new technology while 32.5% have some kind of procedure.

5.8   ICT Influence on Business and Products

[38] Stated that organizations are made up of people from different backgrounds, talents, characters, and visions. Organizational culture is a big determining factor on the adoption of mobile ICT. This can be seen from the 92.5% of the SMEs that agreed that mobile ICT influences their culture while 5% disagreed and 2.5% find it irrelevant. The benefits of ICT applications cover a vast array of business processes as well as transactions. IT is conduit of improved information and management of knowledge, increase the rate of transactions, transaction reliability and potentially can reduce transaction costs [1].

5.9   ICT Dynamism

Product offerings are affected by the use of mobile technology. Therefore 57.5% agreed and only 42.5% disagreed that mobility affects product offerings, product life cycle and product economics. On the scale of influence that mobility has on the enterprise, 12.5% responded that there was no influence, 50% said that the influence was high and 37.5% said the influence was medium. In essence it is noticeable that SMEs are aware that mobility has an influence on the enterprise and its products. 77.5% of the SMEs agreed to have to adapt to the dynamic nature of the mobile environment and 12.5% find it irrelevant and 10% are oblivious to the dynamism of mobile ICT. 40% of the SMEs have innovative approaches towards mobility while 60% have no innovative approaches toward mobility. The dynamism of mobile ICT is gaining momentum and has spread across all countries, industries and socio-economic zones. Therefore for SMEs to gain competitive edge it is important to adopt mobile ICT said [39].

5.10 Data Security

An ICT revolution would not be effective without addressing risks that emanates from IT security that may lead to compromised integrity of data. To this 84.6% of the SMEs said that data security is a high priority and they use various forms of data protection mechanisms such as encryption, malware, antivirus, etc. for data protection. 12.8% said it is normal and 2.6% said it is not a concern. Notably so 68.4% said that they use data protection methods, 47.4% use antivirus, 47.4% restrict data access, 5% use backups particular method to manage security in mobility. A weak IT security subjects the organization to vulnerabilities such as virus attacks and malware. The low security levels can compromise confidentiality, integrity and privacy [40].

6 Mobile ICT Adoption Conceptual Model

The *conceptual model for mobile ICT adoption* depicts the different concepts that are vital in the adoption process of ICT by an [25]. This model is an attempt to clarify the different levels in the process of ICT adoption. The model points out the three fundamental stages of ICT adoption. Firstly the pilot phase, which deals with the analyses and requirements gathering of the adoption. Secondly, the rollout phase which deals with the going live and highlights all the stakeholders that need to participate or support. Finally, the confirmation phase, which deals with evaluating the adopted system to assess if it meets organisation needs and if/when it needs to be upgraded [31, 41–44]. The three fundamental stages are further elaborated below:

6.1 Pilot Phase

The adoption process of M-ICT is initiated by an organisation who identifies the need to innovate and gain competitive advantage. Such idea can only be sustained by predominant factors that need to be carefully strategized upon. The *CEO/management* being the governing body provides plan, run and monitors project, as well as appointing external expertise that align the stakeholder needs to the dynamic capability needed enhances the adoption process. The adoption of M-ICT is only possible with available *resources* be it infrastructure, software, funds and technology. Moreover, there is a need for *internal skill* to operate the infrastructure or the software, therefore a *skill assessment* during the project must be done in order to analyse the skills gap. Although skills shortage can be a hindrance to the successful adoption, adoption is also highly affected by the *organisation ethics and culture*. Once all of the above components are addressed the organisation can be said to be *e-ready.* [45–47].

6.2   Implementation

During the rollout phase, the support of *management/CEO* is vital. They are expected to provide a strategic plan and motivate the *participating employee* as well as *internal staff*. The *vendor's* role in this phase is primarily to set up the infrastructure. A successful adoption is made up of components adherence such as: regulating policies, professional assistance and government sponsorship [48–50].

6.3   Post Adoption

The post adoption phase focuses on the closure of the project in which continuous feedback and hand over the environment to the participating employees by means of training, monitoring, controlling, and reviewing and system evaluation. This may also contain future upgrade of the system [51–54].

The entire Mobile ICT adoption model can help organisation wishing to adopt mobile ICT to understand the vital concepts of the adoption process and managers to delineate relevant strategies and prioritise to enhance the chances of successful adoption of mobile ICT [55, 56]. Therefore the rationale behind, is to afford organisations the ability to identify new resources, renew existing ones, and to create advantages in the dynamic mobile ICT market [57].

While SME adoption of mobile ICT is an important part of Namibian economy, its uptake has been slow due to various reasons. Enterprises in Namibia can benefit from it as discussed below. The Namibian SMEs will be able to transact and collaborate anywhere, any time. The ever changing nature of mobile ICT can shape, reshape and reconfigure the business relationships among Namibian SMEs. The use of modern technology devices such as wireless networks provides mobility, technology access and reaches out to the public. This in turn increases customer satisfaction, easy communication across business units of these SMEs, improved chain of command and convenience.

It is also evident that a number of enterprises are not aware of the factors affecting the low rate of benefits enjoyed from mobile ICT. This low awareness affects the usage of mobile ICT. The adoption of ICT mobility has seen a growing number of workers adhering to the Bring-Your-Own-Device (BYOD) concept to access enterprise resources. This concept is cost effective and affords the enterprise benefits such as management flexibility, maximized employee performance, greater employee contentment and simplified IT Infrastructure [59].

Namibian SMEs should create standard procedures to research and identify new mobile technologies and create a culture that embraces changes and experimentation. They should also strive for competitive advantages which is normally in the form of support services, competitive advantage, strategic support and performance [49] (Fig. 1).

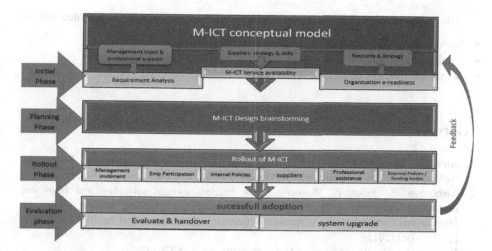

Fig. 1. Mobile ICT adoption conceptual model adopted from [46]

7 Conclusions and Recommendations

Mobile ICT is a clear propeller for the growth of the economy of a country. Innovative technology is an important role player in the improvement of enterprise competitiveness, customer relationship and products. Therefore the process of evaluating the impact of a research is likened to the understanding of the consequences or effects the benefits is able to foster to its community [60]. The effects of this study could not sideline the need for SMEs to create strategies that enhance competitive gain. Such strategy include the following:

Create an operations-efficient environment, Quality service delivery, Unique customer service, Reduce operational costs, Enhance communication, Reduced service delivery times, Enable business dynamism, Strengthen data security, Enforce employee training, Create company visibility, Enable innovative ICT service delivery modes.

Therefore, the researcher recommends that:

- Governing authorities of Namibian SMEs should enforce policies that facilitate the adoption of mobile ICT and sponsor local SMEs as conduit for economic advancement
- Owners of SMEs adopt mobile ICT as a means to gain competitive advantage
- SMEs with existing mobile ICT infrastructure should look into ways of adopting diverse dynamic capabilities of mobile ICT, thus creating a better environment for faster service delivery
- SMEs should adopt the culture of ICT training to enable employees to effectively use mobile ICT
- In order to reduce software costs SMEs can opt for open source applications
- As means to gain visibility and increase customer base, SMEs should make use of mobile technology to market its services/products.

The researcher therefore welcomes further studies in the areas as highlighted below:

- Identification of DCs specific to a give industry/sector
- Challenges of mobile ICT DC adoption in Namibia
- Namibian Internet service provider should specific mobility values

References

1. Airwatch. Enabling Bring Your Own Device (BYOD) In the Enterprise : Leveraging AirWatch to Create a Secure and Convenient BYOD Program, Airwatch (2012)
2. Alshorman, S., Jaber, F., Bensaali, F.: A wireless oxygen saturation and heart rate monitoring and alarming system based on the qatar early warning scoring system. In: International Conference on Computational Science and Computational Intelligence (CSCI), pp. 787–790 (2015)
3. Kearney, A.: The Rising Stars of IT Outsourcing, pp. 1–8 (2014)
4. Basole, R., et al.: Challenges and opportunities for enterprise transformation research. J. Enterp. Transform. 3(4), 330–352 (2013)
5. Basole, R.: Mobilizing the Enterprise: A Conceptual Model of Transformational Value and Enterprise Readiness, pp. 365–372 (2015)
6. Basole, R.: Strategic planning for enterprise mobility: a readiness-centric approach. In: 13th Americas Conference on Information Systems, vol. 6, pp. 3967–3979 (2007)
7. Blackberry, "THE CIO' S Guide to Enterprise Mobillity Management," Blackberry (2012)
8. Chairoel, L., Widyarto, S., Pujanic, V.: ICT adoption in affecting organizational performance among Indonesian SMEs. Int. Technol. Manag. Rev. 5(2), 82–93 (2015)
9. Palladium, Overarching Information Communications Technology (ICT) and Broadcasting Policy for the Republic of Namibia, Windhoek (2008)
10. Dholakia, N., Zwick, D.: Cultural contradictions of the anytime, anywhere economy: reframing communication technology. Telemat. Inform. 135–141 (2011)
11. Scornavacca, S.: The strategic value of enterprise mobility: case study insights. Inf. Knowl. Syst. Manag. 7, 227–241 (2008)
12. Ernest and Young, Driving ICT innovation and security, Ernest and Young (2014)
13. Ghobakhloo, M., Hong, T., Sabouri, M., Zulkifli, N.: Strategies for successful information technology adoption in small and medium-sized enterprises. Information 3, 36–67 (2012)
14. Johnston, S., Cox, S.: The Raspberry Pi: a technology disrupter, and the enabler of dreams. Electronics 6, 51 (2017)
15. Kambwale, J., Chisoro, C., Karodia, M.: Investigation into the causes of small and medium enterprise failure in Windhoek. Namibia. Arab. J. Bus. Manag. Rev. 4(7), 80–109 (2015)
16. Khidzir, Z., Mohamed, A., Arshad, N.: ICT outsourcing information security risk factors: an exploratory analysis of threat risks factor for critical project characteristics. J. Ind. Intell. Inf. 1(4), 218–222 (2013)
17. McDermott, Y.: Conceptualising the right to data protection in an era of Big Data. Big Data Soc. 4 (2017)
18. Namibia Economy Society, CAN SME's BENEFITS FROM FDIs (Foreign Direct Investment), Namibia Economy Society, Windhoek (2004)
19. Namibia Ministry of ICT, Information Technology Policy for the Republic of Namibia, Namibia Ministry of ICT, Windhoek (2009)
20. Namibia Ministry of Industrialisation Trade, National Policy on Micro, Small and Medium Enterprises in Namibia, Namibia Ministry of Industrialisation Trade, Windhoek (2016)

21. Nuamah-Gyambrah, K., Martin, O., Florence, A.: Role of CT in the survival of small and medium scale enterprises in ghana evidence from selected small and medium scale enterprises in New Juaben Municipality Koforidua. Int. J. Manag. Public Sect. Inf. Commun. Technol. 7 (2016)
22. Ogbokor, C., Ngeendepi, E.: Investigating the challenges faced by SMEs in Namibia, pp. 1–20 (2012)
23. Ogbomo, M., Ogbomo, F., Abraka, N.: Importance of information and communication technologies (ICTs) in making a heathy information society: a case study of Ethiope East Local Government Area of Delta State, Nigeria. Libr. Philos. Pract. 219 (2008)
24. Pisano, P.: A Normative Theory of Dynamic Capabilities: Connecting Strategy, Know-How, and Competition, pp. 16–36 (2015)
25. Porter, M., Millar, V.: How information gives you competitive advantage. Harv. Bus. Rev. **63**, 149–160 (2017)
26. Proctor, C.: Effective Organizational Communication Affects Employee Attitude, Happiness, and Job Satisfaction (2014)
27. Rabie, C., Cant, C., Wiid, J.: Training and development in SMEs: South Africa's key to survival and success? J. Appl. Bus. Res. **32**(4), 1009–1024 (2016)
28. Rindova, V., Kotha, S.: Continuous "morphing": competing through dynamic capabilities, form, and function. Acad. Manag. J. **44**, 1263–1280 (2011)
29. Ruairi, Q.: ICT Action Plan, Minister for Education & Skills, Ireland (2010)
30. Rufaro, T., Chiware, E., Dick, A.: The use of ICTs in Namibia's SME sector to access business information services. Electron. Libr. **26**(2), 145–157 (2008)
31. Savulescu, C.: Dynamics of ICT development in the EU. In: 2nd Global Conference on Business, Economics, Management and Tourism, Romania (2014)
32. Sherif, K.: E-Strategies for Technological Diffusion and Adoption: National ICT Approaches for Socioeconomic Development (2010)
33. SMEReports, Small Business Mobility, Australia (2008)
34. Tiwari, M.: Competitiveness of SMEs through different strategies. IOSR J. Bus. Manag. **16**(3), 63–68 (2014)
35. Varshney, U., Vetter, R.: Emerging mobile and wireless networks. Commun. ACM **43**, 73–81 (2010)
36. Bank of Namibia, 12th Annual Symposium 2010 of the Bank of Namibia - SME Development in Namibia, Bank of Namibia, Windhoek (2010)
37. Ahenkora, K., Adjei, E.: A dynamic capabilities perspective on the strategic management of an industry organisation. J. Manag. Strat. **3**(3), 21–27 (2012)

Robotic Autonomy

3D Scene Reconstruction Based on a 2D Moving LiDAR

Harold F. Murcia$^{(\boxtimes)}$, Maria Fernanda Monroy, and Luis Fernando Mora

Facultad de Ingeniería, Grupo de Investigación D+TEC,
Programa de Ingeniería Electrónica, Universidad de Ibagué,
Carrera 22 calle 67, Ibagué 730001, Colombia
harold.murcia@unibague.edu.co

Abstract. A real-world reconstruction from a computer graphics tool is one of the main issues in two different communities: robotics and artificial intelligence, both of them under different points of view such as computer science, perception and machine vision. A real scene can be reconstructed by generating of point clouds with the help of depth sensors, rotational elements and mathematical transformations according to the mechanical design. This paper presents the development of a three-dimensional laser range finder based on a two-dimensional laser scanner Hokuyo URG-04LX-UG01 and a step motor. The design and kinematic model of the system to generate 3D point clouds are presented with an experimental acquisition algorithm implemented on Robotic Operative System ROS in Python language. The quality of the generated reconstruction is improved with a calibration algorithm based on a model parameter optimization from a reference surface, the results from the calibrated model were compared with a commercial low-cost device. The concurrent application of the system permits the viewing of the scene from different perspectives. The output files can be easily visualized with Python or MATLAB and used for surface reconstruction, scene classification or mapping. In this way, typical robotic tasks can be realized, highlighting autonomous navigation, collision avoidance, grasp calculation and handling of objects.

Keywords: 3D reconstruction · Terrestrial LiDAR · 3D point clouds
Intrinsic calibration · Machine vision

1 Introduction

For humans, the rich understanding of our world is mainly guided by visual perception which allows us to distinguish objects, colors, textures, shapes and spatial location. After process this information we can conclude about the number of objects in a scene, type of materials, obstacles detection, distances and size of objects, which impact in how we interact with the scene. Consequently,

Supported by Universidad de Ibagué.

the imitation of these human capabilities in theory, design, and implementation allows to Intelligent Systems to "know" important information from the real world for many applications, involving different sensor types and formats such as conventional images, thermal pictures, multispectral images and 3D point clouds. Considering a real-world scene scanned with a specific sensor, which generates specific data formats, is possible to use different computational processing techniques depending on the tasks and applications (see Fig. 1).

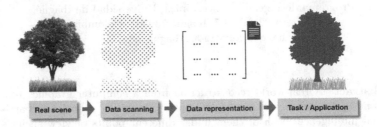

Fig. 1. General relation between scene, acquisition, data representation and task, e.g.: scene = tree; acquisition = LiDAR; data representation = 3D point Cloud and task = scene classification.

Over the last years, the 3D point clouds have gained popularity among engineers and researchers in fields such as: Automated navigation [1], robotic applications [2], mapping and reconstruction [3], airborne tasks [4], among others, given that this data provides more information than a conventional picture by adding new information dimensions, for example: depth, intensity, pulse width or light echo information depending on the sensors used for the reconstruction. Currently, many common off-the-shelf sensors provide 3D point clouds data, these available sensors are based on stereo or multiview vision cameras, laser scanners, time-of-flight cameras and structured light sensors.

LiDAR 3D point clouds can be generated with different sensors, on the one hand, the most employed commercial 3D rangefinders in mobile robotics are the Velodyne family devices with multi-beam models HDL-64E and RobotEye RE08. The main advantage of these sensors is the high acquisition rate that makes them suitable for applications moving at high speeds. However, these sensors are not easily access given their high costs, which range from 8000 USD. On the other hand, a 3D point cloud can be acquired by rotating or translating one or more 2D LiDARs. In this work, a single 2D LiDAR with a rotating platform is considered, as shown in Fig. 2. Regarding these scanning systems, it is important to highlight that their performance strongly depend on their parameters and their calibrations. Most applications require an extraction of high frequency spatial features, where extraction determination of these features can be difficult, unreliable or impossible when the sensor is badly calibrated. In other words, imprecise calibration can result in inaccurate digital reconstruction, and thus erroneous interpretations of the scene.

This paper presents the design and development of a lightweight and low-cost 3D laser scanner determined by spinning an off-the-shelf 2D rangefinder, in

Fig. 2. Configuration of the 3D scanning system based on a 2D LiDAR rotated by a step motor.

the same way, it provides a technique for the calibration of the system determined by a scan of a reference scene. The paper is organized as follows: next section describes the related work, Sect. 3 offers a camera calibration method for the developed system. The application of the sensor to scene reconstruction is presented in Sect. 4. The paper ends with conclusions, acknowledgments and references.

2   Related Work

A lot of work has been done on the 3D reconstruction based on 2D LiDAR sensors [5,6]. Despite some of them don't use any calibration process to improve the point clouds, some authors have reported zero reference offsets or angular deviations with respect to the manufacturer information and methods to correct the measurement errors by means of laboratory experiments as in [7]. However, this idea implies the need to have adequate laboratory conditions and elements, bearing in mind that a millimeter error can generate a bad calibration. Other authors use different techniques and targets to adjust the parameters tuning in a reconstruction model, most of them starting from a set of inaccurate hand-measured extrinsic calibration parameters, updating their values by comparing the scanned data respect to a reference scene in iterative algorithms, for example a corner, a wall or a spherical object.

In [8], the calibration method implemented for the LiDAR and camera is a board with white and black bands in movement, the camera detects the translation between the colors using image processing techniques, and differences of reflection for the LiDAR, in this case ten measurements from the sensors are needed for the calibration. On the basis of this principle, the association of both sensors is possible through geometric and analytic relations. Finally, two methods for calibration are implemented: the Least-Squares Solution and Minimal Problem Solution, the results are analyzed through a function cost and this is used to define the minimal problem solution as the method with the minimum error at calibration. In [9], the experimental calibrations consist in to realize a 2D scan of a small room with stairs without rotating, then the system takes various 3D scans of the same room, but in this case is importantly implemented the rotation, and finally, the sensor make another 2D scan without rotating, then this data is processed through two cost functions for 3-DOF rotation and other 3-DOF translation. In [10], the first step for calibrating the data acquired is maximizing the flatness of the 3D scan taken by the 2D sensor, this method is known as Nelder-Mead, and is implemented for optimization of no linear systems. The processed begin acquiring the point cloud of a planar scene, then separate the planes and this is evaluated on a cost function to finally conclude in a simplex optimization, all the process are iterative until obtaining an optimal solution. Other works focus on calibration with reference systems [11] or without use specific targets [12, 13], e.g. in [14], the system starts by scanning a no specific plane, this space can be obtained easily anywhere, then the data is analyzed and processed for 6-DOF and then those are divided in 3-DOF of rotation and 3-DOF translation, finally a cost function for each one obtain the calibration values. The Table 1 summarizes the main contributions and methods for 3D reconstruction systems based on LiDAR sensors for camera calibration process.

Table 1. Calibration process on 3D camera systems

Sensor	Calibration target	Reference
Hokuyo UBG-04LX-F0 and Chameleon CMLN13S2M	Black and white moving bands Planar scene	[8]
Hokuyo UTM30LX-EX	Small room with stairs	[9]
Hokuyo UTM-30LX		[10]
Hokuyo UTM-30LX	Simple, no specific target	[14]

3   Acquisition System

To create a point cloud which describes a 3D space is necessary to scan that space, this implies the combination of a sensing device and a moving device. Our 3D system is composed of a LiDAR sensor and a motion control device with one degree of freedom and this section presents the main characterization and adaptation of both devices to synchronize and jointly acquire point clouds.

3.1 Sensor Characterization

The Hokuyo URG-04LX is a Laser RangeFinder LRF categorized as an Amplitude Modulated Continuous Wave AMCW sensor. Basically, the laser emits an infrared beam on a rotating mirror which changes the beam's direction, then a scene region is illuminated, providing the return light with the scene information in response according to the flight times, the number of peaks, the pulse width, and signal intensities [15]. The main specifications of the sensor are presented in Table 2. Some authors have studied in detail the performance of the sensor in properties such as incidence angle, color, brightness, and material, by measuring the distance respect to a target and establishing comparisons with similar references under identical test conditions [16].

Table 2. key specifications for the used LiDAR.

	Hokuyo URG-04LX-UG01
Measurement distance	20 to 5600 mm
Resolution	1 mm
Scan angle	240°
Angular resolution	0.36° (360° /1.024 steps)
Accuracy	±30 mm (For distance above < 10000 mm)
Scanning time	100 ms/scan
Power source	5 VDC ± 5% (USB Bus power)

For an initial validation of the sensor features, we conducted an experiment by measuring a wall in a fixed position several times and analyze the results. In this way, we can quantify the data dispersion respect to the surface and the horizontal angle (ϕ) of the LiDAR, which ranges from $-120°$ to $+120°$ in steps of $0.3306°$ when the option of 726 values per scan is set. Figure 3 presents the mean and standard deviation (std) of each horizontal angle from the LiDAR and a partial XY representation in a room corner.

Corners from the room present a higher deviation respect to the beams that illuminated flat surfaces. Overall, the standard deviation of 100 scan measurements in a room for the radial distance r was around 4×10^{-3} m. However, the impact of the dispersion on reconstruction depends on the horizontal angle. In the simplest raw data transformation, the XY coordinates in a Hokuyo frame reference is given as:

$$X_i = (r + r_{error}) \cdot sin(\phi) = r \cdot sin(\phi) + r_{error} \cdot sin(\phi) \qquad (1)$$
$$Y_i = (r + r_{error}) \cdot cos(\phi) = r \cdot cos(\phi) + r_{error} \cdot cos(\phi) \qquad (2)$$

where X_i, Y_i are the Cartesian coordinates for an acquired point in the sensor reference, ϕ is the horizontal angle of the sensor, r is the radial distance obtained from the sensor and r_{error} is the dispersion representation given a normal measurement error. From Eqs. 1 and 2 is possible to observe that the error impact on

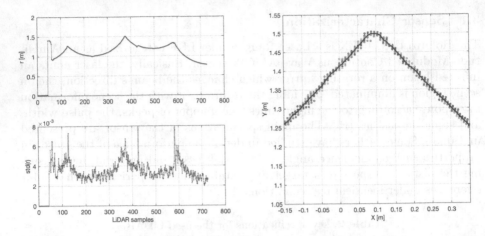

Fig. 3. Mean and standard deviation of the distance measurements: (left top) mean of 100 2D radial distance measurements, (left bottom) standard deviation of 100 2D radial distance measurements, (right) top view of one of the corners of the room.

X_i at high ϕ angle values and by the opposite on Y_i impact around zero angles given the *cos*, *sin* functions, which amplifies or attenuate both, the radial distance and its measurement error. This implies a measurement error with more pronunciation in some reconstructed regions than others.

3.2   3D Scanner

A functional diagram of the acquisition system is shown in Fig. 4. The 2D sensor and the motion controller can be accessed independently by the computer through a ROS Kinetic node which collects the data form the Hokuyo and define the motor actions. Considering that is a simple and low-cost system, neither Inertial Measurement Unit IMU sensors nor encoders are used to know the Hokuyo orientation, this information is only estimated from the motor actions recorded. The used motor is a step motor with approximately 160.000 steps per revolution given its high gear reduction, thus, the vertical angular resolution for the 3D system is around 0.0022°. The motion controller is composed by an Arduino nano which receives commands from the ROS node and generates the voltage signal for the motor driver SparkFun "EasyDriver - Stepper Motor Driver". The ROS node was developed based on URG driver for ROS available on: wiki URG node website. The developed acquisition software obtain the initial, final and increment scanning angles from the user, once the last scan is collected at the final vertical angle, the system generates a flat text file with three columns separated: vertical angle ϕ, horizontal angle θ and radial distances r. After that, in a second stage, an offline algorithm developed in Python, which contains the tuned parameters converts the raw data to a "xyz" point cloud or a .las file by using "txt2las" executable from LASTools of Rapidlasso.

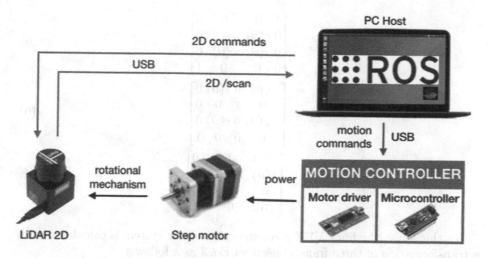

Fig. 4. Functional diagram of the 3D laser rangefinder.

4   3D System Model

4.1   Kinematic Model

The purpose of the sensor system is to acquire the 3D coordinate $P_{initial}$ of LiDAR detection relative to a reference coordinate frame P_o. The final 3D point cloud in P_o consists in a XYZ space in function of LiDAR horizontal angle θ and radial distance r, as well as the motor vertical angle ϕ and system constant parameters which represent the distances between the points and possible angular deviations. With these measurements, the 3D position of p is given by transforming 2D point from P_i to P_1 and then P_1 to P_2 and P_o respectively as shown in Fig. 5. In a general representation, these transformations are formulated from a basic point transformation T_p with $[4 \times 4]$ dimension given it is a square matrix for a 3D space:

$$T_p = R_z \cdot R_y \cdot R_x \cdot T \tag{3}$$

where T is a XYZ translation transformation with three parameters, Rx_p is a rotation matrix around X axis (pitch), Ry_p is a rotation matrix around Y axis (roll) and Rz_p is a rotation matrix around Z axis (yaw), for a total of six parameters per point: three angles and three distances: t_x, t_y and t_z. Each one of these matrix are described as follows:

$$T = \begin{bmatrix} 1 & 0 & 0 & t_x \\ 0 & 1 & 0 & t_y \\ 0 & 0 & 1 & t_z \\ 0 & 0 & 0 & 1 \end{bmatrix} \tag{4}$$

$$R_x = \begin{bmatrix} 1 & 0 & 0 & 0 \\ 0 & c(\vartheta) & -s(\vartheta) & 0 \\ 0 & s(\vartheta) & c(\vartheta) & 0 \\ 0 & 0 & 0 & 1 \end{bmatrix} \tag{5}$$

$$R_y = \begin{bmatrix} c(\vartheta) & 0 & s(\vartheta) & 0 \\ 0 & 1 & 0 & 0 \\ -s(\vartheta) & 0 & c(\vartheta) & 0 \\ 0 & 0 & 0 & 1 \end{bmatrix} \tag{6}$$

$$R_z = \begin{bmatrix} c(\vartheta) & -s(\vartheta) & 0 & 0 \\ s(\vartheta) & c(\vartheta) & 1 & 0 \\ 0 & 1 & 0 & 0 \\ 0 & 0 & 0 & 1 \end{bmatrix} \tag{7}$$

In this sense, the final XYZ reconstruction of our system is calculated with a transformation of three frames based on Eq. 3 as a follows:

$$P_o = Tp_0 \cdot Tp_2 \cdot Rx_\theta \cdot Tp_1 \cdot P_i \tag{8}$$

where P_i corresponds with the initial frame: $[r \cdot sin(\phi); r \cdot cos(\phi); 0; 1]$, Tp_1 is the transformation to point P_1, Rx_θ is the rotation matrix according to variable motor angle θ, Tp_2 is the transformation to point P_2 and Tp_3 is the transformation to the reference frame P_o, which is at ground-level by including the distance of the camera holder to the floor.

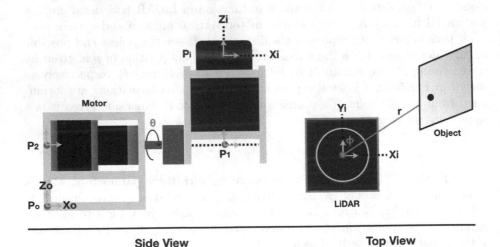

Side View   **Top View**

Fig. 5. Schematic diagram and notations of the sensor system when measuring a 3D point P_i and different coordinated frame points to transform to the reference frame Po.

4.2   Calibration Process

Small errors in the attachment of the 2D device to the rotating mechanism pro-
voke misalignment and in turn generate a distortion in the point cloud computed
with the Eq. 8. Assuming the 3D sensor and the rotational element as a single
system, we propose in this paper an intrinsic calibration process based on a
simple scene reference: a flat ground, which is easy to find in any application,
either terrestrial, aerial, mobile or fixed. The calibration process starts with
a scanning of a flat ground surface and a model with preliminary parameters
defined from simple measurements to generates a first reference reconstruction.
Basically, these parameters represent both, distances between the transformation
points, and inclinations of them which are generally initiated at zero. In this way,
an object/cost function J is defined to quantify the error, this function forms
the basis of the optimization process and is used to compare the acquired 3D
point cloud data respect to the real environment or ground-truth in this case. J
must provide a higher cost when exist a big difference between the reconstructed
point cloud with the vector of parameters W respect to the ground-truth reference, and a lower costs as the match between reconstructed point cloud and the
ground-truth reference improves [17]. The simplest cost function consists in to
calculate the sum of magnitude of residuals between the ground-truth reference
and a fitted plane from the model response. In this way, the iterative method
starts with an initial error between the calculated plane and the reference to
adjust the parameters for the next iteration until an optimal parameters vector
W is defined.

To define the cost function J is important to consider a reconstruction with
n points by using the set of parameters W in an XYZ space as a follows:

$$\begin{bmatrix} X_0 & Y_0 & 1 \\ X_1 & Y_1 & 1 \\ & \cdots & \\ X_n & Y_n & 1 \end{bmatrix} \begin{bmatrix} K_0 \\ K_1 \\ K_2 \end{bmatrix} = \begin{bmatrix} Z_0 \\ Z_1 \\ \cdots \\ Z_n \end{bmatrix} \tag{9}$$

In other words, the Eq. 9 can be represented as:

$$M \cdot K = Z \tag{10}$$

where M is a matrix with XY information from the reconstructed point cloud.
Now, solving for K which represents a coefficients matrix of a fitting plane and
given the system is over-determined the plane coefficients are calculated as:

$$K = (M^T M)^{-1} M^T Z \tag{11}$$

where K is a matrix $[3 \times 1]$ with the best fitting plane coefficients given a set of
points from the modeled reference. Then a cost function J can be expressed in
Eqs. 12 and 13:

$$J = \sum_{i=1}^{n} (M_{[i]} \cdot K - Z_{[i]})^2 \tag{12}$$

The estimation process was splitted in two parts: first the parameters from reference points P_i to P_2 (see Fig. 5) were obtained by using the Eq. 12, then a cost function focuses on find the remaining parameters to define a perfect ground respect to the reference by using the Eq. 13.

$$J = \sum_{i=1}^{n} (M_{[i]} \cdot K)^2 \tag{13}$$

The optimization process was implemented by using the MATLAB function "lsqnonlin" with upper and lower constraints. The computational cost of the optimization process is not of a great concern because the process is done offline and has to be done only once to calibrate the device. The optimization was performed starting from the default calibration data provided by the manufacturer and experimental measurements from the system. Computational resources and costs are presented in next section.

5   Results

5.1   Calibration Results

From a manually segmented region of a scanned ground-truth target, a point cloud was reconstructed by using the nominal parameters. The calibration algorithm was implemented on this point cloud to re-define twelve parameters on the first part of the optimization based on cost function presented in the Eq. 12 and six parameters on the last part of the optimization based on cost function presented in the Eq. 13, for a total of eighteen estimated parameters. The offline optimization was executed on a computer with a memory of 8 GB 1600 MHz DDR3, a processor 2.3 GHz Intel Core i7, and an operative system macOS High Sierra on a MATLAB version R2016a; the algorithm found the parameters in five minutes approximately on a point cloud of 10871 voxels. The Fig. 6 shows a graphical comparison of the reconstructed point cloud of a segment of ground with nominal parameters and with the optimal parameters. 3D reconstruction with the nominal parameters presented inclinations, deviations and uneven ground along the point cloud. However, the second 3D reconstruction reduces these effects on the point cloud with geometry flatter and with a level around zero.

5.2   Point Cloud Comparison

A comparison process was performed once the parameter estimation had finished. The process consisted in scanning a reference object with a second 3D scanner from different distances to compare both reconstructed point clouds. The Kinect V2 was chosen as the second scanner given it is a system with an easy calibration and low-cost. For this purpose, measurements were made every 50 cm between 0.5 and 4.5 m with respect to the reference object. The object of reference was

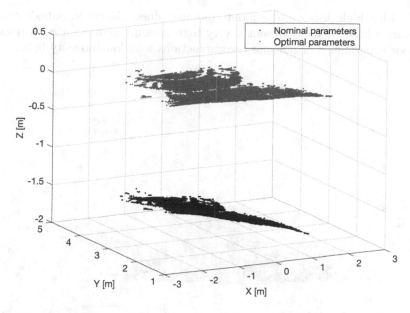

Fig. 6. 3D reconstructions, with nominal parameters (black) and with optimal parameters (blue). (Color figure online)

manufactured by cutting a square window in a depth window of 50 cm section with a laser cutter on a flat wooden surface, the Fig. 7 shows an example of a 3D reconstruction of the object reference with both systems. The Kinect V2 has a limitation on the aperture angles and the range, 60° for the vertical angle and 70° for the horizontal angle with a range R: 0.5>R≥4.5 m. On the other hand, our system has a horizontal aperture of 240° and 360° for vertical aperture with a range R: 0.02>R≥5.6 m. Moreover, our 3D reconstructions presented much less noise measurement on the generated point clouds.

To compare our system and prove its performance, two parameters were calculated from point clouds on every measurement: the window area estimation and the resolution calculated as the number of voxels in a square meter. The Fig. 8a shows the area measurement obtained from the point cloud in each distance. In general, the Kinect V2 presented a measurement error of 4.96% and the developed system a measurement error of 6.72%. Moreover, the Fig. 8b shows the change of voxels number per square meter with a distance variation, for this parameter the Kinect V2 presented around four times more resolution than our system.

5.3   Reconstruction Results

The results for the 3D laser scanner as the terrestrial moving platform are presented in Fig. 9. It shows the reconstructed point clouds which were filtered with the function "pcdenoise" from MATLAB. The shiny objects or elements illuminated with high incidence angles generate measurement error which converts in points with a high dispersion or indeterminate values. Moreover, outside experiments with high sunlight present a very high measurement error with respect to indoor experiments or outdoor reconstructions with low-intensity light.

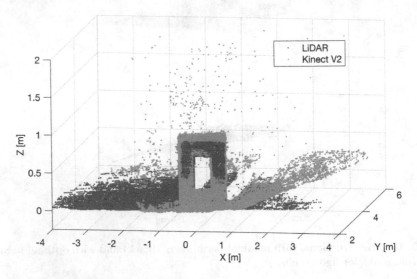

Fig. 7. Point cloud reconstruction of the object reference with the developed system and with a MS Kinect V2.

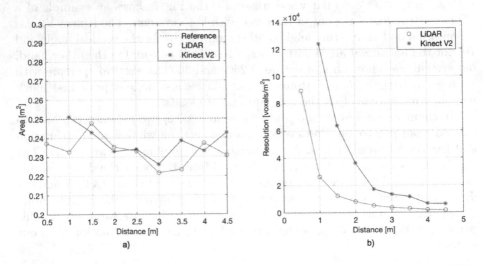

Fig. 8. Reconstruction comparison with a MS Kinect V2. (a) area comparison; and (b) resolution comparison.

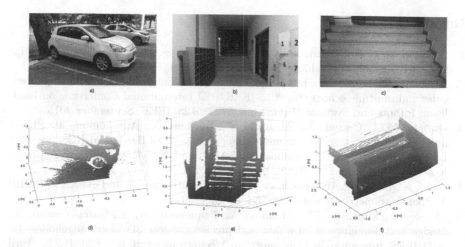

Fig. 9. Reconstructed 3D Point clouds: (a) outside car, (b) indoor scene, (c) high spatial frequency scene, (d) outside car point cloud with around 192.000 voxels, (e) indoor scene point cloud with around 578.600 voxels and (f) stairs point cloud with around 14.5000 voxels.

6   Conclusions

This paper has described the development of a low-cost 3D laser scanner based on a 3D LiDAR and a rotational element without an orientation sensor, with a total price around 1200 USD. Calibration has been performed from a ground-truth target to obtain both temporal and geometric parameters of the new sensor. High spatial frequency presented bigger dispersion compared with planar objects in scenes, thus, an average of ten measurements was implemented to reduce the measurement noise effect. Calibration process improved the quality of geometric constructions, especially on high frequency elements of the scene. The Hokuyo URG-04LX-UG01 presented a better performance in indoor scenes, low light intensity and on non-shiny objects. 3D system reconstructs a profile between 0.1 and 1 s, so that, total acquisition time depends on vertical resolution and number of averaged 2D profiles.

We believe that this result can support different low-cost applications that use a 2D LiDAR and a simple step motor to generate point cloud reconstructions. Future work includes the migration of the optimization algorithms from MATLAB to Python or C++ and then uses the calibration process faster, in an online execution.

Acknowledgments. This research is being developed with the partial support of the "Gobernación del Tolima" under "Proyecto Talento Humano" - Research Culture. The results presented in this paper have been obtained with the assistance of students from the Research Hotbed on Robotics (SI2C), Research Group D+TEC, Universidad de Ibagué, Ibagué-Colombia.

References

1. Levinson, J., et al.: Towards fully autonomous driving: systems and algorithms. In: 2011 IEEE Intelligent Vehicles Symposium (IV), pp. 163–168. IEEE, June 2011
2. Reymann, C., Lacroix, S.: Improving LiDAR point cloud classification using intensities and multiple echoes. In: 2015 IEEE/RSJ International Conference on Intelligent Robots and Systems (IROS), pp. 5122–5128. IEEE, September 2015
3. Ocando, M.G., Certad, N., Alvarado, S., Terrones, A.: Autonomous 2D SLAM and 3D mapping of an environment using a single 2D LIDAR and ROS. In: 2017 Latin American Robotics Symposium (LARS) and 2017 Brazilian Symposium on Robotics (SBR), pp. 1–6. IEEE, November 2017
4. Wehr, A., Lohr, U.: Airborne laser scanning-an introduction and overview. ISPRS J. Photogrammetry Remote Sens. **54**, 68–82 (1999)
5. Morales, J., Martinez, J.L., Mandow, A., Pequeno-Boter, A., Garcia-Cerezo, A.: Design and development of a fast and precise low-cost 3D laser rangefinder. In: 2011 IEEE International Conference on Mechatronics, pp. 621–626. IEEE, April 2011
6. Klimentjew, D., Arli, M., Zhang, J.: 3D scene reconstruction based on a moving 2D laser range finder for service-robots
7. Park, C.-S., Kim, D., You, B.-J., Oh, S.-R.: Characterization of the Hokuyo UBG-04LX-F01 2D laser rangefinder. In: 19th International Symposium in Robot and Human Interactive Communication, pp. 385–390. IEEE, September 2010
8. Guo, C.X., Roumeliotis, S.I.: An analytical least-squares solution to the line scan LIDAR-camera extrinsic calibration problem. In: 2013 IEEE International Conference on Robotics and Automation, pp. 2943–2948. IEEE, May 2013
9. Martínez, J.L., Morales, J., Reina, A.J., Mandow, A., Pequeño-Boter, A., García-Cerezo, A.: Construction and calibration of a low-cost 3D laser scanner with 360° field of view for mobile robots
10. Morales, J., Martínez, J., Mandow, A., Reina, A., Pequeño-Boter, A., García-Cerezo, A.: Boresight calibration of construction misalignments for 3D scanners built with a 2D laser rangefinder rotating on its optical center. Sensors **14**, 20025–20040 (2014)
11. Zeng, Y., et al.: An improved calibration method for a rotating 2D LIDAR system. Sensors **18**, 497 (2018)
12. Mader, D., Westfeld, P., Maas, H.-G.: An Integrated flexible self-calibration approach for 2D laser scanning range finders applied to the Hokuyo UTM-30LX-EW
13. Olivka, P., Krumnikl, M., Moravec, P., Seidl, D.: Calibration of short range 2D laser range finder for 3D SLAM usage. J. Sens. **2016**, 1–13 (2016)
14. Kang, J., Doh, N.L.: Full-DOF calibration of a rotating 2-D LIDAR with a simple plane measurement. IEEE Trans. Robot. **32**, 1245–1263 (2016)
15. Mallet, C., Bretar, F.: Full-waveform topographic lidar: state-of-the-art. ISPRS J. Photogramm. Remote Sens. **64**, 1–16 (2009)
16. Okubo, Y., Okubo, Y., Ye, C., Borenstein, J.: Characterization of the Hokuyo URG-04LX laser rangefinder for mobile robot obstacle negotiation. Spie Def., sec.+sens.; Unmanned Sys. Tech. XI, Conf. 7332: Unmanned, Robotic, and Layered Systems (2009)
17. Muhammad, N., Lacroix, S.: Calibration of a rotating multi-beam Lidar. In: 2010 IEEE/RSJ International Conference on Intelligent Robots and Systems, pp. 5648–5653. IEEE, October 2010

GPU-Implementation of a Sequential Monte Carlo Technique for the Localization of an Ackerman Robot

Olmer García[1(✉)], David Acosta[2], and Cesar Diaz[1]

[1] Universidad de Bogotá Jorge Tadeo Lozano, Bogota, Colombia
olmer.garciab@utadeo.edu.co
[2] Universidad del Norte, Barranquilla, Colombia

Abstract. This article presents the parallel implementation, using a graphical processing unit (GPU), of a Sequential Monte Carlo Method, which is a sophisticated model estimation technique based on simulations, also known as Particle Filter. The particle filter is applied to the localization of a simulated Ackerman mobile robot with a simplified kinematic model. The inputs for the model are the linear displacement of the car and the steering angle, subject to additive white Gaussian noise disturbances. The car model integrates a simulated GPS and a compass which also present Gaussian noise. The program was designed using a client/server architecture, considering that the energy constraints of embedded systems used in mobile robotics favor the separation of the tasks of visualization and localization. The client is a web program responsible for the task of visualization, developed in HTML5 using JS and AJAX, and the server implements the particle filter algorithm using the libraries CUDA and Thrust, improving considerably the performance time of the particle filter. The performance is approximately 9 times faster in GPU over CPU in the tested architecture. This opens the possibility to embed this type in simulations in real-time systems.

Keywords: Particle filters · CUDA · THRUST

1 Introduction

The tendency towards the development of automated, semiautonomous and autonomous advanced driver-assistance systems (ADAS) has been driven by significant technological advances and the need to improve vehicle safety and security automation [1].

For a mobile robotic architecture like the one described in [2], an intelligent, autonomous system consists of three main modules: perception, planning and motion control. Each module seeks to answer specific questions related to tasks performed by the automatic system, as shown in Fig. 1.

Autonomous robotic vehicles are often designed using concept of layers and functional groups taking account that, this type of architecture facilitates the separation of functions and development, allowing for the definition of interfaces between the various subsystems [3]. According to [4], the six major functional groups are Interface Sensors, Perception, Control, Vehicle Interface and User Interface. The task of each

© Springer Nature Switzerland AG 2018
H. Florez et al. (Eds.): ICAI 2018, CCIS 942, pp. 309–320, 2018.
https://doi.org/10.1007/978-3-030-01535-0_23

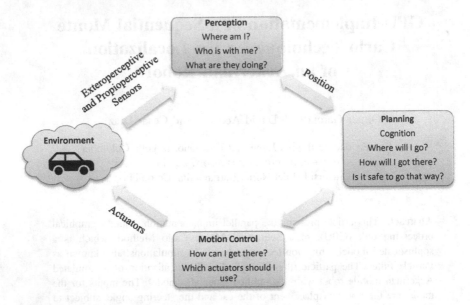

Fig. 1. Layers in the autonomous mobile robotics architecture.

layer of the software are answered by the software architecture. This research is part of the project of the autonomous vehicle VILMA01(First Intelligent Vehicle of Laboratory of Autonomous Mobility) [5] to improve the perception layer.

Within the framework of this work, the Perception layer is addressed, specifically the spatial localization of the vehicle using sensor information. For this purpose, a benchmark case where two sensors are available is studied, a GPS and a compass. Information from both sensors is fused to improve the accuracy of the localization. Sensor fusion combines different sources of sensory information into one representational format [6] and has proven to be an effective method to provide robust information for mobile robot localization.

The method described hereafter requires a mathematical model of the vehicle as well as an algorithm, which incorporates the Bayesian inference process to account for sensor data. In the next section the mathematical background for both methods is explained, then, the software architecture designed for this work is presented. Subsequently, the parallel implementation of the algorithms in the Graphics Processing Unit (GPU) using the CUDA platform and the Thrust library is explained in detail. Finally, some conclusions are discussed.

2 Mathematical Background

2.1 Ackerman Vehicle Kinematic Model

The car robot model is described by the kinematic simplified model of an Ackerman car in the plane xy, which can be described by (1) [7]. This type of robot is a non-holonomic mechanical system, which can be expanded to obtain here dynamics [8].

The position of the vehicle can be described by three variables x, y and θ known as the state vector of the car $\mathbf{x}$. The discrete time state equation can be approximated to

$$\begin{bmatrix} x_k \\ y_k \\ \theta_k \end{bmatrix} = \begin{bmatrix} x_{k-1} + d \cdot cos(\theta_{k-1}) \\ y_{k-1} + d \cdot sin(\theta_{k-1}) \\ \theta_{k-1} + \frac{d}{L} \cdot tan(\psi) \end{bmatrix} \quad (1)$$

where, L is the distance between tires of the car, d is an input composed by the displacement distance with additive Gaussian noise $N(0, dist_{noise})$, ψ is an input composed by the steer angle also perturbed with Gaussian noise $N(0, steering_{noise})$. The Fig. 2 presents the schematic of the Ackerman robot.

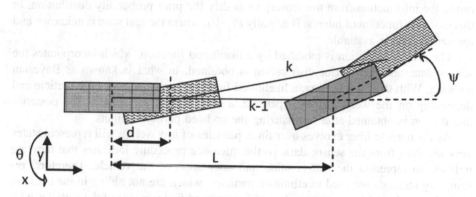

Fig. 2. Bicycle model for the Ackerman robot.

The GPS and the compass data are contained in the measure vector $\mathbf{y}$ which is described by

$$\mathbf{y_k} = \begin{bmatrix} x_k + N(0, gps_{noise}) \\ y_k + N(0, gps_{noise}) \\ \theta_k + N(0, compass_{noise}) \end{bmatrix} \quad (2)$$

2.2   Particle Filter Algorithm

The objective of the Sequential Monte Carlo method employed in this article is to obtain a better approximation of the real position and orientation of the vehicle, and it is based on an iterative procedure in which sensor data is used to update and improve the approximation of a probability distribution given by a set of particles, each of which represent a possible state of the vehicle.

Every time step each particle is generated, where the particle's position and orientation depends both on the probability density function and the sensor data. The weight of every particle is based on a likelihood function, which also employs information from the sensor observations. In a final task, a resampling technique allows for modified versions of high weight particles to replace low weight particles, thus improving over time the approximation for the position of the vehicle.

The actual position and orientation of the vehicle in a state space, given in this case by a cartesian square and an angle, is given by a probability density function over the state-space and describes the probability that any given position and angle are the real target. In this article a uniform random distribution is used as a prior distribution of the particles. Furthermore, both sensors, the compass and the GPS, are represented with normal distributions and the measurements are assumed to be independent.

A likelihood function is given, for instance, by a function $P(\cdot|x_k)$, which describes the probability of obtaining a determined sensor information for a target state x_k. But for the tracking problem, the concept of Bayesian inference is employed by incorporating the information from the sensors to modify the prior probability distribution. In this case, the function of interest is actually $P(y_k|\cdot)$, where the real state is unknown and the sensor data is available.

The prior distribution is modified by a likelihood function, which incorporates the sensor data, and a posterior distribution is obtained, in what is known as Bayesian tracking. With the particle filter, a likelihood function is obtained for each particle and depending on the weight of each particle, a new weight is obtained. The posterior distribution is obtained after normalizing the updated particle weights.

As the particle filter evolves over time, particles of low weight will represent states very different from the sensor data, so the inference procedure indicates that they are unlikely to represent the real position and orientation of the vehicle. Therefore, re-sampling methods are used to eliminate particles, which are not aiding in the tracking procedure and to obtain new particles, which are modified versions of the particles with higher weights.

Many algorithms exist, which can be classified in multinomial, residual, stratified and systematic re-sampling [9]. This segment of the algorithm is crucial to analyze, considering its parallel form, for which different approaches have been studied [6, 10]. In this project the residual method described in [11] is used. In this implementation, the probability of each particle to be copied depends on its weight. More copies are created from particles with higher weights. Nonetheless, for the copy operation to be a parallel implementation in CUDA, the position in memory of each particle copy must be stored. For which a sum of weights is calculated, and every copy made by each thread is stored in a contiguous block of memory. An improvement of this uncoalesced memory access escapes the scope of this work.

To summarize, the steps involved in the mathematical algorithm are described analytically:

1. Generate the state $\mathbf{x}^p$ for P particles using uniform random distribution

$$\mathbf{x}^p = \begin{bmatrix} U(x_{min}, x_{max}) \\ U(y_{min}, y_{max}) \\ U(0, 2\pi) \end{bmatrix} \tag{3}$$

2. Obtain x_k and y_k

3. For each particle p, obtain x_k^p and y_k^p and probability $P(x_k^p|y_k) = w^p$. In this problem, the sensor data is obtained from a normal distribution $N(0, \sigma)$ and the sensor measurements are independent, so the probability is just the product of each sensor i.

$$w^p = \prod_{i=1}^{N_{sensor}} \left(\frac{1}{\sqrt{2\pi}\sigma_i} e^{\frac{1}{2}\left(\frac{y_{ki}^p - y_{ki}}{\sigma_i}\right)^2} \right) \tag{4}$$

where σ_i is the standard deviation for each sensor.

4. Re-sampling the particles. This part of the algorithm was not trivial to be parallelized due to the data allocation constraints of the GPU, in this project, the residual method described in [11] is used. It can be implemented with the Eqs. (5) and (6).

$$\bar{w}^p = \frac{P}{\sum_{j=0}^{P} w^j} w^p \tag{5}$$

$$\hat{w}^p = floor\left(\sum_{j=0}^{P} \bar{w}^p\right) \tag{6}$$

5. Generate the new particles for the next step.

$$x_{k-1}^p = x_k^{\hat{w}^p} \tag{7}$$

6. Return to step 2.

3   Software Architecture

The software is designed in client-server architecture, considering that localization and visualization in mobile robotics should be separated since energy constraints from the embedded systems of the robot normally require low power consumption.

Consequently, a visualization interface was developed in the client using the canvas of HTML5 and JavaScript. It reads the data from the server using Ajax. The graphical user interface is based on the program for particle filters realized by Aleksandr Motsjonov and programmed in coffee-script[1]. This code implements in the client the visualization using html5 and a particle filter where the sensors are measurements to Landmarks using coffee-script (JavaScript). The JavaScript program manipulates the field and the canvas object of the Html page, and request data from the server using the object *XMLHttpRequest*. The animation is made using *requestAnimationFrame*. Other information about the simulation is also rendered in the client side, which save

---

[1] http://soswow.github.io/Various-JS-and-Python/JS/ParticleFilter/, accessed June/2018

Fig. 3. Visualization of the particle filter at Canvas (a) During initialization (b) after some iterations. The red circle represents the real position of the robot. (Color figure online)

resources in the server side. Figure 3 presents the visualization of the particle filter over some iterations.

In the server, the initial idea was to use an Apache server which would host a Fast-Common Gateway Interface program written in C/C++, which by a thread would implement the particle filter. However, since the computer in which the implementation was developed must run the CUDA program over OPTIRUN environment, it was not possible to host the CUDA program in the Apache server.

The architecture implemented is similar to the one proposed in [12], and executes two programs: One is the Apache HTML server, which executes a script called Data. cgi using the Fast-Common Gateway Interface (FCGI). The script reads a Linux IPC (Inter-Process Communication) shared memory using a semaphore and prints it in JSON format using C language. The second one is the particle filter program, which is explained in the next section in detail. The diagram in Fig. 4 represents the architecture for the software.

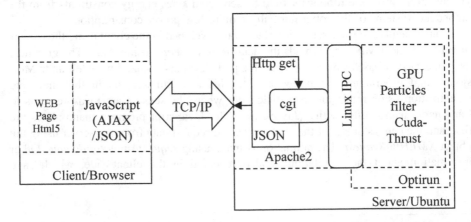

Fig. 4. Architecture of the software implemented.

4   GPU-Implementation

The CUDA program is made in C/C++ using the CUDA platform and library Thrust.
This library is a parallel template used to implement high performance applications
with minimal programming effort [14]. Based on the C++ Standard Template Library
(STL), Thrust brings a familiar high-level interface to the realm of GPU Computing
while remaining fully interoperable with the rest of the CUDA software ecosystem[x2].
The diagram of which data/process is in the host (CPU) or in the device (GPU) is
presented in Fig. 6. The pseudocode of the GPU program is presented in the Fig. 5,
which can be explained by the next stages.

Algorithm 1: GPU algorithm

Data: N,max_l,σ_{gps},$\sigma_{compass}$ $\sigma_{steering}$,$\sigma_{displacement}$
Result: $Robots_x^{host}$

1   $Robots_x^{host} \leftarrow rand_{uniform}(max_l)$
2   $Robots_x^{device} \leftarrow Robots_x^{host}$
3   $robot.init(\sigma_{gps},\sigma_{compass},$
4         $\sigma_{steering},\sigma_{displacement})$
5   $robot.set\_initial\_position()$
6   **while** $true$ **do**
7 | $robot.move()$
8 | $robot.sense()$
9 | **foreach** $r,w \leftarrow zip(Robots_x^{device}, Robots_w^{device})$ **do**
10 | | $r.move()$
11 | | $r.sense()$
12 | | $\Delta \leftarrow robot.y - r.y$
13 | | $w \leftarrow \prod\limits_{i=1}^{Nsensor} \left(\frac{1}{\sqrt{2\pi}\sigma_i} e^{\frac{1}{2}\left(\frac{\Delta}{\sigma_i}\right)^2} \right)$
14 | **end**
15 | $s_w \leftarrow \sum \left(Robots_w^{device} \right)$
16 | $Robots_w^{device} \leftarrow Robots_w^{device}(N/s_w)$
17 | $Robots_w^{device} \leftarrow tfloor(Robots_w^{device})$
18 | $Robots_{index}^{device} \leftarrow Robots_w^{device}$
19 | **for** $index \leftarrow 0 : N$ **do**
20 | | $resample_{start} \leftarrow index == 0 ? 0 : (Robots_w^{device}[index-1])$
21 | | $resample_n = Robots_w^{device}[index] - resample_{start}$
22 | | $Robots_{index}^{device}[resample_{start} : resample_n] \leftarrow index$
23 | **end**
24 | thrust::make_permutation_iterator$(Robots_x^{device},Robots_{index})$ **return**
        $(Robots_x^{device})$
25 | **foreach** $r \leftarrow Robots_x^{device}$ **do**
26 | | $rand_{gaussian}.discard(3*thread\_id)$
27 | | $r.x \leftarrow fmod(r.x + rand_{gaussian})$
28 | **end**
29 **end**

Fig. 5. Pseudocode of the GPU program.

1. Generate N particles in all the space (max_l) using a uniform random distribution. Also, initialize the variables of the *robot*, through the standard deviations of the gps sensor (σ_{gps}), compass sensor $(\sigma_{compass})$, and the state space input variables, in this case steering $(\sigma_{steering})$ and displacement $(\sigma_{displacement})$. Note, that in a real time system the robot initialization will consist in initializing the hardware associated to sensors and actuators. Therefore, this part of the code is performed in the CPU (host), like it is presented in Fig. 6.

2. Move and sense the *robot* to obtain **x** and **y** (lines 7 and 8 of the pseudocode). Like it is shown in the Unified Model diagram (UML) of the Fig. 7, this part was implemented inside the *struct Trobot* through CPU methods (__*host*__) *move_robot* and *sense_robot*. The vector **x** is implemented through the variables x, y, and th; and the vector **y** is implemented through the *struct Measure* which contains an array of *Nsensors*, three in this case, with the actual measurement and the predefined standard deviation (σ) of the sensor.

3. Simulate the movement and the sensors of each particle on the GPU to obtain the weights w^p for each particle. This operation is implemented by the *struct Trobot* through the kernel implemented in the function *operator*. This kernel is totally parallelized, and the information shared are the measurements **y** of the real robot and the displacement input data, like d (*move_dist*) and ψ (*move_orient*). The Eq. (4) is implemented in the method *measure_prob* with the *struct Measure*, which enables the algorithm to be scaled to incorporate more sensors. The data which represent the vector **x** of each particle $\left(Robots_\mathbf{x}^{device}\right)$, is implemented by three arrays which form a tuple to iterate with the operation. This section corresponds to the lines 9 to 13 of the pseudocode of the Fig. 5.

4. Through a new kernel applied to array **w**, the Eqs. (5) and (6) are implemented like it is presented in the lines 15 to 18 of the pseudocode. This step generates the sum of weights used to select the particles, which better describe the robot.

5. Resampling is the technique to reduce the number of particles with low weights by replacing them with perturbed copies of particles with high weight. The probability of each particle to be copied depends on its weight. A transformation is applied to particle weights **w** to obtain the number of copies to make of each particle. For the parallel implementation, the second algorithm of re-sampling presented in [11] transformed to CUDA was used. Considering that each particle must also know where in global memory its copies should be placed and using the cumulative sum from step 4, each thread overwrites $\hat{w}_{i-1}$ through $\widehat{w_i}$ with its index. Then, it allocates them in the contiguous block of memory from $\hat{w}_{i-1} - \widehat{w_i}$. Note that the access to these continuous blocks at *index* array reduces the performance of the GPU processing.

6. Permute the $Robots_\mathbf{x}^{device}$ to select the particles which will be used in the next stage. This is performed by a Thrust function.

7. Transfer $Robots_\mathbf{x}^{device}$ to host. In this stage the data is shared through the IPC memory to the web server to enable the visualization. Note that in a real robot scenery some criteria should be applied to find the estimate of the localization $\hat{\mathbf{x}}$ of the robot to be used in the other layers of an autonomous robot.

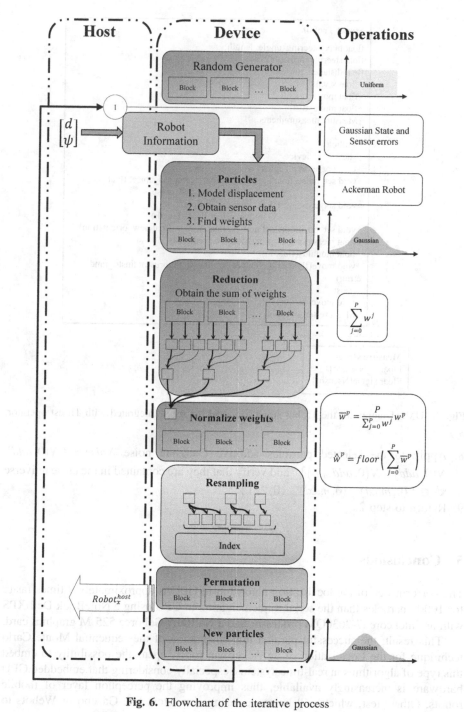

Fig. 6. Flowchart of the iterative process

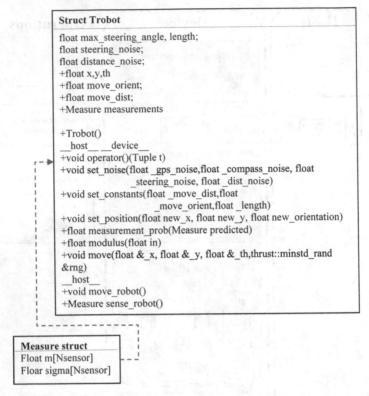

Struct Trobot

float max_steering_angle, length;
float steering_noise;
float distance_noise;
+float x,y,th
+float move_orient;
+float move_dist;
+Measure measurements

+Trobot()
__host__ __device__
+void operator()(Tuple t)
+void set_noise(float _gps_noise,float _compass_noise, float
                _steering_noise, float _dist_noise)
+void set_constants(float _move_dist,float
                    _move_orient,float _length)
+void set_position(float new_x, float new_y, float new_orientation)
+float measurement_prob(Measure predicted)
+float modulus(float in)
+void move(float &_x, float &_y, float &_th,thrust::minstd_rand
&rng)
__host__
+void move_robot()
+Measure sense_robot()

Measure struct
Float m[Nsensor]
Floar sigma[Nsensor]

Fig. 7. UML Diagram of the Trobot struct to model the robot integrated with Thrust operator.

8. Apply to the selected particles additive Gaussian noise $Noise = \{ N(0, add)$ $N(0, add) \quad N(0, add_{angle})\}^T$ and verify that they are contained in the close universe $\mathbf{x}^P \in \{ (0, maxl) \quad (0, maxl) \quad (0, 2\pi) \}$.
9. Return to step 2.

5 Conclusions

The performance of the localization algorithm in GPU is approximately 9 times faster for 10000 particles than the serial implementation in CPU using a NoteBook Dell XPS with an Intel core i7-2630QM processor and a NVIDIA GeForce 525 M graphics card.

This result, the successful parallel implementation of the sequential Monte Carlo technique for the Localization of an Ackerman robot, opens the possibility to embed this type of algorithms in real-time systems, especially considering that embedded GPU hardware is increasingly available, thus improving the perception layer of mobile robots. Others test, which will be made, using simulators like Gazebo or Webots to validate the convergence of the algorithm.

From the viewpoint of the implementation, the use of the random generator in Thrust was considerably challenging, and the difficulty lied in understanding that in the algorithm in the library the seed in not shared between threads.

Additionally, it is worthy to note that the Visualization work very good in Google Chrome, the convergence of the algorithm is fast and after few iterations a better estimation is obtained.

Moreover, the use of Object oriented programming in CUDA using the Thrust library allows for the integration of GPU programming in a predefined software architecture seamlessly and efficiently. Furthermore, it reduces the code needed for tasks like initializations and common functions and the encapsulation resulting from this programming paradigm ease faster code reusability.

Finally, future work include the alternative to use different sensors like lasers or odometers and to replace the Ackerman robot model by including a dynamic model of the robot, which can be implemented using the Boost library [13] which can be adapted to be used with Thrust. Also, different re-sampling techniques could be studied and implemented to avoid the uncoalesced memory access and improve the performance of the algorithm.

Acknowledgements. This work was supported by Universidad de Bogotá Jorge Tadeo Lozano and Universidad del Norte. D. Acosta was funded by Colciencias through Grant 727-2015 and O. Garcia was funded by Ph.D. Scholarship PEC/PG CAPES/CNPq-Brazil during part of the project.

References

1. NHTSA, US Department of Transportation Releases Policy on Automated Vehicle Development (2013)
2. Siegwart, R., Nourbakhsh, I.R., Scaramuzza, D.: Introduction to Autonomous Mobile Robots, 2nd edn. MIT press, Cambridge (2011)
3. Chen, Y.-L., et al.: TerraMax: team Oshkosh urban robot. J. Field Robot. **25**, 841–860 (2008)
4. Thrun, S., et al.: Stanley: the robot that won the DARPA grand challenge. J. Field Robot. **23**, 661–692 (2006)
5. Garcia, O., et al.: The VILMA intelligent vehicle: an architectural design for cooperative control between driver and automated system. J. Mod. Transp. **26**, 220–229 (2018). https://doi.org/10.1007/s40534-018-0160-3
6. Chao, M.-A., Chu, C.-Y., Chao, C.-H., Wu, A.-Y.: Efficient parallelized particle filter design on CUDA. In: IEEE Workshop on Signal Processing Systems (SIPS) 2010 (2010)
7. Snider, J.M.: Automatic Steering Methods for Autonomous Automobile Path Tracking (2009)
8. Guida, D., Pappalardo, C.M.: Forward and inverse dynamics of nonholonomic mechanical systems. Meccanica **49**(7), 1547–1559 (2014)

9. Douc, R., Cappe, O.: Comparison of resampling schemes for particle filtering. In: Proceedings of the 4th International Symposium on Image and Signal Processing and Analysis, 2005, ISPA 2005 (2005)
10. Jin, N.G., Li, F.M., Li, Z.X.: Quasi-Monte Carlo Gaussian particle filtering acceleration using CUDA. Appl. Mech. Mater. **130**, 3311–3315 (2012)
11. Ulman, G.: Bayesian Particle Filter Tracking with CUDA (2012)
12. Garcia, O., Solaque, L., Aviles, O., Niño, P.: Hardware and software architecture of a mobile robot with anthropomorphic arm. In: ANDESCON, 2010 IEEE (2010)
13. Ahnert, K., Mulansky, M.: Odeint–solving ordinary differential equations in C ++. In: IP Conference Proceedings (2011)
14. Bell, N., Hoberock, J.: Thrust: a productivity-oriented library for CUDA. In: GPUComputing Gems Jade Edition, pp. 359–371. Elsevier (2011)

Modulation of Central Pattern Generators (CPG) for the Locomotion Planning of an Articulated Robot

Edgar Mario Rico Mesa[1](✉) iD
and Jesús-Antonio Hernández-Riveros[2](✉) iD

[1] SENA, Medellín, Colombia
emrico@sena.edu.co
[2] Universidad Nacional de Colombia, Medellín, Colombia
jahernan@unal.edu.co

Abstract. The present paper proposes the approach of locomotion in mammals to be applied in articulated robotics. This is achieved using Central Pattern Generators by amplitude modulation of oscillatory signals to communicate the angle of rotation of each of the joints that are involved in a specific type of locomotion. Performing simulations to determine viability by frequency and amplitude, a better response was found in the amplitude modulation. A series of locomotion data with dogs were compiled and used as a reference for the amplitude modulation of the differential equation systems that replicate the Central Pattern Generators of the articulations of the quadrupedal robot. Recurrent neural networks in continuous time were used to represent the CPG. The angle was modulated as a function of the amplitude of the cyclic signal produced by the Central Pattern Generators allowing to manage the setpoints (angles) for a given articulation, between 0° and 90°. Other works, although related to Central Pattern Generators, and some focused on reproducing the model, none of them deals with the construction of modulated signals that represent joint angles based on data obtained from biomechanical studies of locomotion by quadrupeds. A distributed autonomous control architecture based on modular and hierarchical Central Pattern Generators, organized in two layers, that simultaneously synchronizes and executes the movement of each joint from each leg, and for the total movement production is proposed.

Keywords: Locomotion · Modulation · Central pattern generator
Robotics · Oscillator

1 Introduction

Biologists have found patterns in the behavior of a series of internal and external processes of living beings through successive experiments analyzing the electrical signals of the central nervous system [1]. The analysis of the different tests has allowed to configure a theory that explains and describes the functioning of biological and chemical processes in living beings, that has been called central pattern generator (CPG) [2].

© Springer Nature Switzerland AG 2018
H. Florez et al. (Eds.): ICAI 2018, CCIS 942, pp. 321–334, 2018.
https://doi.org/10.1007/978-3-030-01535-0_24

Sten Grillner is one of the authors that proposed the central generators of patterns. In [3], he poses networks of autonomous cells as responsible for executing specific functions in an organ or in a biological system of the living being. CPG are specialized systems that generate signals to produce voluntary rhythmic movements such as walking, flying, swimming and even involuntary movements such as heartbeat, eye blinking, etc. Vertebrate animals have CPG in their spinal cord. For the moving processes in a robot, the observed procedure in CPG is a natural learning approach. A CPG could be developed for one leg and then could be replicated in the other legs. Regardless the number of legs, another CPG could be developed to coordinate the triggering of each one. The CPG approach reduces the effort from the analyst training a robot for an action eliminating the detailed step by step programming of traditional cinematics, mainly when the action is repetitive or rhythmic.

Currently, this approach has tried to reproduce in robotics a specific function such as the locomotion by air, land, and water seeking to optimize and simplify the complex movements that occur in the movement of the robot [4].

The application of CPG in robotics has been possible with the implementation of mathematical expressions whose behavior is a continuous oscillation without the presence of external excitations.

In a robotics project [5], own CPGs have been generated using integro-differential mathematical expressions as a model proposed by biologists to construct oscillators of two and four neurons.

In this paper, we have formulated systems of differential equations for 2, 3, 4, 5 and 6 neurons. These equations have been used for the simultaneous operation of several articulations (among 2 and 6 joints) required for the locomotion of a quadrupedal robotic system.

In this work, a series of locomotion data with dogs have been compiled and used as a reference for the amplitude modulation of the differential equation systems that replicate the CPGs of the articulations of the quadrupedal robot.

The paper has the following chapters:

An introductory chapter used to expose the technologies that are being developed based on CPGs in quadrupedal robots in several parts of the world.

Conceptual Framework: chapter to define and explain key theoretical concepts that are related to the project.

Results: chapter presenting the achieved scopes in the development of a prototype.

Data analysis: an interpretation of the data obtained in the start-up of the prototype is shown.

2   Brief Review of Works on Locomotion with CPG in Articulated Robots

A brief review of published works related to the implementation of CPG in articulated robot locomotion in the last 5 years has been made. In [6], a work in which the signals that synchronize the legs and controlling the joints are performed through CPG reproduced by neural networks is presented. In [7], a project on the locomotion of a quadruped robot based on the kinematics considering the lateral position and the speed of the anterior swinging leg is shown. The balance is achieved by finding the angle of roll by means of inertial and the forces resultant of support legs. In [8], CPGs are proposed to perform locomotion with transitions that allow the change of speed in the same type of locomotion obtaining simulation results that guarantee the viability of the developed algorithms. In [9], a CPG is proposed consisting of two network levels: Hopf oscillators coupled in phase for the generation of movement and matrix formation networks to obtain the frequency and phase parameters of the oscillators. In [10], a CPG is proposed to control the locomotion of the robot formed by a Recurrent Neural Network as oscillator to generate simple periodic harmonic signals and an approximate Fourier series is used to transform these simple signals mentioned in arbitrary outputs under the restrictions of phase in the locomotion of the quadruped robot. In [11], a Natural Learning CPG neural network system was capable of generating any complex movement through the first layer. In the second layer, it learned rhythmic trajectories. In [12], a simulation of biologic neural networks is performed using the Morris - Lecar model. The intention is to verify if the changes generated in a neuron affect the neuromodulation in the neural network. Then, the set of parameters is modified depending on its state. Each one of the neurons shows that if the current state is stable, it can affect the behavior of the network. However, in the state new, it does not change the net. In [13] a procedure is established to reduce the times of frequency adaptation of CPG systems developed with oscillators such as van der Pol and Hopf. It allows having speed and precision in the generation of the oscillation frequency required to reproduce a specific movement in the robotic system. In [14], it proposes the understanding of locomotion from a simple quadruped model with muscles and nerves simplified under simulation, this system put into operation with a central mathematical generator module of patterns that are formed by four neuronal oscillators based on in the Matsuoka model, they are responsible for developing the locomotion of the trot and the gallop. In [15], it presents the behavior and comparison of oscillators focused on its implementation as part of the CPG system by simulating the Hopf models as an example of a harmonic oscillator, a reflective oscillator using the Van der Pol oscillator and the ACPO (phase oscillator coupled to the amplitude) corresponding to the type of phase oscillators. In [16] the behavior of the CPG presented starting from mathematical models proposed by biologists. The Central Pattern Generator (GPC) explained as a nervous circuit that endogenously generates periodic motor patterns. The CPG composed of neurons with irregular intrinsic activity. Using mathematical models of CPG models of two and three neurons based on Hindmarsh-Rose or Hodgkin-Huxley. The behavior irregular of a network generates periodic oscillations addressed.

3 Conceptual Framework

3.1 The Biological Mechanisms in the Robotics

In [17], for development of the coordination of movements in articulated robotics, have been used algorithms inspired by biological theories such as the central pattern generators (CPG). The CPGs are represented by systems of differential equations of first order. On the other hand, in the construction of CPG, the coupled oscillators (ACPO) have also been applied by trigonometric functions. The behavior of the synapse in the neuron is modeled in the RNA by means of a mechanism of weights, which are adjusted during the learning phase. Thus, in a trained RNA, the set of weights determines the knowledge of such RNA necessary to solve the problem for which it has been conformed. For this reason, when implemented, they are very fast and require, in general, lower computing power.

3.2   Recurrent Neural Networks

Recurrent Neural Networks in Continuous Time (RNNCT) have been used for the implementation of CPG. RNNCT consist of RNA that have bidirectional connections between the nodes (Fig. 1) in such a way that they allow reproducing oscillatory and transient signals in the absence of an external signal (Model Hertz, Krogh and Palmer) [18].

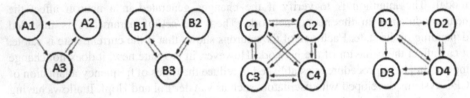

Fig. 1. Some structures of recurrent neural networks for CPG

3.3   Mathematical Configuration of the RNN

The recurrent neural networks are a system of first-order differential equations, such as the one expressed in Eq. 1.

$$\tau_i \frac{dy}{dt} = -y_i + \sum_{j=1}^{M} w_{ji}\, \sigma(y_j + \theta_j) + I_i, \ i = 1 \ldots M \tag{1}$$

The status function of each neuron, based on the Chiel-Beer Model [19], is shaped in general terms by the following parameters: time constant (τ) associated with the permittivity of the cell membrane, weights of synaptic connections between neurons (w), point of operation of each node (θ), transfer function of each neuron (σ), and an external input to the system (I).

4   Results

4.1   The Biomechanics of Dogs

In order clarity about quadrupedal locomotion, in [20], it presents a work developed with a series of dogs of different breeds that were subjected to displacement tests to perform the three types of locomotion (walking, trotting, galloping). This procedure studied ten breeds of dogs to establish behavior energetic of the muscles in function of the speed displacement. The paper proposes model energetic that describe the behavior static and dynamic of the locomotion of dogs. Additionally, in this work, data of sweeping angles are collected for the three joints (hip, knee, and ankle) as a function of locomotion. Information that allows having the certainty of the movements of each leg in the three modes of locomotion (see Fig. 2).

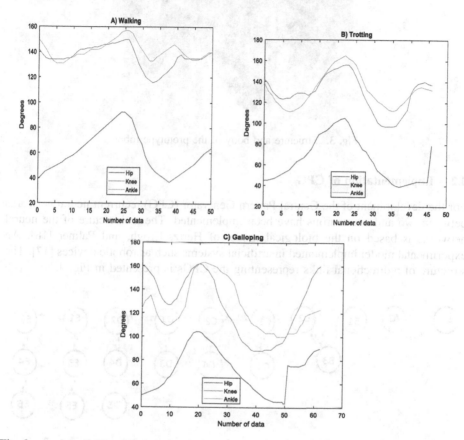

Fig. 2. Angles of Hip (blue), knee (red) and ankle (green) for Locomotion. (A) Walking (B) Trotting (C) Galloping Data taken from [20]

The study carried out in [20] presents variations of speed in the three types of locomotion. It shows cases transition locomotion. The reason for collecting locomotion data in dogs is that their morphology is similar to the quadruped robot developed in the present project (see Fig. 3). The project searches to emulate the locomotion quadruped. The locomotion system of the living beings is the most efficient. This database of Fig. 2 is the seed to adjust the locomotion CPGs of the quadruped robot, which it modulates in amplitude in the joints of the robot's legs.

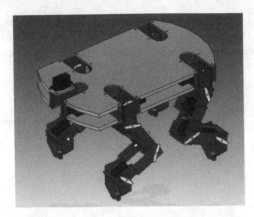

Fig. 3. Structure and body of the prototype robot

4.2   Implementation of CPG

For the development of the Central Pattern Generator (CPG) recurrent neural networks between two and six neurons have been implemented. The architecture of the neural networks is based on the biological model of Hertz, Krogh, and Palmer [18]. An experimental model implemented in artificial systems such as robotic devices [17]. The structure of bidirectional links representing the CPGs is presented in Fig. 4.

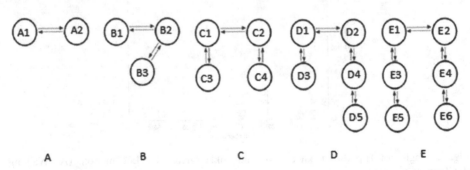

Fig. 4. Structure of Recurrent Neural Networks. (A) 2 neurons (B) 3 neurons (C) 4 neurons (D) 5 neurons (E) 6 neurons

The mathematical expression developed is for systems of differential equations of first order can be observed in Eq. 1. This system is based on the Chiel-Beer model [19]. Each neuron is represented by a first-order differential equation whose response in time is the reproduction of a cyclic signal of low frequency, its behavior corresponds to an oscillator. The intention is to have different recurrent neural networks that can adapt to the requirements of the movements that make up the locomotion that is proposed to execute. Each of the systems of differential equations of the first order are presented in the equations from 2 to 22.

Recurrent Neural Networks of 2 neurons

$$\tau_1 \frac{dy_1}{dt} = -y_1 + \frac{A(k_1 - Dy_2)^2}{(k_1 + Dy_2)^2 + (k_1 + Dy_1)^4} \tag{2}$$

$$\tau_2 \frac{dy_2}{dt} = -y_2 + \frac{A(k_2 - Dy_1)^2}{(k_2 + Dy_1)^2 + (k_2 + Dy_2)^4} \tag{3}$$

Recurrent Neural Networks of 3 neurons

$$\tau_1 \frac{dy_1}{dt} = -y_1 + \frac{A(k_1 - Dy_2)^2}{(k_1 + Dy_2)^2 + (k_1 + Dy_1)^4} \tag{4}$$

$$\tau_2 \frac{dy_2}{dt} = -y_2 + \frac{A(k_2 - Dy_1)^2}{(k_2 + Dy_1)^2 + (k_2 + Dy_2)^4} \tag{5}$$

$$\tau_3 \frac{dy_3}{dt} = -y_3 + \frac{A(B - Cy_2)^2}{(B + Cy_2)^2 + (B + Cy_3)^4} \tag{6}$$

Recurrent Neural Networks of 4 neurons

$$\tau_1 \frac{dy_1}{dt} = -y_1 + \frac{A(k_1 - Dy_2)^3}{(B + by_3)^2 + (k_1 - Dy_2)^2} \tag{7}$$

$$\tau_2 \frac{dy_2}{dt} = -y_2 + \frac{A(k_2 - Dy_1)^3}{(B + by_4)^2 + (k_2 - Dy_1)^2} \tag{8}$$

$$\tau_3 \frac{dy_3}{dt} = -y_3 + Cy_1^2 \tag{9}$$

$$\tau_4 \frac{dy_4}{dt} = -y_4 + Cy_2^2 \tag{10}$$

Recurrent Neural Networks of 5 neurons

$$\tau_1 \frac{dy_1}{dt} = -y_1 + \frac{A(k_1 - Dy_2)^3}{(B + by_3)^2 + (k_1 - Dy_2)^2} \tag{11}$$

$$\tau_2 \frac{dy_2}{dt} = -y_2 + \frac{A(k_2 - Dy_1)^3}{(B + by_4)^2 + (k_2 - Dy_1)^2} \tag{12}$$

$$\tau_3 \frac{dy_3}{dt} = -y_3 + Cy_1^2 \tag{13}$$

$$\tau_4 \frac{dy_4}{dt} = -y_4 + \frac{A(k_2 - Dy_2)^2}{(B + by_5)^2 + (k_2 - Dy_2)^2} \tag{14}$$

$$\tau_5 \frac{dy_5}{dt} = -y_5 + Cy_4^2 \tag{15}$$

Recurrent Neural Networks of 6 neurons

$$\tau_1 \frac{dy_1}{dt} = -y_1 + \frac{A(k_1 - Dy_2)^3}{(B + by_3)^2 + (k_1 - Dy_2)^2} \tag{16}$$

$$\tau_2 \frac{dy_2}{dt} = -y_2 + \frac{A(k_2 - Dy_1)^3}{(B + by_4)^2 + (k_2 - Dy_1)^2} \tag{17}$$

$$\tau_3 \frac{dy_3}{dt} = -y_3 + \frac{A(k_2 - Dy_1)^2}{(B + by_5)^2 + (k_2 - Dy_1)^2} \tag{18}$$

$$\tau_4 \frac{dy_4}{dt} = -y_4 + \frac{A(k_2 - Dy_2)^2}{(B + by_6)^2 + (k_2 - Dy_2)^2} \tag{20}$$

$$\tau_5 \frac{dy_5}{dt} = -y_5 + Cy_4^2 \tag{21}$$

$$\tau_6 \frac{dy_6}{dt} = -y_6 + Cy_3^2 \tag{22}$$

4.3   Obtaining Modulated CPG

To apply the database of angles per articulation of the locomotion of dogs to the system of differential equations of first order, we analyzed the parameters of the system of differential equations that having a small change generates a change of maximum cubic order in the oscillatory signal.

By performing a series of simulations to determine viability by frequency and amplitude, a better response was found in the amplitude modulation. The relationship between angle and amplitude of the signal is established by Eq. 23.

$$Amplitude = A_0 + A_1 * angle + A_2 * angle^2 + A_3 * angle^3 \tag{23}$$

Equation 23 is applied to the systems of equations with 2, 3, 4, 5 and 6 neurons that allow modulating the angle for each joint of the robot as a function of the amplitude of the oscillatory signal. Results are presented in Table 1.

Table 1. Values of the coefficients of the Eq. 23

Number of neurons/coefficients	A0	A1	A2	A3
CPG 6 neurons	−556.9218	329.3312	8.7931	0
CPG 5 neurons	−548.7067	434.3898	0.1677	0
CPG 4 neurons	−159.9939	7.7061	−0.0530	0
CPG 3 neurons	−1941.9	1557.2	0	0
CPG 2 neurons	−3476.4	9833.2	0	0

Recurrent Neural Network of 2 neurons. The signals produced by the system of two differential equations of first order are applied in the locomotion of the prototype robot to cyclically reproduce dead times that are necessary within the process and in which the simultaneous movement of several articulations with a specific angle is required.

The control action for each joint is represented by the amplitude of the cyclic signal indicating the angle to be executed (see Fig. 5).

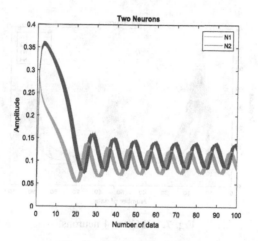

Fig. 5. CPG for 2 neurons

Recurrent Neural Network of 3 neurons. The signals produced by the system of three differential equations of first order are applied to carry out a sequence of three consecutive movements that a certain articulation of the prototype robot must execute.

Therefore, it has been possible to modulate the angle as a function of the amplitude of the cyclic signal of three neurons that allows to manage three setpoints (angles) for a given articulation, between 0° and 90° (see Fig. 6).

Recurrent Neural Network of 4 neurons. The signals produced by the system of four differential equations of first order are applied to perform the execution of consecutive movements of several joints that are in series.

In addition, there are applications of robotics and specifically locomotion in articulated robotics in which it is important to have multiple signals synchronized in an

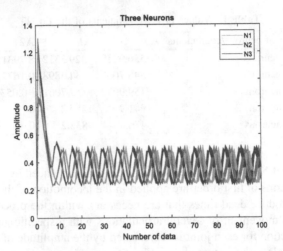

Fig. 6. CPG for 3 neurons

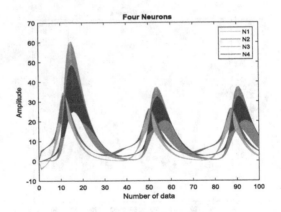

Fig. 7. CPG for 4 neurons

order of at least 4 signals (see Fig. 7) to be able to manipulate the angle per articulation to coordinate the complex movements of the leg.

Recurrent Neural Network of 5 neurons. The signals produced by the system of five first-order differential equations are applied to achieve synchronization between non-consecutive joints.

Therefore, when 5 signals are applied (see Fig. 8), it is necessary to have a single source of signal generation to facilitate its application, having significant phase differences between them allowing to generate a sequence in a movement of great complexity that in the case of the locomotion would be the synchronization of the starting of movement of each leg.

Recurrent Neural Network of 6 neurons. The signals produced by the system of six differential equations of first order are applied to make changes in cyclical routines.

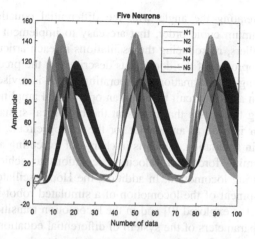

Fig. 8. CPG for 5 neurons

The rhythmic movements in different applications of living beings and robots are not very common to find 6 signals (see Fig. 9) used to achieve the development of a specific action. However, it is important to have this type of oscillator thinking about specific situations such as the implementation of transitions between types of locomotion.

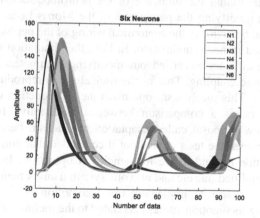

Fig. 9. CPG for 6 neurons

5 Data Analysis

The systems of differential equations of first order, described before, correspond to new expressions produced in a project to reproduce the oscillators as they are described in the biological theory, therefore they are original expressions for CPGs.

The equations relating the angle with the differential equations correspond to expressions of maximum cubic order, that are easy to implement in control devices such as microcontrollers, reproducing the oscillations in each articulation.

Therefore, the approach of the documents described in the preceding brief review regarding the handling of information incorporating CPGs is revised as follows:

In [6], there is an analog circuit based on an operational amplifier and a RC circuit that allow producing the pulses that represent the biological signals of the CPGs. In addition, a transistor is used as an enabler for the analog circuit. In [7], a kinematic model is presented in simulation, which is in charge of executing an operation similar to the CPG, performing force and velocity calculations to achieve stability of the quadruped robot during locomotion. In addition, the Hopf oscillator is presented as a CPG for the development of the locomotion of a simulated robot in which the tactile behavior of an insect is explored [9] and in the locomotion transitions of a quadruped [8], modifying the parameters of the system of differential equations that are based on sine and cosine functions. In [10], a recurrent neural network is proposed in terms of sine and cosine as the unit of generation of simple oscillatory signals and the Fourier transform is used to modify the output signal towards the articulation according to the type of locomotion movement that perform the quadruped robot. In [11], it is proposed a learning system for neural networks based on the type of signal that is reproduced. Additionally, it adds as many neurons as are necessary to obtain the desired waveform, then they are defined and the weights of coupling tuned allowing to configure such signal. In [12], the behavior of biological neurons was reproduced in simulation, with the intention of determining the influence of the neuromodulation of a neuron in a network of neurons modifying the parameters of the Morris-Lecar model. The paper describes the internal behavior in the anatomical wiring of the net indicating changes in the circuit determined in neuromodulation. In [13], the simulation of CPG with Hopf and Van der Pol oscillators is carried out modifying parameters of the model and obtaining fast dynamic coupling. That is, the oscillator can reproduce the cyclic input signal to the system. This mechanism optimizes the reproduction of locomotion in a robot. The paper makes a comparison between the adaptive frequency standard oscillators and a new proposal called adaptation mechanism based on the dynamic coupling forces, between the tests carried out it concluded that both the speed and the accuracy of adaptation depend to the frequencies of operation. In [14], a quadruped robot in which a simplified muscle and nervous system using 4 neurons based on Hopf and van der Pol oscillators to implement trot locomotion is simulated. The paper, indicates that trotting locomotion success is related to the inclination of the body called vestibular modulation. The oscillators are Hopf, Van del pol and ACPO. Cautions must be taken with the connections of the net. It could lead to undesired values in the training that would compromise the correct generation of the locomotion. In [15], simulation tools with three types of oscillators are used to establish their benefits and problems in the construction of the CPG in the locomotion. The oscillators used are Hopf, Van del pol, ACPO. In [16], the behavior of biological models for CPG of two and three neurons constructed with Hindmarsh-Rose or Hodgkin-Huxley are presented. The model simulated the response of the system by changing the parameters of the neurons. It observes intrinsic dynamic behavior of the neurons in their transitions with irregular amplitudes during the synapse (bursting and tonic), typical in biologic neurons. This paper proposes that neurons are in a dynamic state in which there coul be an "objective dynamic" instead of an objective parameter, which maintains a specific mode of operation of the neural network.

However, in all works previously referenced, although they are related to CPGs, some focused on reproducing the model and others in describing their behavior biologically, none of them deals with the construction of modulated signals that represent joint angles based on data obtained from biomechanical studies of locomotion by quadrupeds.

6 Conclusions

It has been considered for the planning of the locomotion of an articulated robot with four articulated legs the optimal locomotion system in living beings and specifically in mammals; information obtained by biomechanics focused on the description of locomotion of quadrupeds has been taken into account.

The procedure proposed in this paper has been largely achieved by the appropriation of knowledge during the development of the project of building a prototype, allowing the consolidation of systems of differential equations of first order (CPGs) as viable tools for the implementation of locomotion in a quadruped robot.

The approach described to obtain the amplitude-angle relationship in terms of the parameters of the system of differential equations for 2, 3, 4, 5 and 6 neurons, according to operating criteria, as an oscillator, is relevant for the development of central generators of patterns in the locomotion of articulated robots.

References

1. Eve, M., Dirk, B.: Central pattern generators and the control of rhythmic movements. Curr. Biol. 11(23), 986–996 (2001)
2. Cohen, A.H., Rossignol, S., Grillner, S.: Neural Control of Rhythmic Movements in Vertebrate, pp 1–500. Wiley (1988)
3. Grillner, S., Wallen, P.: Central pattern generators for locomotion, with special reference to vertebrates. Ann. rev. Neurosci. 8, 233–261 (1985)
4. Buchli, J., Ijspeert, A.J.: Distributed central pattern generator model for robotics application based on phase sensitivity analysis. In: Ijspeert, A.J., Murata, M., Wakamiya, N. (eds.) BioADIT 2004. LNCS, vol. 3141, pp. 333–349. Springer, Heidelberg (2004). https://doi.org/10.1007/978-3-540-27835-1_25
5. Protopapas, A., Bower, J.M.: Dynamics of cerebral cortical networks. In: The Book of GENESIS, pp. 149–168. Springer, New York (1998). https://doi.org/10.1007/978-1-4612-1634-6_9
6. Abe, M., Iwama, K., Takato, M., Saito, K., Uchikoba, F.: Hardware neural network models of CPG and PWM for controlling servomotor system in quadruped robot. Artif. Life Robot. 22(3), 391–397 (2017)
7. Gonzalez-Luchena, I., Gonzalez-Rodriguez, A.G., Gonzalez-Rodriguez, A., Adame-Sanchez, C., Castillo-Garcia, F.J.: A new algorithm to maintain lateral stabilization during the running gait of a quadruped robot. Robot. Auton. Syst. 83, 57–72 (2016)

8. Li, X., Wang, W., Yi, J., Gait transition based on CPG modulation for quadruped locomotion. In: IEEE/ASME International Conference on Advanced Intelligent Mechatronics, AIM, 2015 August, art. no. 7222583, pp. 500–505 (2015)
9. Harischandra, N.R., Krause, A.F., Dürr, V.: Stable phase-shift despite quasi-rhythmic movements: a CPG-driven dynamic model of active tactile exploration in an insect. Front. Comput. Neurosci. **9**, 107, 16 p (2015)
10. Tran, D.T., et al.: Central pattern generator based reflexive control of quadruped walking robots using a recurrent neural network. Robot. Auton. Syst. **62**(10), 1497–1516 (2014)
11. Shahbazi, H., Parandeh, R., Jamshidi, K.: Implementation of imitation learning using natural learner central pattern generator neural networks. Neural Netw. **83**, 94–108 (2016)
12. Gutierrez, Gabrielle J., Marder, E.: Modulation of a single neuron has state- dependent actions on circuit dynamics. eNeuro **1**, 1–12 (2014)
13. Nachstedt, T., Tetzlaff, C., Manoonpong, P.: Fast dynamical coupling enhances frequency adaptation of oscillators for robotic locomotion control. Front. Neurorobot. **11**, 1–14 (2017)
14. Fukuoka, Y., Habu, Y., Fukui, T.: Analysis of the gait generation principle by a simulated quadruped model with a CPG incorporating vestibular modulation. Biol. Cybern. **107**, 695–710 (2013)
15. Ralev, D., Cappelletto, J., Grieco, J.C., Certad, N., Cabrera, M. E.: Analysis of oscillators for the generation of rhythmic patterns in legged robot locomotion. In: IEEE Latin American Robotics Symposium, pp 125–128 (2013)
16. Reyes, M.B., Carelli, P.V., Sartorelli, J.C., Pinto, R.D.: A modeling approach on why simple central pattern generators are built of irregular neurons. Plus One **10**, 1–22 (2015)
17. Rojas, R.: Neural Networks, p. 509. Springer, Berlin (1996). https://doi.org/10.1007/978-3-642-61068-4
18. Rico, E.M., Hernandez, J.A.: Analysis and application of a displacement CPG-based method on articulated frames. In: Solano, A., Ordoñez, H. (eds.) CCC 2017. CCIS, vol. 735, pp. 495–510. Springer, Cham (2017). https://doi.org/10.1007/978-3-319-66562-7_36
19. Cappelletto, J., Estévez, P., Grieco, J.C., Medina-Meléndez, W., Fernández-López, G.: Gait synthesis in legged robot locomotion using a CPG-based model. In: Journa Bioinspiration and Robotics: Walking and Climbing Robots, Vienna, pp 227–246 (2007)
20. Goslow, G.E., Seeherman, H.J., Taylor, C.R., McCutchln, M.N., Heglund, N.C.: Electrical activity and relative length changes of dog limb muscles as a function of speed and gait. Exp. Biol. **94**, 15–42 (1981)

Software Design Engineering

Methodology for the Retrofitting of Manufacturing Resources for Migration of SME Towards Industry 4.0

Juan David Contreras Pérez[1]([⊠]) [iD], Ruth Edmy Cano Buitrón[2] [iD], and José Isidro García Melo[2] [iD]

[1] Pontificia Universidad Javeriana, 760031 Cali, Colombia
juandavid.contreras@javerianacali.edu.co
[2] Universidad del Valle, 760001 Cali, Colombia
{ruth.cano,jose.i.garcia}@correounivalle.edu.co

Abstract. Small and medium enterprises (SMEs) represent one of the main forces in economic development and employment generation. It is expected that these SMEs can turn towards new manufacturing paradigms such as Industry 4.0 to ensure their competitiveness in a future market. Nevertheless, these companies regard Industry 4.0 more as a challenge rather than a chance or as enabler for new value added opportunities. For this reason, in this article a literature review of Industry 4.0 officials reports and standards is carried out, in order to define a step by step the procedure of manufacturing resources migration towards Industry 4.0 by means of digital retrofitting, specifying both hardware and software requirements, the systems structure and required technology mapping for the Industry 4.0 implementation over traditional manufacturing resources. The main objective is to obtain the benefits of applying the Industry 4.0 paradigm without incurring in huge investments and provide technologic tools to SMEs that allow them to participate in globalized markets. Finally, the proposed methodology is applied in the retrofitting of a CNC machine given as result an industry 4.0 component ready to be integrated on a high-level application.

Keywords: Small and medium enterprises · Industry 4.0 ·
Retrofitting of a CNC machine

1 Introduction

One of the key elements during the transformation of emergent economies countries, as Latin Americans, it is the start-up and development of small and medium enterprises (SMEs). They represent one of the economic development main forces, in fact they have been important players under global economy, and experience a generalized increase in production and employment, and, in some countries, even increased their productivity relative to that of larger firms [9]. As in Colombia case, the SMEs constitute more than 90% of the enterprise and these will generate around 80% employment [11]. The previous idea shows how important are the contribution of SMEs to the country economy, nevertheless, the SME tend to be less competitive when they

© Springer Nature Switzerland AG 2018
H. Florez et al. (Eds.): ICAI 2018, CCIS 942, pp. 337–351, 2018.
https://doi.org/10.1007/978-3-030-01535-0_25

confront globalized markets, due to common factors such as: lack of information technologies and non-formal jobs [25]. As a result, statistics show that on average 75% of SMEs close after two years and 25% only remain until the fifth year. [25].

On the other hand, the evolution of information technology has enabled new business paradigms like the Industry 4.0 (I.40). This forth industrial revolution defines an organization and control model of the value supply chain through the product life cycle and throughout manufacturer systems supported by the information technology [21]. This new approach for the organization and implementation of manufacturing systems offer new capabilities, such as, decentralized decision-making, mass customization, horizontal and vertical integration and end-to-end engineering [19]. Allowing companies perform on a higher level and also having a competitive advantage throughout time on a globalized market and increasing opportunities for value creation [22].

However, company migration, mainly in emergent economies, towards the I4.0 paradigm is not trivial and requires the deployment of theories and technological tools, such as: the Internet of Things (IoT), connectivity, digitalization, automation, big data among others, to ensure the proper integration [10].

According to the PricewaterhouseCoopers (PwC), Industry 4.0 report [24], the 33% of the global industrial company have an advanced digitalization level and is being expected this percentage reaches even a 72% at 2020. However, in Latin America the process is complex and slow, especially, when it comes to the transition of SME towards the I4.0 [13]. Several are the factors that have effect in this critical scenario such as the lack of economic and technological resources, cultural barriers, among others. Besides, it is also identified the risk involved in innovation for SME, due to the inclusion of new technologies requires a significant economic effort, which under a poor management could mean meaningful losses for small company and the lack of incentive from government in many regions of Latin America. From a cultural point of view, several SMEs underestimate the importance of acquire and adopt digital technologies in the short term in order to reduce remarkable barriers to compete on globalized markets [8, 13, 15].

Industry 4.0 offers new solution approaches, product innovations, product-related services and improve with a combination of already existing technologies. On the other hand, I4.0 can aid companies in reduce production costs. Furthermore, an increase in sales can be achieved through the enhanced utility and value of their own products [23].

Although the embracement of new technologies allows more efficient process, they also could have a negative impact if those changes are not adjusted on time or not properly implemented. For the above-mentioned is necessary to establish a standard procedure which can enable the migration towards the usage of this new technology. the above considering that, to be truly effective, it is necessary to be focused on improved some concrete technologies proportionally to the company's capabilities, so it fulfils the greatest possible benefit, on a performance level, and at the same time should be translated into a short-term positive impact on the company's income [15].

Several research about I4.0 applications has been published since 2015, but few of them are focused on provide well define procedures for supporting the SME in the adoption of Industry 4.0. As an example, there are applications that do not use standards and not define a system architecture such as in [6, 20]. There are projects which propose a system architecture but do not integrate formal standards such as on [14, 17, 30]. Finally, there are projects which defines a system architecture and integrate some standard such as quoted on [16].

The previous works lack the adoption of the standards defined by the platform Industrie 4.0, therefore, if in the future they wish to fit into the world network conceived by I4.0 (see connect world Fig. 1), they must rethink their current architectures. In this context, a methodology that integrates formal standards defined by the Platform Industrie 4.0 to define a system architecture for supporting the SMEs in the adoption of I4.0 paradigm is proposed in this article. This methodology ensures that SMEs can be easily coupled to the global network. In addition, it is based on the use of Open Source tools to achieve it, allowing cost reduction in the acquisition of specialized software and providing open architecture solutions. To implement this methodology, it is required manual and routine activities, such as the completion of databases and the linking of the native function of the system with the OPC UA methods.

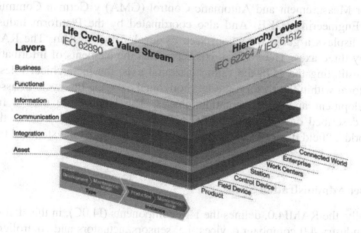

Fig. 1. Reference architecture model for I4.0. **Source:** [2].

The methodology proposed in this article is being evaluated in different areas of manufacturing. Currently, it has been implemented in machining processes, chemical products mix, robotics systems and assembly stations, as well as different field devices. As an example, this article presents a case of study, where this methodology is applied to retrofitting an industrial CNC.

This article is constituted by four sections. First, a formal definition of industry 4.0 is shown. Afterwards, a procedure for the migration from traditional manufacturing to I4.0 is proposed. Next, it is exposed a retrofitting of an industrial CNC machine compliant with I4.0 as application example. Finally, conclusions are stated

2 Formal Definition of I4.0

Since the concept of Industry 4.0 was introduced in 2011, many authors, researchers and companies have contributed to the construction of the concept with new proposals on architecture, dynamics and implementation of manufacturing systems. However, considering standardization as one of the pillars of this revolution [31], not every contribution can be accepted as a correct solution in the I4.0 context. In order to present a right definition of the concept, the sources of fundamental information for the architecture definition, dynamics and implementation of an I4.0 manufacturing systems should be limited to the official agents, which conforms the Plattform Industrie 4.0. This section shows some important concepts of I4.0 concerning to the implementation of new applications.

2.1 Reference Architecture Model for I4.0

In a report presented in 2015 [2] is submitted the reference Architecture Model Industrie 4.0 (RAMI 4.0) (see Fig. 1), developed among many Institutions such as the Society for Measurement and Automatic Control (GMA) y German Commission for Electrical Engineering (DKE) And also coordinated by the Plattform Industrie 4.0. RAMI4.0 displays a guide for whom seek to develop I4.0 system. The RAMI4.0 is depicted by three axes. The vertical axis represents the elements of information technology constituting the I4.0; the right horizontal axis, the hierarchical roles that the assets perform within the factory; the left horizontal axis, the life cycle of assets along their development and implementation phases. The architecture uses a functional hierarchy described on the standard IEC 62264, adding as new elements the "Connected world", "field device" and "product" in order to extend the standard to the I4.0 features.

2.2 Asset Administration Shell

Additionally, the RAMI4.0, defines the I4.0 components (I4.0C), in this definition sets that non-industry 4.0 compliant devices, i.e. sensors, actuators and controllers, can be turn into I4.0C by adding an Asset Administration Shell (AAS). This AAS is a virtual element, which encapsulates the information technology layers of the RAMI 4.0. The AAS allows the communication among other AAS through the I4.0 compliant communication, using the RAMI4.0 communication layer, and encapsulates the functionality of the system. (see Fig. 2). As an example, Adolphs poses on [4] an axis positioning electric system where it is shown how a I4.0C can be composed by the integration of the physical assets and the AAS. This data belong to the RAMI4.0 information layer.

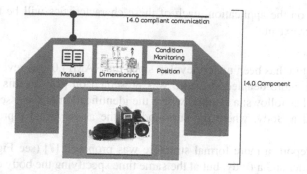

Fig. 2. Example of an I4.0C and the administration. **Source:** Own

3   Procedure for the Migration from Traditional Manufacturing to Industrie 4.0

According to the DIN SPEC 91345 [1], an Industrie 4.0 component consists of an asset and its virtual representation, this asset virtualization is implemented in the "administration shell", which turns a conventional object into an I4.0C. In this way, the procedure proposed for the SMEs migration to I4.0 has to be established in order to integrate the AAS into their manufacturing resources.

3.1   Prerequisites

To begin the migration procedure, it is necessary that the SME has an adequate infrastructure, defines the target system architecture, and have the technologies that will allow the correct implementation of said architecture. This could be achieved guaranteeing the following three steps:

Enable Information and Communication Technology (ICT) Capabilities
Afirst step for the implementation of the AdmonShell is to integrate the physical resource with a physical computational system (e.g. single board computer) or a virtual computational system (e.g. cloud computing) able to withstand the AAS requirements. Regarding of the implementation requirements of the communication, information and functional layers of RAMI4.0, the computational systems where the AAS is planned to be implemented should fulfill the following:

- IP communication for implementation of the communication layer
- Data storage in relational and non-relational databases for implementation of the information layer. Note: Some micro and nano embed devices just need some bits of storage for the state of sensors and actuators.
- Data acquisition and control through physical ports for the implementation of the integration layer. An example of this can be GPIO ports or serial communication, as well as other type of digital or analog inputs and outputs.
- Information processing through software functions for the implementation of the functional Layer.

Depending on the application, each of these characteristics will be necessary to a greater or lesser extent.

ASS Structure

The AAS structure has been under develop since the RAMI4.0 was revealing on 2015. Subsequently a more detailed structure was presented on [4]. On this depiction, the AAS is divided as follows: a Header, where the identification of the asset and the AAS are stored; and a Body, where the sub-models (the asset virtual representation) are stored.

In a later report, a more formal structure was proposed [7] (see Fig. 3). Here the ASS has a Header and a Body, but at the same time specifying the body composition as an integration of multiple data elements, collections of data elements, views, services, collection of services and references. It is also specified the relation between these elements, as well as the standards that must be followed.

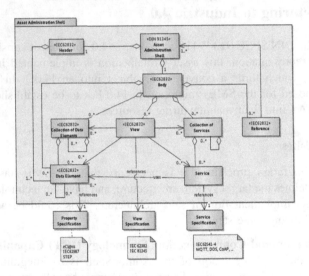

Fig. 3. AAS formal structure. **Source:** [7].

This structure (see Fig. 3) is generic and depends on the device and its application. Different sub-models should be selected, which integrate relevant data elements and services. For instance, in the Fig. 4 an AAS includes a sub-model for the P&ID plan, circuit diagram, mechanical CAD, among others.

Technology Mappings

The models of the AAS structure above shown are technology-agnostic and need to be mapped into different technological tools in order to be deployed as a real application.

Bedenbender exposed on [7] some alternatives for technology mapping such as the OPC UA for devices, MQTT, OpenASS and NAMUR MTP. On [28] a methodology for the migration towards I4.0 using OPC UA is presented. Also, several projects as [12, 18, 26, 27] agreed with the usage of OPC UA to implement I4.0 applications.

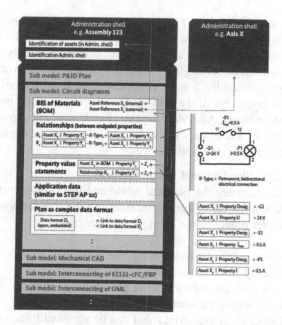

Fig. 4. AAS sub-model example. **Source:** [32]

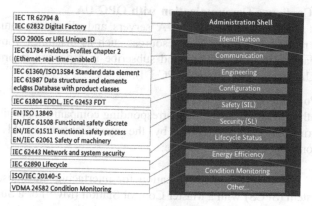

Fig. 5. Generic sub-models standardized by the ASS. **Source:** [4].

According to this, on this article will be used OPC UA as the technology on which the AAS will be mapped following by methodology proposed on [7].

3.2 Migration to Industry 4.0 Procedure

A systematic migration procedure is proposed based on the following conditions:

- The requirements of RAMI 4.0 must be fulfilled [3].
- Implement the AAS using the architecture exposed on Fig. 3 [7].
- Implement the I4.0 communication using the OPC UA guideline [28].

Starting from RAMI 4.0 (see Fig. 1), the migration procedure consists of performing a sequential implementation from the integration layer to the functional layer, since it is not possible to implement a layer without having previously implemented the adjacent layer immediately below. Firstly, the physical and virtual world are integrated (i.g integration layer). Secondly, a basic communication is configured using OPC UA (i.g communication layer). Next, the OPC UA server is populated using, information model (i.g information layer). After this, the asset functionality is implement as services (i.g functional layer). As a later step, the views and references are deployed considering that they need the previous data and services.

First Step: Integrate Physical and Virtual World

First, the connection between the physical world and the virtual world must be guaranteed, this will depend on the nature of the asset and the computational system where virtualization is implemented. Some examples of integration are:

- Sensors and actuators can be monitoring and controlled directly using, the GPIO ports of a Raspberry Pi board with the correct interface.
- PLC memory registers can be monitored and modified from a computer using, an industrial protocol through a serial port.
- Functions and state of an industrial robot can be accessed from a cloud computing application deployed in a thin client PC connected to the robot control unit.

Second Step: Configure Communication with OPC UA

In this step, it is deployed the OPC UA servers and clients to communicate the manufacturing resources allowing that resources such as machines, robots or people can browse, read, write, call methods and subscribe in a generic information model such as OPC UA Device Integration (OPC DI).

Third Step: Populate OPC UA Server

Depending on the virtualized asset, the corresponding companion specification and the extended information model provided by the manufacturer should select. Some examples of companion specifications are:

- MDIS OPC UA Companion Specification for interfacing the Subsea Production Control System (SPCS) with a Master Control Station (MCS) or a Subsea Gateway to the Distributed Control System (DCS)-
- OPC Unified Architecture for CNC Systems for the information model Computerized Numerical Control (CNC) systems.
- OPC Unified Architecture for FDT for network representation using the FDT® standard.
- OPC UA PackML Companion Specification for packing machines.

It is important to mention that both the companion specifications and the extended information model are in current development, this decreases the possibility of finding a companion specification for unconventional manufacturing systems.

In addition to the particular representation of the asset, some generic and standardized sub-models can be added depending on the application of the asset within the

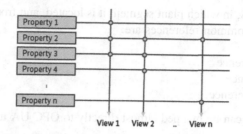

Fig. 6. Pre-defined properties as views. **Sources:** [4].

manufacturing system. In the Fig. 6, some examples of sub-models with its corresponding standard are presented.

Some models such as AutomationML (AML) and FDI are used to integrate different system points of view. However, they use data formats that not compliant with OPC UA, for this reason, there are standards that define the mapping rules that allow migrating the AML and FDI models to the OPC UA information model, an example of this can be found on [10] (Fig. 5).

Forth Step: Define and Implement the Services
Services are the gate to execute AAS functionality. They would refer both higher logic level and asset-specific functionality (e.g. "open grip", "lubricate", "drill hole"). This may include administrative services to retrieve historical data or alarm conditions.

These services should be implemented using the preferred programing language and defining the inputs, outputs and the information required from the information model. In order to relate with the service, interaction paradigm needs to be defined regarding the requirement of the RAMI 4.0 that sets *"A high level of cohesion is to prevail within the layers, with loose connections between them. Events may only be exchanged between two adjacent layers and within each layer"*. This means that the services can interact between them using a web service platform or triggering events from the information layer through OPC UA.

The services should be grouped according to their application as follows: communication, transformation, administrative, and data visualization among others.

Fifth Step: Define and add the Views
Depending on the context, some view can be added to the information model facilitating the access to relevant information. Views allow automating the access to some pre-defined properties avoiding the navigation along the information model. According to Fig. 6 the view 1 is related with the properties 1, 2 and 3.

As an example, for maintenance proposes, a view can be assigned to the supervisory system to access directly to relevant properties like temperature or pressure.

Sixth Step: Add References According to the Context References depicts information about AAS external connections. These connections can refer to other assets connected to the AAS, in which plant segment it is located, and from which other asset it is derived. Some common references are:

• Containment reference
• Inheritance reference
• Type-Instance reference

These references can be mapped almost directly to OPC UA using ReferenceType instances.

Seventh Step: Implement the identification of the AAS
In the last step, the ASS Header should be implemented by adding to the AAS and the asset a unique identifier based in standards like ISO 29002-5.

This identifier items can be added as properties in the top of the OPC UA information model. Other option consists on use the identification variables of OPC DI.

4 Retrofitting of an CNC Machine Compliant with Industry 4.0

Considering the SMEs as an essential part of the economy, the VDMA German Engineering Federation, proposed a Guideline that aims to *"support small and medium sized companies of the German mechanical engineering industry in identifying potentials for products and production with a systematic process in relation to I4.0 and in developing their own specific ideas in this respect"*. To achieve this goal, a Toolbox Industry 4.0 is proposed in [29]. Different levels of application are presented on it and each broken down into five technological and sequential development stages.

As a case of study, a CNC Lathe that is part of a flexible manufacturing cell was used (see Fig. 8). Using the Toolbox Industry 4.0, the Machine-to-Machine Communication layer (M2 M) is selected as roadmap, where, as shown in Fig. 9, the CNC lathe is in the second stage of development and the objective of this application example is to take the system to the fifth stage using the methodology proposed in the previous section (Fig. 7).

4.1 Results

Addition of ICT Capacities
In order to retrofit the CNC Lathe to accomplish the I4.0 requirements, a computational module was added to the machine (see Fig. 10). This module is conforming by a Raspberry Pi Zero W, this device allows the IP communication through a Wi-Fi network; a MAX3232 board that allows the Raspberry to use industrial RS232 interface to communicate with the machine's serial port; finally, a optocopler interface which allows the GPIO of the Raspberry board to write and read the digital inputs and outputs of the machine.

Fig. 7. Case of study: flexible manufacturing cell

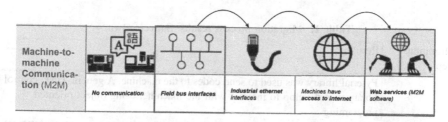

Fig. 8. M2M layer of the Toolbox Industry 4.0

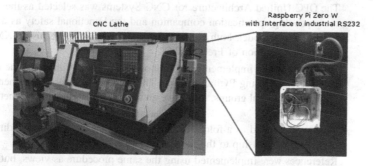

Fig. 9. Computational module linked to the CNC. **Source:** Own.

ASS Implementation

The ASS was implemented using the Python programing language for each migration process step. The result of each step is presented in Table 1.

The final result will be an OPC UA server that the other ASSs can access using I4.0 compliant communication. The resulting server is in accordance with the ASS structure. Due to lack of space, not all the OPC UA server elements were presented on this model (see Fig. 8).

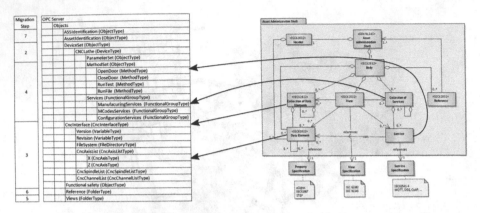

Fig. 10. Resulting OPC UA server from the migration procedure. **Source:** Own.

Table 1. Migration process results. **Source:** Own.

Migration step	Results
1	Pyserial library was used to send codes to the machine. A generic DNC control library was develop to interact with the machine, using object oriented programing
2	A OPC UA server was deployed, using FreeOpcUa Li-brery and the OPC DI information model. The communication was proved using the UAExpert Client
3	The OPC Unified Architecture for CNC Systems was selected as the corresponding specification companion and the Functional safety as a additional sub model, both are added to the OPC UA server using XML importation function of FreeOpcUa
4	All services were implemented as Python functions and linked to the method set of OPC DI using Python threads. The method sets were implemented as OPC DI functional groups, they have an organize relation with the methods in the MethodSet
5	Views were added as a folder that contains the view names and adding an organized relationship to the model properties
6	References were implemented using the same procedure as views, but adding hierarchical and non-hierarchical references, such as association, composition, aggregation and dependency
7	The ASS identification was carried out as two separate objects, whose contained identification variables and it was accomplished according to ISO 29002-5

5   Conclusions

Considering the impacts of SMEs in emerging economies, such as Colombia, it's necessary to support this sector of the industry with a correct implementation of international models that leads to the fourth industrial revolution, Industry 4.0. This economic force can be integrated into the value chain with a global impact, minimizing the risks of market variability. At this point, this article presented an approach of migration from the productive infrastructure, in the context of the SMEs, towards a globalized model defined by the I4.0 standard. The strategy defined for the evaluation of the proposed procedure was through experimentation. Appling this, the components of a flexible manufacturing cell where turn into I4.0 Components. As a result of this migration, new development opportunities for this industrial sector were evidenced. For example, at present, the working group is using the resulting I4.0 system in testing adaptive manufacturing strategies, order controlled production and other application scenarios of the industry 4.0 defined in [5].

An important result of this project is the demonstration that the adoption of industry 4.0 in SMEs does not imply a high investment in new equipment and technologies, but can be achieved through a retrofitting of existing equipment using mostly open hardware and software. For instance, a certified commercial solution for the implementation of OPC Communication in CNC machines, such as Fanuc Focas Ethernet driver, has a cost of USD 1356 for each machine, while the developed application had a unique development cost of USD 800 and an implementation cost for each machine of USD 100.

In this article, it has been clearly demonstrated that Industry 4.0 is an issue that has been correctly developed by organizations such as the *Plattform Industrie 4.0*, which providing the open reports and documentation facilitate implementation in SMEs, as it is the case of the Toolbox Industry 4.0 using as a guide in this project.

In the development of this project, it was evidenced that many of the activities necessary for the implementation of an application of industry 4.0 require manual and routine activities, such as the completion of databases and the linking of the native function of the system with the OPC UA methods. For this reason, it is recommended as future work the development of a framework that facilitates the implementation of this applications by automating generic and monotonous tasks.

Acknowledgements. The authors are grateful to the Vicerectoria de Investigacion of Universidad del Valle for the finantial sopport of this project and the Process Automation Center of Pontificia Universidad Javeriana for the provision of the equipment using in this article.

References

1. Adolphs, P., et al.: DIN SPEC 91345 (2016)
2. Adolphs, P.: RAMI 4.0 IoT for manufacturing (2015)
3. Adolphs, P., et al.: Reference Architecture Model Industrie 4.0 (RAMI4.0) (2015)
4. Adolphs, P., et al.: Structure of the Administration Shell Continuation of the Development of the Reference Model for the Industrie 4.0 Component (2016)
5. Anderl, R., et al.: Aspects of the Research Roadmap in Application Scenarios (2016)

6. Baena, F., et al.: Learning factory!: the path to industry 4.0. Procedia Manuf. **9**, 73–80 (2017)
7. Bedenbender, H., et al.: Industrie 4.0 Plug-and-Produce for Adaptable Factories: Example Use Case Definition, Models, and Implementation. (2017)
8. Beltrán, A.: Los 20 problemas de la pequeña y mediana empresa. Sotavento M.B.A. **7**, 8–15 (2006)
9. Chisari, O.O., et al.: Economy-wide effects of improving small and medium enterprises' acces to capital markets: an applied general equilibrium assessment. Rev. análisis económico **31**(1), 15–35 (2016)
10. Contreras, J.D., et al.: Developing of industry 4.0 applications. Int. J. Online Eng. **13**, 10 (2017)
11. Cristina, S. et al.: Inversión en Tecnologías de la Información y las Comunicaciones y su relación con en el direccionamiento estratégico de las PYMES de Santiago de Cali - Colombia. Rev. Ibérica Sist. y Tecnol. la Inf. 1–17 (2016)
12. García, M.V., et al.: Integración Vertical en plantas industriales utilizando OPC UA e IEC-61499 (Vertical Integration in factories using OPC-UA and IEC-61499). Enfoque UTE **1**(1), 287–299 (2017)
13. Gligo, N.: Innovación en las pymes de América Latina., Santiago de Chile (2016)
14. Grangel-gonzález, I., et al.: An RDF-Based Approach for Implementing Industry 4.0 Components with Administration Shells. IEEE Access (2016)
15. Guerrero, J.C., et al.: Análisis de la problemática en el uso de las TIC. Cienc. y Tecnol. **4**(1), 130–133 (2015)
16. Hoffmann, M., Büscher, C.: Continuous integration of field level production data into top-level information systems using the OPC interface standard. Procedia CIRP **41**, 496–501 (2016)
17. Wan, J., et al.: Mobile services for customization manufacturing systems!: an example of industry 4.0. IEEE Access **4**, 8977–8986 (2017)
18. Liao, Y., et al.: Past, present and future of Industry 4.0 - a systematic literature review and research agenda proposal. Int. J. Prod. Res. **55**(12), 3609–3629 (2017)
19. MacDougall, W.: Industrie 4.0- Smart Manufacturing for the Future. GTIA- Ger. Trade Invest. 40 (2013)
20. Marilungo, E., et al.: From PSS to CPS design!: a real industrial use case toward Industry 4.0. Procedia CIRP **64**, 357–362 (2017)
21. Mendizábal, G., López, E.: ¿Nuevo modelo de seguridad social en el contexto de la industria 4.0? Rev. Int. y Comp. Relac. laborales y derecho del Empl. **5**(2), 22 (2017)
22. Montoya, A., et al.: Situación de la competitividad de las Pyme en Colombia: elementos actuales y retos Current competitiveness of Colombian SMEs: determining factors and future challenges. Agron. Colomb. **28**(1), 107–117 (2010)
23. Plattform Industrie 4.0, VDMA (German Mechanical Engineering Industry Association): Guideline Industrie 4.0 - Guiding principles for the implementation of Industrie 4.0 in small and medium sized businesses, 30 (2016)
24. PwC (PricewaterhouseCoopers Asesores de Negocios): Informe Industria 4.0 (2016)
25. Sánchez, C., et al.: Algunas aproximaciones al problema de financiamiento de las pymes en Colombia. Cienc. y Tecnol. **34**, 321–324 (2007)
26. Schlechtendahl, J., et al.: Making existing production systems Industry 4.0-ready: Holistic approach to the integration of existing production systems in Industry 4.0 environments. Prod. Eng. **9**(1), 143–148 (2014)
27. Schleipen, M., et al.: OPC UA Industrie enabling technology with high diversity and variability. Procedia CIRP **57**, 315–320 (2016)
28. VDMA: Industrie 4.0 Communication Guideline - Based on OPC UA (2017)

29. VDMA and Partners: Guideline Industrie 4.0 Guiding principles for the implementation of Industrie 4.0 in small and medium sized businesses (2016)
30. Weyer, S., et al.: Future modeling and simulation of CPS-based factories: an example from the automotive industry. IFAC Pap. **49**(31), 97–102 (2016)
31. Weyer, S., et al.: Towards Industry 4.0 - standardization as the crucial challenge for highly modular, multi-vendor production systems. Int. Fed. Autom. Control **48**(3), 579–584 (2015)
32. Bedenbender, H., et al.: Relationships between I4.0 Components - Composite Components and Smart Production (2017)

Model Driven Engineering Approach to Configure Software Reusable Components

Hector Florez[1]([⊠])(iD) and Marcelo Leon[2]

[1] Universidad Distrital Francisco Jose de Caldas, Bogotá, Colombia
haflorezf@udistrital.edu.co
[2] Universidad Estatal Peninsula de Santa Elena, Santa Elena, Ecuador
marceloleon11@hotmail.com

Abstract. Currently, there are a lot of enterprises around the world dedicated to the same business e.g. banking, academy, trading, etc. All of those enterprises require specific information systems; however, information systems in the same business have several similar or equal features. Consequently, it is possible to create one information system for one specific business reusing components developed previously in another information system of the same specific business. Since enterprises from the same business are different, their information systems are different (e.g., academic institutions). In this paper, we present an approach to offer the capability to reuse software components that have been created for solving some specific processes. So, for this approach, it is necessary to have some core components and several auxiliary components. Based on this set of components, it is possible to combine them in order to get a functional information system for one specific enterprise in one specific business.

Keywords: Model Driven Engineering (MDE) · Model
Transformation Chain (MTC) · Eclipse Modeling Framework (EMF)

1 Introduction

Enterprises in the same context usually require information systems with several similar features. However, if the business is very complex, it requires a big quantity of components and the management of this big set of components becomes a problem. Some solutions based on Software Product Lines (SPLs) [2,4,12] have been created in order to offer the capability to reuse software components. One SPL must be created in one platform (e.g. JEE Java Enterprise Edition); consequently, all components must been developed in that platform and the connections between components are usually created when one new information system must be built using the SPL; as a result, the process of creating a new information system becomes complex as well. In addition, if someone requires creating several information systems simultaneously, due to all enterprises are

© Springer Nature Switzerland AG 2018
H. Florez et al. (Eds.): ICAI 2018, CCIS 942, pp. 352–363, 2018.
https://doi.org/10.1007/978-3-030-01535-0_26

different, the process of creation the final information systems would be dilatory and complex [14].

In addition, in Model Driven Engineering (MDE), one metamodel is used to abstract one specific domain and one model is used to represent a specific case in the domain [3, 9, 10]. Thus, the model must conform to the corresponding metamodel and thus it has to follow the metamodels' structure and constraints [6]. Furthermore, one model transformation chain consists in collecting and running some individual transformations in order to get a specific result. In this case, each transformation adds valuable components to the model. Usually, the final result when running a model transformation chain is the source code of a final project.

In this paper, we present one model transformation chain to automatically connect components in order to create a software application that belongs to one specific business domain. This model transformation chain has three main elements: the first element is the context metamodel with the abstraction of the business domain, the second element is the architecture metamodel with the abstraction of the business architecture, and the third element is the context model that conforms to the context metamodel and has the description of one specific product to be created by connecting the required software components.

In addition, the model transformation chain has two transformations: the first transformation transforms the context model in the architecture model and the second transformation transforms the architecture model in the source code required to make the needed connections between the required components for the final information system that has been described by the context model.

The approach has been evaluated by creating a model transformation chain for the construction of information systems in the academy domain. In this domain, there are a lot of features that would be controlled through the model transformation chain. The modeler must establish these features when he creates the context model. Some of these features can be the following:

1. Creation of faculties and departments.
   - In the first case, some universities have several faculties and each faculty has several departments.
   - In the second case, some other universities have several faculties, but each faculty has just one department; as a result, this kind of universities can work without departments.
   - In the third case, some other universities have several faculties, but some faculties have several departments and some other faculties have just one department; consequently, this kind of universities have a combination of the previous two situations.
2. Grades.
   - In the first case, some universities have numerical grades, but they do not approximate the grade.
   - In the second case, some universities have numerical grades, but they approximate the grade; for instance, if the grade is 3.8, this grade in some universities is approximated to 4.0.

- In the third case, some universities use alphabetic grades where the best grade is A and the worst grade is F.
- In the fourth case, some other universities use just two linguistic grades, which are Approved and Failed.
- In the fifth case, some other universities uses a combination of some kind of grades presented above; for instance, they use numerical grades for regular subjects (e.g. calculus, physics) and linguistic grades for subjects related to final projects (e.g. thesis).

The paper is structured as follows. Section 2 presents the context in order to explain the related concepts in the paper. Section 3 presents the solution strategy. Section 4 presents a case study of the model transformation chain. Finally the conclusions are presented in Section 5.

2   Context

2.1   Model Driven Engineering

In Model Driven Engineering (MDE) there are two main artifacts: models and metamodels. A model is a set of statements about a system which is under study. These statements are related to the abstraction of an element that can be considered true or false. In software engineering, a model refers to an artifact developed in a modeling language, which describes a system through different types of diagrams. One model requires three key features [9]:

1. *mapping*, indicating that a model is based on an original concept
2. *reduction*, indicating that the model reflects a specific selected part of the original concept
3. *pragmatic concept*, indicating that the model needs to be used taking the specific purpose of the original concept.

Moreover, a model in engineering areas must contain the following features [10]:

- *abstraction*, indicating that the model is a reduced representation of a desired system
- *understanding*, indicating that the model must maintain a way that directly invokes to the intuition
- *precision*, indicating that the model should provide a true representation of the interesting features of the modeled system
- *predictive*, indicating that the model is to predict the interest but not the obvious properties of the modeled system
- *low expression*, indicating that the model must be economically significant for the construction and analysis.

In MDE a model conforms to its metamodel, which implies that said model is an instance of the corresponding metamodel. The interpretation of a model can be obtained by mapping the model elements with elements from the original concept, which can determine the level of accuracy in the statements with the elements. The main use of a metamodel is to facilitate the separation of concerns of a domain [3,5].

Figure 1 shows the classical architecture of the Object Management Group (OMG). In the low level, M0 layer is the actual system. The level M1 represents the model. The M1 level model is conformed to the metamodel defined at the M2 and it is conformed to the meta metamodel of the level M3. The meta metamodel is conformed to itself.

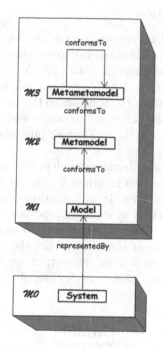

Fig. 1. MDE four level architecture.

2.2 Model Restrictions

At the time of building a metamodel, the conforming models must attend all characteristics defined. However, in several cases the metamodel cannot specify certain characteristics as constraints obtained by abstraction of the original modeled concepts.

Object Constraint Language (OCL) [15] allows setting restrictions on metamodels. The model that tries to be consistent with the metamodel that contains such restrictions must satisfy these restrictions. Thus, applying to the metamodel a few OCL sentences, it is possible to define a set of additional features to the metamodel. On the one hand, OCL queries are defined as a set of elements that satisfy a restrictive expression. On the other hand, it is possible to apply special operators to interact with the relations.

An OCL expression, which can be invariant, should be true for all models that conform to the metamodel to which is applied the restriction. Likewise, an expression can contain preconditions and postconditions in a condition associated with a method. In this way, it is necessary to satisfy the condition specified in the postcondition if the precondition is met. OCL contains a large set of functions and operators that allow setting any restrictions on a metamodel that must be satisfied by the model conformed to the metamodel.

2.3   Model Transformation

A model transformation, allows converting a model M_a that conforms to a metamodel MM_a to a model M_b that conforms to a metamodel MM_b. The transformation is defined by a transformation model M_t that conforms to a transformation metamodel MM_t. MM_a and MM_b metamodels must have direct relationships between concepts to allow the solution to the requirements established for a particular project [13]. The three metamodels must conform to a metamodel such us MOF (Meta Object Facility). Figure 2 presents the elements of a model transformation.

To perform transformations between models, it is necessary to use a specialized language for this task. Two common languages are Atlas Transformation Language (ATL) and Query View Transformation Operational (QVTO) [8].

ATL allows transformations by defining modules. A module must contain a name, an output metamodel and an input metamodel. Furthermore, a module can define rules. Each rule must contain a name, the class from the input metamodel and one or more classes from the output metamodel. Each rule allows assigning the attribute information of each class of output metamodel [7].

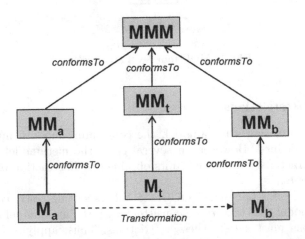

Fig. 2. Model transformation.

QVTO allows transformations by creating functions of mapping models. It is necessary to include metamodels through the keyword `modeltype`. The execution of the transformation is initiated through a main function in which it can appeal to the mapping functions required for transformation [8].

2.4 Model to Text Transformation

Model to text transformation allows generating source code in any language [1]. The transformations generate text files with the desired content and desired extension. The model to text transformation always has an input model and an input metamodel. The output is the set of source code files generated in the language selected to deploy the final application.

Acceleo is a project that allows model to text transformations. It allows to build a set of *templates* that are components where the decisions of transformations are implemented [11]. It has a statement `@main` indicating which templates will be run. If a template does not contain the statement `@main`, it must be called since another template for its execution.

3 Solution Strategy

The solution strategy consists in two main ideas.

1. The first idea is the approach to connect several assets that refers software components or artifacts for allowing the creation of several software products that belongs to one specific business domain.
2. The second idea is the component that represents the model transformation chain, which serves to configure all assets that will be included in the final software product.

Thus, users just need to provide all assets already developed as inputs; then, users can run the model transformation chain, which provides as output all required connections between assets that are described in the context model. Figure 3 presents the complete strategy.

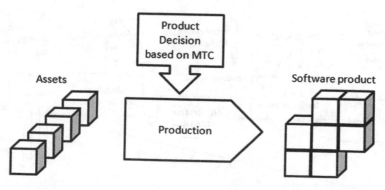

Fig. 3. Solution Strategy.

To build the model transformation chain, it is necessary to create the next artifacts:

- Context metamodel. This metamodel contains all concepts related with the specific business domain that is going to be used for creating the final application. It includes some domain constraints developed using OCL. These constraints are necessary in order to avoid inconsistencies when creating the context model.
- Architecture metamodel. This metamodel contains all elements from the context metamodel; however, it also includes some required elements to provide the final application based on the architectural pattern Model View Controller.
- Context model. This model must conform to the context metamodel. It is used to model a specific project in the business domain defined in the context metamodel. Then, all required connections between assets need to be specified in this model.
- ATL Transformation. This artifact has the context metamodel as input and generates the architecture model which conforms to the architecture metamodel. This transformation has the necessary rules to convert the elements from the context model adding the additional characteristics defined in the architecture metamodel.
- Acceleo Transformation. This artifact has the architecture model as input. It has a set of rules that convert the elements in the architecture model to a source code in any language. In this specific case, the source code corresponds with the necessary java classes and configuration files in order to connect the assets involved in the final product.

With this proposal, the context model and the architecture model are platform independent, yet the files generated by the acceleo transformation are platform dependent. As a consequence, it is necessary to create a different acceleo transformation for each platform in the case of generates the project in different programming languages. Figure 4 illustrates the structure of the described model transformation chain.

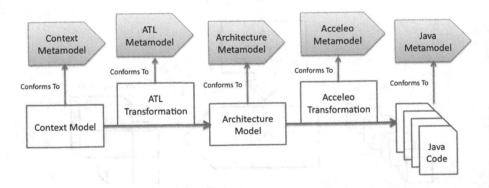

Fig. 4. Model transformation chain.

4   Case Study

The model transformation chain has been evaluated in one approach created for the construction of information systems in the academy domain. In this domain, there are a lot of features that would be controlled through the model transformation chain. The modeler must establish features when he creates the context model. The context metamodel is presented in Fig. 5.

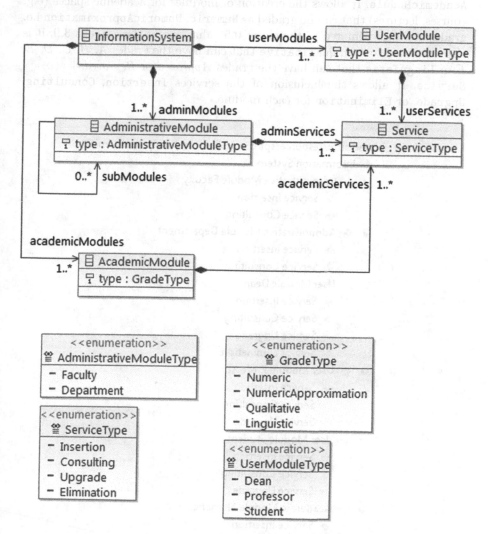

Fig. 5. Context metamodel.

The context metamodel includes the following concepts:

- InformationSystem. It is the container of the metamodel.
- AdministrativeModule. It allows the creation of modules that can be *Faculty* or *Deparment*. One module may contain other modules.
- UserModule. It allows the creation of modules that can be *Dean, Professor* or *Student*.
- AcademicModule. It allows the creation of modules for academic spaces (e.g. courses, lectures) that can be graded as Numeric, NumericApproximation i.e. grades are approximated to the closer 0.5 value (e.g. if the grade is 3.9, it is approximated to 4.0), Qualitative that can have the grades *A, B, C, D, E, F* or Linguistic that can have the grades *Approved* or *Reproved.*
- Service. It allows the inclusion of the services Insertion, Consulting, Upgrade, or Elimination for each module.

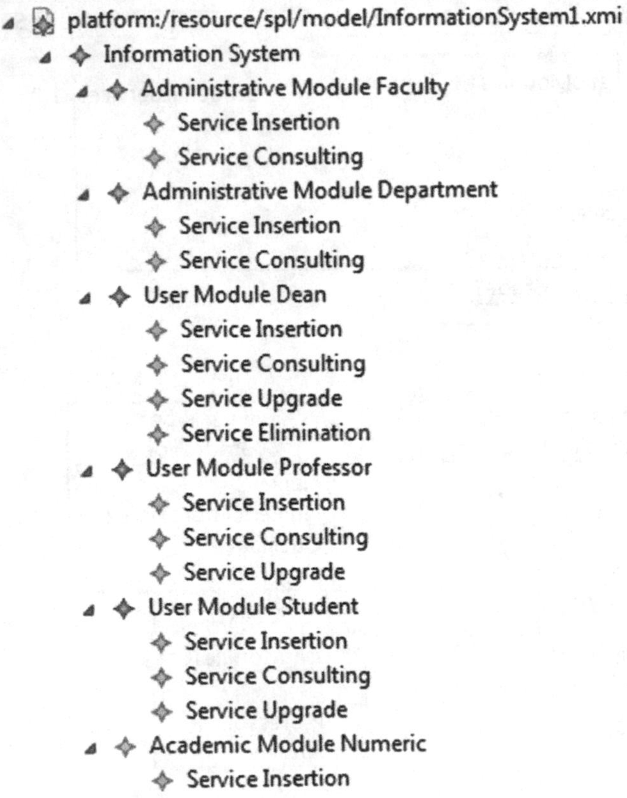

platform:/resource/spl/model/InformationSystem1.xmi
- Information System
  - Administrative Module Faculty
    - Service Insertion
    - Service Consulting
  - Administrative Module Department
    - Service Insertion
    - Service Consulting
  - User Module Dean
    - Service Insertion
    - Service Consulting
    - Service Upgrade
    - Service Elimination
  - User Module Professor
    - Service Insertion
    - Service Consulting
    - Service Upgrade
  - User Module Student
    - Service Insertion
    - Service Consulting
    - Service Upgrade
  - Academic Module Numeric
    - Service Insertion

Fig. 6. Context model case 1.

Based on this context metamodel, it is possible to include the following configurations:

- Faculties with Departments or Faculties without Departments.
- Numeric grades, numeric grades with approximation, qualitative grades for academic spaces such as courses or lectures or Linguistic grades for special academic courses such as thesis.

Figure 6 presents one case in which the information system should have the following features:

- Each faculty has departments. Faculties and departments have the services insertion and consulting.
- There are three kinds of users (dean, professor and student).
- Academic spaces are evaluated with numeric grades.

Figure 7 presents one case in which the information system should have the following features:

- There are faculties that have the services insertion and consulting.
- There are three kinds of users (dean, professor and student)
- Academic spaces are evaluated with qualitative grades.

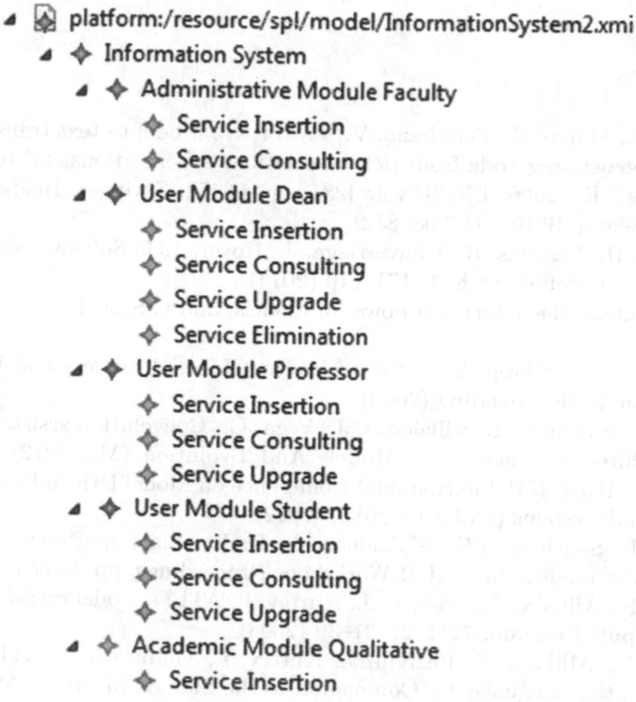

▲ 🗋 platform:/resource/spl/model/InformationSystem2.xmi
    ▲ ✦ Information System
        ▲ ✦ Administrative Module Faculty
            ✦ Service Insertion
            ✦ Service Consulting
        ▲ ✦ User Module Dean
            ✦ Service Insertion
            ✦ Service Consulting
            ✦ Service Upgrade
            ✦ Service Elimination
        ▲ ✦ User Module Professor
            ✦ Service Insertion
            ✦ Service Consulting
            ✦ Service Upgrade
        ▲ ✦ User Module Student
            ✦ Service Insertion
            ✦ Service Consulting
            ✦ Service Upgrade
        ▲ ✦ Academic Module Qualitative
            ✦ Service Insertion

Fig. 7. Context model case 2.

5 Conclusions

Model transformation chains offer advantages related to the development time of software products that are part of the same context, allowing the development team to concentrate on the analysis and design of the product and the particular characteristics that must be implemented based on the infrastructure generated by the model transformation chain.

A model transformation allows adding the project a major set of components that make reference not only to the context, but also to the visualization and control.

The application of a model transformation chain allows semi-automatically generating a final software product. It means that based on the generated elements it is just necessary to implement some specific additional characteristics of each project.

Based on a model transformation chain it is possible to easily configure assets in order to generate a final software product. The model created in the model transformation chain is platform independent aggregating another advantage to the project. However, the final transformation is platform dependent; as a result, it is necessary to create one specific transformation to make the required connections between assets using a specific programming language. Thus, the model transformation chain can be adjusted in order to cover several languages for several platforms.

References

1. Albert, M., Muñoz, J., Pelechano, V., Pastor, Ó.: Model to text transformation in practice: generating code from rich associations specifications. In: Roddick, J.F., et al. (eds.) ER 2006. LNCS, vol. 4231, pp. 63–72. Springer, Heidelberg (2006). https://doi.org/10.1007/11908883_9
2. Arboleda, H., Casallas, R., Chavarriaga, J., Royer, J.C.: Software architecture for product lines. Softw. Arch. **1**, 171–210 (2014)
3. Bézivin, J.: On the unification power of models. Softw. Syst. Model. **4**(2), 171–188 (2005)
4. Clements, P., Northrop, L.: Software Product Lines: Practices and Patterns, vol. 3. Addison-Wesley, Reading (2002)
5. Florez, H., Sanchez, M., Villalobos, J., Vega, G.: Coevolution assistance for enterprise architecture models. In: Models And Evolution (ME 2012) Workshop at The ACM/IEEE 15th International Conference on Model Driven Engineering Languages And Systems (MoDELS 2012) (2012)
6. Florez, H., Sánchez, M.E., Villalobos, J.: Embracing imperfection in enterprise architecture models. In: CEUR Workshops Proceedings, pp. 8–17 (2013)
7. Jouault, F., Allilaire, F., Bézivin, J., Kurtev, I.: ATL: a model transformation tool. Sci. Comput. Program. **72**(1–2), 31–39 (2008)
8. Jouault, F., Allilaire, F., Bézivin, J., Kurtev, I., Valduriez, P.: ATL: a QVT-like transformation language. In: Companion to the 21st ACM SIGPLAN Symposium on Object-Oriented Programming Systems, Languages, and Applications, pp. 719–720. ACM (2006)

9. Kühne, T.: Matters of (meta-) modeling. Softw. Syst. Model. **5**(4), 369–385 (2006)
10. Muller, P.A., Fondement, F., Baudry, B., Combemale, B.: Modeling modeling modeling. Softw. Syst. Model. **11**(3), 347–359 (2012)
11. Musset, J., et al.: Acceleo user guide (2006). http://acceleo.org/doc/obeo/en/acceleo-2.6-user-guide.pdf
12. Pohl, K., Böckle, G., van Der Linden, F.J.: Software Product Line Engineering: Foundations, Principles and Techniques. Springer Science & Business Media, Heidelberg (2005). https://doi.org/10.1007/3-540-28901-1
13. Sanchez, D., Florez, H.: Model driven engineering approach to manage peripherals in mobile devices. In: Gervasi, O., et al. (eds.) ICCSA 2018. LNCS, vol. 10963, pp. 353–364. Springer, Cham (2018). https://doi.org/10.1007/978-3-319-95171-3_28
14. Sanchez, D., Mendez, O., Florez, H.: An approach of a framework to create web applications. In: Gervasi, O., et al. (eds.) ICCSA 2018. LNCS, vol. 10963, pp. 341–352. Springer, Cham (2018). https://doi.org/10.1007/978-3-319-95171-3_27
15. Warmer, J.B., Kleppe, A.G.: The object constraint language: getting your models ready for MDA. Addison-Wesley Professional (2003)

Multi-SPLOT: Supporting Multi-user Configurations with Constraint Programming

Sebastian Velásquez-Guevara[1], Gilberto Pedraza[1],
and Jaime Chavarriaga[2]

[1] Universidad Piloto de Colombia, Bogotá, Colombia
rlxsebas@gmail.com, gilberto-pedraza@unipiloto.edu.co
[2] Universidad de los Andes, Bogotá, Colombia
ja.chavarriaga908@uniandes.edu.co

Abstract. Nowadays, companies have moved from offering a single product for all their clients, to offer different customized for each one. These companies provide Configuration Systems where a user can decide and discard which features she wants in her final product. However, although almost all of these systems support individual decisions, usually they do not offer an special support for decisions made by multiple users for the same product. This paper introduces Multi-SPLOT, a web-based Configuration System that supports simultaneous decisions from multiple users. This system uses off-the-shelf solvers to determine if these decisions are not conflicting among them, and to propose solutions when the decisions of an user conflict with decisions of the others. This paper shows the design of the solution and details of its implementation using Angular, Firebase and the optimization library in Google App Script.

Keywords: Feature models · Configuration systems
Multi-user configuration

1 Introduction

Installing and configuring complex applications may take many months and involve multiple users. For instance, deploying and configuring a system such as SAP takes up an average between 6 to 12 months [8]. Diverse users, with different areas of knowledge and requirements (e.g. engineers, accountants and manufacturing experts) must coordinate their work to achieve a successfull installation.

In a Configuration Systems (a.k.a. a Configurator), users select options that they want to include and enter values for the diverse parameters required by the product. The Software checks if the user selections do not have conflicts among them, i.e. that they can be included in the product at the same time, and offers recommendations to the user if it finds some problems [7]. However, these systems usually consider all the decisions as if they were made by the

© Springer Nature Switzerland AG 2018
H. Florez et al. (Eds.): ICAI 2018, CCIS 942, pp. 364–378, 2018.
https://doi.org/10.1007/978-3-030-01535-0_27

same person, and do not take into account that sometimes several people make decisions about the same product.

Normally, when several people make decisions about the same product, selections by a user may limit the options that other users can choose. The system deactivates the options that conflict with the decisions already made. It is possible that the users who arrive later can not select all the options they want but only those that do not generate conflicts with the decisions of the others. It is also possible that these users do not understand why they can not select certain options or do not feel satisfied with the options they can select. Currently, configurators such as SPLOT[1] and FaMa[2] allow several users to make decisions, but the decisions made by the first users limit what can be taken by the following.

A better alternative may be that each user expresses his selections and preferences freely. An automated process may take the decisions of the different users and, in case of finding a conflict, look for a solution that tries to satisfy all the users in a large extent. This article presents Multi-SPLOT, a Configuration System that allows each user to define the desired characteristics for the product independently, check if the decisions of each user do not conflict with each other, and offers automatic processes that look for a configuration satisfies most of the decisions of all of them.

The rest of this paper is organized as follows: The Sect. 2 presents a background on configuration systems based and feature models. The Sect. 3 describes the problems that occur when several people participate in the configuration process, Sects. 4 and 5 introduce our proposal and describe the corresponding software design. Finally, Sect. 6 concludes the article.

2 Background

2.1 Configuration Processes

The process of specifying the characteristics for a custom product is known as *Configuration*.

The configuration processes are widely used in sectors such as electronic components, the automotive sector and software development. In these sectors, the large number of variants and options (i.e. variability) makes it difficult to specify the customized products correctly.

Nowadays, there are several ways to build these Configuration Systems [7]. For example, they can be built from sets of rules that determine dependencies between the components of the product or through models that represent variability. In Software Engineering, the most used variability models are the feature models [1].

2.2 Feature Models

A *Feature Model* represents the diverse features and properties of a family of products, and their possible combinations [11].

---

[1] http://www.splot-research.org/.
[2] http://www.isa.us.es/fama/.

Table 1. Feature model elements

Element	Figure	Description
Root	Root	Concept or Product to Configure. It must be selected all the time.
Mandatory	X ● Y	If X is selected, Y must be selected.
Optional	X ○ Y	If X is selected, Y may be selected (or not).
Or groups	X Y_1 ... Y_i	If X is selected, one or more of $Y_1, ..., Y_n$ must be selected.
Alternative groups	X Y_1 ... Y_i	If X is selected, one (and just one) of $Y_1, ..., Y_n$ must be selected.

Relationship	Figure	Description
Requires	X --→ Y	If X is selected, Y must be selected.
Excludes	X ←--→ Y	If X is selected, Y cannot be selected.

Syntax: A Feature Model is represented as a hierarchical structure, i.e. a tree. Each element in the tree is a feature or a feature-group. Table 1 shows the elements that may comprise a feature model:

- The *Root*, known as the *Concept*, represents the product to configure.
- *Mandatory Features* represent features that must be selected when the parent feature is selected,
- *Optional Features* are features that may be selected or not when the parent feature is selected,
- *Or-Groups*, feature groups where one or more features can be selected, and
- *Alternative Groups*, groups where just one feature can be selected at the same time.

In addition, a model may include relationships to denote constraints:

- *Requires* relationships, stating that a features must be selected when other is selected, and

– *Excludes* relationships, representing two features that cannot be selected at the same time.

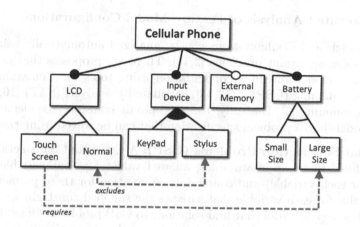

Fig. 1. Example feature model

Figure 1 shows a Feature Model for Cellular Phones. It comprises a root feature *Cellular Phone*; three mandatory features, *LCD*, *Input Device* and *Battery*; and an optional feature *External Memory*. In turn, an alternative group indicates that a *LCD* may be a *Touch Screen* or a *Normal* one, but not both. An Or-Group, shows that the *Input Device* may be *Keypad*, *Stylus*, or both. Another alternative group shows that the *Battery* may be *Small Size* or *Large Size*. In addition, the model includes an *excludes* relationship denoting that phones including a *Stylus* cannot include a *Normal* LCD (they must contain a *Touch Screen*). Finally, a *requires* relationship shows that, if a phone has a *Touch Screen*, it must include a *Large Size* battery.

Semantics: Each Feature Model represents a set of configurations.

A *Feature Configuration* (a.k.a. a Configuration) is a selection of the features in a Feature Model.

A *Valid Configuration* is configuration that satisfies the constraints defined in the corresponding feature model. For instance, considering the model shown above in Fig. 1, the following configuration C_v, is a valid configuration that satisfies the constraints in the model.

$$C_v = \{CellularPhone, LCD, TouchScreen, InputDevice, Stylus,$$
$$Battery, LargeSize\}$$

In contrast, the following configuration C_x is invalid. It includes *TouchScreen* and *SmallSize* battery. It is an invalid configuration because the model states that a *TouchScreen* requires a *LargeSize* battery.

$$C_x = \{\,CellularPhone, LCD, TouchScreen, InputDevice, Stylus,$$
$$Battery, SmallSize\,\}$$

2.3   Automated Analysis of Feature Model Configurations

Feature Models and Configurations can be analyzed automatically using techniques to solve constraint problems [2,16]. There are proposals that determine conflicts in a model and in a configuration using tools for Constraint Satisfaction Programming (CSP) [3,12,13], satisfiability analysis (SAT) [10,14] and linear programming [4]. Basically, these proposals translate the elements in a feature models into a problem specification that can be solved using these tools.

Constraint Satisfaction Problems (CSP): A Constraint Satisfaction Problem is defined in terms of variables, allowed values for that variables (i.e. a domain for each variable) and constraints. A solution for these problems comprises a value for each variable that satisfies the supplied constraints.

A *CSP solver* is a tool that find solutions to CSP problems. Basically, these tools use diverse techniques and heuristics to search the solution in the problem space, i.e. in all the possible combinations of values for the variables. A problem is *feasible* if it has, at least, a solution. A problem is *unfeasible* if it does not have any solution.

Translating a Feature Model to a CSP: To analyze a feature model, the elements therein must be translated to a constraint satisfaction problem [3]:

- the features are translated to variables;
- the domain for all of these variables is: $\{0, 1\}$, where 0 represent a not selected feature and 1 represents the selected ones; and
- the diverse types of features and relationships are translated to constraints on these variables.

The elements in a feature model are translated to constraints according to the following rules [3]:

- *Children features:* each X feature parent of a Y feature is translated to $X \leq Y$
- *Mandatory features:* when X is parent of a Y mandatory feature, it is translated to $Y = X$
- *Optional features:* when X is parent of a Y optional feature, is is translated to $X \geq Y$
- *Or-group:* each X feature parent of an *Or*-group comprised by $Y_1, ..., Y_i$ features is translated to $X = 1 \leq \sum Y_i$
- *Alternative group:* each X feature parent of an alternative group comprised by $Y_1, ..., Y_i$ features is translated to $X = \sum Y_i$
- *Requires:* a relationship $X \xrightarrow{requires} Y$ translates to $X \leq Y$
- *Excludes:* a relationship $X \xrightarrow{excludes} Y$ is translated to $X + Y \leq 1$

Table 2. Rules to translate a feature model to CSP constraints

Element	Figure	Translation
Root	Root	$r = 1$
Mandatory	X / Y	$x = y$
Optional	X / Y	$x \geq y$
Or groups	X / $Y_1 \ldots Y_i$	$x \leq \sum y_i$ (i.e. $x \to \sum y_i \geq 1$) $x \geq y_i$
Alternative groups	X / $Y_1 \ldots Y_i$	$x = \sum y_i$ (i.e. $x \to \sum y_i = 1$) $x \geq y_i$

Relationship	Figure	Translation
Requires	X ---> Y	$x \leq y$
Excludes	X <--> Y	$x + y \leq 1$

Table 2 shows the translation of the feature model elements into expressions that represent the corresponding constraints.

For example, consider the feature model depicted in Fig. 1. It may be translated as the following constraints:

$CellularPhone = 1$
$CellularPhone = LCD$
$LCD \leq (TouchScreen + Normal)$
$TouchScreen \geq LCD$
$Normal \geq LCD$
$CellularPhone = InputDevice$
$InputDevice \leq (KeyPad + Stylus)$
$KeyPad \geq InputDevice$
$Stylus \geq InputDevice$

$ExternalMemory \geq CellularPhone$
$CellularPhone = Battery$
$Battery \leq (Small + Large)$
$Small \geq Battery$
$Large \geq Battery$

Using a *solver*, it is possible to determine if the problem has a solution (and the feature model is valid). Given a problem P, we say *feasible*(P) returns *TRUE* if the problem has a solution or *FALSE* if it has not.

Validating a Configuration: It is possible to use *feasible*(P) to determine if a configuration is valid. Basically, we must add new constraints according to the selections from the users: (1) First, we must translate the feature model to a set of constraints and variables, (2) then, we must assign 1 to the variables representing each selected feature, and (3) finally, assign 0 to each not-selected feature. If the problem has a solution, the configuration is valid. Algorithm 1 shows the process to validate a configuration.

Algorithm 1. Validate a Configuration

1: **procedure** IsVALIDCONFIGURATION(c, fm)
2:     $P = encode(fm)$ ▷ Translate using the above rules
3:     **for all** $f_s \in c$ **do**
4:         $addConstraint(P, f_s = 1)$ ▷ Assign 1 to the selected features
5:     **end for**
6:     **for all** $f_r \in (fm \setminus c)$ **do**
7:         $addConstraint(P, f_r = 0)$ ▷ Assign 0 to the others
8:     **end for**
9:     **return** $feasible(P)$ ▷ Check if the values satisfies the constraints
10: **end procedure**

Auto-completing a Configuration: In addition to validate a configuration, a solver can be used to complete or optimize a partial configuration.

A CSP solver determines that a problem is feasible if it finds a solution for it. When feature models are translated to CSP problems, that solutions correspond to valid configurations to that model.

Basically, to complete a configuration, (1) First, we must translate the feature model to a set of constraints and variables, and (2) Then, we must assign 1 to the variables representing each selected feature. Here, we consider that the not-selected features are not decided by the user and, therefore, we do not assign 0 to the corresponding variables. Instead of *feasible*(P), we use a *findSolution*(P) procedure that returns the solution found.

Algorithm 2. Auto-complete a Configuration

1: **procedure** COMPLETECONFIGURATION(c, fm)
2:     $P = encode(fm)$ ▷ Translate using the above rules
3:     **for all** $f_s \in c$ **do**
4:         $addConstraint(P, f_s = 1)$ ▷ Assign 1 to the selected features
5:     **end for**
6:     **return** $findSolution(P)$ ▷ Return a solution that includes the selected features
7: **end procedure**

Optimizing a Configuration: Optimizing a configuration is a special kind of auto-completion. While the typical auto-completion returns any solution, the optimization looks for a configuration that maximizes some predefined criteria.

Linear Programming solvers allow developers to specify a *optimization function* in addition to the variables, domains and constraints. These solvers returns a solution that satisfies the constraints and maximizes that optimization function. In addition, there are some CSP and SAT solvers that may obtain solutions that maximize the number of satisfied constraints too. To implement a procedure that optimizes configurations, it is necessary to determine what is the optimization function to use [4].

2.4   Types of Multi-user Configuration

In some scenarios the configurations processes imply the participation of multiple users, each one deciding on some or all of the features for the intended product.

Configuration processes involving multiple users can be classified according to the way that the decisions are made by the diverse users [6,8]:

Staged Configuration: When the decisions of all the users are consolidated into a single set. In these processes, the decisions made first by any user limit the decisions of the others [5]. Basically, it works like an interactive configuration for a single person. After a decision is made, the software propagates the decision enabling and disabling other features according to the defined constraints.

Multi-view Configuration: When each user made decisions on a subset of the features. Here, each user has an assigned view of the configuration that contains only the features that are of her concern [9]. Although the users decide on their own views of the model, decisions made by a user affect the decisions that the others may make. The user decisions are propagated just like in a staged configuration.

Simultaneous Configuration: When each user make decisions independently. In this type of configurations, decisions made by a user does not affect the decisions that the other may make. After all the users made their decisions, an additional automated process consolidates the decisions and tries to solve the conflicts that may occur.

While existing software and libraries such as SPLOT and FAMA supports staged configuration and multi-view configuration, they do not support simultaneous configuration. These software may propagate a single set of decisions but do not support multiple set of decisions that must be consolidated and where possible conflicts must be detected and resolved.

3   Conflicts in Simultaneous Configuration

When multiple users participate in a configuration process, it is possible that selections made by a user do conflict with users made by the others.

For instance, it is possible that a user decide to include a feature while other user has decided to exclude it. Consider a process where two user are configuring a cellular phone according to the feature model in Fig. 1. Suppose that the first user decides to include an *External Memory* while the other decides to exclude that option. It is not possible to obtain a single product that satisfies the constraints defined by both users.

Also, it is possible that a user decide to include features that conflict with the features selected by the others. For instance, in the same process, a user may decide to include a *Small Size* battery while the other decides to include a *Large Size* one.

In both cases, it is necessary to revisit the decisions, detect the conflicts and propose solutions.

4   Proposal to Support Simultaneous Configuration

Our proposal focuses on proposing automatically solutions that can solve the conflicts.

4.1   Solution Strategies

We have identified three strategies to propose solutions to conflicts:

Maximize selections: Look for a solution that includes the largest number of features selected by all the users. Here, if a user selects *ExternalMemory* while the others do not, the system will propose a solution trying to include that feature.

Minimize the conflicting selections: Look for a solution that includes (1) all the features selected by the users that do not have conflicts among them, and (2) the smallest number of the selected features that have conflicts. In this case, if a user selects *ExternalMemory*, the system includes that feature in the solution if it does not have a conflict with any other selected feature.

Prioritize the decisions from some users: Given a priority or a weight for each user, look for a solution that satisfies in greater measure to the users with higher height. In this case, the system will propose solutions that tries to include the largest number of features selected by the users with the higher priorities.

4.2   Automated Processing

Our solution uses linear programming to find solutions to the conflicts.

Linear Programming (LP): A linear programming problem looks for an optimal solution to a constraint satisfaction problem according to a given criteria. In these problems, besides the variables, domains and constraints; it is necessary to define an objective function. These constraints and objective function must be defined in terms of linear equations.

Strategies Implementation: To implement each solution strategy, it is possible to define a linear programming problem using the variables and constraints as defined in the Sect. 2. It is only necessary to define the objective function in each case.

Consider a configuration process where n users are involved. Each user provides a C_i configuration, where $i \in \{1 \ldots n\}$. Given that all the provided configuration are valid, a subset of features without conflicts $\mathcal{F}_{nc}$ is the set of features selected by all the users at the same time, i.e. $\mathcal{F}_{nc} = \bigcap_{i \in \{1 \ldots n\}} C_i$. The set of features that may have conflicts $\mathcal{F}_c$ are the remaing, i.e. let $\mathcal{F}_{fm}$ all the features in the model, $C_c = \mathcal{F}_{fm} \setminus C_{nc} = \{f \in \mathcal{F}_{fm} \mid f \notin \mathcal{F}_{fm}\}$.

The subset of features selected by a user that may have conflicts CC_i corresponds to the features in the C_i configuration that are not in the subset of features without conflicts, i.e. $CC_i = C_i \setminus \mathcal{F}_{nc}$.

Maximize selections: To look for the solution with the largest number of selected features, the objective function must be defined to maximize the inclusion of the features that may have conflicts. The objective function is:

$$maximize: \quad \sum (1 * f), \; \forall f \in \bigcup_{i \in \{1 \ldots n\}} CC_i$$

Minimize the conflicting selections: In this case, the objective function looks for minimizing the inclusion of features that may have conflicts. The objective function is:

$$minimize: \quad \sum (1 * f), \; \forall f \in \bigcup_{i \in \{1 \ldots n\}} CC_i$$

Prioritize the decisions from some users: In this case, it looks for maximize the decisions from the users with a higher weight. Let r_i as the relative weight assigned to the decisions of the user i, the objective function is:

$$maximize: \quad \sum_{i \in \{1 \ldots n\}} (r_i * f_i), \; \forall f_i \in CC_i$$

5   Design and Implementation

Multi-SPLOT is the implementation of our strategies[3]. It is a single-page web application developed using technologies such as Javascript, Angular and Firebase that allow us to deploy the software using freely-available web hosting services, such as the Github pages, and low-cost infrastructures.

---

[3] The source code is available at: https://github.com/SebasG22/SPLOT.

5.1   Overview

Our application comprises three components:

1. **A web application to configure products** that supports (1) a administrator users defining configuration projects and assigning configuration tasks to diverse users, and (2) configurator users that select options from the features models in each of these projects.
2. **A module for the automated analysis of configurations** that supports (1) determining the validity of the configurations defined by each user, (2) determining the conflicts among the configurations from the diverse users, if they exist; and (3) proposing solutions to these conflicts, i.e. proposing configurations that use some of the above presented strategies to solve multi-user conflicts.

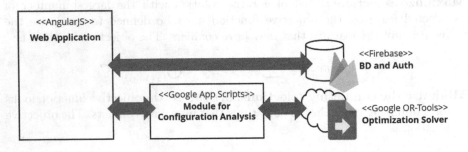

Fig. 2. Application Architecture

Figure 2 shows an overview of the application.

The *web application for configuring products* was developed using Javascript and Angular[4]. It is structured using modules, controllers, views and services, following the recommended practices in the framework. The application stores the information in a Google Firebase database[5] and execute analysis operations using the module for automated analysis of configurations we developed.

The *module for the automated analysis of configurations* was developed using Javascript and Google App Script[6], a cloud based development platform that supports an special version of the Google Optimization Tools[7] library. Using this library, we can process constraint satisfaction and linear programming problems in the cloud.

The following sections shows two aspects of the solution design. They present: (1) the database schema used to represent the configuration projects, the feature models and configurations; and (2) the implementation of the service on Google App Script.

---

[4] https://angularjs.org/.
[5] https://firebase.google.com/.
[6] https://developers.google.com/apps-script/.
[7] https://developers.google.com/optimization/.

5.2 Database Schema

One of the design decisions was focused on the representation of the feature models and configurations. The development of the project required the creation of objects in Javascript that can be interchanged as REST messages and that can be stored in the Firebase database.

Data of Projects and Users: Figure 3 shows a class diagram representing the structure used to store the data of projects and users.

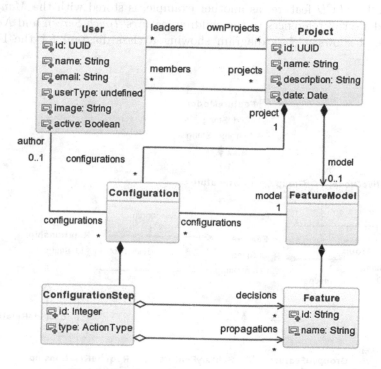

Fig. 3. Configuration project class diagram

Project stores the information of each configuration project, including an identifier, a name, the set of project members, the feature model and the configurations provided by each user.
User includes information of the name, email, and a photo of each user. In addition, it includes a set of flags. For instance, it includes a flag that determines
   if the user is active or not. The user password is not stored here because we
   used the authentication service provided by Google Firebase.
Feature Model stores the feature models includes in the project. All the users
   in a configuration project provide configurations for the same feature model.
Configuration keeps information of all the configurations provided by the users
   in all the projects.

The data is stored in Firebase using a *flatten structure*, i.e., the relationships among the objects are not stored as object collections, but by using lists of identifiers. This is the recommended practice in Firebase[8].

Feature Models Data. The structure of the feature models are stored in Firebase too. For each model, the application stores all the features, their type and children features. For instance, considering the feature model shown in Fig. 1, it stores the *CellularPhone* feature with a *Root* type and a set of identifiers (references) to their children features: *LCD, InputDevice, ExternalMemory* and *Battery*. The *LCD* feature, as another example, is stored with the *Mandatory* type and a set of references to the children features *Touch Screen* and *Normal*.

Figure 4 shows a class diagram showing a class diagram for the Feature Models.

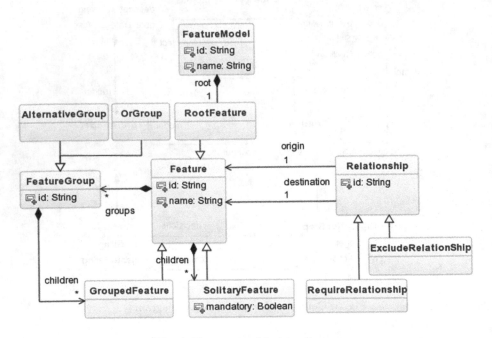

Fig. 4. Feature model class diagram

Configuration Data. Configurations provided by each user are stored as lists of features. Note that, each time a user decide to include a feature, the decision is propagated automatically. Therefore, each configuration includes not only the list of features selected by the user but also other constraints that were selected automatically.

---

[8] https://firebase.google.com/docs/database/web/structure-data.

5.3   Module for Analyzing Configurations

Each time a user configures a product or decides to find conflicts among the configurations provided by the users, the web application uses a module to analyze all the configurations in the project we developed in Google App Script.

Google App Script is a web platform for creating applications and web services. These applications run on Google infrastructure and have restrictions about the libraries that can be used. To build the service we used a special library to access the Firebase database and a special version of the Google Optimization Tools that run on App Script.

6   Conclusions

This paper introduces our proposal to support simultaneous configuration processes. On the one hand, it offers automated strategies to propose solutions when a configuration provided by a user has conflicts with configurations provided by the others. On the other hand, it offers a web application that supports the tasks for creating configuration processes and deciding the configurations.

Regarding the solutions for the detected conflicts, this paper presents three strategies we propose. Basically, these strategies look for a configuration that keeps all the features selected by all the users and (1) that maximizes the number of features selected by some of the users, or (2) that keeps the minimum of these other selections, or (3) that considers the priority assigned to the decisions of the diverse users. All these strategies were implemented using our own javascript library to analyze feature models and configurations using linear programming [15].

Regarding the software, we developed (1) a web-based application to define and run the configuration processes, and (2) a module that use the above mentioned library to analyze the configurations and find solutions to any detected conflict. We used technologies such as Javascript and Google App Script that allow companies to run the solution in free- and low-cost web infrastructures. We expect this encourages the use of our solution in the future.

Nowadays, our solution supports only feature models without attributes. That means that it is not possible to define values for attributes such as price, product weight or size for the features in the model. This impedes the definition of more complex configuration scenarios and constraints. Future work is planned to extend our solution and support attributed feature models. In addition, we are interested on using our solution in real-life scenarios and exploring which other strategies can be proposed to solve conflicts in simultaenous configuration processes.

References

1. Benavides, D., Felfernig, A., Galindo, J.A., Reinfrank, F.: Automated analysis in feature modelling and product configuration. In: Favaro, J., Morisio, M. (eds.) ICSR 2013. LNCS, vol. 7925, pp. 160–175. Springer, Heidelberg (2013). https://doi.org/10.1007/978-3-642-38977-1_11
2. Benavides, D., Segura, S., Ruiz-Cortés, A.: Automated analysis of feature models 20 years later: a literature review. Inf. Syst. **35**(6), 615–636 (2010)
3. Benavides, D., Segura, S., Trinidad, P., Ruiz-Cortés, A.: Using Java CSP solvers in the automated analyses of feature models. In: Lämmel, R., Saraiva, J., Visser, J. (eds.) GTTSE 2005. LNCS, vol. 4143, pp. 399–408. Springer, Heidelberg (2006). https://doi.org/10.1007/11877028_16
4. van den Broek, P.: Optimization of product instantiation using integer programming. In: 14th International Software Product Line Conference (SPLC 2011), pp. 107–111 (2011)
5. Czarnecki, K., Helsen, S., Eisenecker, U.: Staged configuration using feature models. In: Nord, R.L. (ed.) SPLC 2004. LNCS, vol. 3154, pp. 266–283. Springer, Heidelberg (2004). https://doi.org/10.1007/978-3-540-28630-1_17
6. Czarnecki, K., Helsen, S., Eisenecker, U.: Staged configuration through specialization and multilevel configuration of feature models. Softw. Process. Improv. Pract. **10**(2), 143–169 (2005)
7. Felfernig, A., Hotz, L., Bagley, C., Tiihonen, J.: Knowledge-based Configuration: From Research to Business Cases. Morgan Kaufmann (2014)
8. Hubaux, A., Tun, T.T., Heymans, P.: Separation of concerns in feature diagram languages: a systematic survey. ACM Comput. Surv. **45**(4), 51:1–51:23 (2013)
9. Hubaux, A., Heymans, P., Schobbens, P.Y., Deridder, D., Abbasi, E.: Supporting multiple perspectives in feature-based configuration. Softw. Syst. Model. (SoSyM) **12**(3), 641–663 (2013)
10. Janota, M.: SAT Solving in Interactive Configuration. Ph.D. thesis, University College of Dublin (2010)
11. Kang, K.C., Cohen, S.G., Hess, J.A., Novak, W.E., Peterson, A.S.: Feature-Oriented Domain Analysis (FODA) Feasibility Study. Technical report, Software Engineering Institute, Carnegie-Mellon University, November 1990
12. Karataş, A.S., Oğuztüzün, H., Doğru, A.: Mapping extended feature models to constraint logic programming over finite domains. In: Bosch, J., Lee, J. (eds.) SPLC 2010. LNCS, vol. 6287, pp. 286–299. Springer, Heidelberg (2010). https://doi.org/10.1007/978-3-642-15579-6_20
13. Mazo, R., Salinesi, C., Diaz, D., Lora-Michiels, A.: Transforming attribute and clone-enabled feature models into constraint programs over finite domains. In: 6th International Conference on Evaluation of Novel Approaches to Software Engineering (ENASE 2011). Springer (2011)
14. Mendonca, M., Wasowski, A., Czarnecki, K.: SAT-based analysis of feature models is easy. In: 13th International Software Product Line Conference (SPLC 2009), pp. 231–240 (2009)
15. Navarro, J.C., Chavarriaga, J.: Using microsoft solver foundation to analyse feature models and configurations. In: 2016 8th Euro American Conference on Telematics and Information Systems (EATIS), pp. 1–8 (2016)
16. Ochoa, L., González-Rojas, O., Juliana, A.P., Castro, H., Saake, G.: A systematic literature review on the semi-automatic configuration of extended product lines. J. Syst. Softw. **144**, 511–532 (2018)

Author Index

Printed in the United States
By Bookmasters

Printed in the United States
By Bookmasters